I HAD TO GO THERE TO GET HERE

A Wandering Knight's Tale

Ken Holmes

Matador
5 Weir Road
Kibworth Beauchamp
Leicester LE8 0LQ, UK
Tel: (+44) 116 279 2299
Fax: (+44) 116 279 2277
Email: books@troubador.co.uk
Web: www.troubador.co.uk/matador

ISBN 978 1848766 860

Cover photography by Richard Mayfield, Venture Photography

British Library Cataloguing in Publication Data.
A catalogue record for this book is available from the British Library.

Typeset in 11pt Adobe Garamond Pro by Troubador Publishing Ltd, Leicester, UK
Printed and bound in the UK by TJ International, Padstow, Cornwall

Matador is an imprint of Troubador Publishing Ltd

To Denise, without whom this story would not have been written; without whom there wouldn't have been one.

CONTENTS

PREFACE

At seventeen I'd saved up enough Green Shield Stamps to get a cigarette case, a tan pigskin cigarette case. I filled it full of Passing Cloud cigarettes and became the biggest pull on the planet... it didn't work.

At eighteen I bought a suit. A made to measure suit. A tonic mohair made to measure suit. I became James Bond, the biggest pull on the planet... it didn't work.

At twenty-one I bought a car. A Vauxhall Victor. It was old, but it was beautiful. Now I'd become the biggest pull on the planet... it didn't work. I needed the Big One.

Thirty-five years later I invented Kiasu, the greatest invention ever. Then everything changed, but stayed the same, but in a kind of a way it was different.

The Journey

There are times in your life when against all the odds
You know you're right and with the help of the Gods
You will win

You'll scorn the advice from all your advisers
You'll ignore your friends and risk their despises
You'll get blooded and torn. They'll say just forget it
You'll become battle-worn and still don't regret it

It'll take all you've got
And don't you forget it
The whole fucking lot
And still you don't get it

Is this how it ends? Are you sorry you started?
'A bit mad, but he tried. Now he's dearly departed'.
But you're not going yet
So you learn to dig deeper
I for one would have bet
You'd fool the Grim Reaper

So you're not gonna die
But what's the conclusion?
As tears fill your eyes
And amid the confusion

From out of the skies
As you breathe in the air
The truth fills your soul –
You're becoming aware

The journey you're on, the one you have chosen
Did never exist
In the present you're frozen

Your dreams are your path; your journeys your vision
Dismiss all the fools
Ignore their derision
There aren't any rules
You make the decision

Live life to the full and never abuse it
Be true to your heart and never refuse it
You've got what you've got for a reason...

... Now use it.

PART I

MANIC IN WONDERLAND

CHAPTER 1

Could try harder. Could do better. Even when I got it right I couldn't see the point. I left school at fifteen armed with the sure-fire knowledge that the Battle of Hastings was 1066, and that was about it. I hoped no-one was going to ask me why, or who, or how they got on.

School was pointless. I just did enough to keep people off my back. Didn't always work. I did make a pretty feeble attempt to walk away from it once. I'd be about ten, I think – anyway I was still in the Juniors. I left for school at the usual time, walked down Bankfield Road and, instead of turning right towards the Jolly Miller and the bus to school, I turned left towards Tuebrook. In my pocket were a few shillings, school dinner money for the week.

I bought a packet of cigarettes and a bag of currant buns. I got the ones with icing on. I don't know why I bought the cigarettes – I threw them away on the grass verge. I had a couple of buns while I walked the four miles or so to my nan's. I told her I'd been to the dentist that day and, because I'd been a good boy, Mum had given me the rest of the day off.

I went to Nan's again the next day, making sure I got home at the proper time.

On Wednesday, again at Nan's, there was a knock on the front door. I opened it. My mother was standing there. Well, all hell broke loose. I didn't get spanked – it was far more serious than that: big public enquiry at the school, everybody involved. 'Truancy? Why? Was he upset about something?' All that sort of stuff. To me it had just seemed a good idea at the time. It must have been a bit of a shock for my mother; she was probably making her normal Wednesday visit to Nan's, and I opened the front door. I couldn't have done my research very well. I didn't do it again – it wasn't worth the fuss.

Life outside school was cool enough. When I was five we'd moved to a pretty big house on the outskirts of West Derby, Liverpool. I'd stand at the end of the garden with my imaginary trumpet: *Da-da-daah! Da-da da-da da-daah!* Wait a little while, and repeat it: *Da-da-daah! Da-da da-da da-daah!* Then the chickens came, scurrying along as fast as their little legs would go. I'd throw bread, trying to make sure each one got some, but it always ran out. Some of the twigs on the ground were special – they had white spongey stuff in the middle that looked like bread. But they weren't interested, and scuttered off. How did they know it wasn't bread?

Then there was the field with the cows. In one corner there were apple trees and bushes, all overgrown. A broken-down fence stopped the cows getting at this bit. Perfect place to build the hut. Great care had to be taken to make sure it was waterproof, and plenty of dry grass on the floor, so we could sit and plan stuff. At the far end of the field were the holly bushes. You had to take great care crossing the field. Cow pats had to be avoided at all costs, but the biggest danger was the cows – by the looks on their faces as they turned, you could see they were going to charge at any moment. The holly bushes were dense and full of prickles, no way through. You had to go all the way round to get to the castle. A narrow hole in the wall led to the underground passage. Dark, smelly, damp. You had to stoop down in places. It was best to stoop down all the way through, just in case. Daylight appeared as we got towards the end, which meant we could just about see the hole in the ground. Backs flattened against the wall, we'd shuffle past. Sometimes a bit of rubble fell in; moments later a splash. Once we got past the hole and safe we threw stones in and waited for the splash. We knew our mission was dangerous but we had to do it.

There were a lot of trees in the field, mostly round the edge by the backs of the houses. Somebody told me if you cut the bark all the way round the trunk the tree would die. I chose the tree carefully. It had to be the right kind of bark, and big. I don't know how big it was, but I had to lean all the way back to see the top – and then I couldn't. It took a long time. I used a stone. It took several stones before I got the right one to hold and chop. It probably took two or three years to die. The ring I cut wasn't nice and neat as I expected, it was jagged and rough. Why didn't I believe what I was told? It wasn't so difficult to understand,

4

if only I had asked why. I've never told anybody, but the chickens knew.

I asked my mother how much money I would get if I jumped off the roof on to a bed of prickles. That was about the most dangerous, scariest thing I could imagine.

I used to have a recurring dream. I was in the Isle of Man, part of a gang. All my gang were Labi Siffre, a popstar at the time. We were always being chased by this other gang. If we were caught we were all lined up and they'd come along and kick our kneecaps off. They chased us through the streets until we dived into this big hotel. It was on several floors, with several rooms per floor, and it had one main television on the ground floor. The television picture was transmitted from room to room by a series of convex and concave mirrors. A small mirror, placed in the top corner of the ground floor room where the television was, bounced the image up and down and along to every room on every floor of the hotel. It was a brilliant idea. Not many people had tellies then; we didn't. I knew I had discovered something very clever. Every time the dream recurred I couldn't wait to get to the hotel. The other gang ceased to be a threat. There was much bigger stuff going on. The enormity of my discovery totally occupied my thinking time – how to cope with the thicknesses of the floors and ceilings, how to cope with somebody passing across the beam. Until slowly but surely came the realisation – the whole thing was stupid, and the recurring dream stopped.

There was another dream: I was breeding chickens for the dinner table. These chickens very quickly became sought after. People travelled great distances for my chickens. They were the best chickens by far, but where was my fortune? I was charging a lot for them, but I was feeding them on Alpen muesli, the posh breakfast cereal, and it just did not add up. Back to the drawing board.

Was there a lust for fame and fortune at such a young age? Enough to penetrate my dreams? I longed to have the great idea, the big trick, the one that would bring all the glory. But why? Then in my teens the reason hit me like a tornado, and never let up. Girls.

Lavinia Ridell was true love. Sometimes we would get the same bus home from school, and if you added up the numbers on the bus tickets, took away your birth date, times it by the number you thought of in the first place, if the answer came to seven it meant it was true love as deemed by the Universe. I don't think we ever spoke, apart from one time as she got off the bus before me at Threebutt Lane she said, 'Can I get past?' I know it wasn't much of a conversation, but it was absolute, undisputable proof.

When I left school I was given a card that listed my achievements, or lack of them. It concluded, 'A lively interest and some skill in art and handicraft'. In other words, he liked doing it but wasn't really very good at it. Not much to say for ten years. Why didn't school tell us about girls? They didn't tell us anything about life and the wonderland we were about to walk into. *When a man mouse likes a lady mouse they have a baby mouse.* Nothing about girls. *Pythagorus had a theory. Hypotenuse* – need that one. *Pi-r-squared* – that's a good one. It was totally beyond their comprehension to warn the kids that any minute now puberty was going to kick in and sex was going to occupy their thinking time for the rest of their life. And so it did. And the real education started.

I got a job with British Road Services Parcels. Women all over the place. My job was post boy. Everybody started there. I was sent around all the different departments to collect the letters of the day. Every office had a function in the overall scheme, and things started to make sense for the first time in my life – and I was a part of it. Then came the Christmas party – and lechery erupted. Apparently I wasn't the only one obsessed with sex. As the alcohol kicked in, so the pent-up emotions that had been locked up in a pressure cooker for the last twelve months exploded, especially among some of the older ones. They must have been thinking about nothing else. A woman from the adjoining office, probably in her mid-thirties, gripped me. Can't remember her name – probably just as well. My boss, George Eddisbury, came and peeled her off. I don't know whether I'd have got lucky or not; George wasn't going to let me find out. It did my ego no harm, though, and come January I quietly started planning for the next Christmas party, along with everybody else.

The following Christmas it was Heather. I remember when I was saying good night to her behind her house, she said, 'Stop it. People can see from those houses over there,' and what did I think about the fact that she'd got a boyfriend? Nothing at all. I wasn't planning marriage.

The following Christmas it was somebody else. And so the games continued.

George was a good man. Forty-seven. He occasionally made references to his girlfriend. How could anybody that old have a girlfriend? It seemed obscene. I'd started on three pounds fourteen shillings, which put me the highest paid of all my mates. If I'd hung on twenty years I would probably have got George's job, but twenty-seven pounds a week wasn't going to change the world.

At eighteen I left, and was told by the branch manager that, should I wish, I could return at any time. Apparently that was unheard of – the company policy was not to re-employ. I must have made some impression despite my obsession with the typing pool.

During my stint at BRS there was an annual day out, as those places tended to do. One trip took us to Bangor on Dee Races. I became smitten. I must have bagged the odd winner and thought, 'This is it!' I was probably always reasonably good at maths, but now it had a purpose. I would study the form books every night; big thick books the size of a bible, with a lot more meaning. In hindsight, I became very good at mental arithmetic, but not as good as some of the men in the warehouses. Those guys could work out an each-way Yankee bet. Doesn't matter if you don't know what a Yankee bet is. Suffice to say it was complicated.

Probably as a result of my love of horseracing, I got a Saturday job working at a bookie's. The betting shop I worked for had three or four partners, well educated, university – not your stereotypical bookmaker. I learnt more in that short stint at the bookie's and at BRS than I ever learnt at school.

On a Saturday there could be six or more race meetings, hundreds of horses setting off within a few minutes of each other. There were no timed receipts for bets taken; bets were scribbled on the back of fag packets. When one guy passed me his bet I said to him with some regret, 'Oh, that horse has just won'. He grabbed his bet back off me and told me to go and do something indecent. I looked at him in amazement: he was cheating! I couldn't believe it.

The bookies wanted me to go and work with them full time when I left BRS, but I opted for what I considered to be the more exciting alternative, and went to work with my brother in law, who was a shopfitter. This meant travelling round the country, modernising and reorganising various offices to make way for the computers that were starting to come in.

The first place was Mexborough in South Yorkshire. I don't remember anything about the job, but I remember the landlady's daughter. My designs in that area, though, were not to happen – not then anyway. When Dave and I came back for our first evening meal the landlady brought in two big dinner plates filled to the edge with what I found out later was a Yorkshire pudding. I thought that didn't look like much of a meal, but it tasted nice and it was certainly filling. Then, when we had finished, the dinner came in: same sized plate piled up with potatoes, meat and all the rest. It was enormous. How the hell was I going to eat that? Back at the BRS I'd had something of a reputation as a big eater: I was eighteen and growing fast. But I wasn't in the same league as Mexborough. I don't know whether I finished the meal or not; my mind was elsewhere.

While I was considering how best to approach the object of my desires, the decision had already been made for me. Her friend registered her claim. Not as pretty, but what the hell. So with me and the friend, we came to that time of night: the time I'd been thinking about all evening. While I was thinking about the best approach, a little voice in my head said: 'Go for the tits', and I obeyed, only to find the bra was hollow. Not stuffed with a pair of socks or a hankie, like you're supposed to. When I moved my hand away, she promptly put it back. I should have savoured that moment more than I did – it was to be a long time before it happened again. I popped the dints back out of her bra when it was time to go. It seemed the gentlemanly thing to do. Call me old-fashioned if you like. I've heard that girls these days are likely to use a chicken fillet by way of bridging the gap. Chicken fillets hadn't found their way to the kitchen in Mexborough in those days, never mind as an artificial substitute, and thank God they hadn't. In the mind of an emotional boy learning how to cross the road, if I'd have pulled out a chicken fillet it could have killed me.

The job in Mexborough only lasted two or three weeks, then back in the suitcase. As I said goodbye to Mexborough, the landlady's daughter kissed me at the garden gate. Why did I not do something about it before the last farewell? Why? That wasted opportunity plagued me.

Scotland, Uttoxeter, London and many more over the next two or three years. I was out of my depth in London. The stumbling Scouse charm was no match for confidence, sophistication, style and class. But it would be one day.

Uttoxeter was a lot of fun, apart from the bit where my heart got broken for the first time. Excluding Lavinia Ridell. It was the JCB site at Uttoxeter. Awe-inspiring. Joseph Cecil Bamford – the factory was known as Joey's Place to the locals. There was a row of wooden offices – shacks – that were about to be pulled down to make way for this futuristic citadel. Outside the wooden shacks were ten cars with number plates JCB 1 to 10. Rolls Royces, Cadillacs. I think JCB 9 was a Vauxhall Victor. We were building the new computer room; Joey's latest toy.

Alongside the site were enormous earth movers, the ones that bounce along the side of the motorway, tyres the size of a house, as if just borrowed from Star Wars. They were rearranging the landscape of the surrounding countryside, creating an enormous lake purely to add to the panache of the citadel.

We were staying in digs in Uttoxeter about seven or eight miles from the JCB site. When we finished working our ten-hour day we went to a pub near the site, and that was where I fell in love. When it became time to leave the pub the van headed back to Uttoxeter and I stayed on with my Juliet, contemplating the stars, the moon and the universe (as you do). That takes about an hour. So now what? I couldn't get back to Uttoxeter – the van had gone. I walked back to the digs that night, but never again. I acquired the keys to the site stores just in case it was going to happen again – and it was going to happen again, I was damn sure about that.

The following night I let myself into the site stores. There were four-foot high rolls of fibreglass insulation. I stood alongside one roll and wrapped it round me until I had three or four layers, then fell over in the corner and slept. I was wearing a black turtle-neck sweater that twelve hours earlier had seemed pretty cool, but in the morning had become a hedgehog, and for months I was washing fibreglass needles out of me and the jumper. Not one of my best ideas. As the site progressed I got keys to the computer room. Five star luxury. Part of the construction in the computer room was a suspended ceiling, and placed on top of each of the two-foot square tiles was a fibreglass cushion encased in polythene. There were thousands of these in one of the rooms, just heaped ready for use. I could dive into them and disappear into a cushion of luxury.

One night, fast asleep in my gossamer cocoon, I was awoken by the key turning in the lock. Somebody entered the computer room and the lights came on, and voices. I was terrified of being caught. I knew I would be publicly whipped by Joey himself. A couple of men on the night shift must have acquired the same keys as me, and were just having a nose. They came into my room. I could see them through the slit in my cocoon. They chatted between themselves about this and that, unaware of my terror. They left, and I breathed again.

This arrangement went on for some time, and I was as happy as Larry. My nightly visitors never returned – not to my knowledge anyway. All was well, until the computer manager started to work in his own office during the day. He had his own kettle, his own stash of coffee and sugar. This became my morning coffee while I waited for the van to arrive from Uttoxeter. I wonder if he ever noticed his coffee was going down. One morning he arrived at his office early while I was still in my midden. The only way I could have got there was to have passed his office, and the only way to get out was to pass his office. I was stuck. This was more terrifying than the night visitors. And now it was daylight. My only hope was to wait for the van to arrive and mix myself in with the hustle and bustle of the lads starting their day. I waited and waited. The enormity of my crime, and the inevitable punishment, racing through my mind.

The van didn't get in until about ten o'clock. It had broken down – got a puncture. I tried quietly but forcibly to explain the torture they'd put me through. They just thought it was funny, and it wasn't.

Joey visited the computer room every day with his entourage of yes men. This was his new toy. If the biggest pull on the planet had to be the richest man on the planet, surely Joey must be shortlisted, though he didn't look it. He wore the same mid-blue suit every day, sometimes with the collar turned up as if he just hadn't bothered fixing it. He'd walk around barking orders to the man behind him, and the orders got passed down the line to the last of the yes men – who went and did it. In one room there was a unit attached to the surface of the partition, something to do with the air conditioning. He barked, 'That shouldn't be sitting on the surface – that should be sunk in!'

'Sunk in',
'Sunk in',
'Sunk in',
'Sunk in',

got passed down the line, until one of our guys went and sank it in. Nobody had the guts to tell him that if it was sunk in one side it would come out the other. But that's what got done, and then a hardwood panel had to be fitted on the other side to hide the bodge. Nobody argued with Joey. Strange way for the biggest pull on the planet to behave.

When I become the biggest pull on the planet I'll do it differently. I know that. But in the eyes of the world he was something. Bright yellow gleaming earthmovers, 'JCB' emblazoned on the side, emerged from the end of the citadel – very impressive. Immaculate drivers in spotless white boiler suits and hard hats took these machines worldwide.

I was never going to be anywhere near as good at shop-fitting as Dave, and Dave wasn't going to change the world anyway. I wanted the power of Joseph Cecil Bamford, and I knew I would treat it with more respect.

When our part of the site at JCB was complete we went to Scotland. There I phoned my love from a telephone box, and was told it was not to be. Those words sank deep into my soul, and I was crucified. As important as it was in my vulnerable years, I cannot recall her name. And yet I had remembered Lavinia Ridell – probably because her name was more Hollywood.

I went back to visit BRS on one occasion, which was a mistake. I acted big-headed, obnoxious, bragged about how much I'd achieved while they were still pushing paper. I probably wasn't as bad as that but came away not liking myself very much.

Towards the end of my career in shopfitting I was working at a building society in Derby. There I became close to a pretty girl who worked in the office. One evening we were in a pub having a drink. I'd gone to the bar. When I came back she was sitting looking down at the table. She said without looking up, 'You're the nicest person I've ever known.' That little cameo has stayed with me all these years, and my behaviour at BRS – that needs to be eliminated. And whatever I said to that pretty girl in Derby needs to be encouraged, if I only knew what it was I said.

If I was not to be the greatest professional gambler, or the finest shopfitter in Christendom, perhaps my future was in Hollywood? I knew the world was waiting for me in some guise or other, so I decided I would become a film star.

Hollywood. How d'you get there? Whenever I'd been to London the only place to go was Soho, and the erotic delights of forbidden fruit. In wandering around Soho on my own, terrified, I had stumbled across Wardour Street. That's where the film studios' offices were. That was the place to start. I thought about it for an age. Then I packed my bag and headed for London to start my film career. I walked up and down Wardour Street, wearing out the shoe leather. All the film studios were there. Hammer Studios (no, don't want to be Dracula or Frankenstein – I'm better than that). Can't remember the others. By far the biggest was Rank. That'll do, that's more me.

I called in a pub for some courage, then walked boldly up to Rank... and past it and back to the pub for some more courage. I wasn't going to be a film star if I chickened out at this point. I gave myself a good talking-to during the second bit of courage. As I went through the doors of Rank I was faced with acres of thick carpet. Didn't expect that. At the far end was a reception desk. I tried to walk purposefully over to the man at the desk. Probably fooled nobody. I told him I was a student doing work on film studios, and asked him if I could get a pass to go round theirs. I suppose I must have rehearsed that during the courage bit. Anyway it seemed to make sense when I said it. He advised me to go and visit Pinewood Studios. They were coming towards the end of filming 'Casino Royale'. I left with this snippet of information, duly proud of myself – my film career was on its way. Now, where's Pinewood Studios? I couldn't ask him – that would have been stupid.

I was staying in a cheap hotel in Gower Street. I'd ask them. I didn't see anybody until breakfast. Breakfast was basic – so was the English being spoken by European waiters. There were two men at the next table, one American, the other East European. Every time the American spoke, the East European said, 'It's propaganda… it's just propaganda… it's all propaganda.' I couldn't ask them if they knew where Pinewood Studios were. They'd say it was propaganda. Was it propaganda? Was everything propaganda?

I went to Euston Station and found out Pinewood Studios were a lot further than I thought. I don't know what had made me think it was going to be round the corner.

It took hours and hours. Trains and tubes and long walks. There was a lady sitting opposite me on the train – middle aged, a bit older maybe. There was something about her – overpainted face, too much jewellery. I was mesmerised, fascinated. Funny, the things you remember. I'd caught a headline in the paper: Alma Cogan had died. I knew this lady must have been going to the funeral. She was certainly theatrical. I wondered why she was going on her own. Alma Cogan was big, there would have been thousands there. Not my sort of stuff. It was 1966, or thereabouts. The Beatles had just burst into my soul. The lady got off the train before me, I think.

It was a long walk down Pinewood Lane to the studio. I think it was Pinewood Lane – certainly it was a tree-lined road, which may have been pines. It gave me time to practise what I was going to do or say when I got there. Would there be a pub to help me decide? *Perhaps I shouldn't – might need a pee.* Eventually I got to the man on the gate, I dropped the student idea and told him I was a joiner looking for work on the sets. He was very friendly, told me I needed an Equity Card. Equity Card? That made me an actor, didn't it? He told me the studios were about to close for the day. He said there was a bus going from there shortly, taking them back into London – I could get a lift if I wanted. I told him I'd be alright, thank you. I was 'alright, thank you'! How stupid was that? I could have gone back into London with them. I don't know who 'them' were, but they were in – and I blew it. It had taken me a whole day to get there, just to turn round and walk back again. The walk back, and the buses and train journeys, were even longer.

I don't know whether it was the next day, or the day after that, I decided to go to Elstree Studios. Elstree, a busy suburb of shops and businesses. The Elstree Studio was a big, daunting office block. No

Pinewood walk, no friendly man at the gatehouse. By this time my bottle had gone. So I went to the pictures.

I made enquiries about an Equity Card. You needed to be recommended by somebody who carried an Equity Card. Catch 22. So all the thrills and the terrifying moments of my film career came to an abrupt end. What would have happened if I had got the bus with 'them'? I can only take this moment to apologise to my public for cutting my film career so brutally short.

I saw an ad in the paper that said, 'Do you need to earn £100 a week?' or something like that – whatever the equivalent was before inflation started making a mockery of money. I had to go round door to door asking the unsuspecting housewives if they would answer a few questions. The questions were carefully loaded to prove their children could have a far better education and, as they had been selected as one of a few in their area, they were entitled to an extremely special offer – a free extremely special offer. The free offer consisted of the first three volumes of a very expensive set of encyclopaedias, but then they had to pay twenty-nine pounds-odd to cover some waffle about administration costs or packaging. They were conned into paying thirty pounds for this extremely special offer. Well, twenty-nine pounds odd – something to do with their protection (or lack of it) under the law if the amount was under thirty pounds. It sounds an awful lot of money in relative terms, but that's how I remember it. These people were con men and extremely clever at what they did. I fell for it for a while. We were supposed to get £4 for every sucker we could persuade to sign up, then the big boys got £6 for doing nothing, and their bosses would get something, and so it went on. Once they had signed for the special offer, the big guns went in with the real con. It wasn't long before I realised that I and the rest of the door-to-door low life in the Liverpool office of Caxton Publishing were being conned just as much as we were conning others. Our commission seldom materialised as expected, but what really stank was the way the deal was struck.

Instead of heading for our designated areas and preying on the unsuspecting, a group of us went back to one guy's flat. I don't know who sparked the idea, but we decided to swap clothes. The sexes were roughly evenly split, and enough of us did it to cause a riot when we went out to the pub.

And so the figures from the Liverpool office diminished, and we were called to account by the powers that be at the head office in Manchester.

The big boss of Caxton wasn't there – the one that drove the same flash sports car as The Saint on television. But there were about six of his lieutenants on the platform from where they delivered the Sermon on the Mount, and barked out the ten commandments before the summoned flock. It wasn't just the Liverpool office. We weren't the only cretins brought to book. I suppose there would have been about forty or fifty people there, all being publicly whipped for not obeying the high priest. I could feel my blood beginning to boil.

As Liverpool office came to its day of reckoning, the red mist came down. I stood up and said: 'If it's all free, why are they paying twenty-nine pounds?' and, 'That's a lie!', and all that sort of stuff.

There was muttering on the higher level: 'I can see there'll be one person not working for Caxton tomorrow'. I kind of sensed the support of the serfs around me, and said, 'Well here's one not working for Caxton now – and you can tell that to Simon Templar as well.' The meeting descended into chaos.

The Liverpool office closed. I don't know what happened to the rest of the company, but I hope that closed as well. Their operation may not have been illegal but it was highly immoral.

There was a method of door-to-door selling in Liverpool at the time, by which photographers would take portraits of babies and children in their own homes. Unlike Caxton, this was legitimate business A couple of my friends were doing it. These were the days before colour photography, or when it was in its infancy, so they would take black and white photographs, making a note of the colour of the cardigan and clothes that the children were wearing, and then painting it in afterwards. Very crude, but effective. This kind of enterprise sold a lot of photograph frames. I taught myself how to make the frames.

I was only making a few pence out of each one. I must have been mad, when you think that the four pieces of picture frame moulding had to be cut and joined, and the glass, back and stand cut and fitted, but rumbling around in the back of my mind wasn't the amount that I'd get for one frame – it was the amount I'd get for ten, then one hundred. And what about a thousand?

One of the biggest companies in Liverpool doing this sort of photography was Watsons in Huyton. They had two small offices above a chippie – this was real big business to me. After several meetings with Watsons, we had agreed samples and prices. 'Oh, and of course Purchase Tax,' they said. 'Yes, of course Purchase Tax,' I agreed, wondering what the hell they were talking about.

Purchase Tax was the forerunner of VAT and it was levied at one source by the manufacturer – not on the cost of materials or by the shops who were selling the goods, just by the manufacturer. Because it was just being levied at one link in the chain, it was a lot. The rate at that time was a colossal fifty-five percent. I couldn't let Watsons know that I hadn't a clue what Purchase Tax was or how you actually handled it, I mean I was a proper company. I had invoice forms printed with a box for Purchase Tax, and just stuck 55% on the bottom of every invoice. So if I invoiced £50, that became £77.10s. 0d. I suppose I made about ten pounds on the fifty pounds – and then got another twenty-seven pounds for doing nothing. One time they gave me a cheque for one hundred and twelve pounds. I remember the cheque sitting in my inside pocket while I was in church (the first of my mates was getting married). I wasn't interested in the ceremony, of course – I had one hundred and twelve pounds in my pocket, and more than half of it was treasonable. I'd now decided I was defrauding the Crown and was likely to be beheaded. I'd spent all these fifty-five percents, of course. Even had I gone cap in hand to the Government, I couldn't pay it back. The pressure of all this fraud wore me down. I went to Watsons with some cock and bull story, and stopped supplying them.

I had to find out what Purchase Tax was, and how to sort it. I'd tasted blood – or rather my imagination had. But in the meantime I had to get work of some sort.

I had a hammer and a saw, from working with Dave, so I tried to get work pretending I was a joiner. They said, 'Where's your card?' Card. That dreaded word again. This time it was an ASW card. The Amalgamated Society of Woodworkers. I needed an ASW card to prove I was a joiner. Prove I was a joiner? That was a joke. I knew a nail went in pointed end first, and that was about it.

The local headquarters of the ASW held their meetings every other Tuesday night. There were about thirty hard-bitten trade unionists at the meeting. I went to ask them for a card. They asked me where I'd been working. I gave the name of a company in Stockport that was the last place I'd worked with Dave. They said, 'OK, we'll write to the company.' 'Please, God. Don't,' I thought. Dave had had a major falling out with this company, and I had been a casualty. I was told by the throng of thirty good men and true to attend their next meeting.

Not knowing what to expect, but fearing the worst, I returned two weeks later. The worst happened. They'd had a reply from Stockport along the lines of, 'I never employed this boy in the first place, and I would never employ him again', and so on. The thirty good men and true rose in uproar. I thought I was going to be lynched. Instead, they turned on this firm in Stockport screaming that they were not treating a young apprentice with due respect, and that firms like this shouldn't be allowed to operate. I was asked to leave the room while I was discussed. Those few minutes seemed like an age. I wasn't waiting in a plush reception with a pretty girl taking telephone calls. It was a dark, dingy corridor, ten coats of khaki and brown paint on top of anaglypta wallpaper. Why I didn't walk down the corridor and out of the door, I don't know. But I didn't, I waited. After some time I was summoned back in. I don't recall what I said, it was all a bit of a blur. I just remember leaving the building with an ASW card, and going to the pub.

I made myself a joiners' wooden tool box. It wasn't as good as Dave's, but it looked something like it, and I bought a few tools from second-hand shops, and one or two new ones. The new ones stuck out like a sore thumb, so I battered them against a wall and kicked them around the floor a bit to make them look used. It didn't work – that sort of thing never does. But now I had my trusty ASW card in my hot and sweaty.

I bluffed my way on to a building site, a job with William Thornton, one of the big construction companies. The job was concrete shuttering – minimal joinery skills required. A hammer, a crowbar, and an ability to work hard just about covered that. They were building those enormous concrete towers, multi-storey flats, that were all the fashion in the sixties; enormous prisons rising out of the ground – some of them up to twenty-two storeys. The engineering that produced these was very clever. I still marvel at it today. It was called sliding shuttering.

The shutters were metal panels, three foot high by about four foot, bolted to each other like Lego in a form that created the layout for the whole ground floor. The whole system was then connected to hydraulic jacks and the process started – each shutter was filled with concrete then jacked up hydraulically, continuously moving and continuously being filled. It seemed a snail's pace but effectively it climbed two and a half storeys a week. Once all the ground work was in, the shell of the whole building leapt from ground to twenty-two storeys in eight weeks. The neighbours must have looked on in amazement. I certainly did.

Every time a building topped-off we had the Big Night Out. There were three gangs on the site – the joiners, the steel fixers and the navvies. Once it was decided where the night out was going to be, it was left to the joiners to arrange it. I suppose they had the most O-levels. We decided to book the Garrick in Leigh, one of the big cabaret clubs at the time. There would be about forty of us, a full coach-load anyway. To make sure we were treated with the due respect, Ernie had told the Garrick that we were the Crosby Rotary Club – which probably delighted the Garrick, who also suggested we go on to their sister night club afterwards.

We set off for the Garrick about six o'clock. Some of us had had a couple of pints, then of course there were the three or four crates on the coach. We were put on the top table, the full width of the stage. The star of the show was Diana Dors – blonde, busty, brassy, perfect. It would be about nine-thirty when her stint came on. By this time Crosby Rotary Club was well-oiled.

As Diana Dors walked on the stage, Big Henry, the boss navvy, instantly fell in love and stood up calling to Diana – a plea from the heart. She pretended not to notice, but he was only four feet away, and Henry wasn't going to be deterred. He stood on his chair, on to the table and from that point leapt on to the stage. These guys were big, strong, and very fit. He could be ignored no longer. Diana said, 'Isn't it time little boys went home?' Henry walked towards her, arms out in front like the Return of the Mummy. 'Diana, Diana'. Diana knew discretion was the better part of valour and backed off stage. Henry became the cabaret, to the encouragement of all the Crosby Rotary Club. If had been the Crosby Rotary Club somebody would have stepped up to resolve the situation. But we weren't, so there were shouts of, 'Go on 'Enry!' and 'Give her one 'Enry!' The bouncers could do nothing. Henry was mob-handed, and it would have been a very stupid bouncer who tried to intervene. It was hilarious. I was sitting next to Ernie when the manager came over and politely said, 'Er, there's a bit of a problem with the night club...' We instantly knew what he meant, and just said to him, 'Don't worry about it'. I knew by the time the Garrick Club was closing it would have been a successful night.

Henry wasn't quite the biggest navvy. That was Tommy Keaton. At a Chinese one night, Tommy and about three or four others decided the meal wasn't worth paying for and decided to leave. The others got out OK and looked back for Tommy. He emerged in the doorway with about five Chinamen hanging on to him. Tommy just roared and bowled them all off as if they were skittles in a Popeye cartoon.

Once, a food fight broke out in the works canteen. Somebody smacked Tommy on the back of the head with his unwanted sandwich. Tommy lost it and threw a boiling hot pot of tea in the general direction. I got most of it. I flew at him and bounced off like a ping pong ball hitting a steel door. 'Don't do it, Kenny!' he said. He was right.

We went on to build multi-storey flats on different sites, Macketts Lane, Netherley, replacing the back-to-back terraced houses. What a social catastrophe – no more unlocked doors, or nipping next door for a cup of sugar, or sitting on the step watching the world go by. I think all the flats have been pulled down now.

Then there was a major project, a big new wing was being added at Walton Hospital. The whole project was estimated at £2.5 million. Wouldn't buy you a footballer's leg now.

Good times, but it wasn't going to contribute to the Almighty Plan. I was never going to be the boss of William Thornton, neither in ability nor inclination.

CHAPTER 2

The first flat I had was in Crosby. A big old house, with three or four rooms as bedsits, shared kitchen. The owner of the house was a big man in a wheelchair – moved around like Ironside. His domain was the ground floor, for obvious reasons. I moved in on a Saturday afternoon. There was a man in a suit in one room – I didn't see him much, and two girls across the corridor – a fat one with brown hair and a thin one with blonde hair. Before I had unpacked my meagre possessions, the fat one knocked on the door to say welcome, and she was going to the shops, did I need anything. Within ten minutes we were lying flat on the bed. It wasn't my idea. Nice welcome to Crosby, though. It became alternate nights: one brown, the next blonde.

The blonde girl had a boyfriend. He'd call for her from time to time, and sneer at me if I passed him on the path – I was low-life. *If you only knew.*

One thing that BRS had taught me was how to save. One of the old biddies in the office, Joyce I think, came around every Thursday payday and insisted, and I mean insisted, I put some money in the bank she ran. I left BRS with about £300 in the bank – an absolute fortune. And the building sites had paid well. So, despite playing hard, the bank balance was creeping up.

While I was in Macketts Lane I'd taken driving lessons. The instructor picked me up outside the site, and my lesson conveniently drove me home and saved me the bus fare. I passed first time, more by luck than anything else.

Buying your first car is more important than your first girlfriend – a lot more. It happened to be a Vauxhall Victor, and it happened to be from Leighton Motors in Hoylake. My mate from William Thorntons,

Ray, took me over to Hoylake to pick it up. I hadn't realised that I'd picked a night when Liverpool were playing at home, and all the streets approaching the tunnel were chock-a-block, cars bumper to bumper.

As I was crawling towards the Birkenhead entrance to the tunnel I could see smoke coming out of the bonnet. I convinced myself it was the exhaust from the car in front. He moved off, and left the smoke. I tried to ignore it and when I got to the pay booth I got out and said to the guy in the booth, 'I don't think I'm going to get through.' He looked down at the car and said, 'God, you're on fire! Quick, pull the car over there.' I panicked, got in the car, took the handbrake off and rolled back into the car behind me. I got out to apologise. No damage. He understood. I parked my car over there. Didn't know what to do. I know the first thing you're supposed to do is lift up the bonnet. I didn't even know how to do that. I asked some guys, who had also broken down. They lifted the bonnet up and said, 'You're overheating. Let it cool down, take the cap off the radiator – there, and put some water in. But wait for it to cool first… There's the water, over there. We've overheated as well. It happens.' Some consolation – I'm not the only idiot on the block.

What to do while I'm waiting for it to cool down? I looked around: all I could see were cars disappearing into the tunnel, eager to get to the match. Outside the tunnel complex I could see a pub. So I went for a pint. I don't think it touched the sides. I can't remember whether I had another one or not – it wasn't a big no-no then.

Back to the car, calmer now. Put some water into the radiator, slammed the bonnet down, and looked into the big black hole of the tunnel. I glanced back at the pay booth. I hadn't paid. Didn't care about that. I tried to start the car. It wouldn't. A policeman came over: 'Is your starter motor jammed?'

I must have looked at him, blank. 'I'll give you a push', he said, looking down the slope towards the tunnel. He must have seen the panic on my face: 'Don't worry', he said, 'it'll start. Put it in gear, put your foot on the clutch, and when you get up to a speed it'll start.' I thought I'm not hearing this, but a copper had told me to do it, so I had to. The car started to roll into the tunnel, picking up speed. I knew eventually somewhere in the middle it would level off and start to climb up the other side, and I'd go backwards and forwards for a bit – until I came to a standstill at the bottom, causing chaos. Two hands gripping the steering wheel like a vice, as if that's going to help. Down, faster and faster. I took my foot off the clutch and the car bumped a bit and started – a miracle!

When I got home Ray had been waiting for me for about an hour. If this was driving, I didn't want anything to do with it. I just wanted to drop the keys down a grid and never ever drive again.

If this picture framing thing was going to work it had to be taken seriously. In every spare moment I learned more about picture framing. I left the flat in Crosby, went back to live at my parents' house for a while and set up a workshop in their garage. I found out where the wholesale suppliers were – businesses solely dedicated to supplying bits and pieces to the picture framing industry – and wandered round in awe like a kid in Aladdin's Cave; every little screw, every little fitting, a *eureka* moment.

I even started to find out about the dark mysteries of Purchase Tax. I'd contacted Customs and Excise, and a Mr Longmore came to see me. Mr Longmore not only taught me how to keep the books as required by Customs and Excise, he taught me a lot about book-keeping generally. He was very intelligent and took the time to explain it in language I understood, and became a good friend. He was a writer in his spare time. He'd written a play for radio. I was an avid listener to the Third Programme and the Home Service, and I'd heard the play before I met him. I thought it was a great story. It was about a man who was receiving messages from outer space through an orange he'd fitted antennae to. I'd told my mates in the pub about it, so then to actually meet the guy who wrote it was pretty awesome for me, especially as I knew I was going to be a writer one day.

I bought my first workshop in Day Street, Old Swan – well, put the deposit on it anyway. Half shop, half house, in the middle of a terraced block. It had been what they called a dairy in its day. I suppose they were the forerunner of the open-all-hours shop that sold everything. This purchase met with disapproval from my old fella. How could anybody possibly make a living out of making picture frames? It was the best encouragement he could have given me, making me determined to prove him wrong.

I decided to call the shop 'The House at Pooh Corner'. I'd become hooked on Winnie the Pooh from listening to it on the radio, brilliantly read by David Davies. I think this must have confused the neighbours – it wasn't even on a corner. Confusing people appears to be one of my functions in life. I lived in the house and rented the upstairs to a young family.

The House at Pooh Corner was where Eeyore lived. Eeyore got the short end of the stick most of the time, so I decided he needed a champion. 'House at Pooh Corner' and 'Eeyore' went on my business cards, and I knew the company would develop into a row of girls answering the telephone: 'Good morning. Eeyore International'.

Business expanded. The family upstairs moved out which gave more workshop space. I started supplying Max Spielmann, high street photo-processing shops, and serious about frames. They had about seven shops. To me, that was enormous.

One by one, all my mates got married, until I was the last one by a long way. You start to wonder is there something wrong – especially when people are saying 'Don't worry, you'll find somebody one day'. How on earth are you supposed to know whether or not it's love and therefore cast in stone?

It seemed the right thing to do when I met Pat. We bought a house in West Derby, and my tiny empire started to grow.

Our house had a big garden, and I started to see plants and shrubs for the first time. I was amazed at how a tiny little bud or shoot could turn into something so beautiful. Gardening became a passion. We went for a walk around Calderstones Park, and there we discovered the Japanese Garden. The peace, tranquillity and simple beauty of the place took my breath away. The effect was almost spiritual. I just wandered round slowly, trying to absorb whatever it was. I left, knowing I had to build my own Japanese garden.

A Japanese garden needed hills and paths, and streams and ponds. My imagination was running riot. But no matter how much money I was going to make I would never afford a garden in Liverpool big enough for my ideas. A lot of my customers were around the Merseyside area, but so long as I could deliver I could manufacture anywhere. I didn't need Liverpool as a base.

I had a small trade counter in Day Street. Occasionally one or two of the locals would drift in for a frame – curiosity as much as anything else. One day a little old lady came in thinking it was still a dairy. She asked me for a pint of steri (sterilized milk). 'I haven't got any steri,' I told her. 'Give us a pint of fresh then, lad.' There was no point in explaining to her that I didn't do milk. I just went to the back, and got a pint of milk out of the fridge to give to her. When I got back, she said, 'What are you doing here?' I told her. 'Oh, I want a frame,' she said, 'How much are they?' A look of horror on her face when I told her. I said, 'But there's Little Old Ladies' Discount' and I gave it to her half price. She came in again a while later. She said, 'I need another frame, for my son-in-law. He's got plenty of money – don't give him Little Old Ladies' Discount.'

A regular customer was an Irish priest, from Aintree somewhere. He'd phone me up, 'Hello Ken! It's Father O'Flagherty here. I need some more of those lovely frames of yours.' I found myself replying in an Irish accent. Couldn't help it – it just seemed compulsive. He was framing Papal Blessings, or something like that. It probably helped towards his whiskey bill. He would buy about twenty frames at a time and come in to collect. 'How much do I owe you, Ken?' I told him the price, plus VAT. 'Oh you don't need to bother with the VAT – them people have got enough money already.'

I didn't really have a lot to do with my neighbours in Day Street. I was probably seen as something of a weirdo and to be avoided. But one day a neighbour did come in. She'd seen a man behaving very suspiciously around a house a couple of doors up. I went upstairs, where one of my windows overlooked a few of the houses. I saw a man coming out of a back door carrying a bin bag well-laden with something. I thought, 'God – he's just robbed them'. I ran down the stairs and into the back entry. He was walking away with the bin bag over his shoulder. I shouted to him to stop. Of course he didn't – he ran, and clambered over a wall into the road. I raced after him, over the wall, and caught up with him in an adjoining street. I grabbed hold of him, and said something like, 'You're under arrest!' I must have seen that in a movie somewhere. He dropped the bin bag and I started to march him down the street, arm up his back as you're supposed to do, round the corner and back to my shop. He came along quietly for a while, until he started to think this wasn't a very good idea. And I'm thinking, 'How am I going to sit him down to wait while I phone the police'; and what would we talk about for the hour and a half it would take for the police to get there? He struggled to break free. I can't say a fight took place – it was more handbags. Anyway, he ran off.

Having lost my robber, I went back to get the bin bag. I needed something for all my effort. It wasn't there. The insurance man doing his rounds got out of his car and said, 'A woman grabbed the bin bag. She ran into that block of flats.' I told him to go and call the police. He shot off in his car, and I went into the block of flats. I walked around until I found an open door, and there was the bin bag on the living room floor. A woman was spreading out all the gear – record players and stuff. I went in and started grabbing the booty. I said. 'That's stolen!' She said, 'Ah, piss off, lad. They'll be insured.' 'I nearly got my head kicked in for that!' Wasn't true, of course, but I thought I was entitled to colour it a bit. I grabbed everything up off the floor and shoved it back in the bin bag. I left the woman still cursing me and went back to my shop. The man from the Pru came back. He couldn't find a telephone box working. I phoned the police from the shop. Two CID officers came round and the investigation started.

The guy whose house was robbed was a painter and decorator, and the description of the robber fitted somebody he'd sacked a few days earlier.

The coppers said the suspect signed on at Walton dole office and if I went with them when he signed on and spotted him in the crowd it would be far stronger evidence than picking him out of a line-up. 'Christ, I'm busy,' I thought, 'I've got Max Spielmann's frames to get out on Thursday.' Time was tight; it always was. But I agreed to go. You've got to do your bit, I suppose. They picked me up, and we drove the five miles or so to Walton. They were chatting about the football match, or whatever. My heart was pounding like an animal facing its enemy. We pulled up outside Walton dole and thousands of people were walking past, in and out. We seeemed to wait an age. I thought, 'I'm never going to recognise him amongst all this lot.' Then he appeared. Unmistakable.

'That's him!' I said.

'Are you sure?'

'Definitely.'

They waited for him to go in the dole office, then followed him in to tell the staff not to delay him. My heart was still pounding. They told me what would happen: 'We let him come out. We stop him, and this is what you say. It's important to get the wording right…' The pressure's building. My heart's going faster.

He came out and started walking down the street, unaware of us. Then we went after him. They ran the car on to the pavement blocking his path. They both jumped out and grabbed him. (I think they'd been watching the same movie as me.) I did my bit, and they arrested him. The four of us got back in the car and headed back to Old Swan nick. 'We'll drop Ken off first – he's got to get his frames out.' I'd forgotten all about Max Spielmann. This is all matter of fact for them – they're in the front chatting about the football, trying to involve me, and I'm in the back sitting right next to a hardened criminal that I've just sent to prison for a very long time. I pretended to be cool and join in the banter, my eyes glued straight ahead, mind racing like a train – is this fellah next to me going to put a contract out on me? That's what they do, isn't it? Am I dead? And now they've just reminded me about Max Spielmann.

The case came to trial two or three times and was adjourned on a technicality. Each time, I was dragged away from the business at the wrong time. It always would be the wrong time. When it did finally come to trial I was in the Court on my own, and there was the accused with his gang of friends and brothers, all looking like they beat people up for fun. I had to pass them in the corridor. He recognised me, and said, 'Alright there – How're you doing?' He greeted me like a drinking buddy instead of the guy who was going to hang him. He wasn't a bit bothered. He did recognise me, that's for sure. That might have put me at ease a bit, but I was still scared stiff. He had his gang for moral support; I didn't even have the two coppers now.

The prosecution said, 'If it wasn't for the brave action of a neighbour,' *that's me*, 'apprehending the accused until he broke free,' *that's me*. I was rising in stature as my moment of glory was read out before the Court. My moment of glory was short-lived, though, when the defence said that I wasn't so brave, I was told to do it by a neighbour, and had no alternative. My ego deflated like a cheap balloon when the party's over. In the end he was found guilty, of course. He apparently felt the neighbour had owed him a week's wages, and he was taking it in kind. His kind of justice. Anyway, he got off with a conditional discharge, and I got a few shillings' expenses.

The cost of all this must have been colossal. I swore I'd never do it again, but then you never know. For some reason, the two coppers seemed well impressed with me. If they could ever help me out... they said. That might come in handy one day.

I never did see the neighbour who got robbed. No thanks or anything like that. He would probably have preferred the insurance money, just like the woman said.

I had a regular customer for frames over in Northwich. Lawrie Sands. I was running late on Lawrie's order. I did my deliveries in a battered old Anglia van I had at the time. It was just about roadworthy. I was heading to Northwich, desperately short of petrol and no time to fill up. The Gods would look after me.

The route took me over Runcorn Bridge. Roadworks. Typical. One-way traffic crawling bumper to bumper. Please, God, don't let me run out of petrol. Eyes fixed on the needle reading Empty. As we climbed over the bridge the engine stuttered, and stopped. I started it up. We moved a yard or so and stopped again. I started it again, and it stopped. I tried and tried again, hoping for some sort of miracle. It wasn't going to happen. I got out of the van. I'm now on the top of Runcorn Bridge and I've stopped the traffic completely. Both ways.

From the brow of the bridge I could see clearly all around. I searched for the petrol station that wasn't there. Behind me out of the corner of my eye I could see there was a lorry – luckily enough he was blocking all other prying eyes and angry faces. The trick is not to make eye contact, but I could see he was leaning on his steering wheel, bemused: now what's he going to do? Lying against the railings was a battered old gallon can. You could just about make out 'Mazola Cooking Oil' although the can had been rearranged by the passing traffic. I picked it up – at least I had something to put petrol in. There was some liquid in it. I took the cap off – it smelled like petrol. I shook the can and sniffed it again – definitely smelled like petrol. I opened the back of the van, tore a piece of cardboard and made a funnel, and poured the contents of the can into the place where you put petrol. This must have been very entertaining for the lorry driver, but I wasn't looking that way. I closed the back of the van and got back in and tried to start it. It wouldn't start. I tried and tried, but it wouldn't start. I knew now with absolute certainty I'd poured cooking oil into the engine. *That's it… I'm dead.* I tried again, knowing it was no use. I knew sooner or later the police and some sort of emergency service would arrive, and I'd have to tell them I'd run out of petrol so I thought I'd try Mazola Cooking Oil. I've done some stupid things before. This had to be right up there with the best of them. I tried the engine again as I tried to make some sort of coherent sense out of what I'd just done. The engine started, spluttered, and stopped. But then it started again, and we started to move, along the totally empty road in front of me. I assume one by one the traffic was moving behind me, but I wasn't looking. My eyes fixed on the road ahead. I had to get away before the cavalry arrived.

I got off the bridge and found a petrol station and filled up. I told everybody in the petrol station what had just happened, though they weren't interested. I carried that battered Mazola Cooking Oil can around for months as if it was some kind of guardian angel, telling everybody. I don't think anybody believed me.

CHAPTER 3

Pat never saw herself as maternal – she was a career girl – or was that just what other people said. She became pregnant with twins. She was secretary to David Rowlands, personnel director of Littlewoods. We went over for dinner at his house a couple of times. He was a big man in every respect. We got on very well. He took me under his wing and became a bit of a mentor. He told me how he used to raise his voice when negotiating with the unions, building to a crescendo. It was all theatre.

He used it on me once. I had a couple of part-time girls, one of whom was messing me about – coming in when she felt like it, bad attitude – so I sacked her. She threatened to take me to a industrial tribunal for unfair dismissal. I gave her a couple of weeks' wages to buy her off. David Rowlands wiped the floor with me. I can hear him now on the telephone: 'What right have you got to do that?' as if I was setting a precedent that was going to rebound on Littlewoods. His words have stayed with me all these years. He was right.

Twin girls, Anna Soularn and Sara Vivell. Soularn came from *Magnolia Soulangeana* and Vivell from *Erica Carnea Vivellii*.

I started to wonder where I could build my Japanese garden. North Wales was an obvious choice. You could draw a circle around the commuter distance of Liverpool and, say, Manchester and outside that circle property prices were much lower.

We looked for a long time before we found the house in Berwyn, a few miles outside Llangollen, North Wales. Hen Pandy was set in two and a half acres of mountain. Perfect, apart from it was too expensive. It was owned by Mrs Barnett. Leathery skin, gypsy-like, impossible to say how old. She lived there with her brother, and Toma – a black guy in

ties. She had spent a lot of her life in Africa. That's where
nd Toma. Toma was put out of his tribe as a young child to die;
us pelvis was damaged and he could only move by dragging himself
along with his hands. He became known as the Grasshopper Boy. She
adopted him and brought him back to the UK, and tried every way she
could to raise money to pay for the numerous operations he needed.
Now he had grown to be the handsome young man I saw. Liverpool
supporter, and working in the library at Bangor University. People were
wary of this lady. They looked on her with suspicion, believing she was
touting a poor cripple around to make money for herself. How cruel
people can be when they just don't understand.

Hen Pandy was perfect alright, but out of our reach. But I was
determined to beg, borrow or steal whatever it took to get it. I got to
know Mrs Barnett's family quite well before we finished the deal. Every
weekend we'd go there, each week raising a little bit more money
towards the asking price, and each week she was reducing the price.
One time there was snow on the ground and she took me up the
mountain to the edge of the property where the copse of trees was. I
looked down, back to the house, with some trepidation. Going up was
one thing. She must have noticed my concern and said, 'Oh you sit on
your bum for this bit,' and promptly sat down and slid down the tricky
bit. What a star!

She needed to sell the house because her brother, Jack, had cut his
arm off repairing an enormous bandsaw at the local timber yard. The
accident had affected his mind. You could be talking with him and tears
would fill his eyes as he recalled the war, and the loss of his brothers and
father back in Poland. She needed to sell Hen Pandy and move, and try
to give his mind something new to focus on.

She left us the carpet in the lounge when she moved, even though
she said it was an heirloom. She couldn't see us moving in on bare
boards, and she knew the move had taken every penny we had. I wanted
her to leave the pelmet in the dining room too, which was a fourteen
foot snakeskin. She'd persuaded a tribeswomen not to slice it up and fry
it in the normal way, until she skinned it first. She pointed to two holes
at one end of the snake and told us that was where the dart had killed it.
I think I knew which holes she meant, though there were holes all over it
from drawing pins and stuff. Oh, and the ghost – she left us the ghost.

We moved on a Friday. It took all day. Moving's always a nightmare. I needed a drink. I went into Llangollen to find the local pubs. Millions of people all over the place – pubs chock-a-block, bouncers on the doors. It was like Mardi Gras. Great! I found out later that I'd moved in the middle of Eisteddfod week, the international music festival held in Llangollen every year. On the Friday night, thousands and thousands of people came in from miles around for no other reason but to get drunk and party.

When we'd settled in, my local pub was the Conquering Hero in Llantysilio. It was about two miles from Hen Pandy, across the bridge over the River Dee and along the back road towards Corwen.

The first time I went into the Conq was a Saturday afternoon. Hywel Gyfelia, local farmer, came in. He was shearing the next day, and he was a catcher short. I was picking up bits of the conversation: there were three shearers arriving. Johnnie Keeper was a catcher, but he needed another. 'I can do that,' I said. Hywel looked at me, a half smile on his face. 'OK,' he said. I don't think I expected that. No turning back now – I was about to become a catcher.

I got to Hywel's farmyard at seven o'clock on Sunday morning. There was a buzz about the place, loads of people chattering away in Welsh, an air of expectancy. Warm welcome from Hywel, who introduced me to Johnnie Keeper. Johnnie, shortish, looked a bit like a bull. Bleating sheep all over the place, looking a bit nervous, like me. The three shearers made themselves ready in their preferred place – like gladiators. Then it started.

'Follow Johnnie,' I was told. Johnnie went into the pen full of frightened sheep, grabbed hold of one, swung it round like a rag doll, hauled it off to the head shearer, then headed back for another. That's what a catcher does! He grabbed another sheep, and so did I. To my amazement I'm stronger than the sheep.

I grabbed another, and then another. I'd got the hang of it now, or so I thought. 'No! Not that one, Ken!' Hywel shouts. Apparently I'd picked up a lamb. That's one thing a catcher must know – the difference between a sheep and a lamb: it looked about the same size to me – I just thought it had taken better care of itself.

The shearers set about turning all these woolly monsters into skeletons. From time to time blood was drawn. Somebody had a stick with a big blue swab on the end of it and dabbed it, turning the red scar to blue, and the sheep was shoved off and panicked its way to the next bit.

In among the sheep there were two or three with horns. All had to be sheared. I had to get one to make up for the lamb cock-up. I did. I heard Hywel shout, 'He's got him!' Honour restored, and now I'm in the zone. Johnnie came out of the pen, swung his sheep round – crack! Its head hit the gatepost. 'What did you do that for?' 'He butted me.' Must remember not to cross Johnnie Keeper. Once sheared, the skeletons ran through a trough of sheep dip and into the next field.

We broke for dinner. There would be about eight of us in the big farmhouse kitchen. All the chat over the meal was in Welsh. I didn't mind that at all. I was just enjoying the crack. Well, until they started trying to translate some of the funny stories into English for my benefit.

Back on with the shearing. The head shearer did as much as the others put together, but all these years of shearing were taking their toll on his hands. It's gripping those vibrating shears that ultimately causes permanent damage – and what was he, thirty-odd?

The shearing and sheep-dip finished, what's next? Animated gesticulation and chatter in Welsh. I worked out that the shearers were paid per head, and now the count had to be done. This was achieved by letting thrutches of sheep gallop through the farmyard. A thrutch can be anything from fifteen, or thirty or more, at a time. We all positioned ourselves at vantage points to count. I climbed on a fence, focused, concentrating on what was about to happen, determined to do my job for Liverpool and St George. Then it started. The sheep charged into the farmyard, some went into the shippen and out through the windows, into the wagon and back out again, back into the shippen, all the time playing leap-frog over each other. 'I've counted that one twice, so I'll miss that one. Perhaps I didn't – I'll count that one again,' and so on. This anarchy continued until one by one the counters dropped out. Two shearers, Johnnie Keep, one or two farmhands – all lost count. I'd lost count forty-four times, but there was still a number of sorts running round my head. At the end the only two people left with the count were Hywel and the head shearer, and perhaps little old me sitting on the fence. An heated argument ensued between Hywel and the shearer over the disputed figures. Hywel looked at me and said, 'Well Ken's got a count.' He looked at me, expecting support. I can't remember whether the count was four hundred and forty, or four million and twenty-one, but it was a lot. Hywel asked me, 'How many, Ken?' knowing I'd be on his side. I gave him my figure, and he said, 'Shut up, Ken. You're saying more than the shearer.' Oops.

If they had been counted when they went through the sheep dip trough, for instance, in single file... there wouldn't have been any dispute. But no, they were right – they had to be counted galloping like the clappers through the farmyard, otherwise the day would have lost a lot of its magic.

I was told I would now sleep for a fortnight. But I didn't. I had to make the pub that night. There are some things you've just got to do.

For months after, I was pulling needles out of my forearms. Johnnie told me it was the gorse matted in the sheep's wool. It made the fibreglass itching back in JCB days a non-event.

It was probably twenty-five years later, when I was leaving Llantysilio, that Glyn Ty Isa, another farmer carved out of the mountain, said, 'You've been here a long time now, boy.'

'Twenty-five years, Glyn.'

'Is it, be God?'

'Am I accepted now, Glyn?'

'You were day one, boy.'

I'd moved to Llangollen fully intending to move the business there. Finding the right house would be the difficult bit, finding a workshop would be easy – or so I thought. Each day I travelled to Liverpool. Forty-five miles if I went through the tunnel, a bit longer if I went over Runcorn bridge, but same time. I had to make sure I got to Liverpool for seven o'clock so I could cut the glass needed for the day before the two or three girls started. They needed the same table. Getting back to Llangollen about seven-thirty, eight o'clock. Easy pease. Every night I parked the van in the driveway. Not the Anglia van any more – this was three times the size, and newer. I would stand for an age, staring across the river towards Velvet Mountain, stunned by the beauty of the place. I loved the house. Three bedrooms, two staircases, and a ghost.

We had the ghost for a while before we realised – I mean before we admitted it. It was too bizarre. We couldn't light a fire for the first few weeks because there was something wrong with the back boiler, so it wasn't that. Just every now and then there would be this overpowering smell of woodsmoke. I would wander around the house trying to locate it. I went up to the loft just in case. Nothing was burning. We never actually saw anything, we just knew something was there. I didn't know ghosts could appear like that, until somebody told me. We'd be sitting quietly in the living room when Smokey would come. It would be very local. Pat would just say, 'Smokey', and I'd get up and walk past her chair, and the sweet smell of woodsmoke would hit me. Then it would go just as quickly. Each night when I got home the first thing I'd say to Pat was, 'Has Smokey been today?' She'd say, 'No,' or, 'Once,' or, 'Twice.' I felt quite chuffed to think we had a ghost, at least while the lights were on – I didn't fancy coming downstairs in the middle of the night in the black and confronting Smokey, but we didn't have a lot of choice. The house looked conventional from the outside but inside it had two staircases: one led to two bedrooms, and another led to a third. Anna and Sara slept in their cot in the third. It sounds a weird arrangement, but it made sense at the time.

We linked a baby alarm between the two bedrooms so we could hear them if they woke, then down one set of stairs, through the living room, and up the other. Smokey never turned up.

We didn't just get the baby cries, we got police messages when they were in the area. Every now and then we'd hear, 'OK Panda 3, make your way over…' loud and clear.

One night we heard the police on a stake-out at the Chainbridge Hotel which was just about a quarter of a mile away. We could hear clearly as different cars moved into position. There were two or three ways to get out of the Chainbridge. I started to feel sorry for the poor fellow inside who probably had no idea. I felt like going to give him a warning – it didn't seem fair – but I didn't. I don't know what happened, but it brightened up my evening. All on the baby alarm.

When we were able to get the fire going in the living room we only burned logs. I'd sit in my comfy armchair, watching the big logs slowly, slowly smouldering. I was sitting in that chair when John Lennon died

Smokey appeared less and less – moved on to pastures new, or melted into the smell of the real woodsmoke.

The girls were no more than two years old when Jake came along. Jake Matthew – no flowery middle name. His name came from Derek Jacoby, actor in 'I, Claudius'.

The novelty of travelling back and forth to Liverpool had worn thin. Finding a workshop hadn't been as easy as I'd thought, by a long way, but in searching I got to know one or two of the local estate agents, in particular Roland Jones of Kent Jones. He phoned me up one day and told me there was a property about to come on the market, 'But it's not ready yet'. I prised the details out of him: the old Post Office and Sorting Office in Ruabon. I'd driven past this building many times and mused over how perfect it looked. Now it was coming on the market. I had to have it. I persuaded Roly to arrange a visit and he, in turn, persuaded the old Postmaster who very reluctantly agreed on the understanding I would see past the mess in one or two of the apartments upstairs. I assured him that wouldn't influence my opinion of the place whatsoever. Even so I was a bit taken aback to see ashtrays literally overflowing with cigarette stumps. The apartment had been occupied by one of the professors from the nearby Lindisfarne College. The building was perfect.

I hired a wagon to move the stuff from Old Swan. Easy, I thought. I think it was a 7.5 ton – anyway the biggest wagon you can drive on a standard licence. I don't know whether it was overloaded or not. We had to use a shoe horn to get all the bits in. Driving that from Old Swan to Ruabon was scary. The wagon moved OK, and went where you pointed it, and the brakes worked – too well at times. Going round corners was the scary bit: it seemed to lean over about forty-five degrees. How we never fell over I don't know.

It was while we were still unloading at Ruabon, that I first met Hywel Bellis. Driving past he'd seen the changes going on at the old Post Office, and called in to introduce himself. I told him I didn't change banks like I changed underpants – why should I consider Barclays?

My old accountant in Liverpool, whom I'd been with since I'd started, sadly died, and I had switched to Michael Coxey, in Wrexham. I phoned Michael and told him Barclays were offering me 1.5% over base. 'Get that in writing,' he said, 'and snap his fingers off.'

35

I got a good feeling from Hywel from the start, and it was about time I was on first name terms with my bank manager. I moved to Barclays.

The business settled in very quickly and began to have the makings of an well-oiled machine. Sometimes. Though the reality was far from it. Occasionally I got glimpses of what a well-oiled machine looked like, but the more I tried to grasp it, the more it seeped through my fingers like fine sand. It would be easy to blame the staff, four or five at this stage – well-meaning, honest, reliable(ish), but no get-up-and-go. How different it had been in Liverpool. They had the get-up-and-go, they could run with the pack, but not always reliable. All in all, about the same.

I found quicker and more efficient methods of production, building good relationships with suppliers, paying people on time – and being paid on time.

Of an evening when light permitted, and at weekends, I'd wander round my 2.5 acre estate and plan, with my Japanese garden hat on. The first problem was that my 2.5 acre estate was on a forty-five degree angle. Hills are great, but they mean nothing if they haven't got a valley.

A chunk of hill had been cut out at some stage to give a level footing for the house, and that's what I'd have to do again for the garden. I knew what JCBs could do; to cut a lump out of part of the landscape wouldn't difficult. Not for a JCB. Once my imagination took hold of a JCB, I could do anything. As well as rearranging the hillside, why not cut another wedge out and make the house bigger?

We needed a bigger house now. While Jake was barely toddling, Pat became pregnant again. Totally unexpected, and it was twins again. Jo Magda and Tom Nathan. Nobody's going to mess with a guy called Nathan – and Magda, mysterious, a Russian spy. That meant five kids now, and Anna and Sara were not yet five for another month.

By now I'd got to know the locals and who did what, a mix of beautiful and crazy people, and the guys for the JCB were the Claybrooks, Ian and Lester. Sometimes you instinctively know when people are right for the job; honest, reliable and good at what they do – all the bits. The same applied to John Miles, architect. John helped me redesign the house. I turned the modest three-bedroomed house into something much bigger and more in keeping with my delusions of grandeur.

Grandeur cost money. That shouldn't be difficult. The business was expanding nicely.

We had to dig out a big chunk of mountain to sit the extension in. A little knowledge is a dangerous thing. Ian and Lester weren't so sure. We could well hit rock, they said. We agreed to start it with a 'suck it and see' approach. If we hit rock, it couldn't be done. The first thing I got wrong was the amount of mountain we had to move. I thought we'd spread it out over 2.5 acres. No chance. Lorry after lorry took it away. Just when the end was in sight, we hit rock. Lester never gave up, bashing it, scratching it, chiselling at the rock, breaking teeth on his beloved JCB, until eventually we got the hole we needed. There we sat the extension and turned our three-bedroomed house with two staircases into a five-bedroomed, three bathroom house, including an enormous play room for the kids, and one staircase. No expense spared, hardwood doors, skirting and architrave, brass light fittings and hinges. We put three hinges on the doors, pretending they were carrying weight. I stained and polished them, putting highlights in the centre of the panels, as if they'd had hundreds of years of polishing. Absolute minute attention to detail, the slots on all the screws everywhere running North-South.

I got the Claybrooks to cut two flat areas in the hillside in preparation for the Japanese garden. When they finished, it looked like they'd just cut out two flat areas with the JCB. I knew that was what they'd done, but I didn't want it to look like that. In fifty years it wouldn't – no rush.

Max Spielmann were opening more shops every year. They now had thirty. David Edwards knew exactly how to give the high street shoppers what they wanted – and frames were a decent part of it.

We weren't their biggest supplier – that was Heritage. Heritage were using the cheapest materials available. There was no way I was going to beat them on price, and I had no intention of trying.

Pretty well the only way to make one frame different from the next was the moulding – the four pieces that joined to make the frame. There were thousands of different patterns of moulding, and I'd seen them all. So had all the other manufacturers, and so had David Edwards. You could put a cut-out mount in the frame which made it look better, but that had been done before.

I came up with a unique way of cutting the mount. It involved quite a bit of work in cutting out the mountboard, spraying the cut-out bit a different colour, cutting the centre out of that bit and fitting it back inside the first mount. Then when fitted in the frame the effect was better than a double mount, and without the bulk. It was labour-intensive, but we overcame that with practice.

Up to then, all frames being sold anywhere were traditional, golds and browns, and had been for a long time. I began making samples of frames in pink with cream/pink mounts, powder blue, bright red with black/red mounts. I sprayed some of the frames with metallic paint – black or bronze with cream and bronze mounts. The effect was electric.

But was David going to buy this? He was visionary, but he knew his customers weren't. 'I'm not sure,' he said. He liked them, I could see that, but I was charging over twice the price of Heritage. 'Let me think about it.'

I decided to submit the new frames with the double mount trick to the Design Council, the benchmark for excellence in design in those days.

The Design Council wrote to me. Our frames had been approved. I kind of expected that – I knew they were good – but it wasn't until I had the letter that I realised the enormity of what I'd achieved. I was chuffed to bits.

I told my staff, expecting to fill them with pride, and pinned the letter from the Design Council on the noticeboard. I'm not sure anybody read it.

It meant I could put the highly prestigious kite mark on the frames. This would help David make up his mind. I went round to see him – I was the excited schoolboy again.

'Mrs Jones in Rotherham won't see it,' he said. He must have seen my balloon starting to deflate. 'Look, I'll tell you what we'll do. Next month we're having our annual meeting of all the managers. We've got thirty-five shops now. Come along and sell it to them.'

Sell it to them? I'd never done that sort of thing before. Public speaking.

'Course I will. Love to.'

Manufacturing in Wales allowed me to apply to the Design Council in Cardiff, thinking the Welsh office would be an easier route. I don't think it made any difference, but apparently it now entitled me to put the Prince of Wales' Feathers on the frames as well. The American market would like that.

I phoned up the Design Council office in Cardiff and said we'd just received Design Council recognition.

'Oh, you're Ken Holmes are you?' she said.

'Yes, how did you know?'

'You're the only one who's ever won it from this office.'

I found that hard to believe, but that's what she said.

The Design Council had their own shop in the Haymarket in London, and being awarded recognition meant I could target that shop to sell them some frames. I arranged a meeting and went down to see them. Not a huge shop, but full of some of the best designs the United Kingdom had to offer.

I showed three or four frames to the buyer who said, 'Oh they're nice, aren't they? We might be able to find some room for them.'

'I'd be quite pleased if you could... What am I talking about – I'd be over the moon!'

He laughed. He knew how much it meant. We were in. We were also in the Design Council magazine that year, along with Jaguar, and some sort of wine rack.

While I was in London I went to see Liberty's. Walking into Liberty's is an experience in itself, but then sitting down with the buyer and listening to him place an order – I can't describe it. We delivered the frames on a Friday, and on the Monday morning we had a phone call from Liberty's: they'd sold out over the weekend and could they have some more.

Max Spielmann had hired a conference room in a big hotel in Wallasey for their annual do. David was serious about business, and so was I, but if I was going to talk seriously about frames it could be boring. It had to be funny, and that was risky.

It seemed like there were hundreds of people there when I arrived, but it was probably more like fifty. The only one I knew was David. No alcohol for anybody, just soft drinks until afterwards. That was David's way.

He showed me to a big empty room. 'Go and practise while it's empty if you like.' Now I was scared. Practise what? No script, no notes: I was just going to wing it.

There was one speaker on before me, a smart rep-looking type, talking about film, or paper, I can't remember. He didn't speak for long, and he was boring. And now me.

My audience was mostly female. David knew they were the best work force for his shops. I started to tell them a story about Mrs Smith who lived in Bolton. How her life hadn't turned out the way she had expected. Two young kids and another on the way. And him – he was a waste of time. Never did anything around the house. She decided to cheer herself up and go round to Max Spielmann's and buy a photo frame. She looked longingly at those modern, beautiful, elegant photo frames in pink and powder blue, but the girl in the shop persuaded her to buy a Heritage one because they were half the price. So she bought a Heritage frame, of course, but during that afternoon she looked at the frame and a tear ran down her cheek. She wished she'd been braver and chosen one of mine. How nice the pink one might have looked in the bedroom…

I went on like this for some time. I glanced towards the back of the room where the directors were standing. David was laughing, along with everyone else. I've no idea how long the story went on – I think Mrs Smith finished up getting divorced because she'd bought the wrong frame.

The following week David gave me an order for the new frames.

Another way to sell a frame is to put a picture in it. I'd always avoided producing framed prints. The market was flooded with cheap, just like the photo frames. But now we had our double mount trick.

I selected what I considered to be art of quality, and subjects that would be complimented by my frames. I decided to approach House of Fraser which was the top end. I arranged a meeting with the buyer in King Street, Manchester, just behind Kendalls in Deansgate. I now had a range of about sixty framed prints, and took most of them with me. He was bowled over.

'Are these samples saleable?' he asked.

'They're all of saleable quality,' I said.

'Right, I want them all now.' He picked up the phone. After a few moments he said, 'I've got a young man with me with some framed prints. I want you to make room for him on the ground floor.'

I couldn't believe what he was saying. And who was he saying it to? And am I the 'young man' he's talking about?

He put the phone down, and said 'Right, I want you to take all of these over to Kendalls'.

Kendalls? Kendalls? The phrase echoed around my head. *He did say Kendalls, didn't he?* '…The manager will meet you there.'

Of course he will.

We had discussed the prices briefly. I'd told him the prices of the various options, which gave us a very healthy margin.

'But how much to us? We are talking about Kendalls.'

'I'd rather talk about quality and service'.

'What if we give you the whole group?'

'I'd still rather talk about quality and service.'

I went over to Kendalls, literally round the corner. I was met by the store manager, and the manageress of the gifts department. I was greeted and treated like a VIP. The three of us wandered around the ground floor, discussing various positions for the display. We agreed on a prime position, and I floated on air all the way back to the car… and for some time after.

I had to come up with a new name for the company. 'Ken Holmes' wasn't swish enough as a label, apparently. I don't know why I came up with Genesis – it wasn't for religious or pop group reasons. The House of Fraser buyer liked it, and so it stuck.

We were quickly given more stores throughout House of Fraser: Rackhams Birmingham, Dingles South Wales, Peter Jones London, Frasers Edinburgh, and so on. I built display stands, stylish and elegant, in House of Fraser grey. The margins could easily afford that. The only down side was that repeat orders had to be canvassed at store level; each individual store decided which pictures they wanted replacing and how many.

The House of Fraser business gave us an excellent additional marketplace to Max Spielmann. One of the unwritten laws is you don't sell to your customer's competitors. House of Fraser couldn't have been more different.

The best prints we were framing were being created by Ken and Yuriko Morita. Japanese art – prints, some of them large limited editions, down to greetings cards. They were stunning and fitted in with our framing style perfectly. This was the sort of quality that got us into House of Fraser – but they weren't the ones that sold the best. The best sellers were kittens and puppy dogs in pink and powder blue.

I became good friends with Yuriko and Ken. Yuriko was Japanese. I was spending a lot of time in London then, and their studio in Chalk Farm became something of my London office.

We were supplying some of the most prestigious stores – that helped. I mentioned to one pretty barmaid that I was going to Barkers in Kensington, tomorrow. She turned to her mate and said, 'He just keeps coming out with it, doesn't he?' *Oh that's what does it, is it?* But I still didn't know what 'it' was.

Exciting times, business growing steadily, the almighty plan coming together.

I suppose when a company expands fast it presses buttons, with the likes of the VAT office, for instance. Two officers arrived, one overseeing the other. I left them alone in a separate office to absorb whatever they wished. They emerged a couple of hours later, asking why I was claiming the VAT back on my home telephone bill. I said, 'Because a lot of my business is done from home.' But he wouldn't allow it. He wasn't going to charge me back-tax, but I wasn't to do it again. He picked up and queried a credit note from our major supplier.

I said, 'The way we run our stock system, every time a frame is made we calculate all the materials used, and that's reduced off our stock. If our system shows a shortfall in stock our supplier issues us with a credit.'

He seemed surprised, 'Even if you've used it all up?'

'Yes,' I said.

'You must be an honest man.'

I looked at him, amazed, 'I didn't think I'd hear that from the VAT man.'

'Well – pretty honest,' he said.

Everybody has a photograph or a certificate lying in a drawer somewhere that needs framing, and the VAT man said, 'How much are frames?'

'What size?'

He gestured with his hands. Everybody does that – they never know the actual size. I gave him the basic price we'd charge Max Spielmann for an A4 frame.

'Plus VAT?' he said.

'No, we'll scrub the VAT for pound notes.'

There was a look of horror on his face. The senior officer saw the funny side.

'Of course plus VAT,' I said, 'D'you think I'm stupid?'

VAT men aren't stupid, either, and contrary to popular belief they do have a sense of humour.

CHAPTER 4

If I had any skills in framing, Yuriko and Ken brought them out. Ken and I started to promote jointly. I knew nothing about art, and still don't, but that didn't matter – they did. The limited editions were superb, and big – some three feet by four feet – and very expensive. Mostly too big for the English market, their real market would be America. Our first joint promotion was a trade show at the National Exhibition Centre in Birmingham: the Spring Fair. Hundreds of exhibitors displaying everything to do with art and picture framing.

Our exhibition stand was meticulously designed by Ken, with a bit of input from me, in his studio at Chalk Farm. It was something like twenty-five feet by fifteen. Each panel interlocked with the next and was carefully marked with the art to go on it. It wasn't just big stuff; greetings cards, small photo frames, all with subtle shades of pink, lilac, beige and black. We had a day to set up our stand at the NEC, and I had pretty well completed the display by the time Ken arrived. His silent reaction said it all.

Our stand stood out like an oasis in the desert. A good old friend of mine, Dave Bakesef, came to visit. He just said, 'You've cracked it haven't you?' That was all.

Some of the other exhibitors and suppliers walked by trying to be casual, just to see. I was as proud as a peacock. Most of the serious interest was from interior designers, exclusive gift shops, that sort of thing. Then there was Alan. His company had five casinos in London, seven in the provinces, hotels at home and abroad. He wanted gifts to give to his Arab customers. That's what he said. I assumed it was a gesture after they'd just parted with the odd oil well in one of his casinos. I arranged to meet Alan two weeks later in London.

My car was off the road at the time. Mal, a good friend of mine, drove me down. He didn't fancy driving through the London traffic so we parked at Ken's in Chalk Farm and got a cab to Alan's address in Mayfair.

'Isn't it quiet?' Mal said, as we drove through Mayfair. I had to smile, but he was right – not much traffic – but what was going on behind those hardwood doors? I was glad Mal was with me because I had about a dozen framed prints to show Alan and they were pretty heavy.

I needn't have worried about how we were going to park and get the samples in. There was a car park under the building, looking like a Mercedes showroom, with a lift straight up to reception. We sat down and chatted to the two girls at the desk while we waited for Alan. Immaculate pin-striped suits walked in and out. This was serious wealth; you could feel it. *And I'm part of it.* Alan arrived and said, 'We need to be pretty quick if we can. There's a board meeting about to start.'

We quickly moved all our frames into an adjoining room.

'Not that one,' he said, 'Nor that one… But those two – and we'll try those three.' The whole meeting lasted no more than five minutes, and that was that. *We were in Mayfair.*

We'd arrived at his office in a battered old mini-cab, and the boot where we had to put the samples was full of rubbish. One of the girls rang for a taxi to take us back to Chalk Farm. Now we were in Mayfair, so a limousine turned up. The driver opened the boot – I could have fitted the workshop in there, never mind the samples.

We never did get the order confirmed, though. It turned out that our pictures weren't quite 'Arab' enough. I'd tried to persuade him that behind that particular picture of Mount Fuji was an oil well, but he didn't buy it.

I had a phone call from the House of Fraser buyer. He went ballistic – something about how dare we sell the same framed pictures to some tat shop opposite Kendalls. I had no idea what he was talking about. He was fuming. I tried to say there must be some mistake, but he wasn't going to be pacified.

Max Spielmann had a shop opposite Kendalls, a big one, but

they didn't sell pictures. Then I realised it must be the modern frames, the frames I'd sold Max Spielmann in pink and powder blue with the double mount trick. They weren't pictures, they were photo frames, but the frames and mounts were so distinctively us – they were why we had received Design Council recognition; they were unique.

I don't think he could have seen them himself, or he'd have known they weren't pictures. Either way, it was a gross overreaction, but I had to do something. I explained the problem to David and asked him if he wouldn't mind putting a few frames in the back until the heat died down. It was the same overreaction that had got me into the House of Fraser in the first place.

Our next exhibition was in Frankfurt. I thought the NEC Spring Fair was glitz and glamour, but the Ambiente show did the same thing with German efficiency. We had exactly the same reaction as we'd had at the NEC. We were attracting the posh buyers, from posh shops, interior designers. It was kind of summed up with a group of five Americans who arrived on the stand. They wandered round looking at each panel individually. The big pictures – they all nodded. The small pictures – they all nodded again. The photo frames – yes, they agreed. They all looked round at each other and agreed – all of it. The guy who looked like the boss came to me and handed over his card. 'Send me your package after the show.' They were serious.

Ken said, 'Who were they?'

I handed him the card, which gave nothing away.

'What did they want?'

'All of it, I think. We're to send them our package.'

'What did you tell him?'

'I said I would.'

I thought about it for a long time, but I wasn't sure what a 'package' was, or whether we had one. We had prices for everything, and literature for everything, but it didn't amount to a 'package'. He obviously thought we were a seriously big company – that's what we looked like – but we weren't, it was just little old us.

They knew what they saw was good, we knew it was good. A package, though, involved logistics, distribution, and he was in America.

That would involve warehousing. We weren't ready for that. I never did send a package.

America was certainly our target in the long-term. Ken was already selling a lot of unframed artwork there. He had a trip to America planned, and asked me to go with him. He'd gained a lot of air miles over the years, so that would pay for my flight. It was going to take me away from Genesis for a week or so, but Genesis could cope.

We flew into Los Angeles, picked up the hire car and headed to our hotel in West Hollywood. The hotel was small, but decent enough, apart from our room: it had one double bed. We asked the receptionist to change it for two singles. He looked at us sympathetically, 'Have you fallen out?'

We went out to explore the local bars. One was called Trunks. I thought it must be something to do with lorry drivers. It was busy, plenty of people, seemed OK. While I was fighting my way to the bar Ken tapped me on the shoulder. I turned. Through clenched teeth he whispered, 'It's a gay bar!' I looked from side to side, 'Shit! You're right!' and started to back out – as you do – moving a bit quicker as we got towards the door. It seemed like all the bars in West Hollywood were gay.

We got in the car and drove up Sunset Strip. I looked out for number 77. I think I found it, but it was all a bit like that. Ken pulled up by a bar as if he'd been there before, or perhaps he just knew how to recognise these bars. Scantily clad girls trying to look sexy, clinging to poles. Leering men sat on stools surrounding the low stage – so the girls could stoop while the gawping onlookers put a few dollars in their G-strings. Totally pathetic in my view. Ken may have spent a dollar or two – I certainly wasn't going to. I didn't see anything sexy about it in the slightest.

We bought a bottle of booze, took it back to the hotel, and went up to the rooftop swimming pool and jacuzzi. We're in LA so it's still warm at ten o'clock at night. After a while we were joined by two guys. We offered them a drink, and one of them went back to his room and brought some whacky baccy to the party. It must have gone on for a couple of hours. I knew they were gay, but it didn't matter, it was a good laugh. The big guy – and he was huge – started bad-mouthing Britain. 'Wales? Where's Wales? I've never heard of that.' I reached under the water and pulled his feet, under he went. Then it all kicked off. He got up and started knocking me all over the place – forearm smashes. I tried and tried to get back at him, but he was a monster. I knew it was all lighthearted; if he'd wanted to he could have killed me. Somebody from the hotel came up complaining about the noise, and switched off the jacuzzi. The big guy went mad at him, telling him to switch it back on again. He got up and went over to the phone. We could hear him telling somebody on the other end, 'Get the jacuzzi back on again or you'll get no more business from us.' He was pointing to a skyscraper with '316' in big neon on the top. That was the radio station they worked for.

His mate told me quietly, 'Be careful with him – he's an all in wrestler.' But it was all good fun – until they wanted to carry on the party in our room. We finished up having to throw them out. They weren't keen on going, and I had to explain: 'In Liverpool we have a phrase for times like this – Fuck off. Or, let me put it another way – Fuck off.' They left. Welcome to West Hollywood.

I woke up in the morning covered in bruises. We were supposed to meet up with them – they were going to show us round the radio station, but we were running late, we'd overslept and we had appointmnt in southern Los Angeles to visit a manufacturer of framed art – the main point of our trip. We were shown round like VIPs. They must have employed about five hundred people – a tad bigger than the ten people I employed, but then we were in America.

One part of the operation was divided into about ten booths. Round the three walls of each booth hung original art, shoulder to shoulder, in various stages of completion. A Mexican artist added a tree trunk to one canvas, took one step to the right and added a tree trunk to the second canvas, and so on until he completed his circuit of brown. Maybe the tree trunks varied slightly – a root appearing here, a different branch there. He changed his paintbrush to green and added the leaves, and so on. Our host told us that if any of the artists came up with an original idea of their own they got a bonus, then the new idea would be copied over and over, again each one appearing to be identical but a sharp eye could spot the difference. A production line creating what were being passed as original works of art.

Our host appeared to be quite proud of this set-up. I just saw it as cheating.

We went across the Mexican border just to see. It was like going from the Garden of Eden to Mars. No more the lavish glitz and splendour of Los Angeles – replaced with shacks and slums, and faces full of deep suspicion.

We wanted to drive up to San Francisco along the Pacific Highway – five hundred miles hugging the ocean coast. We went to Hertz. Ken asked for 'the best car with the best sound system'. He wanted an open topped sports car because that's how it should be done, but because we were leaving the car in San Francisco we weren't allowed one. The sports cars were the top end of their hire stock and they couldn't guarantee to have another hire to bring it back. Still, the car we had was pretty swish in my book. We drove north along the Pacific Highway – the way you're supposed to, and stayed overnight at Big Sur with the enormous redwood trees – as you're supposed to.

With a bit of effort we got down to the ocean at one point, a beach of sorts, but totally deserted, rough waves, hostile – full of rocks appearing and disappearing. I'm no swimmer, but I had to go in, just so I could say I'd swum in the Pacific. Ken declined. I don't know how long I stayed in – not long – but I crawled out with elbows and knees gashed and bleeding. Those rocks were pretty sharp – but I'd done it.

San Francisco, with its sloping streets, was every bit as dramatic as I'd seen in a thousand car chases. We drove across the Golden Gate Bridge and up to the top of the hill on the other side. A guy was sitting on a bench with his girlfriend.

'That's my house, there,' he said, pointing to a speck in the distance.

'If you live in San Francisco, what are you doing coming up here?'

'The ions, man,' he said, 'the ions,' arms outstretched to channel more of the power.

We sat as near to the edge as I felt like going. A family walked by with two small children and an aged grandmother. From where we were sitting, it looked like a sheer drop to the bay. The family started to walk down and out of sight. Grandma followed, looking frail and unsteady. I couldn't bear to watch. Should I try and grab her back? She wasn't my grandmother. Surely they could see the danger? She was going to fall and then there'd be helicopters and ambulances… I got vertigo for her, and had to go and sit in the car.

On our way back to the UK we had to change at JFK, New York, collect our cases and wait for the connecting flight. While we were waiting for our cases to appear on the carousel, we went for a drink in the bar and got chatting to a lady who happened to be the manager of a big law firm in LA. As the drink flowed, so did the conversation. She convinced us that we should be opening a British pub in America. That must have taken about half an hour or so. When we returned to the carousel we were met by an angry woman in uniform: 'Where have you been?' We explained we'd been chatting to a pretty lady. 'O-oh, that's OK then!' And there, slowly meandering round on the carousel, were just two suitcases – Ken's, and one that looked like mine but wasn't. Security was called. Obviously somebody had picked up my suitcase by mistake. They very carefully opened the wrong suitcase, just in case it was going to explode. And there, inside, was my familiar dirty laundry. I rummaged through, hoping to God to find out it wasn't mine, to save embarrassment. But it was. How could I be so stupid as to not recognise my own suitcase? Years of practice I suppose. Security didn't seem bothered, and we went on our way.

I felt depressed when I got back to the UK – dull grey weather, dull grey back-to-back houses. I'd become intoxicated by the drug called California – the sunny skies and apparent affluence. While we were in LA I saw a school, called Hollywood High maybe. *That's where I want my children to go to school.*

When I'd been back a few days I started to get mixed feelings. Sure it was affluence, you could see that. I'd met a lot of great people – the law manager at the airport, the two gay guys were OK. There was something about the big frame manufacturer in LA, the way he expected me to be impressed, and the deep suspicion on the face of the Mexican guy as he leant on the caravan that sold coffee when we'd just crossed the border. But then why should I care about that? I didn't go there to save the world. I went there for business, and there was plenty of that to be had.

As the business expanded, the stores were demanding more of my time. I tried several times to recruit a manager to run the workshop, but it never worked out. What I had created was a successful company, but complicated. I saw everything as easy to achieve, but of course I would – I'd created it.

The more the business expanded, the more cash we needed to service it. Glyn Price, then my manager at Barclays, could see this, and funded with equal enthusiasm. The borrowings grew, and the cost of borrowing. Glyn said, 'Do you know how much your bank charges were last year?' 'Well, say thank you,' I said. I was riding a very fast train, and Barclays were running with me all the way.

It was apparent that I couldn't do the sales and marketing as well as the production. I recruited Gale, mid-twenties, intelligent, full of energy. She took over the management of the House of Fraser accounts and sales generally. When she was in the office she could write with two pens at the same time – a black and a red – monitoring the sales every bit as well as I could. She travelled around the country visiting the stores, meeting the buyers, encouraging the best lines and deleting the ones that had seen their day. Meanwhile I could concentrate on production.

I introduced Gale to the House of Fraser buyer. I left the meeting to get a couple more samples out of the car. After the meeting Gale told me that while I was away he'd said to her I always filled him with such enthusiasm he couldn't wait to get hold of the new lines, until some time later it would dawn on him – it's just a picture... Oh God, his irrational behaviour was my fault? Life's so bloody complicated.

The kids were the big equaliser; they made everything worthwhile. Playing with them in the snow, for instance. The snow was big in that part of North Wales. I was watching Tom walking precariously on the snow when he suddenly disappearing out of sight. He hadn't fallen down a hole – he'd just been walking on the crust on the top until it couldn't stand his weight. It didn't bother him much, they were at that age when nothing bothered them much.

The Japanese garden was on the back-burner for the moment. I'd turned the bottom level into a play garden. I got Lester to put two long tree trunks in the ground, standing up like telegraph poles, then one across the top, and I fitted a swing, a tyre and a rope ladder.

The kids went to the village school in Llantysilio. They could have gone to the big school, Dinas Bran in Llangollen, but we preferred the village school. There was a government policy at the time to close village schools with less than thirty pupils, for economic reasons. At the time Llantysilio School had twenty-nine, and just about scraped through – five of them were Holmes'.

In the mid-eighties when we had that really bad winter Pat had taken Anna and Sara to school, and on her way back home with the three younger ones she got stuck in the ice in the dip by the Chainbridge and had to trudge back home carrying three children as best she could, and then got them all to bed to get them warm.

I went out and bought a Datsun Patrol, a big seven-seater four-wheel drive, to make sure that would never happen again.

The house was warm – central heating as well as the open fires. All cost money, but that was no problem, there was plenty of that.

CHAPTER 5

If I'd carried on developing what was an excellent product with good margins, and spent time eliminating the complications, it could have been an extremely successful company. But I didn't. I did the opposite and made it more complicated.

I developed a completely different range of framed prints: outrageous, provocative, sexy black and white photographs under the label 'Flash Trash'; and sold the concept to Athena. Athena had shops up and down the country but, as with House of Fraser, we had to call at all the individual stores to canvass orders. Profitable but, again, very time-consuming. Though it gave us more stores in the same towns without them competing with each other.

Male nudes were the big sellers. I thought they were being bought by the girls. Not a bit of it. The store in Hayes, Middlesex: 'Yes, the male nudes please – we're by the airport, we get a lot of gays coming in here.' Brighton: 'Yes, we're by the sea, we get a lot of gays coming in here – we'll have the male nudes.' Leeds: 'Oh yes, industrial north – get a lot of gays coming in here.' And so on.

I didn't get to see Ken and Yuriko as much these days. Their priorities had taken a different turn, and so had mine. Yuriko had always been involved with a Japanese religion. She was translating the book of her religion into English. They had converted one room of their house into a chapel, and once a week the chapel would be open to similar believers. But I did call to see them whenever I could, usually on a Friday, staying overnight with them before driving home.

One Friday I knew Yuriko was going to target me with the religion. I needed the protection, she said.

Ken and Yuriko's house was as traditional Japanese as possible. Shoes were always removed and left in the hallway, we knelt down at the low table for our meal. Yuriko was an excellent cook.

After the meal, Yuriko started to talk about her religion, with examples of how it had protected different people and how it would protect me. I'd kind of been expecting this for some time, and as much as I respected Yuriko I wasn't really convinced. As she talked, her appearance began to change in front of me. Her physical appearance was different. She become slimmer, much younger. She wasn't old or fat, but time takes its toll on all of us. Now she was fifteen years younger. I looked across to Ken – he was slouching on the couch finding it difficult to stay awake. The couple of pints before the meal, and the sake during it, were knocking him out. Yuriko followed my eyes. She looked back at me, stunned, and said, 'Look! Ken's changed. He looks younger. He's lost all his weight.' I couldn't believe what she was saying, because he hadn't. He'd packed up smoking some time before and put on a lot of weight. He looked like a slob. She was seeing him exactly the way I was seeing her.

I didn't say anything at the time. I didn't know what to say.

I normally woke up on a Saturday morning, had some coffee, and set off home. They were late risers. But this Saturday morning I had to wait and tell Ken what had happened the night before. He didn't know what to make of it either. I left and headed home.

I told Pat what had happened. She said it was probably the sake causing the illusion. But Yuriko didn't drink.

A couple of days later I spoke to Ken on the phone. He'd told Yuriko what I'd seen. She didn't seem to think it remarkable; something to do with the religion. It was remarkable to me, and still is. If it had been an illusion caused by beer and sake, why would Yuriko have seen the changes in Ken at the same time I'd seen the changes in her?

Ken and Yuriko became more immersed in their religion, and I became more immersed in my own company. I would like now to have known more about their beliefs. I was still unconvinced; the fact that they believed so passionately made me want to know more, but now wasn't the time.

Business was good, the Athena thing was working well. Gale was doing a superb job with House of Fraser – fast, efficient, she got more business than I did. Soon she'd take over the Athena account as well.

And yet there was something missing. I was working harder than ever, which wasn't a problem, but I felt like a hamster stuck in the proverbial wheel, running like the clappers – for what? I needed a break.

I saw an ad in the paper for an apartment to rent in Puerto Banus, Spain. I'd never heard of it, but it sounded good so I booked it and we all went. We arrived early in the evening and had to go through a customs barrier to get to the port, or that's what it seemed like. Pat explained in French to the uniforms that we had an apartment and they let us through. Now we were special. It was very swish, very upmarket. Every yacht in the harbour told you that. The clothes in the boutiques never had prices on them. As the holiday wore on I became more and more impressed with this facade. I found myself looking in estate agents' windows. When we got back home I had a new energy, a purpose. I wanted an apartment in Puerto Banus. Pat didn't. I had to admit after a while she was right. I realised that the people who didn't have yachts were gawking at the people who did. And the people who did were probably envious of the people who had better ones. It was all false. So, maybe not Puerto Banus, but somewhere. That would make the hard work worthwhile.

I started to feed an additional expense into the management accounts to make sure the company could stand it. This went on for months before the bank manager said, 'What's this on the bottom? £500 a month – FIS.' 'Flat in Spain,' I told him. He laughed. But it seems plans never work out the way you expect.

Gale was driving to a House of Fraser store in South Wales when she had a head-on collision with an army truck. She was rushed to hospital in Cardiff – hours and hours of neuro surgery. For a long time it didn't look like she was going to make it. And then there were months of convalescence. I felt she was going to make a full recovery, but it was going to take years.

Whether I refused to accept that she wasn't coming back or at least not for a very long time, or whether I just didn't want to admit it, either way my priority had to be to keep the production running smoothly. We were busy: if I left the factory production suffered; to spend the necessary time training a replacement for Gale was at the moment unthinkable.

I was kind of between a rock and a hard place: if I didn't spend time on the road the business didn't come in, but then I couldn't leave the workshop. The staff had been with me quite some time now, but without the driving force it didn't work. The runaway train of expansion was starting to stutter, and the borrowings that Glyn Price had warned me about were taking their toll. Meetings with Glyn were becoming somewhat volatile.

Eric Peake was one of our regular customers – an artist. Horses' heads were his thing. We supplied him with the frames. I liked Eric, there was something about him – untamed, a free spirit. Perhaps that was why he was going through a divorce. He told me he had custody of the two rabbits and if I couldn't take them off him he was going to have to leave them on the motorway. I didn't want two rabbits. Half an hour later he'd paid for his frames and gone… and I'd got Peter and Panda. Why did he have to say he'd leave them on the motorway? The kids will love them. My wife won't.

Making a hutch was straightforward enough. Two compartments – one for day time and one to sleep in, with a doorway linking the two. The whole front hinged for cleaning out. I never actually fitted the hinge; the front jammed in between the two sides with a thump, so it wasn't necessary.

Rabbits had been on my mind well before Eric brought them into reception. Wild rabbits were a big problem in Llangollen, on our side of the river anyway. I don't know why it was only on our side. During the recent bad winter they'd destroyed acres of beech forest, gnawing the bark as high as their legs could stretch, killing the trees. It was the only food they could get at with the snow and frozen ground. They were doing it for survival.

In preparation for my Japanese garden I'd put up hundreds of yards of rabbit-proof fencing. This meant digging a trench, ten inches by ten, laying chicken wire along the bottom and up the side, and then two feet out of the ground, and back-filling. The theory was that the rabbit comes up to the fence, digs down, comes across more chicken wire and gives up. And now I've put two rabbits inside the secure compound. Eric had told me they were two males – at least they couldn't breed.

The delusions of grandeur were being replaced with a fight for survival. How to service the borrowings without making the pit deeper?

Glyn Price was a powerful man, with a powerful temper to go with it. There was still a certain amount of mutual respect, though that was running thin. He asked me for the up to date cash flow figures, yet again. I seemed to be spending more time producing financial statistics than running the company. So I sent him a poem instead.

I wandered lonely as a bean
And fell asleep if you see what I mean
I'd been a little tired all the day
Kind of sleepy in a sort of way
And thought I'd have a little doze
And put my head between my toes
About that time there came a cat
I suppose you wonder why I mention that
But this pretty cat she smiled at me
And asked me in to have some tea
She looked across just like a friend
And ate me up. And that's the end

Glyn replied: 'Ken, I'm a very busy man. I don't know what you mean, unless your cat is the two-legged variety.'

It did little to change the situation. We both knew it was serious. A couple of weeks later I came into my office to find my administrator shuffling papers all over the place, looking very distressed, shaking. Glyn Price had just phoned demanding that I be in his office later that morning with all the figures. I was fuming. I phoned him, 'Don't you ever speak to my office like that again. I will be at the bank for eleven-thirty because *I* want to see *you*,' and slammed the phone down.

I don't remember much about the meeting, apart from thumping tables. I don't think I sat down. He wrote to me afterwards saying he'd never seen me so angry.

I couldn't see a way out. The situation was becoming untenable and the pressure unbearable… but I had to bear it, though no matter how much I juggled the figures I couldn't make them add up, but what was the alternative?

I don't know what came first: the extraordinary escape plan by Peter, or Panda becoming pregnant. Well, I suppose there had to be a natural order of things – but Panda was supposed to be a boy.

It started with my first cup of coffee of the day. Through the kitchen window, up four steps was the hutch, but there was something different. *Perhaps I'm not quite awake.* Then I saw it… the front of the hutch was lying on the floor and the two rabbits AWOL. I went outside, hoping for a miracle and they'd be nearby. *They'll see me and jump back in. I'll thump the front back on again and I can get off to work.*

They were still missing when I got home. That was the first thing that greeted me. Apparently a neighbour had seen one of them in the field below. The rabbit netting didn't go round the front of the house. I made a Spartacus net – the sort of thing gladiators used. Me, Pat and the five kids surrounded Panda, closing in all the time until I could swing the net. We'd got them back… for now.

The next morning the front was off again, and the same pattern followed. I know I should have put a hinge on the front, and a catch, but I had to thump so hard to jam it between the sides, whatever force pulled the front off would have pulled the hinges off as well.

We caught Panda with the Spartacus net, but there was no sign of Peter until later that evening when he appeared up by the boundary rabbit netting. He was tearing along as fast as he could, hugging the fence all the way, then suddenly stopped and raced back. But there was something else. On the other side of the netting was another rabbit, a wild one. Peter was pure white; his *doppelganger* was brown and grey. Peter set off again and so did his double, in perfect symmetry. Peter was Steve McQueen on his motorbike in that scene from The Great Escape.

In the morning, Peter was gone. There were no holes in the fence, no burrows dug under it. He'd leapt for freedom and the lure of the wild.

At least the problem now was less by that amount. But I was wrong. It got worse: Panda was pregnant. The first time I was aware of it, he'd started collecting straw to build a nest. But he was pretty stupid. For a start, nobody had told him male rabbits don't get pregnant, and also that if the front of the hutch is off you don't have to go into the living room and through the small hole to get into the bedroom to build your nest – you can just jump straight into the bedroom. Not a lot of difference, unless you're carrying a mouthful of straw which is sticking out five inches either side. You just can't fit through the hole unless you turn your head sideways and guide the straw in that way. And that's what he did.

Panda had his babies: six grey, blind rats.

A few days later, with my morning coffee, I saw the front cover was off the hutch again, and the six little rats had been dumped on the concrete. The hutch was raised about 20 inches, so they'd fallen that far, but they were still alive. I picked them up carefully and put them back. Panda watched from a distance while I covered them in straw to keep them warm. There was no time to play nurse or explain his parental responsibilities. I had to get to the office for my daily skirmishes with the finances.

This became the norm with my morning coffee. I flung the still-blind rats back in, hardly bothering whether they were landing on top of each other or not, and went back into the kitchen. Our cat was busy scratching on the concrete near where the rats had been. I went back out and there was another rat that I'd missed, still on the concrete. The cat was scratching around gathering scraps of straw to cover it up and keep it warm.

Barclays placed a consultant with me to help turn things round. He was intelligent and quickly grasped the situation, and above all he was calm, not volatile like Glyn and I had become. We needed additional sales. We had an excellent product. We had the capability. He could see all that.

Coping with Barclays was easy compared with the rabbits. I now believed the rabbits weren't a consequence of Eric's divorce; they were the cause of it. I saw Panda was up by the perimeter, not tearing along on a motorbike like Peter, just hopping from one clump of grass to another. Probably carrying the rabbit equivalent of a rolling pin.

I sat on one of the kids' swings on the lower level watching Panda up by the netting a good distance away. I began talking to her, telling her she had to look after the babies – it was her job. I talked to her about all sorts – told her about Barclays and House of Fraser, and how everybody's life is shitty from time to time. This must have gone on for a couple of hours; I'd been back to the house twice to fill up my whisky. All the time she was coming nearer and nearer to the swings, so she was just three or four feet away. I thought I'd made a real break-through.

I was at home in a meeting with the consultant when I had a phone call from the office. For the first time in my life three cheques I'd issued had been bounced. Glyn had been away for a week and I'd issued the cheques with the knowledge and consent of another manager. When Glyn returned he overrode this and bounced the cheques. I wanted to phone him there and then, but the consultant stopped me – attacking Glyn when I was angry wasn't the best way. I never would have gone behind Glyn's back, if that's what he thought, but he hadn't been there. The three cheques he'd bounced only amounted to a few hundred pounds, but they were critical and essential in the scheme of things – otherwise I wouldn't have issued them, for Christssake.

One of the bounced cheques was the deposit for a stand at the Photokina trade show in Cologne – the biggest exhibition in Europe for photo frames. I knew our range of frames would go well, and it would have given us the extra business. I could have gone back to the office and worked on the figures late into the night – what if I did this, what if I did that? But I knew what the answer would be – I'd done it a thousand times before. Perhaps bouncing the Photokina cheque was the last straw. It may not sound much of a straw, but then the last straw doesn't have to. I didn't blame Glyn Price – he'd just made me face up to the obvious.

Is this what madness feels like? I called in a liquidator.

The consultant tried to stop me, saying it wasn't necessary, but I'd already done it. He tried to get me to rescind, but it was too late. He knew that. Once that call's made the pack of cards comes down instantly.

By Saturday morning Panda was nowhere to be found. Two of the babies had already died. That left four. I'd never killed anything before, not knowingly, not intentionally. I hope I never have to do it again. I'd heard people had drowned kittens if they'd had to put them down. Baby rabbits are called kittens. It took ages for the bubbles to stop. They fought. I didn't know they'd have that much life left in them.

The burial site, where two cats had gone before, was at the far end of the field. That meant little presents and poems from the children. I didn't have the energy. I was knackered. I told the kids there was an alternative. They hadn't had any great bond with the rabbits, but I didn't expect it to be as easy as it was.

'Hoofing' the kittens meant standing on the patio with your back to the log store, placing a dead kitten on the small shovel we had for topping up the boiler with anthracite. Then with two hands you flung it over your head, over the log store, and down to the overgrown land below.

So they were the basic rules, but we had five kids and only four corpses. I thought the drawing of straws to decide which kid was excused would have been the fairest way, but the one who got the short straw screamed, 'I didn't get the wishbone at Christmas either!'

The first three goes went straight up in the air and we had to scatter. Then two went in the log store. My attempts were no better. Two of them got caught high up in a tree, and are still there now as far as I know. It was hardly the most reverend of burial ceremonies, but somehow a fitting end to a pretty barbaric week.

CHAPTER 6

There wasn't a Plan B. I wasn't prepared for this eventuality. I was devastated, destroyed. All I'd worked for over all this time – gone. No-one to blame, nobody's fault except mine. I suppose what happens in these situations is you go on to some kind of automatic pilot, and make the best of what's left.

David Edwards was shocked when he heard. He'd had no idea – well of course he didn't, you don't let your customers know you're struggling. 'If I give you another lump of our business,' he said, '– a big lump – can you start again?' The lump he was offering me was the down-market, high-volume business. I could do that. Manufacturing that kind of stuff was easy. I'd shied away from that in the past because the margins weren't big enough, but perhaps now they didn't have to be. That was the most magnanimous gesture I've ever come across.

A guy called Vaughan Griffiths came on the scene. He owned a contract packing company about a mile away. We kicked the figures around a bit. Vaughan didn't know the first thing about framing; he didn't need to. He offered a pittance for the company, in the usual way.

The liquidator asked was it in my best interest for Vaughan Griffiths to buy the company. I was shocked. He was supposed to be acting in the best interests of the creditors, not *my* best interests. I could tell by his expression – he was looking for a backhander. He never got it. Vaughan bought the company.

It all came as a blessed relief. I suppose it was because I'd worked so hard to build the company up, and then worked so hard to save it. Anything had to be better than trying to work with that kind of stress.

There was no pressure from Barclays, but I decided to sell Hen Pandy and bought a much smaller house – number one of eight former

Council houses in the village of Llantysilio. If only all Council houses were like that, nobody would ever buy their own. Hills and mountains behind, in front a couple of fields with Hywel Gyfelia's cows and then the River Dee. The kids' school was fifty yards away. I knew everybody there. It was home from home. The sale of the house paid back Barclays. That reduced our overheads considerably. Why didn't I think of that before? Perhaps it had just been unthinkable. The time hadn't been right then; it was now. We carried on manufacturing out of the old Post Office in Ruabon.

With no bank borrowings, and the extra business coming in from Max Spielmann, the new company became viable again. I didn't need the complications of the House of Fraser business, or Athena. Gale wasn't going to return; all that belonged to a previous life. It didn't matter – we'd started up again. My deal with Vaughan was to do the management bit, and receive a percentage of all sales, and a small rent off the new company for use of the Ruabon premises which I had managed to keep hold of.

We learned how to make cheap and cheerful photo frames – low margin, high volume. Easy peasy, really – you've just got to know the tricks. It worked very well for a while. It didn't bother me that I didn't own the business.

Vaughan suggested moving our operations to his industrial unit about a mile away. I sold the old Post Office building on the understanding that we could continue our operations there for the time being pending moving to Vaughan's unit. The arrangement suited the new owner, who had ideas of turning the property into four dwellings, and that took time with planning permission, etc.

A derelict cottage came on the market, up on the mountain about a mile behind our house. Fron Haul was actually two cottages, but you wouldn't think so – they were tiny. Just one more house behind Fron Haul, and then the mountain. [1]

I knew the cottage very well – I often went for walks up that way. Standing outside Fron Haul on the edge of the world, you could see the River Dee winding its way into the far distance, between rolling hills and valleys. Peace and tranquility – what more do you need? At the right time of the year in the early morning Fron Haul was above the clouds: clear blue skies above, and below a blanket of white with the odd mountain top peeking through.

But before I could make an offer on the cottage I made the mistake of mentioning it to the wrong person. It quickly turned into a gold rush, with three people determined to get it – including me. Their way of settling it was a game of cards – winner take all. Not my way of doing things, and I wasn't prepared to be in the risk business.

The selling agent, aware of the sudden interest in the property, said, 'We'll accept the best offer in Monday's post.' I knew the Barber family well; they had owned the cottage for a very long time. Robin Barber, the last occupier, now lived in Bryn Eglwys. On Sunday night I went over to see him and asked him if he would accept £500 on top of the best offer. We shook on that deal. I posted a note through the door of Kent Jones estate agents in Wrexham: 'Last night I agreed a deal with Robin Barber…' I wasn't quite sure if the estate agent was going to approve of my tactics, so I phoned him up at ten o'clock. I needn't have worried; he said he didn't like the other two anyway.

I envisaged the grand house scheme again. The old cottage didn't have any windows overlooking the valley; that wasn't why it was put there. It was originally a quarryman's cottage – shelter and protection from the elements were its functions, not sight-seeing. There was a certain amount of land. We could put an extension on stilts… John Miles gave me an idea of the costs. But then I told myself that was stupid, and filed it all away in the back of my mind and left it as it was.

After some time I thought I may as well sell Fron Haul if I wasn't going to do anything with it, and decided to put it back on the market. I went up to visit it one last time, but found I couldn't bear to sell it and withdrew it.

By far the biggest account in the UK for photo frames was SupaSnaps. I think they had over 400 shops then. A tiny piece of that business would be decent. I went to visit them on a number of occasions and built up a rapport with the buyer. She was concerned that they had just one principal supplier at the time for photo frames, and wanted to spread the load. I had to make sure that was me.

She came up to North Wales to do the factory inspection bit. Now that we were on the point of moving to Vaughan's contract packing site, I could show her a spacious industrial unit which was more than suitable for high-volume production.

She came up with her husband, a management consultant. We went out for a meal in the evening, and was I given the third degree. I wondered how much I should tell them. Honesty's always the best policy – in fact in my book it's the only one. I told them about the liquidation and the selling of the house and all the crap that had gone with it. She already knew – she'd done her homework. They were both firing questions at me all through dinner. 'Will you two get off my back,' I said, 'so I can eat!' At the end of the evening she said: 'Does the SupaSnaps account mean much to you personally?' 'A hell of a lot,' I said, my mind spinning like a fruit machine. 'Good,' she said. Had I passed the inquisition?

The next day I took them to see the new manufacturing site, and to introduce them to Vaughan. He knew I was coming, how important it was, but had decided not to be there. I was furious. I tried to gloss over it but they took it as a personal affront. She said, 'Well, I would have liked to meet the person who signs the cheques.' I tackled Vaughan later about his absence. He said, 'Oh, they've just come up for a jolly.' Had they hell!

She told me that she planned to leave SupaSnaps in a couple of years' time, and buy a hotel on the coast. (That was in confidence, but it's a number of years ago now so I'm sure I'm excused.) 'You've got two years to get your feet under the table, and this is how you do it. Every now and then we have a promotion that will consume eighty thousand frames. You give me your best quote for that, and make sure you supply it on time.' The stage was set. But life had other plans.

Shortly after that meeting she was taken seriously ill and had to leave SupaSnaps prematurely. She was replaced by a smart-arse graduate. A lot of buyers are arrogant and self-opinionated; he was one of them. Vaughan forced me to go in with too high a price. I told him, 'You'll kill it – it's too dear. They're not fools.' I knew what the price should be, but Vaughan wouldn't listen.

The buyer said, 'Your price is well out. You're way above your nearest competitor.' I phoned Vaughan and told him. He just said flippantly, 'Knock fifteen percent off then.'

'What the hell are you talking about?' I said. 'You can't just knock fifteen percent off a quote like that without good reason.'

He tried to change the subject: 'How are the figures looking this week?'

'For Christ's sake, Vaughan, SupaSnaps is going to blow up here!' He wouldn't listen.

I dropped the price to SupaSnaps. It was about the worst phone call I'd ever had to make. The buyer just said, 'I think there's something wrong with your pricing structure,' and that was the end of the discussion. There would be no room for another while that buyer was at the helm.

The buyer was absolutely right. I was furious to see all the work I'd put into SupaSnaps being treated with such contempt. It killed my relationship with Vaughan. I didn't want to work with the man any longer, but for the moment I had no choice.

We went ahead with moving our production from the old Post Office to Vaughan's unit, albeit without the SupaSnaps business. Vaughan's contract packing involved employing large numbers of casual labour from time to time. He tried to introduce this untrained and uncaring work force into frame production, with the assumption that any fool can make a frame. Quality suffered, efficiency went out the window, and we had serious health and safety issues.

Flexi-points held the MDF backing board in the frames, fired in with pneumatic guns. I caught one member of staff firing the gun at another. A flexi-point could have taken his eye out. I wanted that employee summarily dismissed or, at the very least, suspended pending. Instead, nothing happened.

It came to a head when Vaughan forced me to go to David Edwards with a ten percent increase that was unwarranted and unjustifiable. David just said, 'Doesn't Vaughan Griffiths think you've got any competition?'

I told Vaughan I was leaving. At first he said, 'OK, we'll carry on without you.' When David Edwards heard of this, he said, 'If Ken goes, we're going too.' Although there were a good number of other customers, without Max Spielmann there wasn't a company. Vaughan had no alternative but to let me take the company back over in total.

There was another major contributing factor: I'd been working for the last few months with W H Smiths, who were very big in photo frames. Vaughan knew this, of course. What he didn't know was they were about to place their first order, and it was big. And, right now, I wasn't in the mood to tell him.

It was going to cost ten thousand pounds to buy the business back. That was for the stock, equipment… nothing for good will – there wasn't any. I found premises to rent in Llangollen. I didn't have ten thousand pounds. I went back to Barclays. All the people I had known had moved on. Timing was critical, not least because of the position with W H Smith.

The premises in Llangollen were part of Upper Dee Mill, a big old three-storey former seed mill. The sort of place where hundreds of people had been employed in days gone by. I arranged to rent three thousand feet on the top floor from the owner, Graham Bromilow. The stage was set. The business plan was good. I thought the application for a loan from Barclays was academic. The bank refused the loan. I couldn't believe it – it was so right. I decided to sell the cottage, and I put it back on the market again. Right away there was interest, but once again I couldn't sell.

I traced Hywel Bellis-Jones, the guy who had first brought me to Barclays. He was now a senior manager in a different area, but he remembered me. He intervened on my behalf and arranged a meeting with him, me, and the manager who had refused the loan. By clever manipulation of words he got me the loan without causing too much loss of face for the cretin.

There was some delay with the lease arrangements on the old mill – I can't remember what it was, and I finished up moving in a week before the lease was signed. Graham Bromilow saw this opportunity to take advantage of the situation, and charged me an extortionate licence fee for this one week. I asked my lawyer, 'Can he do this?' He said, 'I told you not to move in before the lease was signed.' I'd taken the chance, not knowing that Bromilow was the bastard he later proved himself to be, and his wife wasn't any better. They knew they had me over a barrel and were doing everything possible to extract their pound of flesh. All the suppliers, including the bank, had taken my word as surety. Not the Bromilows. They made me sign a personal guarantee.

In a meeting with Jenny Bromilow, I said, 'If I go out now and walk under a bus you'd take my wife's house off her.'

'Oh, we wouldn't do that!'

'Oh, yes you would.'

The relationship with the Bromilows never got any better. Nevertheless the business was very quickly re-established and firing on all cylinders. Even though we were on the top floor of a three-storey mill, the commercial access was excellent. A conveyor belt ran from the top floor right on to the wagons for loading and unloading.

The first order for W H Smith went out complete and on time, and developed into a regular monthly order. Max Spielmann, and business generally, was booming. Production was simple and efficient. Staff knew what to do and when to do it.

For the first time in a long time it was a pleasure to go to work in a morning.

I don't recall how long we'd been in the building before I had that phone call on Friday night. It would have been about six-thirty. I was getting ready to go out for another drunken Friday night with Jack Ty Canol, Johnnie Keeper and Berwyn. The phone call was from one of the girls I employed. She screamed, 'The factory's on fire!' Hysterical woman, I thought, but I jumped in the car and went to see, feeling a little bit put out – I wanted to go out for a drink with my mates.

There were fire engines all over the place and a large crowd was already gathering. This was serious. I pushed my way through and introduced myself to the fire officers. They hadn't gone in yet – the building was full of smoke. For the time being I just had to wait with the hordes of onlookers. I heard one man in the crowd say it was an insurance job. I felt like smacking him.

A number of times I tried to tell the chief fire officer that there were five or six Calor Gas bottles on the top floor. I thought if they exploded they'd blow a hole in the building – and there were hundreds of people standing round watching. It seemed to take ages for this to sink in before the firemen moved the crowd back.

I told the fire officers, 'There's a conveyor belt on the other side of that green door that runs right up to the top floor.' They broke open the green door and about eight men went in, feeling their way along the belt, in the full gear including breathing apparatus. I knew how cramped it was to try and squeeze alongside the conveyor belt, and they hadn't a clue what they were walking into in the black, acrid smoke. They didn't know whether they were going to bump into a typists' chair, a brick wall or a guillotine. They were only in there a few minutes before a panic button went – one of the officers was in trouble. The officers outside smashed one of the windows on the ground floor and brought him out. The operation had to be aborted. Some time later they broke a window in the far top corner – my area – and, with the conveyor belt access door open at the opposite corner on the ground floor, very slowly the smoke started to vent.

Five fire brigades from all the surrounding districts were involved. I believe it was on the News at Ten.

I don't know whether it was the next day or the day after that before I was allowed back in the building. The place was deserted, black, reeking of smoke, as if I'd just stepped into a war zone. I went up the three flights of stairs to my office. The bottom half of the door had been stoved in where the firemen must have crawled through. I wasn't going to crawl into my own office. I booted the rest of the door in and it smashed off its hinges.

The whole factory floor looked like the aftermath of battle, as if I were viewing it as an old black and white movie: shades of black and grey, and the acrid smell of smoke.

The fire had started on the floor below – ten thousand square feet of stored dried flowers. The actual area that had ignited was very small. The flames, that you expect do the real damage, didn't travel very far. The smoke, however, had penetrated everything on every floor. The actions taken by the firemen to vent the premises very slowly had prevented the whole building from bursting into flames.

The cause of the fire was said to have been electrical, starting on the floor below me. I was never really convinced that was the true cause. We were insured, of course, and the assessors came in. It was then that I realised how inadequate our insurance was. The business had expanded fast, but the insurance hadn't kept up. My priorities had been to maximise the efficiency, set down hard and fast ground rules, and see that they were adhered to rigidly. Stock was coming in and going out. It might have crossed my mind from time to time: 'Am I insured enough for this?' but that was only momentarily. The unthinkable would never happen.

The picture frame moulding came in ten foot cartons. All were contaminated and worthless. The smoke had penetrated even the sealed cartons. Glass, picture frame backs, face papers saying 'Max Spielmann' had to be destroyed, face papers saying 'W H Smith' had to be destroyed. Barcode labels that told W H Smith customers how much the frames were had to be destroyed.

A firm of industrial cleaners was brought in, and the whole building needed re-wiring. It was going to be at least two weeks before there would be any chance to get up and running again.

The insurance assessors understood the situation but we were under-insured. They did what they could, but getting back into production was a nightmare. Furious battles with the bank again. They froze my account, even though I was well within my facility. I was getting blame from all quarters. W H Smiths understood. David Edwards didn't understand at the time. I was now his principal supplier for frames, and the shelves in their shops were running bare.

I needed time to think. From the front of our house, it was only a couple of hundred yards' walk across the field, through the woods and down to the river. I often went there with the kids. We'd make a campfire and cook. It was a very special place. I took a tent down. Hywel Gywelia said, 'Don't put the tent there, Ken. Cows tend to get curious and they could lean on it. Put it there, just on the other side of the fence, at the edge of the woods.' Hywel understood better than the bank.

I'd always written stories. People said the kids' stories always seemed better when I told them. You can never write down the grunts and groans and the delights of your different characters adequately. It's impossible. Down by the river bank, I tried to put the stories on tape. It wasn't very successful, probably because I didn't have my audience, but also my stammer came back. I used to stammer as a child when I was asked to read out loud; talking into the machine was similar I suppose.

The insurance started to pay out, and I began to regroup. The money was far less than I'd claimed, but the insurance assessor pushed it through, and that made the difference.

David Edwards came over and visited the factory. The meeting was pretty aggressive, hostile at times, but at the end we understood each other's position. The mutual respect was still there.

Somehow I survived, business-wise anyway. I can't say my marriage was a casualty of this, but events contributed. The marriage was over, and had been for some time. Pat and I had been like two trains racing along separate tracks – hers the house and the kids, mine the business. The kids meant the world to both of us, but she had the job of looking after their daily needs, doctors, school uniforms, PTA evenings – and there were five of them. I was never allowed near the school – that was the kids as much as Pat; they were a bit scared at what I might say to the teachers. I have my own views on education, and they knew me well. Until now, the kids had meant the trains had been running along parallel tracks. It was the fire in the mill that had brought matters to a head. It devastated me more than I could explain to Pat. She never understood, never saw the destruction the fire caused in the mill. Not blaming her, nobody's fault, but I felt guilty, I felt like a failure. I'd arranged to buy five mountain bikes from a bike shop in Wrexham, I was just waiting to see what sort of discount he could come up with; in the back of the car was the travel agents' blurb on Disneyland, Florida. The fire killed all that, though I put the five bikes on my credit card.

CHAPTER 7

They say it's always darkest before the dawn.

I woke up feeling as if the weight of the world had been lifted off my shoulders. *It's not my fault.* We're only animals, the same as any other on the planet. The marriage had simply run its course.

I'd stopped smoking a few years earlier with the aid of Sarah, a hypnotherapist in Chester. I remember stubbing out my last cigarette on the floor before I knocked on the door. The room was a bit cluttered, but as soon as I sat down it all felt comfortable. 'I'm counting down from ten,' she said, 'You'll feel your arms getting heavy... Now your legs are getting heavy...' *This isn't going to work.* My legs and arms were feeling heavy, but that was just because she was telling them to. I don't think I lost consciousness, I can remember it all quite clearly. What she said just seemed to make sense. I rolled my own cigarettes at the time. That evening I didn't feel like smoking, but my fingers were twitching because they wanted to roll a cigarette. I managed to stop smoking until I saw her again the following week for the second session. Then I didn't smoke again for three years. Clever stuff.

I decided to go back and see Sarah again.

I was all mixed up – call it stress if you like. Under hypnotherapy, she took me along the beach in the early morning sunshine, water gently lapping against the sand. Peaceful, warm, quiet. At the end of the beach there was a big cliff. I went up the cliff until I reached a door. 'Go through the door,' she said. I went through the door and there was a staircase going down, and down, and down. I came to another door. 'This is your room. Turn the golden key and go in. There's a desk, it's your desk. Sit down. On the desk there's a button, and in front of you there's a screen. When you press that button what will come on the screen is exactly what you want. In a moment, I'm going to ask you to press the button, and I'll leave the room… Press the button.'

What came on the screen was the cottage, Fron Haul. There it was, on the screen in front of me. No longer derelict. Not the big grand five-bedroomed house either, just a simple cottage renovated back to its former glory. The only difference from its original appearance was that double doors opened onto a balcony overlooking the beautiful valley and the River Dee disappearing into the distance. I saw myself sitting on the balcony in a chair with a little dictaphone in my hand – I was writing. I remember concentrating with the utmost intensity to bring the children into the picture. One by one they arrived, playing in the garden, running in and out of the house. I was terrified Sarah was going to bring me out of it before all the kids had arrived. They all did.

When she brought me round, I said, 'That's a hell of a trick!' She gave it some name and just said, 'It works – but you have to practise. It'll work quicker if I do it, but you can also practise it yourself.' I don't think she asked me what I'd seen, though I probably told her, because I was so amazed at what had appeared on the screen, and with such vivid clarity.

There's no doubt if I'd been asked at the time why I bought Fron Haul, I'd have said it was to turn it into the family home – but my ideas were far too expensive and so it got shelved. Twice I'd put it back on the market, only to withdraw it.

What I'd seen on the screen in Sarah's flat was really weird, and yet made so much sense. Had I subconsciously all that time wanted the cottage for myself?

I went back to see Sarah a couple more times, and I practised and practised. I found I could take myself very deep very quickly. Each time was different. Each time took me to a different place.

In the meantime the factory was getting back to some normality – whatever normality means.

It made sense for me to use the same electricians that Bromilow had employed in the main part of the building. They weren't very good, to say the least, but they didn't deserve what Bromilow had in mind. He refused to pay them a significant amount and they took him to Court. I was subpoenaed as a witness.

During the Court hearing Bromilow was giving evidence. I was sitting next to Jenny Bromilow. She had his diary out in front of her. Whenever Bromilow made a statement referring to a meeting, Jenny Bromilow made an entry in the diary on the appropriate date so as to confirm it should the diary ever be brought as evidence. She was using different pens to make the falsification look more authentic. Should I have jumped up and said something – but what? I don't remember what the outcome of the trial was. My mind was just preoccupied with what Jenny Bromilow had done. Graham Bromilow was obviously lying through his teeth under oath, which I wouldn't have known if I hadn't been sitting next to Jenny Bromilow and seen her making entries in the diary to corroborate his story. Whatever the electrician had done, he didn't deserve that. Nobody does.

How we survived I don't know. Why we survived I don't know. But I'm not going to argue with whoever governs these things. The fire should have been the killer blow. We did better than survive: the shortfall from the insurance disappeared, and we began to make money again.

The place for me to be in the sixties had been Liverpool. The place to be in the eighties and nineties was Llantysilio. The difference was I didn't know how great a place Liverpool was until twenty years later. I knew how great a place Llantysilio was at the time. Places are people, not architecture or landscape. The community of Llantysilio was a drug. I had absorbed it and become part of it.

I decided to renovate Fron Haul, exactly the way I had seen it under hypnosis. The two cottages became one. All the ground floor was open plan, with doors leading on to the balcony, as it had been on the screen. John Miles produced the plans, and Paul Davies was the builder for the job.

Because everybody knew everybody, and everything about everybody, there was nothing to hide. There was no point. I became the Fool on the Hill, and why not – somebody has to be. There were two pubs nearby, The Conquering Hero (the 'Conq'), and the Sun Rhewl. If I started to try and relate some of the characters and anecdotes from them, we'd need another book.

I saw to it that Pat had all she needed within my means and that the kids were OK. I bought a caravan off Paul for three hundred quid and that became my home during the renovations.

In reality, I probably finished up spending more time with the kids than I had done for a while. Every night one of them would walk up to visit. A meal and a chat in the caravan became a treat for all of us while the renovations progressed. They actually organised their own rota so they each had their turn, occasionally swapping nights with each other if music lessons or parties got in the way.

The renovation of the cottage and Fron Haul itself was ideal therapy. Just a perfect little dwelling. Paul and John knew what perfect was. And there I was, perched on the side of a mountain. [2]

I suppose I became something of a recluse, and went into the garden for a year or two while I tried to come to terms with the point of everything – or anything.

It was the wish to build a Japanese garden that had brought me to Llangollen in the first place and, although it had been shelved, it was now back on the agenda. With the same logistical problem: how to create a Japanese garden full of peace and tranquility… on the side of a mountain?

Every morning I would drive down the track and the five miles to the factory. Each evening I'd come home and plan the garden. Two entirely different worlds. I stretched a rope out in a big, haphazard oval. That would be the pond…

There were only two main tenants at the mill. Apart from me, there was Rick, who ran his dried flower business on the floor below. I'd known Rick for many years and we always got on – always there to lend each other a cup of sugar should we need it. So when Bromilow sold the mill to Rick I welcomed it with open arms. Although Bromilow would still occupy the suite of offices adjoining the mill, I was glad to be rid of him as my landlord.

I'd been playing the recluse feeling sorry for myself for long enough by then. I grabbed myself by the scruff of the neck and began to go out with the lads again of a weekend. One Sunday afternoon I said to Berwyn, 'How many pints did we have last night?' 'Fourteen,' he said, without a moment's hesitation.

The front garden – or top garden – was the first project. I gained a little bit of extra land that wasn't strictly on the deeds but nobody bothered. Stone. I needed stone… smooth glacial stone – the sort of stuff that you find on the beach, but big. Ian and Lester Claybrook had some stone. It was only about five miles away on the other side of the river. Good stone, the sort of proper good stone that I needed, had to be the size of a big fat man, and weigh at least a ton.

I sculpted hills and valleys on the top garden, just like a kid playing in sand. Stones go in threes or fives. I chose three. When the garden was ready for them, Lester brought the stones up one at a time in his dumper truck. He told me if anybody enquired where he was going with that, he'd just put a finger to the side of his head and say, 'Nutty Ken.' That was all the explanation needed. The Japanese believe that to protect the house from devils you bury a grain of rice under your God Stone. I only had American long-grain rice which I hoped would be good enough, and I wasn't sure which was the God Stone so they all got one.

I met somebody who went to a singles' club – one of these organisations that sad people go to, who haven't got a life. He persuaded me to go along with him. It wasn't a bit like I expected. I suppose there are some people like that – there always are, but there was a crowd among them who were mad, exciting, and full of fun.

The Nexus gatherings were every Wednesday evening in Chester. I suppose there'd be about a hundred at each of the gatherings, probably mostly women – they've got more balls for this sort of thing than men. Then there were parties, dinners and various shindigs, mostly good fun and some you'd avoid like the plague. Each time I'd look across a crowded room for eye contact with that someone. Didn't happen. I made a lot of friends – female, good fun, full of life. Then Barbara brought along Denise. She said, 'Denise won't be on her own for long.' I saw what she meant. D and I became very close very quickly. She lived on the Wirral.

I started excavating the bottom garden. I didn't insist on Paul giving me rigid quotes. From time to time I'd ask him, 'How much to get a digger down there?' or 'How long d'you think that bit might take?' There was an instinctive understanding between us of what was right, and how to achieve it in the most efficient way possible.

D would often spend weekends at the cottage. She loved it. I persuaded her to move in.

Business good, the staff were excellent, everybody pulling their weight, in full production just after eight, and finished just before five. High levels of efficiency, despite the odd breakdown of machinery and the constant battle with suppliers, principally moulding not arriving when promised. Apart from that, it was easy.

You never really know how well off you are until something comes along to adjust it.

Rick's business went into liquidation, which meant I no longer had a landlord. The liquidator's job, as always, was to realise the assets – and that was the mill. It was going to be sold. Rick and I had never bothered formalising our arrangement with a lease, but we never thought about him liquidating either. If my activities didn't fit in with the new owner I could be put out on the street.

I searched for suitable premises. I didn't want to move far away from Llangollen because it was so convenient for me and the staff – but there was nothing approaching acceptable. I was travelling further and further afield, to Wrexham fifteen or twenty miles away, to view proper premises, the usual square boxes you get on industrial estates. They looked more appealing: ground floor, no pillars in the way which we had at the moment.

D came round some of the premises with me. It was great to have a second opinion for the first time. *I suppose I could arrange a bus to bring the staff in every morning, take them home every night. Expensive and messy.*

As well as being further away, the nice tidy square units were more expensive, a lot more. Higher rent, rates of course, and the bus maybe – all taking my garden money. How dare Rick go into liquidation and disrupt my plans that I could see so clearly. I suppose he had other concerns.

I started to think the unthinkable. Should I buy the mill? By now it had been on the market for a year, and the price was coming down. What would I do with a thirty thousand foot factory? Where's the comfort zone there? But, frankly, I didn't have any choice.

I wasn't the only one showing interest now the price had come down. It was turning into a bit of a race. But now I'd decided I wanted it, I wasn't taking second place.

When Bromilow heard that I was showing interest in buying the mill, he did everything he could to discredit me. He actually wrote to the agent saying I wasn't a fit person to own the building. The other serious contender was the guy who owned the 'Dr Who' business in Lower Dee Mill across the road. He actually had the effrontery to write a long letter to me explaining in detail why I would not be able to afford the mill. His opinions were based totally on his own arrogant assumptions about what my turnover and profitability were. You can instantly tell with some people that they're shits – almost before they open their mouth. He was one. Bromilow was another.

If anything, all of this pushed the purchase of the building in my favour. The selling agent could see through Bromilow and was also aware of the arrogant attitude of 'Mister Dr Who'. The building was complicated, which raised a number of discussions with the agent. I always found him a fair and reasonable man. It seemed the other interested parties were messing him about, and he actually guided me on what sort of offer might secure the deal. He told me that I'd played it straight all the way down the line. It wasn't unethical; his job was to realise the best price he could get for the building, and that's exactly what he was doing. He just recognised an asshole when he came across one. Most decent people do. And he did something about it.

Now I'd got a thirty thousand foot factory. Why does life have to be so complicated? And what's more, I'd got Bromilow as a tenant. The suite of offices he was occupying were part of the package. He'd negotiated a ten-year lease at £1 per year when he sold the mill to Rick – and he'd still got eight years to go. I'd got to put up with Bromilow for another eight years, and I'd get £1 a year for the privilege. I suppose for a moment I thought the boot's on the other foot, now I can make his life a misery, but I couldn't be bothered. Either your parents were married before you were born or they weren't.

If I love any material more than stone, it's wood. When I'd been round to see the Claybrooks about the stone Ian showed me a load of pitch pine that was outside and would be rotten in a year or two, so I bought it all cheap. Some I turned into fence panels for the top garden, joined to each other by twenty inch square stone pillars.

It's funny, the way life nudges you from time to time into the path of people who are going to have a big influence. I needed steel in these stone pillars formed in such a way that it would present brackets to attach each of the wooden panels. I went to an engineering suppliers in Wrexham to ask them if they knew the man who could make these. Dave Broadhurst was only a couple of miles from the factory. He instantly knew what was required.

I'd stand on the balcony in the morning, looking down at the bottom garden. The first thing we had to do was build a retaining wall so as to make the pond area level. The second thing – *what the hell am I going to do with a thirty thousand foot factory*?

The ten foot high retaining wall consisted of two parallel rows of concrete block, with an eight inch gap between filled with steel and concrete. Serious stuff. It wouldn't do to fill the pond and have the wall collapse and flood whatever got in its way. And that would have to be that, for now, because I had the other enormous blank canvas to consider.

Rick rented back a small part of the mill. That still left an enormous area of empty space that would be difficult to sublet. The cost of improving common access, and in particular the cost of fire escape requirements, and so on, would outstrip any advantage that might come with rental potential.

Under normal circumstances if a neighbour suggested you were creating a disturbance, you'd do your best to resolve the situation amicably. It happened once in my first workshop in Old Swan, where I was in the middle of a block of terraced houses. My neighbour, who was on nights, complained about the constant tap, tap, tap, of the panel pins going in. He was quite angry at first, so I invited him into the workshop and took him around to show him all the bits and pieces we were doing. He said, 'Is that all it is?' He went away happy that I wasn't causing a disturbance at all. He was probably exhausted after his night's work and his imagination blew it up. And that was the end of it. There must be somebody out there who's got a good deal more than their fair share of reasonable understanding – because somebody's got Bromilow's bit.

Bromilow wasn't part of the common access, thank God. Though it didn't stop him wandering in, contaminating things, with that sly grin that went with him. He came up to my office and started on about the noise I was creating and how it was... *Well, anyway.* It was during morning break time, because the staff were in the canteen and they all stayed in there while the confrontation went on. I could feel the rage building up as Bromilow banged on and on, and on. I felt my right fist clench and unclench as the muscles in my right arm grew stronger and stronger like a Popeye cartoon. 'Get out of the building,' I ordered him, pointing towards the door with my left hand. He didn't move. I repeated it. I could feel my voice getting slower and lower. Any moment, my right hand was going to swing. I was praying for him to get out of my sight before it did. Not that I was frightened of hurting him, it was just that if I'd missed I'd have screwed myself into the floor.

He left. The staff wandered out of the canteen. I said to Howard, the workshop supervisor, 'Did you heard that row?'

'Yes,' he said mildly.

'Why didn't you come out to give me some support?'

His look said it all.

I wrote to Bromilow, banning him from entering my part of the building unless he had written permission from me. After all I did own it now.

I moved my operations down to the middle floor, which was called the Ground Floor, although it wasn't – there was another smaller floor below, which we all called the Lower Ground Floor. Believe me, it didn't sound so confusing when you lived there. It's another consequence of building on the side of a hill. This floor offered a much smoother production flow, and a couple of decent sized offices and reception at the main entrance to the mill, like a proper company.

The company D worked for was going through a 'night of the long knives', and her boss had been unceremoniously discharged. I asked her to come and join me in my company. It seemed perfect timing for both of us.

The factory became more efficient, making more frames for less effort. It all seemed obvious to me, to do it that way. I didn't realise how efficient it was until some years later when I visited a number of other large framing set ups and saw chaos and confusion.

Whether I created it, or whether it was thrust upon me, doesn't matter – we now had a hungry animal that wanted feeding. We knew how to make photo frames and had a big space to do it in. Thirty thousand feet.

Where was the additional business going to come from? All the main shops these days were selling frames coming in from Asia. Not the cheap crap that might have been the case a few years before, but well-engineered high quality and – I had to admit it – far better than the frames we were making. Our advantage was selling high volumes with short lead times. That gave us the edge with some buyers, but not all.

We needed a stronger foundation to build our castle – a reason to stand out from the rest. The double mount trick had been great for a few years but that wasn't going to stop what I saw as the 'Asian invasion'. Subconsciously I must have been re-inventing the wheel.

Saturday morning. I'd been in and out of the shed for two or three hours, bending a piece of wire this way, then that way. I drilled a hole in the rebate at the base of a frame and pushed the wire in and the frame leaned back on it and actually stood up. I then rotated the wire, still in the hole, so it lay flat against the back.

I stood the frame up on the table and just looked at it, and there is stood like a magnificent trophy.

D came downstairs.

'Oh, that's a good idea,' she said.

It was a good idea – a bloody good idea.[3]

PART II

GULLIBLE'S TRAVELS

CHAPTER 8

I quickly learned to grab a cloth if Dave Broadhurst passed me something.

Dave, a big bear of a man, with vice-like hands made out of asbestos, had been welding, bending and drilling metal for years and had ceased to realise the metal was sometimes too hot for a mere mortal.

Dave's factory was dark, dingy, always in a mess – and I loved it to bits. In among the mess were lathes, pillar drills, grinders, welders, presses (big beasts that thumped and bent and moulded and punched), all kinds of other machinery and well-worn wooden drawers full of tools, gauges, bits.

I'd shown Dave the photo frame stand on Monday. He knew the bit of bent wire was a good idea. He'd never bought a photo frame in his life, but he knew the existing tie-shaped strut was crap. Everybody knew that.

It was a good idea, but limited to small frames. For it to become a great idea it had to work on all sizes. On any frame bigger than five inches it fell over. The weight just forced the wire to swivel in the hole and the frame fell down. I tried different thicknesses of wire and altered the shape, but whatever I tried failed. And yet I knew the solution was there, somewhere.

What had begun as a desire to give Genesis frames the edge over increasing competition, was now taking on a life of its own and becoming an obsession.

I'd been making photo frames for over thirty years, and they'd always been supported with a strut. When I started out, the strut clicked on to a bracket on the back to stand the frame upright; you could then take the strut off and click it back on another bracket to stand the frame 'landscape'.

Then came the tie-shaped strut hinged to the back so the frame could stand up either way. But the system was far from perfect. It would warp, collapse or bend, and break. Everybody's got a frame that won't stand up any more and is propped up against the clock or something. Nevertheless it had become the industry standard worldwide – and it had been that way for a very long time.

In an effort to stop Bromilow moaning about something else, I insulated the wall that divided our two premises. I took advice from an acoustics engineer. He recommended fitting a particular plasterboard on battens on the wall, making sure it was kept off the floor an inch or two, stuff the gap between the battens with something, and that would do the trick. We already had the saw and the automatic mitering machine on two-inch rubber mats. Still, without my knowledge, Bromilow made an official complaint to the Council. The first I knew about it was when two suits walked in saying they'd received a complaint about the noise. They'd come in unannounced so we couldn't create an artificial environment. They saw our activities warts and all, then went round to Bromilow's. When they came back they told me the noise levels we were producing were perfectly acceptable in what was, after all, an industrial unit. They had apparently told Bromilow that the noise levels he was experiencing were no more than the traffic noise from outside, which was minor.

But then one of them asked, 'What's that smell?' There was a vague whiff of fumes coming from downstairs.

I said, 'Oh, they occasionally spray the dried flowers with a tin of Halfords' – Christmas coming up you know.'

'Oh no, they can't do that.'

'I expect they've got the windows open,' I said.

The other man chipped in, 'No, they can't vent it outside. I'm Environment.'

They both went downstairs and stopped Rick from spraying his Christmas holly. What he was doing was very minor but, courtesy of Bromilow, he had to stop.

Garden plans on the back-burner for now. Most of my weekend time was spent at Dave's. I was about to change the world. Not greatly, yet. Just a little bit. First, I had to stop the bloody thing falling over.

It didn't just have to support all sizes of photo frame; it had to be able to lie flat against the back so the frame could hang on the wall, or for packing.

We created brackets that would fix to the back to receive the wire. We tried squashing the end of the wire to fit into a bracket, bending it, twisting it. We abandoned the wire altogether and tried stamping it out of flat metal, again fitting it in to a bracket. Every new idea involved Dave making new tools. He never charged me much more than the material costs and a packet of fags. But every idea failed for one reason or another. I knew the solution was there; I could taste it, nearly touch it – but it was always just out of reach. I felt like the demented donkey chasing a carrot.

We invested in a Zund computerised mount-cutter. Superb Swiss technology and engineering: tap in the desired shape, size and quantity of mounts, and leave the machine to do the rest. D and I developed a range of small frames for the nursery: Humpty Dumpty had an egg-shaped mount, Twinkle Twinkle star-shaped, and Akey Brakey had a heart shape. All cute and cheerful in bright nursery colours, and supported with our wire stand. Dave made us a few thousand stands to get started.

We booked a stand at the NEC to show our Humpty Dumpty frames. It was all a bit last-minute, so we couldn't get into the Art and Framing Hall and had to settle for a stand in completely the wrong place. I knew the wire stand was leading to something special, but what? I was terrified that somebody else would see the round wire stand and solve the problem before me, and I would have given it away.

Humpty Dumpty sat on the wall
It seemed the safest place.
But he slipped and fell and cracked his shell
And got egg all over his face.

Dave's factory became my second home. I didn't see the mess any more. The place was still dark and dingy, but twinkled with bright ringlets of turned metal shavings and the comforting smell of warm oil. He knew exactly what I was trying to do, and why. Without knowing the first thing about the industry, he knew it was big.

It's strange, sometimes, how ideas develop. They can come to you like a snapshot and go just as quickly. I could even discuss it with Dave during that snapshot and it would go again, until it decided to settle down and become a good idea. And when it did, it was obvious... and I wondered why it caused so much pain to get there.

And that's how it happened. Why not use square wire? [4]

For twenty-odd years, I and the rest of the world had accepted the tie-shaped strut, warts and all. All I knew was I wanted to protect Genesis and its share of the market. The old saying goes 'necessity is the mother of invention', and so it seems to be. But how? Did I wake up with the idea on that Saturday morning? Is the mother of invention that powerful – for me to wake up with a radical alternative to a standard I'd been practising for the last twenty-five years? Did the idea come to me while I was asleep?

W P Thompson, Liverpool, patent attorneys, copyright attorneys. Highly polished hardwood table that could seat fourteen or more, wall to wall bookcases full of leather-bound books in meticulous order. Every patent filed since time began. And I'm going to be numbered among the great and the good.

Mid-January, Robin Bartle at W P Thompson warned me, 'You must *not* tell anyone,' he said, 'You must keep this secret at all costs until it has been registered with the Patent Office.' Something to do with the fact that if it's leaked it ceases to be original thought. D was sitting next to me. *He knows she knows. What about Dave? What if Dave tells his wife? God – who else have I told? I don't know anything about patents. Have I blown it because I've told somebody? I'll keep quiet and try and get away with it.*

Robin Bartle did nothing to dampen my enthusiasm. Quite the opposite. All this cloak and dagger stuff told me I'd discovered something big. If he could see it, so could the whole world. And it was the whole world I was after – too big for Genesis to keep it to itself. Gone was the idea of simply giving Genesis an edge. Genesis couldn't supply the whole world with frames. I needed a new company just for the invention. Besides, no serious framemaker is going to buy anything off another framemaker.

The new company needed a name and an image. The idea for the style of the logo came through scanning design books, and the name

'The Lade-Back Co.' came out of brainstorming with D.

The stage was set for the NEC in Birmingham, the Spring Fair. Anything and everything to do with gifts, from tacky Christmas decorations to fine porcelain figurines, and of course picture frames. The show started on the Sunday. Our Humpty Dumpty frames were of little interest to the buyers who streamed past without giving us a second glance. By the end of Monday, still no interest in Humpty Dumpty. A Belgian company on the stand opposite ours, a bit concerned at our lack of business, asked, 'Where are all your customers?' I told them, 'We're not a customer-based organisation.' One of the rules I've learned is if you can't give a reply to impress, knock them sideways. Our frames were good and the display looked good; we were just in the wrong place.

I didn't care. Tucked away in my little bag was my invention.

On the third day of the show I received confirmation from Robin Bartle that the invention had been filed at the Patent Office. Huge sigh of relief – I could talk about it at last.

That meant it was mine – nobody could steal it, I could tell people, but who? I hadn't really given that a lot of thought. At least Dave could start making some and we could put them on Genesis frames, but that wasn't enough now.

In the picture frame industry there were sizeable companies servicing tiny parts of it. An American company, Craft, manufactured the hinge that attached the tie-shaped strut to the frame – I'd been using their hinges for years. They had to be the best people to talk to. I didn't know them, but they were an established company. Everybody knew that. You don't go to the trade shows year after year with flashy stands selling picture frame hinges unless you're selling a lot of them.

In two weeks' time Craft would be exhibiting at the SACA show in Bologna, Italy – the entire show dedicated solely to the art and picture framing industry. That would be the best opportunity to talk with them. I practised the conversation I was going to have, over and over again, as you do.

D was standing alongside me when we met Armand Roy on the Craft stand in Bologna. I showed him the leg going into the bracket and the frame standing up. Sharp intake of breath. I took the leg out and told him the bracket could also act as a hanger. Another sharp intake. It spoke a thousand words. We were invited into their inner sanctum – the small office some stands have for private talks with important people.

'What d'you want us to do?' asked Armand.

'Work together, I thought, manufacturing, distributing, promotion.'

My fingers and toes were tingling – fame and fortune at last. I don't think there was much more said. I can't remember, apart from he wasn't gushing with enthusiasm, but I suppose I'd given him a lot to think about.

Dave started manufacturing some of the brackets and legs for us. It wasn't the sort of work he specialised in, though Dave's speciality was doing anything – from welding holes in skips to making tiny little bits for model trains.

It was a nightmare trying to find out where to get the square wire, and the steel for the brackets, and then how to get them finished. I didn't think I'd have to learn about engineering – and what quality control is there in a piece of wire shaped a bit like a coathanger? And how complicated can it be just to have it blackened or plated? Very.

It didn't really matter greatly, Dave and I both knew it was short-term. Craft were the boys to make it, we knew that. He was just doing whatever he could to help us get the product out there and tell the rest of the world this is serious.

We had to come up with a name. We settled for 'Curl Up n' Stand'. I don't know why, but there it is.

We did some research on the size of the industry. Despite all the years I'd spent making frames, the numbers that came up staggered me. Eighty million frames a year in the UK, similar in France and Italy, more in Germany. Then any number you come up with in Europe is doubled when you go to the States.

Armand Roy invited D and I out to visit his factory in Massachusetts.

As we came off the plane at Logan Airport in Boston, I saw the few seats reserved for first class customers. *Next time maybe.* Armand, and his sales director Ron Morin, met us at the airport.

Ron took us to the Colonel Blackington Inn in South Attleboro, a warm friendly country hotel. It was about nine o'clock in the evening. Ron said he'd meet us for breakfast in the morning, and left. We headed straight for the bar. I went for a refill about twenty minutes later. The manager looked up at the clock as if to say, 'Another one?' I was planning another three or four. I was excited. I needed to quench some of that excitement, and D wasn't far behind me.

A beautiful spring morning. I was up with the birds. The Colonel Blackington backed on to a cemetery. Cemeteries are magical places, and this was as good as they get – if that's the right expression – winding paths, hillocks and trees hiding what was around the next bend. I kept looking back towards the Blackington. I became mesmerised, pausing at one headstone and then another. Each one told its own story of the dearly departed, and now their stories are finished, or are they? Maybe they're still there, drifting around in the cosmos somewhere.

I lost track of time. An hour or two had gone by. I looked back for the hotel – the Blackington had disappeared and I was completely lost. I tried to retrace my path. It didn't work. Panic started to set in.

Ron's going to arrive for breakfast and I'm not there. I came out of the cemetery by a completely different gate to the one I went in. I couldn't ask anybody where the Colonel Blackington was, because now I couldn't remember the name of the hotel either. I found it eventually, by walking round the perimeter of the cemetery, hugging the wall as best I could, until the hotel appeared.

Bacon, pancakes, eggs – 'Over easy – sunny side up?' Maple syrup. Strange people. A huge stack of pancakes arrived. They were just for Ron.

Ron had prepared a detailed itinerary to occupy our next three days. First the grand tour of the factory.

The Craft factory was a schoolboy's dream. It was superb. The company was started by Armand's father who, now retired, lived in the house adjoining. The factory was purpose-built, dedicated to the manufacture of photo frame hinges – or at least that's how it appeared. As we walked around, press after press thumped out hinges by the million. Very few people about, quietish, a picture of excellence in engineering. Millions of hinges whose sole function was to attach the tie-shaped strut to the back of a photo frame. And I'm saying, 'You don't need all that any more. There's going to be a new standard for picture frame support, and it's here in my pocket.'

We were introduced to everybody, all welcoming and friendly in American accents. Everything's different and all we've done is stepped on a plane at one end and got off at the other.

It was time for lunch. I kept looking at my copy of the itinerary. Where are the business meetings? We were taken to see where the Kennedys spent their summers, we had a beautiful lunch in an harbourside oyster bar in Newport, Rhode Island, we dined in the evening with Ron and Gayle, his wife (the conversation didn't flow – D was finding it difficult to keep awake, so was I – we'd missed about seven hours' sleep somewhere). The next day it was more of the same. Big grand evening meal (the car pulls up under the canopy, money passes over, and the car is parked by the car hop). Armand warmly greeted by the owner as he would any top member of the mafia. Armand's not mafia, but I'm an inventor and allowed a little bit of imagination. Ten inch steaks, two inches thick. Still no business. We went to Armand's beautiful house, we met his beautiful wife. Then we went to his country house, on the beautiful lake. One of his sons had had his twenty-first birthday there a little while before, and they'd actually employed some of the local constabulary to keep out the riff-raff. If the riff-raff had been kept out of my twenty-first birthday party I'd have been on my own. No business. Armand picked me up early next morning in his twenty year-old Corvette Stingray his wife had bought him for Christmas. There was a big family affair at the hotel, a shower. For those of you who are ignorant like me this is where every man and his dog, correction every lady and every lady dog, brings presents for the bride-to-be. No business.

There was one business meeting – pretty short, where I met a less than enthusiastic Jerry. Plant Manager. The whole meeting was less than enthusiastic. Ron Morin said, 'There's room in the market place for a niche product – we know of one company that makes very heavy frames,' out of porcelain or rock, or something. My frustration burst out: 'I want ten percent of the market in twelve months!' That didn't please them.

The simplicity of Curl Up n' Stand makes it cost-effective. That's the whole point of invention. It's got to be commercially competitive against the alternatives. I knew we'd achieved that when I first had the idea. Armand Roy knew that when he first saw it it in Bologna.

We were going to change a fundamental standard, change the way photo frames were going to stand up worldwide. I kind of expected them to be a bit more excited about it.

In amongst all this activity, or lack of it, D and I had a pre-arranged meeting with a patent attorney in downtown Boston, about thirty miles away. Ron dropped us off at the station. Double-decker trains – how clever.

Thomas Smurzinski, patent attorney, was the American link to W P Thompson & Co. in Liverpool. The meeting was on the fortieth floor. He was clearly impressed with the product, and I was impressed as well looking over the vast Boston skyline from his office window. *I could get used to this.* Though Boston itself was a mess; traffic jams trying to negotiate their way from one building site to another. 'We call it the Big Dig,' Thomas said. They'd decided ten years ago to put the city infrastructure underground, but didn't think it through. They started digging a hole here, and another one there, then ran out of money. Got some more money, and started digging another hole, then ran out again. When their own pockets ran dry they went to the Government, and it's become a national joke. They'd get there one day, but it wasn't going to be tomorrow.

After the meeting we took the train back to South Attleboro and Ron picked us up. I thought this little interlude – going to see an American patent attorney – might have hammered home why I was there, but it didn't.

There was no doubt that Armand and his family are nice people and from a social point of view we had a great time while we were there, but I wasn't there for nice. He had concerns about Curl Up n' Stand that I couldn't quite put my finger on, though I should have seen when I told Armand, 'By the way, I'm calling it Curl Up n' Stand.'

'You can call it whatever you like – it's your baby.'

Was he concerned about the name? I asked Thomas Smurzinski if Curl Up n' Stand could mean something different to Americans, but he'd said not really. I knew it was going to compete with the hinge, that was obvious, but I also knew that, if handled right, promoted, and introduced to the market in a positive manner, it would bring them a lot more business. Nevertheless, Armand agreed to start the manufacturing of the brackets, and Craft would stand the cost of the tooling. I would cover the sales and marketing as my share. But there was no enthusiasm, no excitement, no 'Let's change the world'. I just felt that for the last few days I'd been getting patronising pats on the head. Maybe I let my frustration show once or twice, but I'm not making any apologies for that.

It was almost dark as we arrived back at Logan Airport. Way up in the sky were fireflies, mesmerising little dots of light slowly performing a galactic ballet, each one in turn becoming larger as it came in to land, to be replaced by another firefly.

Patent attorneys are expensive, but as in all professions you can come across one who excels and justifies the charges. David Huntingford, one of the senior partners of W P Thompson, one of life's gentlemen. One of the skills of the patent attorney is to convince the Patent Office of original thought, at the same time telling them as little as possible. 'The bracket is 'coupled' to the back,' he said. Coupled. What a brilliant word. It tells you that the bracket is there, but it doesn't tell you how it's fixed, or even if it's fixed. With this skill, though, comes the price. My bank manager, John Pitchford saw the power of Curl Up n' Stand from the beginning. Once, when a loan was being arranged and I'd queried his charges, he said, 'I'll remember that when you're sitting on your yacht'. Yacht. That says it all, doesn't it? *I wonder where you get yacht catalogues from?*

For an invention to be patented you have to claim original thought. Once that claim is filed with the Patent Office you have a priority date, and once that is recorded you can extend the claim worldwide, pretty well, taking each country in turn. In the beginning W P Thompson asked me whether I intended to extend my patent outside the UK. 'Of course,' I said, 'the whole world.' It seemed a strange question. Why wouldn't I want the whole world?

The first trade show with Curl Up n' Stand was in Atlanta, a show dedicated to the art and picture framing industry and all things relating. Craft were exhibiting in Atlanta, as they had done for a long time, and invited me to join them in order to test the water. They organised everything, and I was to meet them there the day before the show started. D stayed back in the UK, and I set off alone, feeling like a little boy on his first day at school.

Atlanta Airport is enormous, and the pits. I came off the plane into organised chaos. At different points orders were barked at me, and I was sent off first this way and then that. I tried to keep focused on some of the faces I'd seen on the plane, but one by one they disappeared. As if by the hand of God I found a carousel taking my suitcase for a ride. I grabbed hold of the case, only to have it taken off me again by a big guy who grunted and threw it through a hole in the wall. I didn't know why, but then it seemed like everybody's bags were going the same way. The nervous apprehension I'd felt as I got off the plane had turned to scary, and now stark terror was setting in. I was carried along by the rush of people. We all got on a train that screeched off at a hundred miles an hour – God knows where. The whole thing seemed too ludicrous to ask anybody why – and what would I say anyway? Nothing made sense. The train stopped and we all got off, and entered another circus of horrors. A load more carousels spinning merrily – all crammed with suitcases, people fighting to get… wherever. But they seemed to know. I didn't. I went from one carousel to the next, knowing my case was lost for ever. Then it appeared, jiggling past me. I grabbed hold of it. I don't know how it had got there, or how I'd got there for that matter, but we were together again. I headed for the exit, which was blocked by big black security guards with big black security dogs. I looked at them and tried to raise a smile. It was wasted. Welcome to Atlanta.

I was staying in the Hyatt in Downtown Atlanta. I dumped my suitcase and went to find the exhibition hall. That was easy enough – ten or fifteen minutes' walk. Boxes, crates, people dashing around, electricians up and down ladders. All this chaos would be turned into the usual glitz and glamour by first thing tomorrow morning. Nobody noticed me.

I found the Craft stand, all finished – clean and professional, and there – my box of tricks sent over a week earlier had arrived safely.

I wandered back to the hotel, now totally at peace with the world, in stark contrast to a couple of hours earlier. It was still early afternoon. I got a map from reception. Time enough to check out the area, find the shops and see what they're selling. Plus I needed to get out of the hotel. It was full of cackling women with blue-rinsed hair. The hotel was hosting the Sweet Adelines Convention, the female equivalent of the barbers' shop quartet.

The map told me if I went over that road… crossed over there… and down there, there was a shopping mall. I turned right outside the hotel, right again at the junction, then came to a very big junction… and it's over there somewhere. I crossed over there somewhere. No sign of any shops. No sign of anything. Didn't like it. I was uneasy.

Behind me, someone shouted: 'You! Hey, you! Stop!'

I didn't stop.

'Hey you! I'm talking to you!'

I could see out of the eyes in the back of my head there were three black men behind me. I kept walking, quicker. A park appeared on my right and I darted in for sanctuary. That was worse – men lying on the ground blocking the path, asleep on park benches. I kept walking purposefully as if I knew where I was going. Couldn't turn back – couldn't look back. I got out of the park and back on to the main road. *I'll get a yellow cab and get out of here.* Cars whizzed up and down both carriageways – not a yellow cab in sight. How can you be on a main road in Atlanta and there not be a yellow cab, full or empty? I kept on walking, further and further away from the hotel, still expecting to find the shopping mall. I'd have a coffee and get a cab back to the hotel. That was the plan. Bound to be taxis there.

The shopping mall appeared at last. There was an eerie silence. No people. The shops were closed. If there had been tumbleweed it would have been bowling down the street. Still no yellow cabs. The only thing I could do was go back the way I came.

I've seen a thousand movies where the good guy has to walk through the canyon where the bad guys are waiting for him. He always gets through OK. I got back to the park where the bodies were lying on the ground and the guys had shouted at me, adrenaline pumping round me all over the place. A big racket started on the other side of the street, and about five black guys ran out in my direction. *Here we go. This is it.* I braced myself for the imminent attack. Instead, four of them started beating up the other one, kicking, shouting, punching. He scrambled to his feet and started to run away. One of the other guys pulled his jacket open and grabbed at his belt to get what I assumed would be a gun. The victim tore past me, pursued by the others. One of his assailants grabbed a long piece of three-by-two and set off after him. He was carrying it across his front, resting on his arms. The end of the wood struck a lamppost and sent him spinning. He crashed to the ground. It was the funniest thing I'd ever seen. *If I laugh now I'm dead… and I'll need new underpants.*

I carried on walking, fast, biting my tongue to stop myself laughing. I got within the sound of the hens clucking – I never thought I'd be so glad to see the blue-rinsed Sweet Adelines again.

Once I got my breath back, and now wrapped in the security of affluent America, I ventured out again down Peachtree between the ostentatious buildings and Starbuck's cafe, making sure I kept the hotel clearly in the rear view mirror – difficult to imagine the ghetto just a few hundred yards away.

The following morning, up early as usual, I went for a walk down Peachtree to find the Starbuck's cafe from yesterday afternoon. I had an hour or so to wait before I met up with the Craft people for breakfast. Starbuck's was closed. Everywhere was closed. Was I too early, or was it just that the Starbuck's cafe wasn't where it had been the night before?

I was about to cross over a junction, when I heard, 'Hey! Wait!' I turned, to see a black guy, scruffy, stained T-shirt, 'You can't cross. The lights are on red.'

Christ, here we go again. The streets were empty, it was six-thirty in the morning. I knew the light was on red, but I wasn't going to wait there for the lights to stop the traffic when there wasn't any traffic to stop.

I turned to walk back. 'That's as far as I'm going,' I said.

He came up alongside me.

'I've just got out of prison. I was charged with murder. Can you imagine what that's like, man? I didn't do it.'

I kept walking, didn't speak. He tried to guide me down an alleyway, dark, dingy, dustbins. On the corner of the alleyway a shop was opening up. I looked at the guy inside for support. He could see exactly what was going on, but there was no support there. I carried on walking, a bit quicker, towards the hotel.

He kept at my shoulder. 'What's the greatest country in the world, man?'

He stank as if he'd working in a kitchen all night, but it was six-thirty in the morning. He'd probably been sleeping in a dumpster.

'It depends how you define great.'

'Oh, you're a clever man. What do you do, clever man?'

The Hyatt was still way off. 'I'm an inventor.'

'What do inventors do, then?'

'Well, that's it. You can never tell. The only thing you can be sure about is it'll be different.'

He hesitated. This seemed to put him on the back foot. I started to spout out words like diarrhoea: 'You think your country's so great, why are you going round like that in a dirty T-shirt? Where's your family? I've just spoken to my family'. I was firing questions at him before he'd had a chance to answer the last one. 'I've just spoken to my family and it's raining.'

'Where's that, then? Where are you from, man?'

'Wales.'

He'd never heard of it. 'Where's that, then?'

When I'd come out of the Hyatt, way up high in the block opposite there was a cracked window and somebody had put tape across the cracks. 'If this country's so great, why is that building injured?' I pointed high up on the block further down the street. I said, 'Look. That building up there. Why is that building injured?' I couldn't see the cracked glass from there, never mind him, but it got me a few steps nearer the Hyatt.

I could see he was getting nervous as we neared the hotel. He didn't like it. Like an idiot, I always carry a wad of money. I pulled it out and peeled off a note and handed it to him. I'd given him a Twenty by mistake. I snatched it back and gave him two Ones and muttered something about getting himself a cup of coffee. I left him, and disappeared into the hotel.

I was born and bred in Liverpool. Multi-racial. Never come across this before. These guys were carrying something that's gone on for generations.

It was still too early for breakfast. The Hyatt Hotel was three tall buildings. The centre one – the posh one – had its lift on the outside of the building. It shot up and down like a glass spaceship. I went and found the posh lift, and pressed the button as high as it would go. The glass capsule started to shoot up the outside of the building, and scared the living daylights out of me. This lift stopped two storeys from the top, for some reason. I had to get to the top. I found the lift that went the final two storeys – I had to do it. I can't remember whether that lift just did the last two floors or not – I was too scared. The lift doors opened, cleaners were busying about, wondering why I'd come to the restaurant at that time of day. I ignored their quizzical looks and decided it was time for breakfast. I went down the two floors and climbed back in the glass pod. I knew it was going to hurtle to the ground floor on the outside of the building. I pressed the button and plastered myself against the wall, gripping the handrail. There was a song going round at the time: 'You should scare yourself once every day'. In the last twenty-four hours I'd had enough to keep me going for a while.

The object of doing this trade show was for us to test the water with Curl Up n' Stand. The big exhibition hall in Atlanta was crammed full of exhibitors selling anything remotely to do with a picture frame. The American framing industry loved Curl Up n' Stand. Ron didn't seem to.

My old dad once said to me, 'You'll never make a living out of making picture frames,' and there I was, going to be a millionaire out of a tiny little part of one.

In the evenings I had dinner with Ron Morin, seven-thirty. Eight-thirty he was off to bed or somewhere. I wanted to play. I found a much livelier bar up the road, and was served by the barmaid with the piercing eyes. I met a couple of guys in there who were also exhibiting. They were the Blue Ridge Moulding Company. What a great name. The three of us got drunk propping up the bar while I told them about wandering in to the ghetto and nearly getting mugged looking for Starbuck's at half past six in the morning… and my terrifying ordeal in the lift. They seemed to think it was the funniest thing they'd ever heard. One of them slid down the bar to the floor as his legs went with laughing. He pleaded for me to stop and help him back up, but I couldn't because I was gripping the brass handrail round the bar for dear life, as I relived my ride in the lift that morning. Earlier in the day somebody had suggested I brought it on myself for not taking more care of where and when I wandered – perhaps not in so many words, but that was the implication.

Between the Blue Ridge boys and Piercing Eyes, that became my bar for the rest of the stay.

The guys had never heard of the song 'The Blue Ridge Mountains of Virginia'. They were much younger than me, but I still found that hard to believe. They were American, for God's sake – the Blue Ridge Mountains of Virginia was Laurel and Hardy's signature tune.

It wasn't that she was pretty; it went much further than that. It wasn't that she was particularly self-confident; it went further than that too. She carried with her her own private universe and was in total control of it. I didn't try to get inside her world; I just observed it from a distance. I don't think I felt out of my depth. I was just fascinated. I hadn't seen anything quite like that before.

Someone came up to the bar and ordered a particular brand of whisky. Expressionless, she just said, 'And your second choice is?' *I must use that one day.* He preened his macho feathers and tried to engage her in some light-hearted tête-a-tête and impress her with his wit. Without changing her expression, 'That'll be five dollars… and I like him.'

Why didn't I see that coming? I prided myself on my powers of observation. *Four nights I've been coming to this bar.* That was my last night. The next day I left Atlanta.

The majority of people who visited the Atlanta show were the 'Mamas and Papas', the independent framers in the high street, graphic designers, photographers, craft shops. All small buyers, and thousands of them. The really big volume – the people making upwards of fifty thousand frames a week, and there's a lot of them – are not so easy to track down, but they were the ones I was really after.

The idea of changing something as fundamental as how a picture frame stood sent my ego into overload.

The major launch of Curl Up n' Stand was at the NEC Birmingham. This time we weren't stuck in an obscure position – we were right where we should be. We put full page, full colour ads in the trade mags blazoned 'A Star is Born'. By now Craft had started making the brackets for us and we put an acknowledgement in the corner to them as manufacturing.

The theme of our stand was 'Oscars Night'. For our show stand we needed an 'Oscar' award. That was a focal point. It was a fifteen inch gold-plated model of Curl Up n' Stand mounted on a base inscribed 'Best Performance in a Supporting Role'. (I'm afraid it got as bad as that.)

Despite the effort Dave and I put into getting the Oscar right, it kept falling over. Whatever we did, the fifteen inch Curl Up n' Stand wanted to break away from the plinth. We just about got it stable enough for the show – so long as too many people didn't try and pick it up. The ads in the magazines worked their magic: everybody swarmed to our stand. It was as though a new flower had arrived in the garden; the bumble bees were buzzing with excitement.

David Edwards came on to the stand, smiling, almost grinning. He shook my hand in both of his. 'You don't need to make frames any more. Where does that leave Max Spielmann?'

'We'll be making frames for the next twelve months at least,' I said, 'and if anything ever happens I'll make sure Max Spielmann are fully covered.'

He knew I meant that, and probably also knew I was thinking, 'Please God, let me get out of frames.' David had once asked me what my ambitions were and I said to buy a shed in the hills of Crete and write the book. He buried his head in his hands – it wasn't what he'd wanted to hear – but he understood.

We received a lot of orders from the show, mostly small, but little acorns produce oak trees.

The cost for using Curl Up n' Stand was a bit cheaper than the traditional strut, and that was going to get better with economies of scale. Nevertheless, I tried to convince David that it was worth more because Curl Up n' Stand looked and did the job better. But he wouldn't have it. How could something be a good idea if it cost more? He had a point.

We agreed to run a trial for Max Spielmanns with Curl Up n' Stand on a few selected items, but I knew that was academic – soon it would be fitted on all Max Spielmann frames and there would be fifteen thousand a week going into the UK on their frames alone. That was the average number of frames we were selling them each week, and that was about fifteen different designs of moulding, each one with up to twelve different sizes. The order would be faxed over to us on a Thursday afternoon, winding out of the fax machine like a toilet roll, spilling off the desk on to the floor, for delivery the following Thursday – and that was what we did. The problems we'd had with the fire and anything else were a distant memory.

I'd recruited various members of staff to help manage this monster. I knew exactly what wanted doing and how we were going to do it, but I was probably a total pain in the arse. I was never able to find somebody with the vision and drive needed. Staff came and went.

To get to the fun side of inventing – the promotion and distributing worldwide, there had to be a legal agreement between manufacturer and inventor. Dave Broadhurst and I didn't have a formal agreement – that was never necessary – but I understood the need for one in the bigger picture. Julie Mogan, my solicitor, had sent over a draft heads of agreement to Craft, outlining the points I had agreed with them in South Attleboro and inviting their comments. A few weeks had passed and we'd had no response. I reminded Ron Morin a few times that Julie was waiting for their reply.

Two weeks after the NEC there was the trade show in Italy. A week after that, Frame-O-rama in New York. At this stage, we knew any orders we received from New York would be from the 'mamas and papas', and would have to be despatched from the UK. It meant bringing the brackets in from Craft in the States, re-packaging them with the appropriate legs, and then shipping them back to the States. Bit of a nonsense, but whatever it took. D and I had worked out the cost of a small starter pack. This included freight back to the States via UPS – a very expensive way of shipping, but wrapped in a starter pack it offered an attractive package. Curl Up n' Stand looked expensive and could stand the cost of the carriage to the small framer. We came back with lots of orders. We now had a foothold in the States, or at least a toe-hold.

After the Spring shows I was talking to Craft regularly, but we still hadn't had their response to the heads of agreement. Julie was pushing for this – it was now a couple of months.

A long letter from Craft's attorneys finally arrived. I was gobsmacked. The language used was very aggressive and hostile, and the letter contradicted a lot of what we had agreed. Gobsmacked is probably not the sort of word to use in a book, but 'flabbergasted' or 'dumbfounded' doesn't do it. The language used was truly offensive. Julie tried to pacify me, saying, 'That's just solicitors' talk.' I didn't care whose talk it was – I wasn't going to be treated like some sort of low-life who'd dared to crawl out of a pond.

The letter said we had no right to use the Craft name or logo and that any implied association with Craft on our advertising must be withdrawn immediately. It questioned my claim for royalties, and said (and this was the killer) that any modifications to the product became the property of Craft. There had been countless modifications taking place so far. Ninety-nine percent of these modifications had been thrashed out in Dave Broadhurst's workshop two miles up the road. The countless hours and days I'd spent at Dave's – Saturday mornings and two or three times during the week, tweaking this, altering that angle slightly, shortening the leg, lengthening the leg, numerous variations on the bracket. Dave never charged me a thing. If a new tool had to be made he charged a little, but at no time did Dave ever suggest he was entitled to any right of ownership. He just wanted, like me, to see it work.

During the one serious meeting that we'd had in South Attleboro, Armand Roy agreed to manufacture the brackets. He, Ron Morin and Jerry the plant manager were all present at the meeting, and so was D. Not only did they agree to manufacture the bracket, they agreed to stand the cost of the tooling, and I would do the sales and promotion as my part of the deal. It was out of respect for Craft that we'd offered to acknowledge in our advertising their part as manufacturers, and they'd happily agreed. Ron Morin even made sure we had the correct Craft logo to use. They knew perfectly well their attorneys were contradicting our agreements. If they didn't, why had it taken them all this time to respond? If I'd offended their world in the manner in which their solicitor was implying, they'd have been down my throat within days.

From the beginning I'd taken to Armand and I thought he felt the same. I thought we were treating each other as equals – and we made each other laugh. Surely agreements must be founded on mutual understanding, and a respect for each other's efforts and input. The needs and wishes of both sides should amount to about the same thing. There was no respect coming from their solicitor, no laughing now. I was furious.

It's only now I realise the full extent of the meaning of that letter. As the term 'Heads of Agreement' suggests, it was an outline of points to be agreed and suggestions in order to formalise the arrangements. There was nothing hostile or confrontational whatsoever in Julie's letter. The delay in their response, and their aggressive manner, spoke volumes. There must have been discussion with Armand Roy and Ron Morin on the wording of that letter – several times, I would imagine, going by the length of time it took them to respond.

If they had wanted to discontinue the association they could have just said so, and that would have been the end of it. But they didn't do that. They tried to bully me and put me on the back foot, while still keeping the relationship alive. '… Keep your enemies closer'. They were concerned, very concerned, about the implications of Curl Up n' Stand.

Armand and Ron were coming to visit me shortly in North Wales. Rather than start a letter war, we'd clear the air then.

I put them up in the Bryn Howel Hotel just up the road from the factory. I was friendly with the owners, who put a small framed 'welcome' notice in reception and in each of their rooms, with Curl Up n' Stand on each of the frames – just a bit of theatre.

The meeting didn't flow. I had thought we were all of the same mind, but I was wrong. I got angry. I said, 'Tell your lawyers never to speak to me like that again.' Ron shuffled around that a bit, but did nothing to explain. While I was full of adrenaline I told them, 'I want ten percent royalty. And not ten percent of manufacturing cost – ten percent of selling price.'

An agreement of sorts came out of that meeting, but I wasn't comfortable with the outcome – far from it. I knew it was going to have a big impact on their own product. They'd had that market for the last twenty-odd years. But things were changing. That was definite. Why could they not see it? They'd have a hand in the new innovation, surely that was the important thing?

After the meeting, Julie Mogan said, 'When you started on them, I could have come over and hugged you.' But was all this table-thumping necessary? Perhaps it was – perhaps that's what you have to do. Whatever it takes.

I needn't have worried. Orders for Curl Up n' Stand were pouring in from every corner of the world. Australia, Asia, even Pakistan and Kuwait – countries I wouldn't have considered in my wildest dreams.

We'd now exported to thirty-two countries. All the trade shows and the patent costs were colossal, but so was the business. John Pitchford at Barclays could see his faith in me justified.

We were short-listed for the Fine Art Trade Guild's Innovation of the Year Award. Black tie dinner in Stratford on Avon. *Not my scene, really, but I've got to get used to it – this is the price of fame.* Dave Broadhurst and his wife Ginnie came with us. The idea of the dinner was to announce the winners in the various categories, and in true Oscars fashion the finalists are read out somewhat sombrely, dramatic pause, then the winner. You then clap enthusiastically when the winner isn't you.

But it was me. A cheer went up, I think – it's all a bit hazy. I seemed to remember saying something like, 'All this fuss over a bit of bent wire...' and took the trophy.

CHAPTER 9

A star was born. I was on cloud nine. Now I could go full belt on the garden.

Paul cut a track down to allow his mini digger to reach the bottom garden from the track – anything bigger would have rolled down the mountain – and the ponds were dug out.

Such a playground for the imagination, and then there'd be bridges. There'd have to be bridges, but I had no idea where, what kind or how.

One large pond, a waterfall – a big one – flowing into a splash pool, a winding stream, and on to another pond.

When the butyl liners arrived, Paul unpacked them on the local football field and brought them back rolled around a long scaffold pole like a carpet.

The waterfall stone had to be placed with utmost care on top of the liner without damaging it, and it must have been close on 1½ tonnes. I'd selected this stone months before. It was one I'd acquired from the Claybrooks. It measured about 5' x 4' x 3' with a smooth flat top, asking for a three foot sheet of water to flow over it. It had to be a lot of water to create the dramatic effect, so we're not talking about a schoolboy having a pee, we're talking about ten rhinos. Before it was positioned we poured barrel after barrel of water on to the stone, timing it to the second in order to achieve the right flow. The water pumps weren't graded in rhino, so Rule 4 applied and I bought the biggest one they had.

Every inch of the liner had to be hidden. We found a quarry on the North Wales coast with smooth glacial boulders of every size and shape, where we could hand-pick them all. Every one told a story. Three wagon-loads arrived. Christmas as a kid was never as exciting as this, but then I've never grown up.

Spielmann's now had one hundred and seventy four shops, and their first one in Paris, and had become something of a monster. David appointed Trish to absorb some of his work load. The first I knew about it was when I found my phone calls to David being picked up by Trish with, 'Tell me. David's busy.' I wasn't in the habit of calling David unless I needed to – weeks could go by – but when I did it was because it was important we had the correct understanding. I'd try to explain it to Trish, and I'd get, 'Leave it with me and I'll speak to David,' but I could tell that the relevance was being missed.

The trial of Curl Up n' Stand had been running for a while now. I'd showed Curl Up n' Stand to Trish. It didn't mean anything to her. She couldn't see it; she just said,

'Won't it scratch the table?'

I tried to put her mind at rest, but she'd sown the seeds of doubt and that was all she could see.

Everything can be misused. A teacup or a wine glass can break, or you could cut your finger on a kitchen knife – but it doesn't stop you buying these things. If she wanted to, she could *make* it scratch the table.

I'd known Trish for a very long time and we'd always got on well. She used to be the manager of the Preston shop. But all I was picking up now was negativity. In hindsight, there may have been a little bit of resentment over whatever special relationship David and I had. I'm not sure.

With some effort I managed to get past Trish to speak to David.

'As the trial has been running for a while now, I'd like to extend Curl Up n' Stand to the whole range if we could.'

'I tell you what,' he said, 'There's a meeting next Friday above the Leigh shop with all the area managers. Get yourself in on the tail end of that.'

At the meeting there were about twenty area managers. If I'm honest, I love being the centre of attention, especially when there's a group of women. They loved it, bar none. They saw it for what it was, a good idea. There was a bit of a mix over whether they thought it was worth any more or not, so no price increase, but it did mean that there'd be fifteen thousand frames per week going out into the UK preaching the gospel. I was absolutely thrilled at the outcome, and couldn't wait to phone Trish after the meeting. She said, 'We'll wait and see when I get their report on Monday.' Her tone sent a shiver down my spine.

On Monday she said, 'The girls weren't as enthusiastic as you made out. We're not going to go with your hangy thing.'

'It's not a hangy thing, Trish. It's a stand.'

'Whatever,' she said.

I was stunned. How could she say such a thing? Was she deliberately trying to kill it? I'd been elated when I left the meeting on Friday, on cloud nine. It wasn't just that the girls had approved it – they were impressed, excited, enthusiastic, and that would have had a knock-on effect. They would have enthused to their managers, and it would have gone down the line to all the shops and on to their customers. With a few short words Trish had killed it. I gave this a lot of thought. I couldn't say anything to David. He seemed to hold her in high regard.

I'd been planning a leaflet to promote Curl Up n' Stand in the Max Spielmann shops. I quickly finished it. No good showing it to Trish. I called David while she was at lunch and told him, 'I've produced a draft leaflet for the shops to promote the prod. If I can just have two minutes in reception, you'll know instantly if it'll work for Max Spielmann's or not.'

I went over right away, even though I was wearing shorts and Jesus sandals. He said, 'OK, change that… make that bigger… take that out – we're not a trade counter. Print ten thousand and get them to the warehouse. We'll distribute.' Job done in thirty seconds. There was a distinguished-looking man at the far side of reception. David called him over.

'Show him your doofy.'

I put Curl Up n' Stand on a frame and stood it up. The man in the suit looked at David: 'Have you got this covered?'

'It's not mine, it's his. He's a millionaire tomorrow – and look at him, I don't know whether he's coming to see me or going to the seaside.'

I had the leaflets printed and they went over to the warehouse.

To make sure all the liner would be completely out of sight the stones that edged the pond went right down the liner thirty inches into the pond hiding any sign of the tell-tale black rubber.

The time had come to fill the ponds. It took two days and two nights – not as long as I'd expected, but more exciting than you could imagine watching the water creep very slowly higher and higher. Paul had done a superb job on the levels. The water crept towards the top of the waterfall stone, then the first drop spilt over into the splash pool below. If ever there was a moment for champagne, this was it, but we settled for a can of lager. The splash pool filled and the water flowed over into the stream, bubbling onward through the stones, and began to trickle into the bottom pond.

When at last the bottom pond was full, it was time to switch the pump on to circulate the water. The pump gurgled and spluttered and kicked into action, and then silence. We waited for an age – had something failed? Then in the distance we heard the gurgle again and the water suddenly came spurting out from the 'source', as though from out of the mountain, flooded the reed bed, and into the top pool. All the fag packet calculations Paul and I had done had worked perfectly. Apart from one.

We knew the two inch pipe pushing the water from one end to the other would take up some water, but the real problem was the water level in the top pond had to rise over one inch before it started to flow at full belt over the waterfall… then fill the splash pool… then the stream, all the time raising the levels. It took thirty minutes for the water to start trickling back into the bottom pond. By that time the bottom pond was practically dry, and we had to switch the pump off. The excitement of thirty minutes before now turned to despair. Once the pump had been switched off the levels settled down again, and very slowly the bottom pond was replenished. What we hadn't considered by any stretch of the imagination was the amount of additional water needed to raise the level of the entire system by about one and a half inches for just the period of time when the pump was running.

I arranged for a load of friends, family, anybody I could grab hold of, to visit Max Spielmann shops and ask about this exciting Curl Up n' Stand they'd heard about. The idea was to enthuse about it and generate some of the excitement that Trish had strangled. If the shops happened to be full at the time then all the better. D's mother went to Chester, Ellesmere Port and two shops on the Wirral, Dave Broadhurst went to

Oswestry and Shrewsbury, and so on. But none of the shops had heard about Curl Up n' Stand.

I found out that the leaflets had never left the warehouse. Ten thousand leaflets, sat on a shelf gathering dust.

It was a new invention; people hadn't seen it before. You can't just stick a new idea in front of your customers without explanation – it needed to be introduced and promoted in the correct manner. When a customer is buying a photo frame and is undecided, they may absent-mindedly turn the frame to look at the back, expecting to see the familiar tie-shaped strut. If they see something unfamiliar without explanation they may well be tempted to put the frame back down again.

I don't know whose fault it was. I'd gone to a lot of trouble to get the leaflets designed, approved by David, printed and delivered to Spielmann's warehouse. The leaflets would have given Curl Up n' Stand some kudos, an element of respect, encourage people to become familiar with the name, and highlight the benefits.

Instead, Curl Up n' Stand was fitted on all Max Spielmann's photo frames, and went out with no introduction and without the planned promotion.

Nevertheless, Curl Up n' Stand was selling well and was now going out on Genesis frames to all our other customers. What I couldn't understand was why some of the really big frame manufacturers would show a lot of interest in using it themselves, and then fade away. I thought the main problem was how to fix the brackets on the back, fast, in high-speed production, but perhaps it was more than that. They'd start out full of enthusiasm, but then they went cold. The same scenario would happen over and over again. If we could grab only one of them, the domino theory would kick in. The general public loved it – that was certain. Surely they'd be the ones to decide ultimately, but they weren't getting the opportunity.

Craft developed the bracket in coil form for us with an automatic feed. It meant they were showing a real commitment at last. On the face of it, a big move for the volume user. But the brackets were slightly the wrong size, making them too tight for the legs, and, although fast, the coils came out far more expensive than I expected. I should have ironed out with Craft the cost that high-speed manufacturers were going to be willing to pay, but I didn't. So many things I could have done better in hindsight; but that's what hindsight's for.

I had various ideas for how to solve the water problem in the garden, but it kept coming back to the same thing. To solve the problem of the bottom pond running dry we needed to build a reservoir to store the extra water needed while the pump was running.

There was just about enough land beyond bottom pond to dig a hole about six feet by seven feet. It had to be about seven feet deep in order to hold the volume of water needed. It involved cutting some of the enormous roots off a nearby tree. I was concerned about how much damage was being done to the tree's stability. It was big and old, and partly dead. Was I killing it and making it unstable? The tree was on neighbouring waste woodland, but the roots were on my land – did that make it alright? While I was contemplating all this, Geordie with the axe kept chopping.

We dug the hole, lined it with butyl, and set the pump in the bottom and switched it on. It worked perfectly – the waterfall was at full belt, flowing down the stream and into the bottom pond and began trickling into the reservoir just in time. But then I realised the water was also seeping over the sides of the bottom pond. We knew that the point at which the water dropped into the reservoir was an inch lower than anywhere else in the bottom pond, but that didn't stop it seeping to waste over the side. Not just a little bit in one place, but in a few places.

It seems that water isn't the simple wet stuff I've taken for granted all these years – I've gained a new respect for it. The water rose at least an inch and a half while in circulation, and only settled down to its original level about an hour after the pump was switched off.

Unlike the top pond, the bottom pond couldn't cope with the rise of an inch and a half. The levels were critical. The stones around the pond had been arranged to form areas for bog-loving plants. An inch and a half higher meant the water flooded the plants and ran to waste. Not a lot, but enough.

I decided to ignore it for the moment, hoping a miracle would happen and the problem would go away. Besides, mentally I'd solved that problem and switched into bridge mode.

The first bridge was a wooden zig-zag across what was going to be the water-filtering reed bed. The Japanese say the devil can only travel in a straight line so he can't follow you – seems devils have been around for a long time. We'll stop the bastards. [6]

Now we'd got to the far side of the pond, we'd need to get back. A lot of the time the pond was making the decisions for itself. The only way back was another bridge – and there was only one place the bridge could start from – and to finish where I wanted it to meant it had to be at least a twenty foot span.

I asked John Miles for advice. He said the only way we were going to be able to do it was with concrete, and it would have to be at least eight inches thick. That horrified me – it would be an ugly monstrosity and destroy what I was trying to achieve. It had to be slim and elegant. I worried John to death trying to find out how we could slim it down.

Determined to solve the high volume production requirements, I developed the slip-on bracket. [7] It just clipped over the edge of the frame back, no fixing machinery needed at all, and received the same leg as the fixed brackets. So simple, so effective, so obvious – why hadn't I thought of that before? Now I needed somebody to manufacture it.

I'd already tried a lot of engineering companies in the UK with no success. The Curl Up n' Stand project needed commitment. None of them had the vision. It seemed I was the only one who could see the vast potential.

I went back to the States to meet with Craft and couldn't wait to show Armand our new slip-on bracket. I had a lot of respect for Armand and he was a brilliant engineer. I knew he'd like it.

A stretch limo met me at Logan Airport to take me to South Attleboro. I didn't need that – I'd rather have sat in the front and talked to the driver.

I expected Armand to be impressed with my new idea, but he wasn't. He just said, 'Let's carry on with what we're doing for now.' He showed me his new machine – this he *was* excited about – the latest development in his easel hinge machines. He showed me how it worked. The machine is loaded with backs and struts and the button pressed. Backs move this way and struts move that way, a hinge is fitted, a hanger stamped on and another adjacent – a completed back falls off the end all ready for the frame, and nobody's touched it.

I watched, mesmerised, fifty percent of me impressed by the engineering, and fifty percent of me wondering why. I knew in my pocket was a slip-on bracket that made all this unnecessary.

This machine was going to their main customer, and that would make number twelve. Twelve machines working 24/7, making millions and millions of photo frame backs.

He wasn't gloating or bragging – he's not like that. He was simply proud of what he'd achieved. He just wanted to show me because he knew my love of all things inventive. I thought my slip-on bracket idea would have brought us closer together but, if anything, it had the opposite effect.

John came up with the solution for the bridge – an idea he'd seen in the penguin enclosure at London Zoo. The edges of the bridge could be four inches, so long as the centre spine was eight inches deep, and with two steel channels at the required arc to give it strength. One of us got the calculations wrong and when the channels arrived on site they were two metres longer than expected. We could have cut them but we tried them in place and, instead of the end of the steel landing where we'd planned, it flew over the waterfall stone and created a much more dramatic effect. One of those magic moments when a mistake turns into a triumph.

Paul built a wooden shutter, wrapped steel mesh around the channels, and filled it with concrete. He returned in the middle of the night when the mix had started to set. Then, by the light of a lamp on his pit helmet, he dressed the concrete to a fine finish.

When the shuttering was stripped, the bridge was smooth, slim and elegant – yet it could still have taken the weight of a car. A work of art. [8]

I wanted to be able to get to every part of the garden, which meant we needed a small bridge over the bottom pond. A hump-back bridge in bright red – the only colour that ever appears in Japanese gardens.

I didn't know how to achieve the hump-back without involving a joiner's workshop, which sounded expensive. So I thought if I could bend thin strips of wood and glue them together in the required arc it might work. I tested four different adhesives on samples of the wood I was intending to use, and left them outside for a few months to see which could best stand the test of time.

Dave Thorpe had been in the framing industry for as long as me, and knew the sort of problems I was having trying to get a good working relationship going with a hardware manufacturer. 'Try Rick Flagg in Taiwan,' he said.

Rick, an American, had been Craft's man in Asia for years, until he became surplus to requirements and was dismissed. He wasn't happy at the manner in which this was done. Good, I thought. No vested interest there. I gave Rick a call. Within a few weeks, Rick was over to visit our factory in North Wales.

Rick was impressed with Curl Up n' Stand, and he could clearly see the potential. He knew the industry in Asia and the engineeers who could make the parts. He got some ball-park prices from engineers in Taiwan. They were less than half the price of Craft.

We never did get a formalised agreement with Craft, so there was never any commitment to stay with them as engineers.

I flew out to Taiwan to meet Rick's engineers. As Benjamin, Rick's assistant, was taking me to the hotel on the outskirts of Taipei, I looked out for a bar to test the night life. Benjamin was horrified that I was thinking of going off into the night, but I did.

The bar consisted of a few spartan tables and chairs. The bar itself was a make-shift pasting table. I guessed they served beer because there were a couple of spent bottles rolling about on the floor. I pointed to a bottle on the shelf, and settled down. It was beer. Nobody took any notice of me, not to start with – a few men laughing and joking about the day, as they would in any working class bar. My phone rang. It was D to see how I was getting on. I told her I was in a bar.

'D'you feel pretty tall there?'

I looked around at the various groups of people engrossed in their various worlds. 'No,' I said, 'I feel pretty insignificant.'

As I got my sea-legs, I took my bottle of beer and went and stood at the doorway looking up and down the street, absorbing the atmosphere of another world. A boy came and stood alongside me. He could speak a bit of English and was glad of an opportunity to practise. I probably had one or two more beers, but it was clear I wasn't going to rock the Casbah tonight.

I'd passed a supermarket on the way to the bar, and decided to investigate it on the way back to the hotel. I went in. No matter what part of the world you're in, supermarkets have a similarity, until you get down to the point of being there. Everything was described and priced in chopsticks. We're driven by the colour and type of packaging that we recognise from years of corporate branding. I bought a small bottle of what I hoped was a nightcap. It was near enough.

The next day we went to a factory owned and run by Mr Gao. It would be impossible to say his age; he was small, busy, industrious, a caricature of himself. The factory was like Dave Broadhurst's, but more hyperactive as if it was on something – all health and safety procedures out the window. His own children, barely teenagers, were operating presses. I cringed, but then it wasn't that long ago we were sending children up chimneys.

I became acclimatised and accepted that was the way it was. The work ethic was in stark contrast to what I'd seen in South Attleboro a few months earlier but, then again, my feeling was exactly the same: *What's in it for me?* I looked around; *he'll need a bigger place.* But I was touched by their warm friendly welcome, their eyes full of curiosity and wonder.

In the evening I went back to the same bar. Sitting down with my bottle of beer, my phone rang again. A broad Welsh accent said, 'Hello, Mr Holmes? This is Wrexham County Borough Council here. We've had a complaint from a Mr Bromilow. There's water coming in and causing severe problems to Mr Bromilow and Mrs Bromilow. The damp's causing chest problems.' I told him I was in Taiwan. 'Oh goodness me,' he said, 'I'm very sorry, I didn't know that.' How would he?

I phoned D to warn her, just in case. We laughed about the stupidity of the situation. My young friend from the night before came to join me in the doorway again. He disappeared, as if to get something. A few minutes later he reappeared, sitting on the wall with another young boy, and beckoning me to join them. His friend was obviously some sort of gift. I brushed away the proposition, and moved on to look for another bar. The two boys looked on, wondering where they'd gone wrong.

The next bar was a much livelier affair, a few Europeans, English spoken. I was joined by a Scandinavian guy. We chatted for a while about meaningless trivia, until I realised he had an agenda similar to the boys in the previous bar. I made my excuses and left, and went back to the hotel and the remains of my supermarket hooch.

The next day, Benjamin was shocked, and related to Rick that last night I went to *two* bars. They were astounded – how did I manage to do that without being killed?

Rick started producing a lot of our growing number of products, in black, brass and nickel finishes, and in particular the slip-on bracket. One of the downsides of this product was that the thickness of photo frame backs varies, so we had to order them in three sizes to accommodate different thicknesses of backs. Nevertheless, the quality was good, and delivery times reliable.

We continued to buy the fixed bracket from Craft. I suppose I still thought that sooner or later they would come round to the inevitability, and America was the biggest market place.

The wooden samples I was testing adhesives on were now looking grey and weathered, but on every one the adhesive was as strong as ever. I bought lengths of 4 x ½ inch tanalized timber, guaranteed for life. Paul set up a former on the factory floor to bend the lengths round to the required arc. It took all his strength to get the wood bent, but nothing broke and I knew once the adhesive set that would be it. We finished up with two arcs of solid 4 x 4 inch timber for the main structure. We completed the bridge in the factory, with short turned posts painted green supporting low side rails. It was now ready to take up to the pond. Although it was small in comparison with the concrete bridge, it still took a lot of manoeuvring to get it out of the factory and up to Fron Haul on the back of Paul's wagon.

I noticed Paul or one of his lads had run a scaffold plank across from the concrete bridge to the side of the pond to make themselves a short-cut while they were working. I thought what a good idea, but how could we do it? Even though the concrete bridge was solid, there was inevitably a bit of movement, so I couldn't attach another bridge to it because eventually that slight movement would cause something to break.

A few months and a jar of paracetamol later, I had the idea for the xylophone bridge – a twelve-foot railway sleeper was solidly anchored into the ground on the garden side and cantilevered over to the concrete bridge, stopping just one inch short of actual contact. We then attached two-foot lengths of timber spars across the sleeper to provide a walkway. Now we had another bridge, and another dimension to the garden. It looked for all the world like a xylophone, and if anybody walked on it and you asked them what was supporting it they'd look down and get very nervous as they realised it wasn't attached. It was solid as a rock, but defied logic. [9]

I don't know whether it was by design, or just the way things worked out, but there were a lot of odd things going on in the garden. I loved it to bits.

We needed a fence on the far side of the pond because there was a ten foot drop, which was a bit scary when the path narrowed to about three feet, but a regular fence wouldn't do – that would look ridiculous.

Probably flushed with the success of the red bridge, I decided to bend some timber laths, something like 3 x ½ inch, soaking them in the pond for a week or two to make them pliable. I was then able to force them into a pretty decent arc. I set them in place overlapping each other. But they just looked like a row of M's – for all the world like an ad for Macdonalds. Back to the drawing board.

The biggest photo frame company in the States by a long way was Burnes of Boston. I'd thought the biggest was Intercraft, but then discovered they were the same company. After some searching, I tracked them down and spoke to Cynthia Zeller. She sounded interested. I sent her a full pack of samples. I felt like a prospector panning for gold. Was this the big one – the motherlode?

I gave her enough time to receive the samples and phoned her, impatient, excited to see what she thought. She was interested. I asked her what she thought of the slip-on bracket. I could tell by the pained reaction that she didn't understand what I meant. I told her, 'I'm in the

States in about two or three weeks' time – can I come by and explain?' I said it casually, as if I was going to the corner shop to get a packet of tea. She pencilled a date in her diary. 'Yes, by all means come by if you're in Boston.'

I hadn't planned on going to America, but I was now. All that way after a somewhat casual five minute phone conversation. All the way to Boston. That's how mad I was, or how important I saw the opportunity to be.

Burnes are just about half an inch away from Craft on the map, and they'd never heard of Curl Up n' Stand – and this was two or three years down the line. Such was the interest Craft had in Curl Up n' Stand. I couldn't go all that way and practically pass Craft's front door without telling them. I phoned Ron Morin and told him I was going to see Burnes next Tuesday.

There was a silence. The significance of my meeting with Burnes hit hard. Ron said, 'But they're just up the road.' I didn't give him the opportunity for conversation. I just said, 'I'll come by and have a coffee with you after the meeting, shall I?'

I hate driving in a foreign country. Driving on the wrong side of the road is not so difficult when you think everything is opposite, but then the next day – opposite of what?

I arrived at Burnes' offices by taxi. Enormous car park, full. 'I have a meeting with Cynthia Zeller,' I said and handed the receptionist my card. It seemed to take an age. *What if she's not there? What if she's had to take the day off because one of the kids has tonsillitis?* Running over and over again the casual conversation that brought about this meeting. She'd said to come over when I'm in the area. She didn't know I'd flown three thousand miles for this meeting.

She was there. I did the demonstration, and it blew her away. 'I'll have to go and get George,' she said, and left the room. She returned with George, product engineer, and somebody else. I did the demo again.

'Well doggone!' he said, 'Have you ever seen the like? We don't need that, we don't need that – and we don't need that! Well doggone!'

That was it – they loved it. We didn't discuss price much. It wasn't necessary. George could see, and so could Cynthia, that simplicity had to make it cost-effective. *I've shown it to the biggest company on the planet, and they love it.*

They told me they didn't make their own photo frame backs. They were made by a company in North Carolina, close to one of their main manufacturing sites. I think he said they had site in Texas, too, and did he also say Durango in Mexico? My head was spinning. I left the meeting with instructions to send samples out to the backs manufacturer, Carolina Component Concepts (CCC), in North Carolina for testing. Outside, my driver was waiting, and we made our way over to Craft. *Ron Morin's not going to like this. Tough.*

The girls in Crafts' office welcomed me as usual, but then I saw Jerry the Plant Manager pass by at the end of the corridor. He scowled at me as if he knew I was the one that had burned down his barn. The meeting with Ron Morin was very hostile – just about the worst meeting I've been in. I had dared to tread on the hallowed turf of Burnes of Boston. He told me that he would handle any further contact with Burnes regarding Curl Up n' Stand. *Him handle it? He's been handling Curl Up n' Stand for the last three years and they don't know anything about it.* 'No,' I said, 'I'll do it.' I was angry. I told him that I would be handling all contact with them. 'They're going to buy,' I told him, 'But if you want any part of it you'd better sharpen your pencil. Your prices are too high.' I left the meeting in disgust, dismissing Ron's suggestion of lunch. I was in no mood for lunch. Not with Ron Morin.

George saw the introduction of Curl Up n' Stand to be with 14 x 11 inch frames fitted with the pressed on bracket. Quite large, but would emphasise the benefits of Curl Up n' Stand over the traditional strut.

I sent a pack of stock over to CCC. That must be the company that Armand Roy had sold twelve of his automatic easel hinge machines to. However big they were, nobody's bigger than Burnes. They were to fix the brackets on the backs and re-submit them to Burnes. Out of my hands a little bit now – I just had to wait and be patient.

The samples took an age to get from North Carolina to Burnes, but at last George rang, concerned about the cost: 'Remind me how much the Curl Up n' Stand is.'

'Six cents,' I said.

'That's what I thought.'

'Why, what's the matter?'

'They've come in from CCC very expensive.'

They'd charged about twenty cents for fitting them on the backs. A ridiculous price.

'That's far too expensive, George.'

'Yes, I know. This sort of thing has happened before. Leave it with me – I'll see what I can do.'

But what could he do? He knew the product was great, he knew it had to be cost-effective, but now we've got a key link in the chain making the whole thing impossible. Did CCC have a vested interest in seeing the Curl Up n' Stand buried?

I had to go back out and see George, and also to find out what was going on in North Carolina. As enthusiastic as George was – and Cynthia too – how hard were they going to fight my corner? If I wasn't careful a ridiculous quote coming back from CCC would just kill it stone dead. No discussions over why, or how can it be improved. George was no fool; he knew the bracket had to be pressed on, and he knew the encumbrances of that – he's an engineer – but he's got a thousand and one demands on his time, like everybody. It just seemed a casual stroke of the pen by some low-life in North Carolina could kill the project without intelligent reason.

I felt as though the whole world was battering me around like a ping-pong ball, and I could never seem to predict where the next bat was coming from, being hurled from one exaggerated scenario to another. If only I could take the time to stand back and look... But that's ridiculous. You can't think of anything so rational when you're peeling potatoes, you just have to keep going.

I went to a trade show in Spain – Madrid, was it? Can't quite remember. I only ever went there once. It wasn't one of the big ones. I needed to see a couple of people. I didn't expect to see Ron Morin.

I came down for breakfast and walked into the dining room. Right in front of me was Ron Morin sitting at a table with another guy I didn't know, and Doreen, I think it was.

Ron said, 'Why don't you come and join us? We're going now.'

His invitation matched the glare of the other guy. Perhaps he was Spanish, he looked a bit latin.

'No, thanks. I'm meeting somebody.' I walked to the other side of the room. It was hardly an invitation anyway. They left the restaurant.

Craft were exhibiting at the show. I had to clear the air, and went over to talk to Ron. He was with somebody, but I could tell it wasn't important. He just ignored me. I waited a few minutes, talking with Doreen. The other guy I'd taken to be Spanish wasn't – he was their American engineer. He continued to glare at me when he could; he'd obviously been briefed on what a low-life I was. I told Doreen I'd come back later, and left.

I did go back later, when Ron wasn't with anybody.

'Hi, Ron. I think we should talk.'

'Yeah,' he drawled, 'I think we should talk.' His manner was straight out of a John Wayne western.

'Shall we go and get a cup of coffee?'

'Yeah. Let's go and get some coffee.'

When we were sitting down I showed him Curl Up n' Stand with the slip-on bracket. That was the first time he'd seen it. He held it for a few moments.

'It's good. It's very good,' he said.

His tone was quiet, almost sombre, sincere. I'd never seen him like that before.

'The thing is, Ron, I'm a customer of yours, but I'm also your biggest competitor.'

'We'll be OK. We can get business from the electronics or the automotive industry.'

I was stunned. I didn't know what to say. Does he think it's that serious? I didn't think anybody saw it as that serious. I didn't think it was *that* serious.

I can't remember much more about the meeting, and I never saw him any more at the show after that, but I was only there a day anyway.

All I ever wanted to do was work *with* Craft, not against them – but surely they knew that? Was Ron saying they'd rather come out of the industry than work together? I found it difficult to come to terms with what he'd said.

My mind tends to switch off if problems become a bit overwhelming. Or maybe the mind just says 'you can't do anything about it now, so stop wasting time pretending you can and concentrate on something you can do something about'.

CCC's business was fitting hinges to photo frame backs by the million – Craft's hinges – for pretty well all the large frame manufacturers in the US. I spoke to them several times. To say that their response was negative would be something of an understatement. 'How the hell are we going to fit those brackets?' Tillison said, in a patronising, condescending way. 'It's *going* to happen,' I said.

Burnes Group could well be CCC's biggest customer. George and Cynthia were still very enthusiastic; I had to keep that going. Sooner or later CCC would have to take their interest seriously and find a way to apply the bracket.

There was another trade show coming up, in Atlanta. We had our own stand. I didn't fancy sharing with Ron Morin and I'm sure he felt the same. I tried to get George or Cynthia to meet up with me there, but that show wasn't part of their schedule, and it was a long way to ask them to go. If I couldn't get them to come to Atlanta, I had to go back to Boston.

D arranged the flights for both of us to go to the Atlanta trade show for four days then, three days after we returned to the UK, I would fly back out to Boston.

The horrors of last year's experiences in Atlanta were embedded, but I was prepared this time; it wouldn't happen again. I'm sure D thought I'd been exaggerating.

'We get our cases from somewhere by here, and then over there they take them off us again and shove them through the hole in the wall. I know about that stuff,' I told her.

We waited and waited by the first carousel but the cases never arrived. We had to accept they weren't going to. Whether they never got on the plane at Manchester, or whether they were wandering round Charles de Gaulle like two aimless souls, I didn't know – but they weren't in Atlanta. Someone gave us a little bag which is supposed to appease the situation. Toothbrush, tiny toothpaste, comb, deodorant, and that was about it. I can get by with that, I just wanted to get to the show and do my party tricks, but D was distraught. Our suitcases arrived at the hotel that evening, but we'd had to do the first day of the show in the clothes we'd set off in thirty-six hours previously.

We didn't stay in the Hyatt Hotel this time, but it was nearby. As we passed the Hyatt, there, high up on the skyscraper opposite, was the bandaged injured window just like it had been twelve months ago.

An easy, pleasant stroll back to the hotel once the first day of the show had finished, along a quiet tree-lined road in the early evening sunshine, chatting about the day. A black saloon car came down the street from behind us and screeched to a halt at the kerbside just in front. A big black guy leapt out and blocked our path, arms outstretched. 'I'm not going to hurt you,' he said. I went into a rage and screamed at him: 'Fuck off!' He repeated, 'I'm not going to hurt you, I just…' 'Just fuck off!' I screamed louder. Both my fists were clenched, every sinew taut. I felt like a raging bull. He hesitated for a moment, then got back in his car and they drove off.

We were laughing about it in the bar later. D said, 'I thought you were going to turn green and burst out of your shirt!' I never saw the guy again, though I did hear he became a Mormon, teaching basket weaving and the art of jam making. What's with these guys? It hadn't been funny at the time, and I don't know whether I would have been quite so brave if I'd been on my own, but this time I had somebody to protect.

He wasn't laughing either, neither was he a real bad man, he was just a chancer. Saw the possibility of perhaps picking up a few dollars, same as the guy twelve months earlier at six-thirty in the morning while I was looking for Starbucks. He wasn't a bad man. Were their lives so wretched that's what they were reduced to? So this is the greatest country in the world… so long as you fit the right criteria.

Earlier in the day inside the show I'd gone to get a tea and a coffee from the kiosk. The guy slapped an iced tea on the counter. I said, 'I didn't ask for iced tea.' He said 'That's tea.'

'Listen pal. We invented tea. You start off with hot tea and then adjust it from that point.'

It seemed to amuse the people behind me, so he changed it.

Everything seems to be a confrontation. Mind you, I was wrong – we didn't invent tea, we may have discovered it at one point, but we didn't hold any rights over it. Perhaps I was becoming over-sensitive.

It always seemed to be the black guys who were carrying this burden. Whatever it was, their angst was going back a long time.

Back in the UK, three days to wash a couple of shirts, bang my suits on the wall, and re-pack the suitcase for Boston.

The meeting with Cynthia and George was enthusiastic as ever – more, if that's possible.

'The big boys are in today, aren't they?' George said.

Cynthia hesitated, 'Yes, but…'

'Don't you think it would be a good idea to introduce them to Ken?'

The big boys? The big boys are in? Who are the big boys? I wanna meet the big boys.

'They are in, but they'll have a very heavy schedule,' she said.

But George didn't let up: 'It'll be a good opportunity for them to meet Ken.'

I'm looking from one to the other, willing George with all my strength to keep going. He won. Cynthia left the room, and returned ten minutes later with Rocco Davanzo. *I was meeting Rocco Davanzo.* In all my wildest dreams I never thought I'd meet somebody called Rocco Davanzo.

'Hi Ken,' he said, 'I believe you've got a cute idea.'

I blurted out my presentation. 'Forgive me if I sound a bit excited, but I am.'

'I'm not surprised,' he said, 'It's a great idea. Hang on a minute, I'm going to get you some names.'

He returned with a piece of paper, 'This is Nicolas Shaw, my counterpart in Europe, and I believe you're going to North Carolina. Call in at the Intercraft factory – I'll tell Curtis Swope to expect you' – and a few more names. 'Lee Cielonko, he's head of purchasing, he'll be useful to you.' I couldn't have been more elated if he'd given me a knighthood.

I hadn't actually planned to go to North Carolina, but I was going now.

'How are you getting to North Carolina?' Cynthia asked.

'I'm not really sure.'

'We can arrange that,' she said. 'I'll get one of the girls to do it'.

A girl came in. 'I've got you a flight. Can I have your credit card?' *Eight hundred dollars.* I must have looked a bit shocked. Somebody said, 'Yeah, internal flights in the States are expensive.' I handed over my card, praying there would be enough left on the plastic.

I phoned D from the airport, told her the meeting was great. 'Good,' she said, 'are you on your way back to New York now?' 'No. I'm on my way to North Carolina.'

I tried to make sense of what was happening in as few words as possible. 'But you're booked in tonight at the Chelsea Hotel in New York.'

'Well, I'm not going to make that. Change it to tomorrow… and try and get me a flight back tomorrow from North Carolina to New York.'

D phoned back a few minutes later: 'Whereabouts in North Carolina?'

It puts it into perspective a bit, how enormous the States are, and some of the states are bigger than the UK. I thought North Carolina was specific enough, but it's like saying North England – could be anywhere. She started studying maps to find out where Greenfield was.

The first appointment was a hastily arranged meeting with CCC, the company that had twelve automatic Craft machines. *I'm now taking Craft head on.* Going by the conversation I'd had with Charles Tillison, I was expecting something of a hostile meeting – I was about to tell them they didn't need those twelve automatic machines any more. But now I've got the backing of Rocco Davanzo. Nobody says no to Rocco.

The meeting opened with, 'You'll find the picture frame market different in the US to Europe.' I thought *here we go, they're going to try and bury it*. But I was wrong – not a bit. 'In Europe frames are hung on the wall. In America we love table-top frames. Your idea is perfect.' They loved it – or that's what came over at the meeting. In particular, they thought the slip-on bracket was brilliant.

CCC could see the benefits and the excellence of Curl Up n' Stand, they could also see how the end user would prefer it, but it was the old story of who's going to put the bell on the cat. Nobody wanted to do it.

The slip-on bracket took away the need to use the fixed bracket. That may have seemed a great solution to me, but their business revolved around fitting a hinge to a back – and I'm showing them something that means they don't need to do that any more. I left on good terms but rather than solving problems I was creating bigger ones.

The Intercraft factory was a stone's throw from CCC. This was the main manufacturing arm of Burnes. The factory that appeared in front of me was what I imagined a Ford car plant would look like; it was enormous. Curtis Swope, the plant manager, was there to meet me, because he was told to by Rocco Davanzo. You've got to love these names – Curtis Swope, Cynthia Zeller, Rocco Davanzo. I must have been with Curtis for an hour. He gave me all the time in the world as if he had nothing else to do. He loved the ingenuity of Curl Up n' Stand, probably because of his production background. He gave me an additional problem to solve: how could the same system be applied to a window back? It doesn't matter what a window back is at this stage, but I couldn't wait to get my teeth into it.

The scheduled flight should have got me to JFK at about seven-thirty; one night in the Chelsea Hotel, then the long-haul flight home. But the weather had other ideas. Freak storms delayed the flight. The take-off time from North Carolina was pushed back further and further, and then cancelled altogether until the next day. D had to cancel the Chelsea Hotel for another night.

The Chelsea Hotel had been recommended by John and Daniel, two guys I got to know through the trade shows. I'd told them I was fed up with staying in downtown Manhattan and all the artificial bits that go with it.

Two days late I arrived at the old, unimposing building that was the Chelsea. A long corridor led to the small reception. 'Glad you finally made it, Mr Holmes.' So was I. The room was spartan, basic, doors not fitting properly. Nothing seemed to fit properly, except me – I loved it. In any hotel I would normally dump the case and get out of the room as quickly as possible, and find the bar. Not here – I just wanted to absorb the atmosphere.

I knew there wasn't a bar, because two girls before me at reception had asked about one and were told, 'there isn't one in the hotel but if you go out, turn left and left again, and down the steps, you'll like the bar there'. I came out, turned left and left again, and down the steps. The doorman politely said, 'Sorry, guests only at the moment, it's a private function.' 'May I be able to come in later?' I said. 'I'm just staying round the corner at the Chelsea.' 'You're at the Chelsea?' he said, 'Come in.'

The bar wasn't particularly glamourous, but I wouldn't have been at all surprised to see David Bowie or Mick Jagger in the corner. 'Enjoy your stay at the Chelsea,' the doorman said as I left a couple of hours later.

During the flight back to Heathrow I had an idea of how to solve the problem Curtis Swope had set me. There's something about long haul flights… it's not the distance or the time… something just wipes your slate clean of all the crap, and allows the ideas to flow.

Back home, I sent the sketches over to Curtis Swope. 'Is this anything like you had in mind,' I asked him.

'That's exactly what I had in mind,' he said.

'What's the next step, then?'

'I guess you get samples made.'

I needed to get more prototypes made like I needed a hole in the head, but Curtis Swope was a vital link in the chain and in any case I wanted to see it work. But it was more money.

I had a meeting with John Pitchford to bring him up to date with the Burnes Group. He said, 'They'll want you to join them. They'll finish up making you an offer.' Make me an offer? I hadn't thought of that. John didn't say things lightly. He was also one of the very few people whose opinion I respected. Were my ideas that good? One thing it seems I'm always able to do is inflate my ego when it's needed.

A good idea may take one or two percent of the market; a great idea takes most of it. Right now I would have settled for one or two percent – it would still make me a millionaire. A good idea is not dangerous – Curl Up n' Stand was. Do all inventors go through this before they have their moment of glory? We only hear about the ones that make it and become household names. How many great ideas never make it because they tread on too many toes?

'We don't need this, and we don't need this, and we don't need that…' That's what George Simmons had said. The trouble was, 'this' and 'that' were CCC's business, and they were going to fight for their lives. As much as they applauded Curl Up n' Stand in North Carolina, they were going to do everything they possibly could to kill it.

The solution came from Cynthia Zeller. 'We only manufacture about fifty percent of our frames in the US,' she said. 'The other fifty percent comes in from Asia, CKK in Hong Kong.' Cynthia introduced me to Iris Chan at CKK to explore the possibilities of getting Curl Up n' Stand fitted there.

I sent samples out to Iris with the brief to look at fitting Curl Up n' Stand on some of Burnes' frames. A month later I was on the plane to Hong Kong.

CKK arranged the hotel – the most luxurious one I've ever stayed in. *May as well start to get used to this.* They sent a limousine to pick me up at nine o'clock in the morning. The familiar tingles started again. At their offices Iris Chan's assistant, Candy, greeted me with that warm Asian smile, and took me to their showroom. It was about the size of my factory floor. Around the walls were a dozen booths, each one displaying a different range of photo frames: porcelain, silver- and gold-plated, solid silver, plastic, wooden… frames of every description. Each frame I passed I could see being stood up by Curl Up n' Stand – that's the way it would be soon. I asked Candy what she thought of Curl Up n' Stand. 'We love it,' she said.

Iris Chan came in to join us, and the meeting started. Right away she said, 'These are the prices: the large one twenty-five cents, and the small one twenty-three.' The red mist came down. I was expecting in the region of four or five cents. Adding those sort of prices on top of the cost of frames for Burnes was ridiculous. I felt my anger building up. 'That's got to be a mistake, Iris. Oh – you mean Hong Kong Dollars?' 'No,' she said, 'US Dollars.' She must have seen the look of horror on my face and just sat there, hardly saying another word. There was no, 'perhaps we can improve the price if the volumes are right,' no attempt whatsoever to bridge the enormous gap.

If anyone knew the cost of manufacturing hardware, CKK did. All the frames in that showroom were manufactured by CKK at their factories in China. Not just the frames, but all the metal fittings that went with them.

She'd killed it stone dead. The price was about five times what I'd expected. It wasn't a question of negotiation. I don't remember much more about the meeting. It closed on a sour note. I think I muttered something like, 'It *will* happen, Iris.'

I'd gone all that way just to see an assassination. Again.

It will happen. Is that going to be my epitaph?

I knew with absolute certainty that what I was doing was right, and found it hard to believe that CKK could treat the Burnes Group with such contempt. But that's what had happened.

On the plane back home, the blunt words at the meeting I'd travelled half way round the world to attend played and replayed. Twenty-five cents: five times the price I was expecting. If I tell anybody, they're going to say I'm stupid. How could I go all that way without nailing the prices first? And yet I did. She hadn't blamed the costs of raw materials or the tooling costs, she hadn't blamed it on being outside their normal production, or a thousand and one other excuses normally associated with inflated prices. She just hit me with twenty-five cents, and killed it stone dead.

'We love it,' Candy had said. *'We love it.'*

Was Curl Up n' Stand that dangerous? Had I discovered the everlasting match – was that the problem? Frames weren't going to fall over any more – and here was me thinking that was a good idea. How naïve was that?

I don't remember much else about the trip or the posh hotel. I suppose I muttered something about UK manufacturing costs and Taiwan manufacturing costs. If I did, it was just a waste of time. The assassination was swift and complete.

I buried my head in the garden for a week or two while I thought about it all.

When you're searching for a solution it's like doing a jigsaw puzzle; you might try several pieces that look close, but only one piece fits, and when you find it you know it's right and all the pain goes away. The correct solution appears to be an exact – not a near enough, nor a compromise.

That's how it was with the fence on the retaining wall. I'd like to think the sunbursts were inspired by the Land of the Rising Sun. I can't remember, but they might have been.

The sunbursts were fitted in pairs, with bamboo planted in pots attached to the outside of the wall between each pair.

CHAPTER 10

I waited a few days before reporting back to Cynthia on CKK. I wasn't quite sure how to say it. She greeted me with, 'There have been some major changes here.' She told me the whole office block in Boston was closing down. Everybody, including Cynthia and George, made redundant unless they wanted to move to Texas. I think the factory in North Carolina went as well.

All those months and years of work, gone up in smoke. How dare they? The administration and some of the production was going to Texas, and there was another facility in Durango, Mexico. Might as well have been on Pluto.

Perhaps I shouldn't have built up my hopes, but isn't that what hopes are for? If you don't have your aspirations and expectations running at maximum, you'll never have the enthusiasm to drive it.

I realised all those years ago when I first saw the Japanese Garden at Calderstones Park in Liverpool how important peace and tranquility were… and now I've built my own. The garden was a spiritual sanctuary. There, nothing was a problem. All I could see were solutions.

I designed a valve that allowed the level in the bottom pond to lower by an inch and a half when the pump was running. A very simple device, and it worked perfectly. It meant the whole system stayed constant throughout. It appears every problem has a solution where there's a will to find it.

Every Japanese garden should have a tea house, but I hadn't known where until now. Sitting the tea house on top of the reservoir not only hid the big hole but the balcony overhung the edge of the pond and the water seemed to disappear beneath your feet as though running on for ever.

The tea house was beautiful, complete with overhanging roof, turned up at the eaves, and cedarwood shingles. [11]

From time to time I'd received blurbs from the Welsh office about trade missions to various exotic places. I always glanced at them but threw them away. Then one came in about Singapore. The idea of doing business in Asia had started with CKK. I liked the irony, considering it was the competition from Asia that started it all in the first place. I'd heard about trade missions and knew they were something to do with the backbone of British industry promoting themselves abroad. I thought they were more for proper companies like ICI and Cadbury's and people like that. But perhaps not. This leaflet was promoting a trade mission to Australia and Singapore, including all the flights and hotels, sponsored by the British Government. If I'm being sponsored by the British Government, surely people are going to take notice then. To my surprise, my application was approved.

And so our little band of warriors took off: twelve missionaries and three Government 'minders'.

A brief stop in Singapore to refuel and a cup of tea, and then Sydney. The day after that we would meet the British High Commissioner. *I left school at fifteen with 'could do better' stamped over everything, and now I'm meeting the High Commissioner!*

We were all to meet in the lobby of the hotel at nine-thirty to get to the Embassy for ten o'clock. Everybody arranged their alarm calls. I didn't need an alarm clock; I'm always awake at six-thirty, raring to go. Not on this occasion. I'd forgotten about the jet-lag you get travelling East. I woke up and looked at the clock with horror: it was a quarter to ten. I didn't bother showering. I grabbed a suit and dashed downstairs. They'd all left in a coach. I found out from reception where the Embassy was and decided to run there. How I found it I don't know, running past big official buildings along big official streets. By some miracle I found it – I was unwashed and sweating – but there in time. They'd tried to wake me apparently but couldn't.

We were introduced to one of the high officials, a lady. One by one she asked our names. *She's not going to remember all these names.* When she got to me I said, 'Hermione'. I don't know why I picked that name. I have a slight stammer, a residue from my childhood that comes back at times like this. Hermione is hard enough to say if you haven't got a stammer. Anyway I stuttered it out. 'Hermione?' she repeated with a smile. I think I picked Hermione because it sounded a bit Ambassadorish. Anyway, she remembered my name. Every now and then through her talk she'd catch my eye, and I could see her whispering 'Hermione' under her breath. I think there might have been a flip chart and a pointer, and there was probably a map of Australia. Somebody probably said something like, 'Australians like buying British products', and that sort of stuff. I was waiting for her to ask, 'Does anybody know when the Battle of Hastings was?' I had my answer prepared on the tip of my tongue. But she never did. Instead she went on at some length about GDP. At the end she asked, 'Has anybody got any questions?' Everybody remained silent. So I asked her what GDP was. She thought it was funny. When it was all over, the Ambassador shook our hands at the door. I thanked him and said, 'Next time, you must come round to ours.'

I had a few meetings in Australia. For a country that's supposed to be so sparsely populated, they still sell a lot of frames. I met two potential distributors, each saying they were the biggest and wanted exclusive, but they all say that. We'd been warned at the Embassy briefing that Australians love to do a bit of pommie-bashing, so I was prepared when at one meeting I was greeted with, 'Oh, you're the pommie bastard I've been hearing about.' I said, 'As we've not been introduced yet, could you call me Mr Pomegranate.' The ice was broken.

My main interest on the trade mission was Singapore. Asia was the biggest manufacturing area in the world, certainly as far as picture frames went.

Meetings had been arranged by the Trade Commission at which the missionaries could meet local businesses with mutual interests. I met a lady who ran an engineering company, a real live-wire, full of energy. The next day I visited her factory. Her husband was the engineer, but she was certainly the mover and shaker. She arranged for me to meet with the Singapore Economic Development Board. I was very impressed. It would have taken six months in the UK to arrange a meeting like that.

The meeting took place on the twenty-fifth floor, overlooking the harbour. The object was to ask for financial support for the development of Curl Up n' Stand, and associated tooling costs. Two officials listened attentively to my presentation. Then one said to me, 'What happens if it fails?' *Fails?* Chinese people sometimes talk loud and a bit animated as though they're cross about something. I stood up and pointed to the Singapore skyline. 'Failure? There's no such thing as failure. *Kiasu!*' They looked at each other and repeated 'Kiasu! He knows Kiasu?' The mood of the meeting changed; they were immediately on my side. I'd learnt the word 'Kiasu' from the taxi driver on the way to the meeting. Singapore was such a fantastic success story, and that was almost their mantra. It means 'Refuse to Fail' – or at least that was my interpretation of it. I had, with that one word, become a brother. When the meeting was over, they took me to a restaurant that was very big, very busy. I appeared to be the only Westerner there. Everybody was chatting away in Chinese. Dish after dish of food appeared, and each time they made sure I approved before we started to eat.

They were impressed with the inventions and their potential, but it wasn't the kind of development that Singapore was looking for. Singapore was a very affluent country with high wage rates. The kind of manufacturing business they were looking for to take Singapore forward had to be high-tech.

I met Gary Lim in Singapore, a marketing consultant, Chinese. It was going to be a while before Curl Up n' Stand was ready for a marketing consultant, but Gary and I just hit it off right away. I thought I travelled through life at a hundred miles an hour, but it was a job to keep up with Gary. On the last day while the rest of the missionaries were sitting on their suitcases in reception waiting, I was sitting by the pool talking with Gary.

He said, 'You're talking about the Pyramid of Needs, the needs of man.'

'What's that?'

'It was something written by a Harvard professor; the Needs of Man. You start with the need to be warm and cosy, then to become the hunter, then the family man, the career, and so on. At the very top of the pyramid is self-realisation.'

That hit home. Isn't that what we're all looking for?

It was difficult to assess the immediate benefits of the trip. I met some very interesting people. I hadn't expected to be so impressed with Sydney or Singapore, and I hadn't realised I was following some sort of pyramid of needs.

Self-realisation – is that what I'm trying to achieve? Self-fulfillment – is that the same thing? Making Curl Up n' Stand the standard for picture frames – is that my mission in life? Seems pretty shallow when I put it like that. Why did Gary Lim have to say that? Life was quite simple – bloody difficult, but simple. It was me against the rest of the world, pretty well. Goodies and baddies. Isn't that the way it's supposed to be?

Over the last two or three years we'd had serious interest from some of the large manufacturers in Europe but, apart from one in Germany, we hadn't pinned any of them down. The big manufacturers in the UK had been all for it in the beginning, then changed and became downright rude. I'd arranged to meet Lee Pevy of Sarah Leigh, one of the UK's big manufacturers, at a trade show. I arrived at the arranged time. He was talking casually to someone one the next stand so I stood back and waited... and waited... and waited. He knew I was there and purposefully kept his back to me.

When Ron and Armand came to visit me in North Wales I knew they'd gone to Liverpool the day before. Mike Pevy's business was in Liverpool. I can't think of any other reason why they would go there, and I couldn't help thinking was there a connection.

The other big companies weren't much better. But there were a lot of volume frame makers in France and Germany – perhaps we'd get more respect there.

D drew up a schedule to go and visit as many of these as we could. She carries an in-built map of Europe from all her travels over the years. I don't – I never know where I am. Doing an itinerary that D and I were happy with was one thing; but slotting it in with the potential customers' schedules was a totally different matter. We finished up having to zig-zag all over the place.

We flew to Dresden. Two meetings and about two hundred miles later we were on the outskirts of Hameln. 'It's over there somewhere,' D pointed out of the window as we hurtled along the autobahn. She was doing all the driving. I do the important bit: like telling prospective customers how Curl Up n' Stand is going to improve their life beyond measure, though I haven't been very successful yet. D told me that Hameln is Hamlin of Pied Piper fame.

We found a hotel just off the autobahn. Perfect. We checked in then found the bar. It was a big bar/restaurant, just about a dozen or so zombies scattered around. Not much of a laugh here. Just a few lonely souls waiting to be called up to be executed.

A pretty fraulein came to take our meal order.

'Have all the mice gone?' I asked.

She looked puzzled.

I said, 'This is a very famous place, you know. We all know about the Pied Piper.'

She smiled in recognition.

'You weren't one of the children, were you? Did your mum and dad let you watch?'

She went off to the kitchen with our order, chuckling. One by one the zombies stirred into life; everybody remembered the Pied Piper story.

At the end of our meal she appeared from the kitchen carrying a big plate. The chefs had made us an ice-cream mouse – complete with tail, almonds for ears and whiskers – I think it had whiskers, but anyway it was certainly a mouse. I know in the story it was the rats, but we were in Germany; I called it a mouse for the sake of *entente cordiale*.

We covered a huge number of miles in three days. How much did we achieve? We waved the flag a lot to people who hadn't really seen the full potential, but the most impressive thing was D's driving, and the most memorable was the ice-cream mouse.

We flew back to the UK from Frankfurt, and the next day we got a flight from Manchester to Barcelona and hired another car.

One meeting in Barcelona, which was a waste of time, and then North to meet with Molduras Hergon. Tomas Corominas spoke perfect English. He'd studied at the LSE in London while he was keeping out of Franco's way. It never ceases to amaze me how big some of these facilities are. His factory was the largest importer of timber in Spain, and they were just producing picture frames – raw wood coming in one end, and frames out the other. 'I can't show you round the factory today,' Tomas said, 'because at the moment we've got thirteen contract engineers installing our new automatic assembly line, and our insurance company won't allow any more. They hold us up as their flagship. In case of fire, the whole factory can be vacated within so many minutes and steel fire-proof shutters come down to isolate the area.'

Tomas was very intelligent, perceptive, and utterly charming. He saw the potential. They had the big Craft easel hinge machine. 'Well, I'll just tell Craft we're going to put it under dust covers.' He was convinced.

'Where are you off to next?'

'Perpignan.' That immediately told him I was going to see one of his competitors.

He looked at his watch, and said, 'Don't stay in Perpignan tonight – there's nothing there, a few castles, but you've got better in the UK. Stay in Figueras and have a meal at Duran, and if you get going now you'll have time to visit the Salvador Dali museum.'

'Do you know of an hotel?' I asked him.

'Stay at Duran,' he said.

We booked in at the hotel and went to the museum. We must have walked round there for about two hours, hardly speaking, mesmerised by the genius of the man.

Dali had designed this museum to house his art works, each one more outrageous. As we wandered round, and up to another floor in the circular gallery, from time to time we glanced down into the inner courtyard. In the centre there was a Cadillac. Standing on the bonnet was a larger than life statue of a woman looking skyward, where the hull of a suspended boat dripped water.

A couple of hours later the museum was closing and we'd been reminded several times. We were now by the old Cadillac. There was a chauffeur in the front, and in the back the elderly businessman accompanied by a scantily clad lady of the night. The Cadillac was mounted on a plinth and D wasn't quite tall enough to see inside so I looked around for something for her to stand on. There was a metal box on the floor which had a slot for a coin. Curiosity got the better of me and I put a coin in. Suddenly music bellowed out and water poured into the car from its ceiling like a torrential rainstorm, saturating everything and every one inside it. An eerie green glow lit up the interior, revealing living ivy creeping up over the passengers. .

We hadn't heard the music during the whole time we'd been in the museum, and I wouldn't have noticed the metal box on the floor either if I hadn't been looking for something for D to stand on.

That evening we had dinner in the hotel. Dali's paintings were all around the walls. The old waiter remembered Dali very well. 'He used to sit over there, with his wife Gala and a few others, two or three times a week.' Their lavish extravagant lifestyle was paid for by rich sponsors, who were repaid with paintings. His presence was tangible.

After our meeting in Perpignan, we were chasing the clock a bit. We had to get back to Barcelona airport for midday, and return the hire car.

At the airport, I thought we'd parked by the Europcar office. I got out, opened the boot and started sorting out our stuff, but then I realised we weren't parked in the right place, so we got back in the car. There were two or three guys walking around, talking on mobile phones. They stood out a bit because there was nobody else around. One of them came over and put his hand up to stop us, pointing towards the back of the car. I got out, thinking I must have left my briefcase on the ground. Two other guys appeared. I couldn't understand what they were saying, and called to D. They were speaking French. One of them was stooping down, pointing at the tyre. I squatted down trying to understand what he was saying and what he was pointing at. There was something wrong with this. Alarm bells rang. *Here we go again.*

I pushed over the one stooping down next to me and screamed to D, 'Back in the car!' She moved like lightening – she knew instantly. We jumped in the car, 'Lock the fucking door!' I shouted, and grabbed my mobile. I screamed down the phone, 'Police! Police!' Angry face, hammering at the window. I shouted at D, 'Drive! Drive! Take 'em out!' Just as well I wasn't driving – they'd have been dead. He had a piece of glass in his hand, he shouted something abusive, threw the glass at the car and was off. When I looked at the phone, I'd been holding it upside down and back to front. I might as well have tried to call the police on the ashtray.

When we'd first picked up the hire car, there was a note lying on the seat. I don't normally read the blurb, but I'd read that. 'There's a team of thieves about, preying on tourists.' They pretend you have a puncture, help you unload your luggage, then rob you.

A police officer was further up the road conducting traffic. I leapt out of the car and started screaming at him in my best Scouse: 'There's robbers there! Go and grab 'em!' He hadn't a clue what I was talking about. I was hysterical, and he was Spanish. His arms became more animated as he tried to guide the traffic while I was pointing first this way, then that. We left him confused and drove to the Europcar office.

I went to the front of the queue shouting, 'We've nearly been robbed!' He took no notice. 'Just now! Here in the airport!' That pressed his panic button. Immediate phone calls: 'They're in the airport! They're in the airport!' But they were probably well gone by now. Three men, smartly dressed, mid-thirties. They drew attention to themselves with their mobile phones, but other than that they'd blend in anywhere. These guys weren't chancers, they were professionals. But what were they going to get? What was our second-hand luggage worth? Curl Up n' Stand was the only valuable thing in there – at least there was somebody who wanted it, even though they went about it in a strange way.

Everybody wanted it really, or at least everybody liked it. Turning it into a firm commitment was a lot harder than I could ever have imagined, though I never lost faith that one day it would happen, and neither did D. Tomas Corominas was going to place an order, but it was still more of a trickle than a flood.

I can't help thinking I'm glad I had the idea for Curl Up n' Stand when I did, and not thirty years before when I was in my early twenties, because I wouldn't have had the confidence or the balls to see it through.

CHAPTER 11

Christmas morning. I had a phone call from Dave Broadhurst. 'I know it's Christmas Day, Ken. I can't wait to tell you.' Last night he'd been at a party and the manageress of Max Spielmann's Shrewsbury had been there. 'She loves it, Ken. She absolutely loves it!' *What a brilliant Christmas present – just what I wanted to hear.*

'I'm glad you called, Dave. I've had an idea.'

'Oh God, what now?'

'I can't tell you over the phone. It's about the garden.'

Dave loved business the same as me, but he knew as soon as I said I'd had an idea it was going to cause pain.

Dave's interest in Christmas was about the same as mine, and he was probably glad to get out of the house, so he came over on Boxing Day.

I used to spend weeks agonising over what presents to buy for people – then probably got it wrong. That year, instead of presents, I gave a donation to the Salvation Army, which didn't go down well either. We'd sold a hell of a lot of frames over Christmas. We always did, so my moral outrage was somewhat two-faced.

I like the idea of celebrations, but I've got to do it in my own way. That year I built a life-sized model of a man. I screwed his shoes on to a small plinth so he could stand up on his own. I dressed him in my dinner suit, with dress shirt, black leather gloves and a cane. He had dark glasses and I hired a top hat from Moss Bros., a necessary expense. His face was made out of papier mâché. If you looked hard you could see the printed line that said Liverpool 2 : Manchester United 0. A good result on the face of it. Mr Dude was our Christmas Tree. [12]

Mike Lister had bought the house just above me. In order for him to build his garden and house plans, he'd put up a fifteen foot retaining wall, which looked absolutely monstrous from my side of it. I'd been struggling for ages on ideas for how to mask this. A conifer hedge would take years, and in the end wouldn't look much better. Now I knew what to do, I thought, but I needed Dave.

When he came round on Boxing Day he watched and listened with pained expression as I gestured a snake-like line on the ground.

'That's it, Dave,' I said. 'That's the line. I want a light steel frame going up from that to the full height of the wall, with something like 1-1/2 x 1/8 inch steel straps running horizontally, snaking in and out, following the pattern on the ground. Then we can fix vertical timber batons.' The line of the top of the fence curved up and down, mirroring the hills and mountains behind. [13]

Dave organised the steel, and Geordie helped me build it. I had to select the right moment to pay Geordie, because as soon as he could he'd get to the pub and turn it into lager. Some mornings you could smell the ale coming out of him. But he was a welder, built for speed and could climb like a monkey.

High up in the left hand side of the screen we fixed a kidney-shaped 'moonstone'. We very carefully cut a hole in the screen to match the contours of the stone, then placed the moonstone so about one-third of it was protruding through the hole into the garden over the reed bed. It took an enormous effort to get the stone up there – it was heavy. The weight of the stone was supported by a steel cradle welded to the angle iron behind and totally invisible.

I'd heard about a spring way up on the mountain side. This had been the sole water supply to the cottage for many years. The pipe bringing the water down had rusted away a long time ago, but there were bits here and there for me to trace way back to the source: a little trickle of water coming out of the ground. I cleared the earth and rocks away until the water ran clear. I looked back at the house; it was a long way. I bought the biggest reel of hose the building suppliers had, and still had to join it. I dragged the hose up the mountainside, over the rocks and gorse bushes, watched from a distance by Glyn Ty Isa's sheep. I built a little sump pool where the spring came out of the mountain, set the end of the hose in there, and watched with the excitement of a child as the water disappeared down into the pipe. Then I ran down the mountain as fast as I could to see if I could get to the other end before the water. I got there first, and waited and waited… but no water came. Disappointed, I traced the hose inch by inch back up to the spring, shaking it here and there in case there was a kink. I was on my own at the time, running up and down the mountain like a mad goat. I gave up, and sat down by the pond, exhausted, contemplating how cruel life can be… and the water began to trickle out.

I acquired a 500 litre tank, one of those big plastic ones in a steel cage, secured it on a platform behind the cottage, out of sight, and connected the spring water to it. A teacher at school used to say, 'small things amuse small minds'. Well, I must have a small mind, because I was thrilled when the mountain water started to trickle into it and slowly started to climb up the sides. I divided the outlet three ways with microbore pipe.

Sometimes when people are planning a big project they'll build a model first. I did it the other way around. I built a miniature replica of the garden alongside the main pond, complete with two ponds, a waterfall, bonsai trees and a tiny stone wall surrounding it all, supporting the miniature hills and valleys of the landscape. I buried the first microbore underground with the end connected to a fine bamboo pipe coming out from a stone wall five feet above the miniature garden. The water trickled out of the bamboo and down into the miniature pond, over a waterfall to the little bottom pond, then finally made its way to the main pond. We had two tiny goldfish in the miniature pond: Pinky and Perky. As they grew a bit, one started chasing the other all around the tiny pond. I decided he must have been the male with tea on his mind, and I changed his name to Pokey. When he didn't let up I released them into the main pond, giving Perky a chance to play hard-to-get if that's what she wanted.

The second microbore went up behind the back of the screen and trickled water over the moonstone to splash down into a stone trough set into the reed bed. It was quite bizarre to see the moonstone perched twelve feet high in the timber screen, dripping water down into the pond. Occasionally people would notice the moonstone and the water dripping off it, and stare at it in disbelief for a moment, then move on to something else. What they were looking at was impossible, too ridiculous to contemplate. Perhaps I'd picked up something from Salvador Dali without realising it.

The screen was sculpted around the outcrop of boulders that formed the Source. At the right hand side I built an eyelet in the screen that was only visible from above, and in the eye I planted a Gingko tree.

The facade was complete. It wouldn't have looked out of place on any Hollywood film set. The grotesque retaining wall was gone.

The third microbore went to service the main pond replacing the natural evaporation of the day.

We received a trial order from Tomas Corominas for a department store in France – a good start to the New Year. We also had an enquiry from Rikard Mansson. Rikard was Swedish, manufacturing partly in Sweden, but mainly in China. Among his customers was IKEA. On the strength of IKEA alone, I went out to meet him in Nyköping, somewhere south of Stockholm. I'd never heard of it before, but one of the budget airlines had.

Nyköping airport was a reclaimed air force base, and tiny. As we bumped to land I could see it certainly wasn't Heathrow. We were bundled off the plane and into Arrivals. The usual groups of excited friends and family, one by one disappearing, until I was left on my own, apart from a boy. This 'boy' as I had thought, was Rikard. His young appearance didn't give a clue to what was going on inside.

We discussed Curl Up n' Stand for a couple of hours in Rikard's office. He knew exactly what he was talking about. I was impressed. He had some business to attend to, so I was to have dinner on my own and meet up with him later in the evening.

The hotel was pleasant enough – the town was pleasant enough. But there was nobody there, not a soul. I walked out into the main street; not a sign of anybody. Not even a cat scavenging a yoghurt pot or a dog peeing on a lamp post. I stood in the main street wondering whether to walk left or right, or cross over. In the distance a car approached. I thought I'd wait for it to pass for something to do. It turned off before it got to me. I was on my own again. I found a bar that had a restaurant. I was amazed to find there were people in it. How did they get there? I took a table in the restaurant and tried to fathom the menu. It might as well have been written in Swahili. We were sufficiently far away from Stockholm for the automatic need for an English translation to be felt unnecessary. I was glad to have some work to do. I scanned the menu. It was bizarre – I couldn't understand a word, but then I saw 'bifstek'. Ah, bifstek, I thought, I like bifstek. Funny way to spell beefsteak, but they're funny people. The waiter came over and I pointed to my chosen dish: 'Bifstek, please.' 'Ah, good,' the waiter said, singsong, 'You have chosen the fish.' He was right: some sort of fish arrived covered in shrimpy things, but it was good. (Back home I met my Swedish friend, Runa, and described the meal. When I said they looked like a kind of torpedo-shaped Kinder egg she recognised the description immediately, 'Yes, I know what they are, they're a kind of skrimp'. So, if you're ever in Nyköping, I can recommend the Bifstek and Skrimp.)

I met up with Rikard a little later. He knew where to go. Boy, did he know where to go. I'd been in the wrong part of town. We met up with some girls, then some boys and girls, and then more girls, and proceeded to get bombed out of our minds. At some point in the early hours my head had reached its artistic conclusion, but where the hell was my hotel? A girl offered to take me back to the hotel. A great night: bifstek, a good drink with Rikard – and I've got lucky. I was wrong about the last bit. She showed me where the hotel was and then took herself off home. Ah well.

Rikard was due to pick me up at 8.30 in the morning. Breakfast was an experience. I hadn't a clue what all the various dishes were. It was a go and help yourself thing. I'm only in Sweden, we're all Europeans, so what's all this stuff? I casually tried to see what other people were doing, but only made myself more conspicuous. I had to have something, so I know I've had breakfast in Sweden. I don't know what it was – I can't describe it, but it was OK.

Eight-thirty came and went. Nine o'clock came and went. I phoned Rikard's office. They had no idea where he was. Ten o'clock, no idea. Ten-thirty, no sign. My plane was leaving at one o'clock and I'd have to be at the airport before then, I knew that much. Reflecting on the night before, I started to think, *I've killed him. He'll be found washed up on some distant shore. What've I done? I mean we haven't finished the business. What about IKEA?* He arrived in some sort of dishevelled state, with just enough time to get me to the airport. On the way I glanced at him from time to time, wondering if I should say, 'A good night?' or, 'Have we covered all we need for the moment?' or, 'You look rough – how are you feeling?' Nothing seemed appropriate.

He'd told me the night before how he first got into China. On his own he'd travelled thousands of miles through forbidding territory to open up a factory in the north of China so as to maximise the economy of the labour rates but also to send the finished product overland to northern Europe by the shortest possible route. During his journey across China, the train was stopped several times by the army. Each time, he was fined for some makeshift reason and the dollars he was carrying were taken off him. On one occasion, he was taken away by the army and locked in a room for twenty-four hours with no explanation, no toilet, nothing. He arrived at his destination penniless – and opened his factory anyway.

One night of drunken debauchery wasn't going to dampen his enthusiasm, especially now he knew about the slip-on bracket. We sent him a trial order of ten thousand pieces. Our manufacturing in Taiwan was good, but China would be better, and he was the guy to do it. He knew engineers – people he'd worked with before. Rikard and I decided to go to China together and visit them. I arranged to meet him in Beijing, or was it Peking then?

I was there about a day before him. What a magnificent city. The happy enthusiastic smiles of the people enjoying the sunshine were intoxicating. Nearby, I watched workers build scaffold out of thirty foot lengths of bamboo. They climbed up the bamboo, lashing the cross-pieces together with rope as they went. On another building, they were taking the bamboo down even faster, the long lengths clacking to the floor. It was all mesmerising.

There was a wide pedestrian walkway, everybody strolling up and down. So I did too. I was joined by a young Chinese man who wanted to be my tour guide. He told me about his young wife and how beautiful her tits were. His guided tour seemed to revolve around his wife's tits. I've no idea why, but thank God that's as far as it got. After quite a long walk going nowhere in particular, he said, 'I go down there now'. I had no idea where we were. I asked him how to get back. He pointed back the way we came, reeled off several landmarks which meant nothing, and disappeared. So I turned round and strolled all the way back to the familiar bamboo scaffolding.

Rikard and I had to get a small plane to take us to our final destination. I hadn't been in a plane with propellers before. The plane started bumbling down the runway before half the passengers were sitting down. The propellers whizzed into their invisible motion, and we took off. Young men propped their feet up on the seat in front, laughing. Not loutish or drunk, just getting themselves comfy. All the time I kept half an eye out of the window, in case the whizz of the propeller became visible again. The cabin crew, if that's what they were, came around with the ubiquitous snack – a biscuit. I took one bite, and my whole body dehydrated. Every tiny drop of liquid disappeared into the biscuit, and my mouth turned to dust. Everybody else seemed to enjoy it. I'd lost the ability to speak.

At the engineering factory we were greeted by three managers, who showed us round. Charles Dickens would have loved it. Thirty or forty people – children, girls, boys, men, beavering away in hazardous conditions. That wasn't for me to say, that was just how it was done. Rik could speak a tiny bit of Chinese, but we had an interpreter from the university for the day. As we walked around I noticed one or two of the workers were following. The more we walked round, the more people joined, the train of curious onlookers getting longer and longer.

After our guided tour, it was time for lunch. They'd hired the banqueting hall in the only hotel in the town. By now there were six of them, the interpreter, Rik and me. Big round dining table, plenty of room for all.

A very heated exchange started between Rik and the others. Shouting flew back and forth as Rik told them in no uncertain manner what the terms and prices should be from one stage to the next, until Rik arrived at the price he'd been after, and everybody was happy. Then the food arrived.

Now, I was brought up in Liverpool. I know what Chinese food is. What came out wasn't proper Chinese food – this was totally alien. And the wine came. Plate after plate of the strangest looking stuff arrived – I was just glad to see none of it appeared to be moving. But their enthusiasm for the food and the wine was infectious and I joined in the affray. The form was to pile as much stuff in your mouth as you could – no matter what it was – and you spat out the bits you didn't want to swallow. I wouldn't say I had the best table manners in the world, but I couldn't spit it out the way they did, in case I brought up something unmentionable. Every now and then one of them would stand up, walk to the corner of the room where the bucket was, wrench something up from the bowels of his stomach and spit it into the bucket. And the wine flowed – bottle after bottle. Now this *was* my territory. Pretty soon they realised I could match them drink for drink, and they started to laugh. It seemed the slightest thing I did sent them into fits of giggles. I don't need much encouragement when I've got an audience like this, so the giggles turned into riotous guffaws, broken periodically by one of them standing up with his glass raised, addressing me: 'Holmez, Holmez – Campai!' which meant I had to drink the full glass of wine down in one. And they weren't delicate wine glasses – these were tumblers. I don't think it was particularly strong wine, but it was our fourteenth bottle.

I think I became something of a hero with them because as far as the food went I tried everything. Rikard couldn't face the crabs: you cracked the shells in your mouth, sucked out the innards, and spat out the rest. He got his own back, though. After the meal Rikard took out his chewing tobacco. They were fascinated as he put a plug of tobacco in his mouth. He handed the tin over to one of the Chinese guys, who took a bite. His face contorted in utter horror, and he screamed at the revolting taste, ran over to the spittoon and despatched it. I stole a gag from Morecambe and Wise, pretending to drink out of a bottle raising my opposite arm in line with the tilting bottle by way of hiding it. Two or three more Campai's – I can't quite remember – and it was time for us to head back to the airport.

They'd borrowed an executive car from the army, just for us. The gleaming car with its special number plates drove fear into any other road users, and our driver took full advantage. We set off to the airport in this Chariot of Fire, followed by our hosts in their little insignificant saloon. Our driver hurled the car through the streets scattering pedestrians, bicycles and other cars aside in his wake. Soon our friends in the saloon car were way behind, and out of sight. The driver shook his fist at anybody not heeding his warnings. I found myself mentally doing the same – I'd become Boadicea also.

We got to the airport and I looked back down the road. Where were my friends? I hadn't said a proper farewell, and now it was too late. We made our way through the Departure Lounge. I'd just handed my ticket in at the point of no return, when I heard: 'Holmez! Holmez!!' I turned round to see three red-faced panting Chinamen come running through the doors. They'd made it.

Rik got samples off to IKEA, who said they liked it and that it would have to be available for all their manufacturing bases in China. At first I thought they were asking for exclusivity, but it wasn't that – they just had a number of factories in China making frames for them and wanted to make sure Curl Up n' Stand was available to them all. Being IKEA, they tested the brackets to destruction, and found if the bracket was bent backwards and forwards five times it would break; if we could strengthen it to achieve seven times it would pass their QC, then they would use it. It wasn't meant to be bent backwards and forwards at all, but they were right. But how to solve it? I didn't know. Not then, anyway. But every problem has a solution. That is a law.

It was difficult to keep in touch with Rik now he was travelling a lot in China. It was a big project, setting up a factory. He brought some of his key workers over to Sweden to train them fully, and he said how fast they were at learning, and how fast they were generally, leaving his Swedish workers behind. He took his trained staff back to China. I couldn't contact him in that part of China – our phones just didn't reach him.

Bit by bit I lost touch with Rik. He stopped replying to emails and phone calls. I was worried about him but, more important, without him I couldn't follow up on the engineers in China, nor IKEA for that matter.

CHAPTER 12

Once, sometimes twice, a year the range of photo frames with Spielmann's was reviewed. At any given time we'd be supplying about twelve or more different designs, which with different colours and sizes amounted to around two hundred and seventy different items. Any slow lines needed to be deleted and replaced with something more electric, more appropriate to the mood of the market place. This had been the form for a number of years. The meeting had always been chaired by David Edwards, but now it was Trish. Frankly, there wasn't the same symmetry of understanding.

She was nervous, a bit edgy. 'You'll remember,' she said, 'I wondered if Curl Up n' Stand was going to scratch the table. Well, somebody else has wondered about that as well. So I'm going to have to ask you to go back to using a strut, I'm afraid.'

'It doesn't scratch the table, Trish.'

'Well I did wonder about it, and now somebody else has mentioned it, so I'm afraid we're going to have to go back to using a strut.'

I was livid, but had to contain it. 'We can't,' I said.

She looked surprised and said, 'I'm sorry, Ken, but I'm afraid you'll have to.'

'In that case then, Trish, you'll have to start a phased withdrawal of all our lines.'

At that moment, I'd pulled the plug on Genesis. She fell silent. I think I did as well. She'd been against Curl Up n' Stand from the beginning. She should have seen it as an asset to her company and promoted it, but she didn't.

If I'd taken Curl Up n' Stand off our frames at that point, I would have been sending the wrong message to the rest of the world. The

Lade-Back Company was promoting Curl Up n' Stand as the modern solution for photo frames. How could I allow its sister company to contradict? I was prepared to see eight people lose their jobs, plus D and me. Genesis could not survive without the Max Spielmann account, but Curl Up n' Stand meant everything to me, it was what my whole life had been about. Trish didn't know what to say. She was stunned.

We were not the only frame supplier to Max Spielmann's, but we were the principal one by a long way. There were many other suppliers snapping at my heels, in an extremely competitive industry, low-tech, not capital-intensive, very little automation. In fact, the reason why I'd invented Curl Up n' Stand in the first place was to give Genesis the edge.

The meeting concluded shortly after that. D was shocked at what I'd just said. But I wasn't going back on it; I was adamant.

I waited for a letter in the post about the structured withdrawal. It didn't arrive. Nothing changed. Trish never mentioned the scratching the table thing again. We carried on supplying Spielmann's just as before, as if nothing had happened.

There was no bitterness with Trish, she wasn't that type of person. She was just being asked to do a job to which she was not suited. But how could I tell David?

Something similar had happened a number of years before. Spielmann's warehouse manager, Andrew, had been with them a very long time. The way he treated his own warehouse staff was appalling. He was a bully. When it came to Christmas time, David would never accept a Christmas gift of any sort. He'd just say, 'Oh, take a bottle or two round to the warehouse lads.' I always took a crate, a couple of bottles of spirits, wines, various bits and pieces, and I gave it to Andrew to distribute to the lads. In January, one of the warehouse lads said to me, 'You know all that booze you brought? He took it home – we never saw any of it.' So the next year I made a big show. I told the warehouse lad, 'I'm coming over with your box of Christmas, if you're hanging round at about three o'clock.' At three o'clock I saw that all the lads got their share.

On one occasion I came into the office to find D upset. 'What's happened?' She said, 'Andrew's just been on the phone and he's threatening to tell David because we're a a bit late with the order. I was furious. He'd upset her. I phoned Andrew immediately. I said, 'Don't you ever speak to my office like that again, and don't threaten me with David. If anybody's going to speak to David, I will. I want you to phone back immediately and apologise to D.' He did.

Some weeks or months later, Phil (number two at the warehouse) phoned me.

'Andrew's gone.'

'Why?'

'I don't know. It all happened quickly. He was just kicked out. Don't tell anyone I've told you, you're not supposed to know.'

Two days later, David told me. There'd been some suspicion over Andrew and a trap was arranged to catch him out. The irony was it was Trish who set the trap.

Craft started running a series of full page ads promoting the use of window- or door-backs for photo frames. This was the system I'd discussed with Curtis Swope, a while ago now. Basically it's a form of picture back that fits over the entire reverse side of the frame, with a window in the centre, cut out on three sides, allowing the customer to lift it up and insert their photograph.

The significance of this was that Curl Up n' Stand was unsuitable, whereas the traditional hinged strut system as promoted by Craft was quite acceptable. That may well have been why Craft had decided to promote the window back. In hindsight, it was fascinating to be involved with such a battle of wits, but at the time I was just doing what had to be done.

I decided to dig out the sketch I'd sent over to Curtis Swope as my variation on a solution. Again, with a lot of Dave Broadhurst's help, we produced the first products of what we decided to call the Scroll System. [14] Slim, elegant – quite expensive to produce, but then so was the window-back. The tricks and tools that Dave came up with to produce the Scroll leg were so clever; some people have such talent, though you'd never know. Everybody should be forced to invent something at some stage in their lives; the anxiety of the process makes the achievement so much more rewarding. Once we were satisfied that we'd developed a new and potentially commercial product, we had it produced in Taiwan.

Taiwan were good manufacturers, and Rick Flagg was doing a great job but there was no real commitment. I thought Rick might have done some promotion, some marketing in Asia – but he didn't appear to be interested. As good as the products were, they still needed to be driven.

AMS was another engineering company in the picture frame industry based in the States. Not in the same league as Craft, but Craft had declined to make the slip-on bracket, so they certainly weren't going to make the Scroll System.

I met Joe Eichert of AMS at a trade show. I didn't like him – there was something about him that made my skin creep. Though I'd liked Armand Roy, and that got me nowhere.

Armand got wind of my talking to AMS, and told me, 'Joe Eichert won't be able to make that bracket, you know.'

'That won't matter,' I said, 'I'm already getting it manufactured.'

'Would you like us to do some marketing in the States for you?'

I couldn't believe what he'd just said. 'I'll need time to think about that.' There was nothing I would have liked better, but where did that come from? Did he want to be a partner after all?

Perhaps I was having a much bigger impact on the industry than I realised. Had Armand Roy come round to the inevitable? But how could I be sure it was going to be marketed the way I wanted it to be, and not to just some niche market – and I've lost control?

Joe Eichert was marketing various metal picture frame fittings, though he didn't do anything with strut- or easel-hinges, so no vested interest. He showed a lot of interest in Curl Up n' Stand. Was he the link I needed in America? I cast aside my concerns about the man (I mean how much can you know about a person after a fifteen minute conversation) and went over to see him in New Jersey.

I arrived at La Guardia airport, New York. No limousine to meet me this time, and no budget for a car and driver. I wandered around outside the airport, nervous, apprehensive. How do I get to Pennsylvania Station? There was a bus parked up, ticking over. I asked the driver, 'Does this go to Penn Station?' He grunted something, which I supposed meant yes, and nodded his head backwards without looking at me. 'Did you get your money back from charm school?' I said, and walked down the bus to find a seat. I felt something hit the back of my foot as

I sat down. My wallet was on the floor. Had somebody tried to lift my wallet, and had I moved before it was gone?

I got to the hustle and bustle of Pennsylvania Station, a place I'd heard of in a dozen movies. Hundreds and hundreds of people dashing around. Everybody seemed to know where they were going except me.

By the miracle of modern transportation I found myself in New Jersey and phoned Joe's office as arranged.

I waited an age outside the station in New Jersey, feeling very much the poor relation, before Joe picked me up. AMS wasn't a facility of excellence. Compared to Craft it was a shambles. But they were servicing the marketplace – mostly with crap, but lots of it.

I needed to keep in close touch with D back home to make sure everything was OK. I'd left her with a pretty heavy production schedule – making frames was easy, even with the deadlines, but the supply of picture frame moulding was erratic and haphazard, and a constant battle. If we didn't get the moulding in time the frames didn't go out. We were stuck with one major supplier, which wasn't a good place to be, but right now there was no alternative. Today I couldn't call her – my mobile phone battery had run down and I'd come away without my American adaptor. The guys at AMS tried to adapt their chargers to fit my phone, but without success, so I went out to a nearby hypermarket. It was massive – of course it was, I was in America. I wandered round until I found what I thought was the appropriate aisle, but couldn't see one. I asked one of the staff, 'Have you got a UK adaptor so I can charge my phone?' He looked at me bewildered, puzzled, then walked away. I think he thought UK was a pop group.

The talk with Joe seemed to go OK. At one point he took me round to his house. I don't remember going in, but he seemed to have animals, a rabbit or something, in the garden, or should I say yard. Perhaps he wasn't that bad after all. He had another facility in Germany, and he wanted to run the ideas by them.

So he came to visit us in North Wales with his European sidekick, Dirk. I wondered should I show them the new developments. I wasn't sure they were 100% covered by the patent, but decided to take a chance. The pair of them looked shifty and gave each other a sidelong glance, which made me more suspicious.

They placed a trial order, a few thousand of the various bits so they could do the necessary tests back in New Jersey. Fair enough.

For an engineer to stamp out metal brackets he needs a tool. Simply, a tool is in two halves, a male and a female. One thumps against the other, and the piece of metal between them is stamped out to the required shape. I had an engineering tool that was actually designed for the fixed bracket, but was never used. It had been built by an engineering company who said they wanted £4,000 for it if I could sell it. I told Joe about this, and agreed to send the tool over to New Jersey with his trial order on the understanding that if it worked with their presses they would pay our engineer. Their order was packed in six boxes, the two halves of the tool being in separate boxes because of the weight. We sent it out to AMS on their UPS account, as per Joe's instructions.

A few days later I received a fax from AMS, 'We've only received five cartons, not six.' The missing carton was one containing half of the tool – the clever half.

We put a search with UPS to trace the missing carton. UPS produced a signature for six cartons. I told AMS, 'UPS have got a signature for six cartons. You must have received a carton destined for somebody else. I'll get UPS to come and collect the wrong carton and search for the correct one.' But AMS then said they'd thrown it away, the sixth carton had just been full of packing waste and they'd thrown it in the skip.

I started to smell a rat. A big one. First of all they said they'd only received five cartons, and when we proved they'd received six they decided the sixth carton had been full of packaging waste. If you do get a wrong delivery, you always keep it because obviously it belongs to somebody else. You don't throw it away. They had received six cartons, which included both halves of the tool. *The lying bastards.*

I tried to speak to Eichert, he wouldn't come to the phone, he was always missing. Then we got a bill from UPS for delivering the six cartons to New Jersey. Joe Eichert, having asked us to send it on their account and given us his account number, had then refused to pay. Then the battle really started. AMS tried to threaten me with some kind of legal ramifications. I was furious and let them know it in no uncertain manner. They paid UPS for the delivery and the stock we sent them, proving that had been the arrangement in the first place, but they weren't going to pay our engineer the £4,000. It was impossible for me to prove they'd received half the tool, so I insisted they return the half of the tool they'd admitted receiving. At least that way the stolen half became worthless.

Where the hell is all this leading?

The suspicions I'd had about Eichert from the very beginning had turned out to be all too real. He had this slight half-smile, half-smirk, exactly the same as Bromilow. George W Bush had the same look – and he went on to be President of the USA for eight years. But then Nixon was President as well... after he'd been caught out, people thought he looked like an iffy second-hand car dealer, not to be trusted. Couldn't they see he'd looked like that all the time? The face reveals a multitude of sins. I was glad I realised when I did what Eichert was like – I just felt sorry for the rabbit.

Were things starting to take a more sinister turn? The ecstatic enthusiasm of the earlier trade shows was still there to some degree, but one by one the big boys were losing interest. No – they just disappeared. I became aware of clandestine meetings between Ron Morin and various other 'godfathers' of the industry. I couldn't hear the conversations, but I could sense it: 'Are you sure we really want this Ken Holmes thing?' It was as though overnight they'd realised that, with Curl Up n' Stand, frames weren't going to fall over any more, and that wouldn't be good. If there were eighty million frames sold in the UK every year, how many of those were replacing perfectly good frames that just didn't stand up any more because the strut had collapsed, or bent or broken? Now we had the slip-on bracket, it meant that the frames that had been broken could easily be repaired and stand up again.

I sensed I was becoming Public Enemy Number One. Was I witnessing some kind of conspiracy as if the whole scenario was being played out in an old fifties black and white movie? It wasn't a conspiracy of course, they're not that clever – but there was a definite closing of ranks.

I'd wander round my garden of an evening, water running, a perfect antidote – totally absorbing, like a symphony. Every time was different.

We started to introduce fish to the pond. Not big fish – we could have chosen big fish, but they were expensive – just small fish so that we could all grow together. Small koi carp, orfes, little goldfish, ghost koi. I was very careful to put them gently into a shallow bit, talking to them in a peaceful, fish kind of way. Then they'd vanish for a couple of days. I thought they'd gone, but they were only in hiding while they grew accustomed to their new world. They settled in and began chasing each other round the pond. I gave them names, Jack the Lad, Darth Vader, Goldilocks, and of course Pinky and Pokey. We had eight or nine orfes, about two and a half inches long, and my knowledge of fish hadn't grown to tell them apart yet, so the names didn't get that far.

In the game of 'Chase' it was always certain ones chasing certain others. I'm sure it was the males chasing the females. But the females didn't like it. I found two dead in the stream. They couldn't have swum over the waterfall, the water wasn't deep enough at that point. They must have flapped their way across the waterfall stone and fallen down into the splash pool, then onwards into the stream. When the pump wasn't running, there wouldn't be sufficient water in the stream for them to survive. Did they go to all that enormous effort just to get away from unwanted advances? I might be wrong, but that's the way it appeared. I didn't know when you bought fish you had to decide was it a little girl fish or a little boy fish… and was that little boy fish sex mad?

Apart from that, the garden was looking more and more beautiful. Traditionally, the ground cover in a Japanese garden would be moss, consistent with the quiet, shady atmosphere of the original gardens in Japan. I tried and tried, and discovered so many different kinds of moss, but I could never cultivate any vigorously enough for the purpose. A ground cover plant called Arenaria thrived, though, and I found that I could divide a ten inch diameter plant into seven or eight smaller plants, and so the Arenaria slowly began to spread forming a soft carpet of gentle mossy mounds of pale, almost lime, green. It would take years, but the effect was better than I could ever have hoped for. They would in time form the lime green carpet underneath the acers. We'd bought fifteen acer cultivars from Westonbirt Arboretum, each one carefully chosen for its size, habit and Autumn colour. We wouldn't live to see them reach full maturity, but every year they would become more majestic.

I'd kept in touch with Dave Thorpe since he'd introduced me to Taiwan. He'd been in the industry for as long as I had, albeit from a different point of view. Dave knew a lot of potential customers in Northern Europe, Scandinavia and so on, and he started to promote Curl Up n' Stand within his region as an addition to his own products.

Ron Morin learned about this association and tried to poach Dave away. He offered Dave a job working for Craft. It was getting more and more bizarre. Craft were prepared to create a position for Dave within their company, just to stop him helping me. Dave realised the sinister motives behind this, and declined. He brought in some business, but not enough to sustain the efforts.

Despite how great Curl Up n' Stand was, the promise of overnight success was being replaced by a long and winding road, full of mines and potholes… and apparently without end.

Our moulding supplier for frames was D & J Simons. I'd known Howard Simons for over twenty-five years; we're about the same age. For a long time I refused to deal with them. At the shows Howard would say, 'When are you going to start buying off us again?' and I'd say, 'When your quality and service improve.' Then they discovered a synthetic material, from which they made picture frame moulding, and called it Emafyl. It was a great product, and the designs and prices were exactly what Max Spielmann was looking for. At the Spring Fair each year David Edwards and I would visit the Simons' stand and discuss the ranges for the coming year, but then from that point there was a constant battle with supply. But Simons never pushed hard for payment, so one kind of compensated the other.

At one of the shows I asked D to go over to the D & J Simons stand to clarify a particular moulding while I looked after our stand. D never liked visiting the Simons stand. She was always ignored. Any questions she put forward, the answer was directed to me. But they were our main supplier and there were certain things we had to put up with. There simply wasn't any alternative.

Simons' was one of the biggest stands at the shows. Always busy with ten reps talking to thirty customers. This time, one of the reps told her Howard Simons wanted to speak to her. Howard, managing director, had invited her in to the inner sanctum. I'd never been in there. Now D was being lectured to by Howard, in a quiet polite manner, but basically telling her that Ken shouldn't be concentrating too much of his efforts on his inventions.

I was furious. How arrogant to send one of his minions to get D and lecture her like some self-appointed godfather. My reaction was to go over and confront him and tell him not to interfere in my business, and how dare he try to get to me through D. But what was that going to achieve if he did have ulterior motives? What was I going to accuse him of? He would say he was just giving D friendly advice, and make me look paranoid. But then if he wanted to give advice why didn't he give it to me? Was he scared because he didn't like the effect Curl Up n' Stand was going to have on the market?

He's never shown any interest in my business. He doesn't know anything about me, he's never been up to visit my factory – he hasn't the foggiest idea how I run my business. He's hardly spoken to me for years. I remember saying to him a few years before, 'Why don't you sell up and make yourself a millionaire?' 'I am already,' he said. It was obviously not enough. He wasn't interested in my welfare – his lecture to D wasn't for my benefit, it was for his.

It was shortly after that when our moulding supply became even more erratic. For the first time ever we started to have some difficulty in getting orders completed and out on time. This had never happened in all the years I'd been producing frames.

At any given time, we could owe Simons two or three months' payment, and always had. And now they wanted it back, and it could amount to fifty or sixty thousand pounds.

Somehow I found the money, not all of it by any means, and I agreed with Simons to send payment, provided our supply was not disrupted. The understanding was that I'd always send them more money than the value of the order I was chasing. I'd send the money and we'd get some moulding, but not the amount I'd been chasing. It was a constant battle.

For years now I'd been practising self-hypnosis, as I call it. Really, it was just a form of meditation, deep relaxation. It helped with problem-solving with the inventions, for instance. It also helped me to keep focused, to understand where we were going and if it was going wrong what to do about it. I'd lost touch with my hypnotherapist some time ago, but felt in need of a top-up. I met Alexandra Sewell.

Alex discovered the power of hypnotherapy when she was studying for her Masters. She became so impressed with the benefits and power of hypnotherapy that she became a therapist.

She took me down some winding steps to the lake. At the far end of the lake the path led to a country lane. Along the lane, until a track appeared on the right. Up the track between the trees. 'Through the trees you can see the flickering embers of a camp fire. That's where the wise man lives. That's where you're going.' I arrived at the camp fire. She told me to put some wood on the fire and, as it flared into life, it lit up the cave where the wise man lived. The wise man came out to greet me. 'Ask the wise man anything you like and he will answer you… Now become the wise man and talk to your visitor.' I changed places; it seemed perfectly natural. 'Look in the cave,' she said, 'and you can see what the wise man does.' Inside the cave there were shelves full of books, and in the corner there were some walking canes that he whittled in his spare time. 'Now it's time to go, but the wise man has a gift for you.' I took the gift. As I left to walk back down the track, she said, 'Wait a moment.' I thought she was going to tell me to turn and say farewell to the wise man, but she didn't. She said, 'Look at your gift. Now become it.' I went down the track, back along the lake, up the steps. The gift that the wise man had given me was a pouch. I knew that every time I opened that pouch I could speak to the wise man. She didn't mention the pouch, she didn't know what the gift was. She just told me to become it.

I got to see Alex quite a lot over the next few months, and practised the walk along the lake to the wise man in my own time. I always followed the same formula, but every time was different.

I wondered what the books were in the cave – I didn't know whether they were his teachings or his learnings – until one time curiosity got the better of me and I went into the cave. The wise man was sitting at his bench with his back to me. He was leaning forward, writing. Long robe, long thin white hair, like a mediaeval mystic. I looked in the books: all the pages were blank. I didn't understand. The next evening it had been the village fete, a special time in Llantysilio. D and I were sitting chatting with friends, drinking beer. I suddenly realised what the blank books had meant: I was to write them.

I reflected constantly on the many times I'd nearly struck the pot of gold and failed. If only one of them had happened, all the pain would go away and then I could learn how to write.

When Cynthia Zeller left Burnes she went to work for another frame company, Fetco. I decided to give her a call and keep in touch. She was really pleased to hear from me. I found out that all Fetco's frames were made in Asia. I was planning another trade mission to Singapore and Australia later in the year. She said, 'Let me know when you're going. We've got an office in Hong Kong – I'll introduce you to Jones, the manager.'

The last time I went to Hong Kong it was at Cynthia's suggestion to go and see CKK, and she knew what a waste of time that had been. But now she's actually got her own office there – that's not going to be a waste of time is it?

There was no definite reason to go on the trade mission this time. Perhaps I was just following every avenue I could, and perhaps the options were running out.

Our favourite pub in Llangollen was the Corn Mill. One Saturday night we went for dinner there with Diane and Ray. I'd known Ray for a few years. Good lad, down to earth. He was a builder, and helped me a lot with the design of the cottage when I first did it up. Towards the end of the meal I said to Ray, 'What are you up to at the weekend?' He said he was going to Preston to see Darren. Ray had two sons from a previous marriage: Wayne, whom I knew quite well, worked for Ray on the building; and Darren, who from what I gathered was a drug addict, a waster – and now in Preston nick.

As Ray was talking about Darren and how he'd tried to help him, and how difficult the situation was, I went into a trance, completely out of it for a few seconds, and came to crying, saying, 'I've just felt Darren's pain,' then immediately went into a trance again, and when I came to the second time I said, 'I can help him.' This was in the middle of our meal in a busy pub where I'm well known. I don't know what it was. It had never happened before. But it was powerful enough to make me cry.

When it subsided we carried on with our meal, as if nothing had happened, I suppose – but it had.

I had no idea what it meant. I do know I had no control over it.

I didn't see Ray for some time after that. We didn't see each other that often, anyway. I didn't know what to say to him. But every day I thought about it. I couldn't talk to D about it. Whenever I tried to mention it, she'd just close up. I couldn't talk to anybody. What had happened that night in the Corn Mill I may never know... but it happened.

Right now, I didn't need some out of body thing. There were more earthly matters to sort. My framing company was struggling with its supply. Every day was becoming more and more of a nightmare.

Stephen Simons was Simons' financial director. He'd phone me up and shout: 'Send me some fucking money!' That's the way he was. They were East End lads, or that's where their business was. Didn't bother me – I'm Liverpool. Similar postcode really. I'd send the money on the understanding that the moulding supplies kept flowing. We needed the right quantities, the right designs, at the right times. That was essential. Anything less than that meant we were struggling to function. Despite all the promises, we were just getting a very sporadic supply, nothing like what we ordered.

I phoned Stephen.

'You remember last time we spoke I said I'd send you the money on the understanding that we got the moulding in?'

'Yes.'

'Well it never came in.'

There was a short silence. I could tell he was sympathetic, but not enough to do anything about it.

Then we'd get a bit of moulding delivered, and things staggered on. We were letting Spielmann down, and other customers as well. One by one, Trish was switching our lines over to another frame maker. Our turnover was dropping every month.

We don't need this crap. Who does? If only we can get a decent commitment for Curl Up n' Stand... because I can't help thinking that's the reason why all this shit's flying around.

During our trips round Europe we discovered picture frame hardware manufactured by a company called Mark in Austria. I sent samples of Curl Up n' Stand over to Mark. They seemed very interested, and invited me over to Austria to visit their factory.

I flew to Vienna, then three train journeys to get to Spital am Pyrhn. Christian Muehringer of Mark phoned me every step of the way, looking after me. He seemed to know me well, and we hadn't met. It was late in the evening when I arrived at Spital. Just one person waiting on the platform: Christian.

'Did everything go OK?' he said.

'Until just now. I've left my briefcase on the train.'

He didn't say anything. He just walked calmly over to the station master, had a short conversation, came back and said, 'The station master is having it collected at the next station. We'll have it in the morning.'

I stayed in a Swiss Chalet type of ski-lodge in the foothills of the mountains. Spital is very big on skiing.

It was a big hotel. Not big like American big – square, and miles high. It was only two or three storeys tall.

After a good night's sleep I came out of my room and everything was new again. How did I get here? The first decision of the day: left or right? I started to wander through a labyrinth of corridors and stairs. I found myself in the company of glowing pink bodies, casually wrapped in white towels. My bewilderment must have been tangible. An enormous Frau said something. She was big, blonde crew cut, and scary. She realised I wasn't capable of saying anything sensible, and swept past.

I'd wandered into a part of the hotel that hadn't existed the day before – swimming pool, gymnasium, solarium. I continued on, hoping that sooner or later something would make sense.

After a process of trial and mostly error, I found myself in a dining room decked out to feed the five thousand. I felt as though I was the only English-speaking person who had ever been to the hotel. I was shown to a table. The restaurant was about half full. Two thousand five hundred sitting over there… and I'm sitting here. On my own. They've all got green napkins… and I've got a red one. Just to let everybody know I was the stupid Englishman who got lost in the solarium. It was a buffet service, so I nonchalantly waited until the masses had thinned out, then casually made my way over, only to to be overtaken by a stampede of new arrivals. Every single one of them knew exactly what they wanted, and were all quite sure they were more important than me. But in true British fashion I stood my ground, put orange juice in my tea cup, dropped my bun on the floor and spilt the orange juice while I tried to pick it up. And so I had my breakfast.

At nine o'clock Christian arrived, carrying my briefcase. On the way to the factory we drove through Spital, Christian explaining that the Mark factory used to be in the town. 'That was one building there,' he said, 'and there's another.' And so on. From time to time I got glimpses of this futuristic-looking construction appearing on the hillside as if it had been placed there from another planet. As we drove out of the town, the construction got nearer and nearer, until eventually I asked Christian, 'What's that?' He said, 'That's where we're going.'

I guess I must have been open-mouthed as we got out of the car and followed the path that led to reception: over the wide bridge across the lake, koi carp on either side. The reception area was enormous. To the left a wide staircase that wrapped itself round what I was to find out later was a very old press weighing, I guess, a few tonnes. At the flick of a switch the press moved slowly up, appearing to be counterbalanced by the weight of engineering parts descending.

One wall of the boardroom was sixty feet of glass, panoramic views of the mountains that would soon be covered in snow. Everybody was a keen skier. Rudolf Mark was part of the mountain rescue squad.

Glass cabinets in the boardroom displayed some of Mark's manufacture. It was the 7 mm round washers that impressed me most. Anybody who can make small parts like that commercially knows how to mass produce at the right price. And some of the other stuff he was doing was extremely technical. All possible avenues covered.

The numbers would come – there was nothing more certain – and Rudolf could see that. His own experience of the industry told him the potential was vast. I came away with a feeling that it was an honour and a privilege to be associated with such a company.

Back home there were more pressing issues.

A company called Eco came on the scene, manufacturing synthetic picture frame mouldings in a lot of ways similar to the Emafyl product coming from Simons.

I spoke to David Edwards and told him, 'I think I've got an idea why I've been giving you such a crappy supply lately.'

'I must admit, Ken, it's not your usual standard.'

'I think I'm being frozen out.'

'Because of your stand?'

'Yes, I think so. Have I got your permission to switch over to Eco?'

He understood exactly what I was going through. He knew from other experiences how difficult Simons could be.

'Yes, yes,' he said. 'Run it by Trish. Take care of yourself.'

Running it by Trish was another matter.

D and I had a meeting with Adam Boot, the managing director of Eco. He understood completely. He was very sympathetic. 'Sure, we'll supply you. You've been treated appallingly.' Eco couldn't exactly produce like for like, not unless there was a lot of investment, and that wasn't on. But we had an alternative supplier of some sort.

Every day I was thinking of Darren and what had happened that night in the Corn Mill. Couldn't talk about it to D – she wouldn't let me. Couldn't talk to anybody. It was nearly twelve months ago now. I knew I could help him. Why I knew that, and how I could help him, I had no idea, but I decided to try. Ray hadn't seen Darren for a few months but I found him through Ray's other son, Wayne. He was staying at his mother's house.

Darren wasn't the vagabond or scallywag I'd expected. A nice man, in his late twenties, working as a plumber, earning just enough money to keep the devil on his back under some sort of control. But I could see the pain in his eyes. I went round to see him most evenings after a day's firefighting with the suppliers. We'd go for a walk in a nearby park for an hour or two, and just talk. He'd started messing about with drugs at the age of fifteen, like thousands of other kids, trying out new things, experimenting like kids do, and drugs were available.

After a couple of weeks I asked him would he consider hypnotherapy. He said he would, he'd like to know where his confidence had gone. 'I used to be a confident man,' he'd say. But hypnotherapy was down the line a bit. As the days and weeks passed he was starting to look better, more alive. The pain was going from his eyes.

I told him, 'You're looking better.' He seemed to be smiling for the first time ever.

'I know, Ken. I'm feeding off you.'

'Good. Keep doing it.' The better he was looking, the more I wanted to help, the more I knew I could help – and all I was doing was talking with a bit of understanding and a determination to make things better.

The trade mission to Singapore and Australia was coming up, which would take me away for a couple of weeks. If I stopped seeing Darren for two weeks he'd go right back. I went to see Alexandra Sewell to see if she could help. She felt confident she could. She was already helping in similar situations, and knew more than I how powerful hypnotherapy could be.

Supplies had started to come in from Eco. Adam Boot had asked for pro forma cash up front for the first two or three orders, which was a bit of a strain on the cash flow, and the materials were costing us a bit more, but at least we were getting them. The quality was good, and it was a blessed relief we were getting some supplies in at last.

It seemed as though our life was getting back into some sort of order.

I was becoming attached to the fish. I'd never realised fish had personalities. When I came down to the pond they'd see me and swim fast up to the other end to hide. Then one by one they'd sneak back, curious to get a glimpse of the one who walked on bridges. Jack the Lad was always one of the bravest – that's how he got his name.

Occasionally the trickle of water from the mountain wasn't enough to keep the pond topped up and I had to use a hosepipe. I threw the hosepipe in the pond and it landed in such a way that when I turned the water on it made a fountain. Once they got used to the initial shock, the fish went to investigate, then gradually one by one they'd swim into the splash and be tumbled down by the water. This became a great game. There was a rock in the shape of a turtle in the water, supported by a pillar of pebbles. The hose had got caught on it and that's why it had made the fountain. Whenever I had to top up the pond with the hose I made sure it landed on the turtle, and sat by the edge to watch. There'd be a queue of excited fish waiting to have their turn. Some bullies jumping the queue – just like a kids in the playground – or perhaps they were just the bravest.

The Japanese Garden Society came to visit a couple of times. I'd joined the Society a few years before. I would normally have shied away from that sort of thing, but membership qualified me for a discount on stone lanterns, bowls, architectural bits. I had mixed feelings about opening the garden to thirty or more people – even if they were enthusiasts. I didn't want anybody telling me how beautiful it all was, and asking me how long it had taken… But they didn't ask stupid questions. Mostly they wandered round in silence, or chatting quietly with each other. I overhead one person say to his friend something like, 'I just feel totally inspired. I want to get back to my garden now'. The secretary of the Society, Brian Jacques, asked me if I'd like to go on the national garden database. 'Do you think the garden qualifies?' I asked him. 'Qualifies?' he repeated, raising his eyebrows. But I decided not to. The garden was my spiritual sanctuary, and I wanted it to stay that way. Occasionally a group of ramblers would appear and line up shoulder to shoulder along the fence, and peer at the different parts of the garden for what seemed like an age. One hand would point towards that, another to something else. I suppose it must have been a curiosity, appearing on the side of a mountain in the middle of their walk. I kept out of sight whenever possible.

D had been renting out her house after she moved into Fron Haul and the tenants, being tenants, never treated it with the respect it warranted. She sold it and bought a house in a village much nearer to Llangollen. This gave D a project of her own, time away from the hassle, and from me for that matter.

We decided to take a week's holiday… D would play house and I would play Japanese gardener for a week. Mike, my neighbour, had other ideas for me. He wanted me to go to Odessa with him. He'd found the love of his life on the internet. I'd been away on holiday with Mike before – we went to Fuerte Ventura with his mate, Martin, and had a riot of a time – but how could I tell D I was going to Odessa to meet all the internet birds?

While I was pondering that dilemma I went round to see Darren and he was in agony. Couldn't walk. He'd put his back out at work. No work meant no drug money. He couldn't take any pain killers because of the Warfarin he was taking as a result of all the years of drug misuse. It was crisis time, and I would be going away for a fortnight shortly on the trade mission. I'd discussed with Darren on many occasions what the programme of rehabilitation might be. He'd tried a number of times to kick the drug and failed. It was no picnic. But now circumstances had brought the situation to a head. I said, 'This is it, Darren. We do it.'

First of all he had to get permission from his doctor to see if his body could stand it. I don't remember the exact form, but he had to take a special medication for twelve days, and then he would take the blocker. The blocker meant heroin would have no effect.

There was no point in starting any of this while he was still living with his mother in Wrexham. Drugs were too easily available – on every street corner apparently. I decided to bring him up to Fron Haul while D was away. No street corners there. I tried to find out what I could about heroin rehabilitation. God, it was heavy. I was told he'd be bouncing off walls – and bouncing on me probably. I had to get shut of all the knives out of the house, dope him with anything I could: whisky, marijuana. Hide anything he could harm himself with. What the hell was I getting into? Didn't matter, it had to be done. Telling Mike I was going to take a rain check on the Russian internet beauties was one thing, but how was I going to tell D this? By coincidence she'd seen a programme on the television that described in gruesome detail exactly what happened when an addict tried to come off heroin. Initially she was furious at the idea of my bringing Darren up to our house, but she knew I had to do it. So, instead of going to Odessa, I was bringing Darren up to Fron Haul for a week.

Darren had a long-time girlfriend, Sharon, who knew him before the heroin so she could see through the crap. I'd met her a couple of times. Nice girl, recently trained as a solicitor. She's got to be a steadying influence.

Am I supposed to clear the house out of what might be danger items? But how do I do that? It's a house, for Christ's sake. I need knives for cooking. What if he hits me with a chair? This is all too ridiculous. I gave up.

I picked Darren up on a Saturday morning and we went to Sainsbury's to buy goodies. I thought Sharon was coming with us to get it started, but no – she was going off to South Wales for some reason. I bought a load of alcohol and comfort food. We tried to go for a little walk along the canal by Fron Haul, but he couldn't walk more than a few feet. The pain was worse now because the heroin was starting to wear off. So we went back to the cottage. He went upstairs. I thought he was going to the loo, but he never came down – he'd fallen asleep. Best thing, probably. The more he could sleep the better. I made some dinner: salmon fillet with a rich cream sauce, mushrooms, a bottle of whisky on the table. I thought I'd keep it warm until he came down. He eventually came down about nine o'clock and said, 'I've got to go, Ken.'

'No, Darren.'

'I just need one more dig, Ken. You know what it's like when you need one more dig… I'll be back.'

'No, Darren. You're not going.'

'I've got to, Ken.'

I stood by the door blocking the way, 'Well you've got to go through me first.' He was half my age, but he was so weak. He started to cry. I probably did as well. He hugged me, said, 'I don't know who's brought you to me, but thank God.'

I was starting to get some indication of what a ferocious grip this heroin had on the mind and body. He went back upstairs and fell asleep again. I ate alone, thoughts racing. *What the hell is the next episode going to be like?*

That was scary. He wasn't aggressive, never tried to harm me, but it frightened the life out of me. I thought I'd prepared as best I could, but I hadn't. I was totally unprepared.

There were two sheds under the balcony, 'Chaos' and 'Confusion', where all the tools were kept. I'd never bothered locking them. I'd tried to find the keys before Darren arrived, and hadn't been able to. *Now* I found them.

Somehow I got through the night. Despite the whisky I was waking at the slightest sound, real or imaginary, but Darren slept through – and most of the next day as well. He came down once for something to eat, then went back to bed.

I was starting to become concerned. I phoned D just for somebody to talk to. She sounded really happy, playing house. I couldn't tell her what I was going through.

As the evening came, I found out why he'd been sleeping so much – he told me he'd come away with twenty-four strong sleeping tablets, enough for two weeks. Now he had four left. We weren't going to make it.

I phoned D to tell her. I needed to try and get more sleeping tablets. I phoned Darren's mother, I even phoned the hospital, but they needed a prescription. If I took Darren there in his state I didn't know what they'd make of it. I realised the mission had to be aborted. I felt strong – I could have coped with a lot more – but it was never going to work. Sleeping tablets may have helped, but they were never going to be the cure. The devil inside him was so powerful. I'd had no idea of the enormous task I was taking on, and yet the formula was typical of a rehabilitation programme. He knew – he'd tried it before.

He asked if he could borrow my car to get home (and there he would get access to a dig). Where he lived was a very respectable part of Wrexham – drugs don't just operate in back streets and slums. He was in no condition to drive, and neither was I – I'd been drinking the whisky. He wanted to start walking down the track. I couldn't let him do that. The track was steep and rough – he'd have fallen, he wouldn't have made it. I phoned his girlfriend, Sharon, who was back from South Wales, and asked her to come and pick him up. She wasn't surprised. She'd known the mission would fail. I knew Darren had no money for drugs, he never asked me for any. When Sharon arrived, he told her he needed to go home to get his record collection and sell it. It was all very emotional.

'Have you given up on me now, Ken?'

'No, Darren. This is just the start.'

In the morning, I came downstairs. The dining table, the two place settings – one used. A poignant reminder.

There are times when you know instinctively something is fundamentally wrong. The regime we'd followed over the last few days, and the ten days before, had been a set procedure for the process of drug addiction rehabilitation, but what I'd experienced over the last few days had to be wrong – there had to be a better way.

It was probably a few weeks later when I was looking for some cement in the garage, there under the bag of cement was an axe I'd hidden before Darren came to stay. I shuddered to think what had been going through my mind.

I met up with the other missionaries in the executive lounge at Heathrow. After all, we were VIPs. Posh seats, comfortably isolated from the usual airport rabble, food and drink – just help yourself.

One of the guys on the mission was John. His company, extremely technical, had developed a system to detect the presence of drugs from a sample of human hair. I had no idea that kind of technology existed. I told John about my experience over the last week or two with Darren. I couldn't help thinking that he was going to be key in my understanding of what course drug rehabilitation could take. There was never going to be a quick fix, I knew that.

Was it just another bizarre coincidence that John and I were brought together? He was about the only one of the missionaries I did talk to.

My mission somehow seemed less important now. How can it be important to change how a picture frame is stood up, when we're killing our children through drug addiction?

Those two or three days I'd spent with Darren at Fron Haul had struck home very deeply. Anyone who says that drug addicts are losers, weak-willed wasters, doesn't know what the hell they're talking about. The grip of heroin goes far deeper than I could have imagined. Why? What is it that grips people so fiercely? I'd been preoccupied with changing the way a frame stands up and keeping my framing company alive. For what? To satisfy my ego? Fame? Fortune? It was difficult to make sense of it all.

The first stop was Australia. We weren't invited to meet the British High Commissioner this time. Had I mortally offended them? There were some big official affairs to which local dignatories were invited. The guest of honour was Rhodri Morgan, First Minister for Wales. I'd met Rhodri on the previous mission. But now I didn't want to talk to him about bits of bent wire. At the reception hundreds of people all wanted to be seen talking to Rhodri Morgan. I knew my five seconds would come, but I was impatient. I fought my way through the crowd of women with their bosoms and hat pins surrounding Rhodri Morgan and asked him if I could have a word when he had a moment, 'I'm over there.' Like the other missionaries I had my table with my bits and pieces and blurb saying how great they were. He came over shortly afterwards. 'How's the invention going?' he asked. 'OK, but I don't want to talk about that; I want to talk about drug addiction.' I told him about Darren and he listened and listened. I told him, 'We're not going to get anywhere throwing twopence-halfpenny do-gooders at it like you're doing.' He didn't walk away. Instead, at the end, he gave me his card with his personal contact details.

I met Jane at a similar soirée. She was the editor of New Ideas magazine – an Australian equivalent to Hello! or OK magazines, and we became good friends. She lived near Bondi Beach. I finished up spending a lot of time on Bondi Beach during this period, just walking, thinking.

It seemed strange to think you get a bus from the middle of Sydney to take you to the beach. I found the bus stop but then on the other side of the road there was another bus stop with the same numbers going the opposite way. There was nobody queuing up with buckets and spades and impatient kids. Was I on the right side of the road? But then there were no screaming kids on the other side either. I couldn't very well ask anybody. All the people passing were business types hurrying here and there to do something important with their briefcases and schedules. I couldn't bring myself to ask, 'Is this the right bus for the beach?' The bus came, and I got on and prayed. I knew sooner or later there'd be strips of leather with blond hair carrying their surfboards and Sheilas. But they didn't get on either. Every now and then the bus stopped and people got off and people got on. I began to wonder if I was the only one that knew there was a beach up here. At last we came to a little town and the name Bondi cropped up over the shop windows. I breathed a sigh of relief. Now there was only me and two other people on the bus. The bus finally came to a halt and the three of us got off. And there was the beach, practically empty. I had it to myself.

I had this idea of a screenplay, a thriller: 'Do you remember '92? So do I.' I suppose I was thinking that if I spent time writing it would take my mind off other things. But that wasn't true. Your mind does what it wants to do; you have no control over it. I had a very clever little mini-disk recorder, so there I was wandering up and down the beach dictating into my little machine. Nobody was there so it didn't matter how stupid I looked.

Danny, the main character, is a dealer, a bit of a Jack the lad, who is about to make his fortune shipping antiques to the States. He meets up with a girlfriend from the distant past. She wants out of her current relationship with a violent boyfriend. Danny comes up with an idea to scare the boyfriend off for ever. But the boyfriend is murdered in horrific circumstances. At the same time our hero's deal goes wrong and the local mafia is after him. But Danny's idea for scaring off the boyfriend seems to be taking on a life of its own.

All the villains were people I'd had the misfortune to deal with in my recent past. It was quite cathartic to see them dealt with and despatched appropriately – but then Danny too was murdered. Gripping stuff – I couldn't wait to know what was going to happen next.

But then my thoughts would go off at a tangent.

Everybody knows when you pack up smoking you put on weight, the popular reason being that you're stuffing your face with sweets. John, a sales guy who worked with me a few years before, suggested another theory: when you're smoking the nicotine creates acids that burn off the fat, acids that your body produces naturally. But as nicotine supplies the acids your body stops producing them. And then when the nicotine stops your body needs time to regenerate these acids, and that's why you put on weight. That seemed to make sense to me. So when I stopped smoking I watched my diet very carefully, especially in the beginning, and avoided the weight gain. Does something similar happen with heroin?

When I'd asked Darren would he consider hypnotherapy he said yes, because he'd lost all his self-confidence. Heroin induces confidence and self-esteem. If it were taken regularly, habitually, over a long period, would the body stop creating those bits that give us the feel-good factor? Is that what happens?

I could see the magic of Bondi Beach, as the waves built up to come crashing down, but I guessed they were only baby ones – there was nobody out there. Jane's husband was a blond-haired strip of leather.

They only lived about a mile away from the beach. She was often there, splitting her duties between running the magazine and looking after their little boy.

We talked about putting an article in her magazine, but Curl Up n' Stand was not available in the shops yet, so that would be going up a blind alley. Nevertheless, New Ideas had a big circulation. Curl Up n' Stand was always loved by the general public – it was the industry that was putting up the barriers. If we could start to create demand at the sharp end, the industry would have to come along. We discussed the possibilities of putting in a little freebie of Curl Up n' Stand, the sort of thing where you get a free shampoo or lipstick with the magazine. It would just cost us a few thousand samples, nothing really.

I didn't seem to spend a lot of time chasing the Curl Up n' Stand rainbow on this trip. I needed time on my own. I didn't spend time with the other missionaries, either, apart from John. He told me about the Stapleford Centre in London, which he knew very well, founded by Dr Collin Brewer. It was a centre specialising in drug rehabilitation. It seems one of the standard treatments for drug addiction is to reduce or stop the supply of heroin, then treat the resulting symptoms, one of which is severe depression. I was convinced there had to be a better way.

I didn't have anything in common with the other missionaries and of an evening they went their way and I went mine. One of them overheard me talking with John about drug addiction. 'What would happen if you locked him up in a room?' he asked. 'He would go mad,' I said angrily. 'Yeah, yeah – but what would happen?' he repeated in a superior manner, as much as to say treat scum like scum. I had to walk away. It wasn't that Darren would have gone mad – it would have been much worse than that, but I didn't know how to explain. I still don't. I just wanted to find some way to help.

When I got to Singapore I tried to be part of the group. I met them in the lobby of the hotel and followed them on their evening jaunt. They knew where they were going, they had it planned: they headed straight for the most English-looking bar with a big screen to watch the football. I've watched football in the past and loved it – but we're in Singapore. I left them there.

I found another part of town – busy, hustle bustle, and away from

1. Fron Haul – the cottage as it was when I first saw it.

2. Fron Haul – the cottage after renovation.

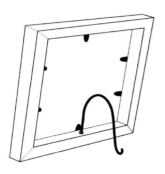

3. The original 'Saturday morning' picture frame stand. A bloody good idea.

4. The first Curl Up n' Stand square wire picture frame stand.

6. The devil-proof zig-zag bridge across the reed bed.

8. Our cat 'Stump' checking the shuttering for the concrete bridge.

7. Curl Up n' Stand square wire stand with the slip-on bracket.

9. The concrete bridge, xylophone bridge, and sunburst fences.

11. Red bridge over the bottom pond, and the tea house.

12. Mr Dude.

14. Curl Up n' Stand scroll system.

13. The timber screen with moonstone.

15. Mighty Mouce press.

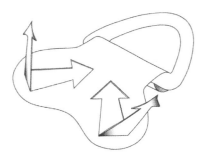

16. Dragonstail D-ring.

18. Kiasu Easel standing a frame.

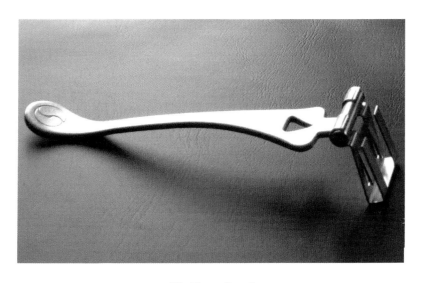

17. Kiasu Easel

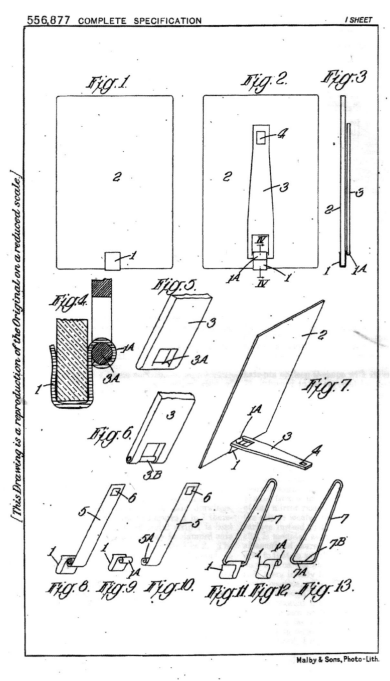

Malby & Sons, Photo-Lith.

19. 1943 patent drawing.

20. Forged signature, with actual signature underneath.

21. My castle at Foxhill.

22, 23. Don Quixote in all his glory.

the tourist trap. I wandered up and down until I found my restaurant. I seemed to be waiting quite a long time for my meal, and said so to the waitress. She said, 'Oh please don't get upset.' I didn't think I had got upset – I was just unfamiliar with the procedure. But everybody became attentive and looked after me. As a special treat they gave me some green tea ice cream – no charge. This seemed to impress the people around me. One chap leaned over and said, 'Oh, I love green tea ice cream.' I didn't really think much of it until I realised it was that special, and then I enjoyed it.

As I came out there was a big line of taxis down the centre of the road. While I was wondering which one to choose and where to go, the waitress who had served me came running out and greeted me like a long lost brother. 'Please come back and see me again. I'm here on Tuesdays and Thursdays.' It's funny the effect you sometimes create without knowing the reason why.

I chose the best looking cab, a sparkling white Mercedes. Benny the driver knew exactly where to take me. Orchard Road is the main avenue for shops, splendid designer outlets in all their glory. Of a night – a different story – enormous bars appeared that were not visible during the day. Cathouses. Six floors of wall to wall girls. Singapore became the forbidden city. Benny took me to one that was a cut above the rest. That was where I met Tang. Young, stunningly beautiful, charming. This was the unspoken Singapore. Benny became my best buddy for the next few days. Tang was from Thailand. She came to Singapore for a couple of weeks when her visa allowed, to earn money to take home to her family.

When you travel around on your own you find special places that you'd never find if all your social life is run by committee. In another restaurant I talked to the head waitress, a very elegant lady, in her forties I'd expect. At eleven o'clock when her shift had finished she'd leave the elegance of the restaurant and drive north to Indonesia to a different world. Singapore is very affluent in stark contrast to the poverty nearby. There must be thousands and thousands of people supporting the facade.

I found a jazz bar in Singapore. A small, intimate kind of place. It seemed a strange mix at first – Chinese and jazz – but I felt at home there and went again the next night. As I arrived the manageress patted me on the stomach and said, 'Get rid of that.' It made me smile. I thought I would have been allowed a little leeway at my age, but apparently not. I found myself sitting at the bar chatting to a very beautiful young woman. I thought she had tattoos on her fingers, but it turned out to be henna. We talked for a long time. I asked her what the rings were. Later on she said it was to deter. Apparently I didn't qualify. I didn't know what henna was, but I do now. She gave me her card. When I got back to the UK, I found the card in my pocket. It read 'Miss Singapore'.

I was hoping to have the opportunity to go to Hong Kong. The key appointment would have been Cynthia Zeller's Hong Kong office, but I hadn't heard back from her before I came away. But now I'd just had a phone call from D; she'd received an email from Cynthia asking me to try and get to see Jones, at their Hong Kong office.

Now I had to get to Hong Kong. I needed to arrange the flight from Singapore. D couldn't do it from back home. Two other calls in Hong Kong as well: Martha Lee at Sun Ngai, and a third one I can't remember.

I thought I would have had some help from the mission organisers to arrange the flight, but it wasn't happening. All the help came from the concierge at the hotel. Billy was tall, skinny, especially tall for a Chinese guy.

There I was, going to Hong Kong to find three addresses – me, who gets lost crossing the road. I was at the airport by six o'clock in the morning, and handed in my ticket and passport. She handed it back and said, 'You're a handsome man, Mr Holmes.' What's going on? Nobody talks to me like this. It was six o'clock in the morning, and I'd had my quota last night. I made some stupid remark like, 'So are you,' and went on my way a few inches taller.

If Atlanta is the worst airport in the world, Hong Kong may be the best. Smiling efficiency, and a short distance to the immaculate train that takes you to Kowloon. Spotlessly clean, twenty five percent full, there in front of me was a map with the bubble moving along as the train progressed at high speed showing you exactly how far you've been and how far to go. Just two or three stations, and I was there.

I found Jones' office. He was expecting me. We spent two hours discussing various options. He understood Cynthia Zeller's enthusiasm perfectly. Then off to meet Martha Lee at Sun Ngai. What a cute address: Tenth Floor, Thriving Industrial Centre. It wasn't a cute place, though. A concrete nightmare. Busy industrial unit workers scurrying back and forth, shouting instructions to one another, all dressed in dark grey and brown to match the labyrinth of concrete. I was the only one who didn't know where to go. I couldn't ask anybody where the lift was – partly because they wouldn't understand, but the real reason was that if I gave the game away the shutters would come down and I'd be captured and sent to some far-off land to work in the mines, never to be seen again.

At last I saw four people appear from a hole in the wall. I dived into the hole before it sealed up again and got off at the tenth floor – another labyrinth of corridors – and then, as if by magic, I saw the words Sun Ngai and knocked on the door and went in, leaving the dark grey of the concrete and entering a grotto of bright lights and sparkling colours – as if I'd entered an Oxford Street showroom. Martha Lee greeted me. She was only small but her enthusiastic personality made her much larger. We'd first met in Bologna a year or two before, and she chatted away about the major benefits and pitfalls. I probably put in the odd word, but it was hardly necessary. Most of her frames were very small and even the neat simplicity of Curl Up n' Stand could look a bit bulky, and the price had to be cheaper – but of course I'm now in China and everything is cheaper.

When I came out it was raining. I mean raining, the kind of heavy rain you see in movies. Three drops fill a small teacup. Everybody had umbrellas. Everybody knew it was going to rain. Except me. I looked down the road, saw a Chinese restaurant and dashed for it. It was a shoe repairers'. I looked up and down the road again and saw that every shop sign looked like a Chinese restaurant – or perhaps they were all cobblers.

I called in a shop to get some tissues to wipe the rain away and stop me sneezing. It had stopped raining by then, and I walked along the street having some difficulty opening my packet of tissues. The smiling faces passing by seemed to be laughing occasionally – did everybody in Hong Kong know I'd just bought a packet of sanitary towels?

I got back to the airport earlier than I needed to. Job done. My flight was at eight-twenty but the airport clocks are all twenty-four hours, which confuses me beyond belief. Every five minutes I'm checking the time and trying to convert it from one logic to the other. Why can't we just decide on whether to have a twenty-four hour clock or a twelve hour one?

I asked one of the officials what time the Singapore flight went. He checked and said, 'Twenty past eight'. He was working on a twelve hour clock, despite all the clocks around him saying different. I sat down and got my calculator out. We should really work on a ten hour day, five o'clock being midday. Ten hour day, one hundred minutes in an hour, one hundred seconds in a minute. That would work out roughly the same and it'd be a lot simpler. Wouldn't have a cat in hell's chance of getting international agreement on that – we can't even agree what side of the road we should be driving on.

Billy was still on duty when I got back to the hotel. He was thrilled at what I'd achieved in that trip, getting to Hong Kong, three appointments and back, in the same day – and that he'd been a part of it.

One more day, and then the mission would be over. Singapore is an island, and I hadn't seen the edge, apart from the harbour, but I didn't really call that the edge. I realised a long time ago all proper islands are roughly the same size as the Isle of Man – thirty by ten. So the edge couldn't be far away.

I went to the concierge's desk to find Billy. He wasn't there; he was off duty. 'I need Billy,' I said, 'This is a job for a man.' Billy appeared behind me as if he was just transported there. 'I'm here,' he said, and went behind the desk to attend to my next project.

'I want to find the edge,' I said.

'The edge?' he repeated, louder than he need have.

'Yes. I've been in Singapore six days now. Tomorrow I go back, and I haven't seen the edge.'

It is essential to get a bus for adventures such as this. A taxi would never do. Not at all. A camel's OK, or a donkey, but certainly not a taxi. The bus dropped me off in the middle of a big wide main road, offices and shops all around. No indication whatsoever whether to go left, right, forwards or backwards. By process of quite a number of trials and errors, I found the edge.

Once again, I was the only one there. Just a short sandy bit, and sparse parkland. I didn't have my swimming costume, but it was just as well – the lapping water was dirty. I don't mean dirt like crisp packets, drink cans and ice cream containers – just flotsam and jetsam. I don't know what flotsam and jetsam are, but I imagine that's what they look like. Every now and again along the edge there were rustic seating areas, ideal for picknickers, just in case. There was one JCB and three builders with spades wondering what to do next. I did think of suggesting they go and clear the flotsam and jetsam, but it wasn't my place. A little way away, I could see the ubiquitous Macdonalds. What a shame. And there was a group of Chinese people walking along, as groups do, with their cameras round their necks. It's not just London, then, where they take photographs?

A couple of hours must have passed – time to make my way back. Where the hell do I start? I do this all the time. I do give myself a good talking to: *look around, know where you are before you wander off, take note of the landmarks.* It seldom works. I can't help it if I get lost in the excitement of the occasion. I got myself to a main road, though it didn't look the same. Where's D? She'd know the way. I started walking along the road, hoping I was going in the right direction. A smart young Chinese man was walking towards me. He'll speak English, I thought. After a few moments of meaningless conversation he pointed to an hotel in the distance. Was he suggesting we get an hotel for the afternoon? We both realised we didn't like the way this conversation was going and walked off in opposite directions – he relieved to get away from this interruption, and me more confused than ever.

The next day it was Mission Complete, though what had been completed I had no idea. I hadn't managed to see Gary Lim either; he was away in China.

I didn't appear to have achieved an awful lot of business, apart from my trip to Hong Kong, but then when Hong Kong did work it would all be worthwhile.

If I'd achieved little in Singapore, Fort Canning Park made it all worthwhile. I went to the park a number of times. Each time I became lost, physically and mentally. I was totally absorbed in the stories the park had to tell. In one part, there were various groups of families with the young bride and groom, dressed in splendour for the occasion. The plaque on one building read something about the solemn vows... Chapel of Solemnity... or something like that. I mused on the literal definition of solemnity. Surely this shouldn't be a solemn occasion?

In another part of the garden, there were big doors cut into the hill, leading to a tunnel. The doors were closed – I wouldn't want to go in anyway. Outside was a brass plaque saying this was where the British surrendered to the Japanese. I shuddered as I reflected on what might have happened during that time of war, and what was going on at the surface while the troops were beneath.

Another time, I came across gravestones, inscribed with the memory of the fallen: 'Fusilier… aged 18'. Such a short life.

Birds twittered in the trees, and if you studied for ages you sometimes got a glimpse of the exotically coloured little creatures. Enormous trees and plants displayed magnificent flowers I'd never seen before. I guess it was the tropical climate. If you put on a clean shirt in Singapore, half an hour later you needed to change it. The flowers loved it, and D would have loved to see the flowers.

I always finished my walk in a different place, and left the park by a different exit, unaware of how I'd got there.

Seven thirty a.m. on the final day, I got in the lift to go down for breakfast. A pretty girl pressed the button to go down, and the lift moved. That shouldn't have happened. I looked at her. She was smiling. They all did – always smiling, always happy. The first day we had arrived at the hotel we couldn't get the lifts to work, until we were told you had to swipe your plastic door key to make the lift operate. I guess it was some kind of security thing. It didn't deter the Orchard Road girls, though. Perhaps it wasn't meant to. I looked at her and said, 'You're special?' Her smile lit up, 'Yes, we're special.'

'None of the others have asked me to help with anything,' Billy told me, a bit sombrely. 'I don't want you to go.' Part of me didn't want to go either.

Back to the UK. Had I nudged the project that bit further? Sooner or later. Please God, let it be sooner. Though there's something much more important. Had I discovered something profound in the rehabilitation of drug addiction? We use the word 'addict' as if it explains everything, but it explains nothing. Why is there an addiction? Some of the greatest minds in history have been addicts of one sort or another. Are we saying they were weak-willed, low-life?

Could it be that use of certain drugs causes elation and, taken habitually over a long period the body ceases to produce the feel-good factors because the drug's doing it? Then when the drug is stopped the body is left like a quivering wreck. Surely that had been thought of before? It seemed obvious to me. I'm sure I'm being simplistic and there are many other factors, but it could be a major contributor to the horrifying effects. I wrote to Rhodri Morgan, who promptly wrote back introducing me to the head of his department in Wales specialising in drug and alcohol abuse.

I also wrote an article and sent it to the Lancet hoping they would publish it, but they declined. I was disappointed but I shouldn't have been surprised. I'm not a doctor. No letters after my name, no qualifications, no twenty years' research. To me it seems obvious, but sometimes the obvious can get overlooked.

Not being part of the educated elite does have its drawbacks. All I learned at school was the Battle of Hastings was 1066. Perhaps if I put that after my name, Ken Holmes BoH, it would make a bit of difference.

During our flight from Australia to Singapore I wasn't seated among the other delegates, although our tickets were all handed in together as a block booking. I was sat between two Chinese girls – much more me. The one next to the window was about fifteen. But the one on my outside, Shelley Xue, was twenty-four. Perfect. She'd been on a seminar representing her Shanghai company. The conversation flowed; I told her about my inventions and also my theories on drug abuse, and how obvious it all seemed… and that I was going to put that on my grave: 'Ken Holmes, Professor of the Bleedin' Obvious'. She laughed so loud, the noise travelled up the plane. The mission leader, Robin, turned round from four rows up to see what the fuss was about. It also brought my young friend next to the window into the conversation.

Perhaps that's my epitaph: Ken Holmes, B.o.H., Professor of the Bleedin' Obvious. Everything is obvious when you know, but it's more than that. How often do we realise that the answer to a difficult problem has been staring us in the face all the time? It just takes the right triggers – or is it bloody minded determination – to see it.

Shelley Xue and I emailed each other a few times afterwards. She was trying to put me in touch with her friend who worked in the buying office for IKEA in China. The Gods move in mysterious ways. I thought they'd done their job putting me between the two Chinese girls and not with the other lot, and now they're introducing me to IKEA.

I wrote to Dr Colin Brewer of the Stapleford Centre. This is part of his reply:

"Thank you for sending me your article. It is a great improvement on the ignorant and prejudiced stuff that passes for public debate on this issue. I particularly approve of your suggestion about linking confidence-building rehabilitation programmes to steady opiate prescriptions or to very slow and manageable reductions."

To receive comments like that from someone of his standing at the front line of rehabilitation, and for him actually to approve of my suggestion about confidence-building during rehabilitation, meant such a lot – but what now?

I spoke to him on the phone and tried to arrange a meeting, but his heavy work schedule could not allow it at the time.

All I want to do is bring my theories and beliefs to wider discussion. We all feel a lack of confidence, low self-esteem, depression from time to time; it seems that 'cold turkey' is a thousand times worse, but why? Everything has a reason – that is a law. Is our body drained of the elements that create our self-esteem, self-confidence, happiness – in other words the very things that make life worth living? If it appears that I'm repeating this, then so be it. I'm repeating it to myself a thousand times, and will continue to do so.

What if Darren's body had stopped creating those chemicals that were supplying the feel-good factors because they didn't need to; heroin was doing it? Now the heroin had stopped, what would happen? The body would need time to re-create the chemicals – time and encouragement. And in the meantime what happens? If you feed in anti-depressants isn't that going to continue to confuse the body?

Drug addiction may be the biggest problem facing modern society. It is all too easy to dismiss drug addicts as wasters, the dregs of society. If there was a bit more understanding – if we cared a bit more – we'd do something about it.

I was impressed with Dr Colin Brewer and the caring attitude he had to the drug addiction problems – and his willingness to listen to me.

Then, some twenty months later, his name and photograph was in all the daily papers. Full page articles appeared saying, 'In the biggest case to come before the General Medical Council, six men and a woman were accused of serious misconduct for their contraversial treatment of drug addicts. It is the first time so many doctors have been jointly charged. They include Colin Brewer who founded the Stapleford Centre in Belgravia and six of his colleagues.'

Six months after that The Times reported the ongoing investigation and twelve-week hearing and named the doctors involved. I don't know how well-founded the allegations were or whether we will ever truly know, but what I do sincerely believe is that Dr Colin Brewer and his colleagues were extremely learned in the field of addiction. The allegations were that they were supplying drugs (methodone) totally irresponsibly, the implications being that they were ignoring best practice for monetary gain.

Is it because I have no formal training, no 'education', that I'm able to see outside the box? I did know Darren had been getting better. After the first two or three weeks he was looking brighter; there was a bit more of a sparkle in his eyes. It was as though the black thunderclouds he carried with him were starting to fade. He wasn't sapping my strength, wasn't taking anything away. If anything, the more I could see him improving the more I wanted to help. Also, and perhaps even more important, I want to explore my belief that habitual drug abuse diminishes the body's ability to create confidence, the feel-good – things the rest of us take for granted.

If I'm right about the effects of drug addiction, it's got to be of help for the addicts to know this and begin to understand why they feel so crap. If it's not that, what is it that makes them feel so wretched? Because something's doing it.

I never got to see Darren after that aborted attempt at Fron Haul. I tried to contact him loads of times after I got back from the trade mission, but he didn't return my calls.

None of this was taking away my ability to turn around the fortunes of the company. We are able to concentrate on a number of projects at the same time without neglecting one, so long as the motivation is strong enough. It's as though the mind is like a muscle: the more it's exercised, the more powerful it becomes.

The advance payment agreement with our new moulding supplier, Eco, was supposed to be a temporary arrangement, and then we'd move to monthly payment terms as in normal business practice. Instead of that they starting asking for payment with order, which was at least one month in advance of delivery. That was punitive. Adam Boot, the director who had been so understanding a few months earlier, refused to come to the phone, and never returned calls. Whenever I phoned his office and asked to speak to him a nervous voice would say, 'Oh, er… he's not here at the moment.' They were lying, and I told them so.

Even when I agreed to pay them up front, they still didn't supply. Their latest excuse was they couldn't accept any new orders because they were 'too busy'. Ridiculous. Companies always accept orders and find a way of producing, especially when prompt payment is involved.

Eco was a subsidiary of a much larger organisation. I contacted the financial director of the parent company and explained the situation. I could tell by his response he considered their behaviour strange business practice, but he could offer little help as Eco was autonomous. Was I scaring the industry that much?

I'd recently been introduced to Simon Wallwork, corporate lawyer, at Wacks Caller in Manchester. Whenever I met with Simon he said very little, never wrote anything down, but I grew to have great respect for him. He knew how powerful the invention was, and was always on the end of the phone for comment. I told him about my very deep concerns over my chain of supply, and asked him if it was possible to take legal action as they were causing restraint of trade. 'There's no such law,' he said.

Howard Simons accused me of taking my eye off the ball. How pompous, how arrogant. Did he think I was that stupid, after all the years he'd known me. Why did I move supply over to Eco when it was going to cost money, if I wasn't forced into it by his own company?

The business I'd built up over the last thirty years was being assassinated. In a matter of months, it had gone from a thriving organisation, affording a healthy salary and a profitable bottom line, into a company that was now struggling for its life.

The only thing left was to realise all the assets I had – sell the house, sell the cars, sell the factory, sell everything. I cut our overheads down to an absolute minimum. I sold my beloved TVR that I'd bought three years before when the future had looked exciting and mind-blowingly prosperous. I put an ad in Auto Trader. The only response I got was from Christopher Neil – the company I'd bought it from in the first place. They gave me what I was asking for. Apparently they were short of good second-hand stock. I allowed my Jeep to be repossessed by the finance company, and I bought an old Mondeo off Dave for £300. It was a bit of a shed, but it worked.

John Pitchford agreed to meet me over breakfast at Carden Park as usual. About the most difficult meeting of my life. John was shocked – he wasn't expecting it – but I hope he knew deep down I had no alternative.

I told him over our bacon and eggs at eight o'clock in the morning that I had to put Genesis into an IVA. If approved, it meant the company could carry on trading – but in order for an IVA to be approved, the company had to receive permission from eighty percent of its creditors, and Barclays Bank were the biggest. John gave his approval.

The meeting ended with the bacon and eggs congealing on my plate. I had a lot of respect for John, he was a friend. Telling him that had hurt.

He told me I'd have to leave Barclays because sooner or later we'd want to borrow money and Barclays would never do it.

An IVA simply meant the debts were frozen and the company could continue to trade and pay what debts it could over a period.

I didn't bear any ill will to anyone for more than a moment or two of self-pity. I don't know whether that was because I'd written the screenplay which despatched them all. If that's the case, perhaps catharsis is much more powerful than it's given credit for. Wouldn't it be far more civilised if, instead of going to war with your enemies, you write a play about it? I bet Shakespeare would have an opinion on that, if I ever get to meet him.

I'm sure there was no malice intended, either. I did feel pity for them; were their lives so trivial, so shallow, so vulnerable, to see Curl Up n' Stand as such a threat?

Neither did I see lack of success as failure on my part, nor regret having to sell my TVR, or what I was facing now – the possibility of having to sell Fron Haul. There was a kind of instinct that told me everything was going to be OK, and that what I was doing was the right thing. I'm sure D felt the same, though we never talked about it – we didn't have to. We just did what had to be done with hardly a cross word.

My next door neighbour, Mike, couldn't believe it when I told him I was thinking of selling Fron Haul. He tried his best to make me change my mind – he couldn't imagine anybody else living there except me – better the fool you know, I suppose.

And that was about it.

Mike bought Fron Haul so nobody else could move in. It's difficult to relate what emotions, what pain, what regret there was in parting with the garden. Perhaps the doing of it was the important thing, or perhaps there was something more important to take its place, or perhaps I'm just trying to say something I want to hear.

The real reasons are often masked, wrapped inside something that's easier to deal with.

We moved into D's house, and I never went back.

The framing company was now hanging by a thread. The two or three full wagon-loads of frames that we'd delivered to Spielmann's every Thursday had diminished to one or two deliveries a month. There was no point in going back to David Edwards. He had approved Plan B when we moved to Eco. There wasn't a Plan C. If I'd told him that now Eco were refusing to deal with us as well he wouldn't have believed it, and I wouldn't blame him. I couldn't make sense of it either.

Thirty years I'd being supplying Spielmanns. All gone. Trish moved any remaining business over to our competitors. There were always scavengers snapping at my heels.

I sold the factory to Nico Breederland and rented a small portion back off him. Survival time. Nico and I got on brilliantly from the start. He had ambitious plans to turn the factory into luxury apartments. I could see the sense in that. But it would take time, with plans to be drawn up and approvals. It suited both of us for me to keep pottering about making what frames we could.

The deal I struck with Nico gave me a bit of survival money that nobody knew about. Not exactly legal, or ethical, but I did it. Not a lot – I can't remember exactly – but if I hadn't we would have been history.

At the close we owed Simons less than six thousand. A couple of years back it would have been fifty or sixty thousand. Eco actually owed us money. We'd sent them payment in advance and they hadn't supplied.

I had a phone call from Brian Simons, another of the brothers, 'Where's my fucking money! Where's my five thousand!' He was going hysterical on the phone. I told him to calm down, 'You'll give yourself a heart attack!' I knew that would make him worse and I didn't give a damn. I didn't feel guilty about that debt in the slightest, I didn't feel guilty about anything in the slightest. The demise of the company was not of my doing – it had been assassinated.

CHAPTER 13

We carried on making frames for what little business we managed to keep hold of, though our main source of income was now reliant on Curl Up n' Stand.

I decided to contact IKEA. They'd said a long time before that they would approve our slip-on bracket once we'd strengthened it to withstand being bent backwards and forwards at least five times. Now the bracket had been redesigned and the problem IKEA saw had been eliminated completely.

I spoke to a Catherina Cronsgø at IKEA in Sweden. She knew about Curl Up n' Stand, but she was away on business for two or three weeks, which included being in London towards the end of the next week. I told her I'd be in London then. 'Would it be possible to meet up?' She agreed, and I arranged to meet her in her hotel at 9 o'clock Friday morning.

I travelled to London by train on the Thursday. D booked me a room in the same hotel as Catherina. As my train pulled into Euston, I looked up at the rack above my head. Something was wrong. My coat was there, but my overnight case was gone. Stolen. Probably at the previous stop which might have been Milton Keynes. I'm not sure… could have been anywhere.

I reported the theft to the railway police but it was a waste of time. They couldn't have cared less. I could manage without the clean shirt and socks, but with no samples I had nothing to show Catherina. D faxed some illustrations to the hotel – sketches, photos – anything to give me some sort of presentation.

I didn't want to bump into Catherina at the wrong time, so I went to another hotel up the road for a drink. I think it was the Lancaster

Gate, a big posh place, with posh people coming in and out. I sat at the bar, being quietly entertained by a group of about twenty businessmen in dinner suits. One of them came over to the bar and asked the barman what whisky he would recommend. I checked on the drinks menu – the one recommended was one hundred pounds a shot. The businessmen began shuffling about, as though making ready to move off somewhere. I heard the head waiter whisper to his colleague, 'Put two more bottles of wine on that table.' He knew full well they were getting ready to move and took the opportunity to put, at a guess, another £140 on the bill.

I met Catherina in the morning. She was very understanding of what had happened on the train. She definitely knew about Curl Up n' Stand. 'A simple solution for everything,' she said. She gave me their UK office address in Stockport and asked me to send the samples to Gaynor there, and keep in close touch. A very successful trip. Apart from my briefcase.

I'd got away without the samples, I didn't care about the shirt, but in the case had been my little mini disk recorder and the full disk with 'Do you remember '92? So do I.' I could get the story back; I'd run through it in my head a thousand times. But you don't get the magic of that original spontaneity. What the hell was that case worth to anybody? A couple of bits of bent wire that they won't understand, a mini disk player they'd get ten quid for... and my underpants.

On the train back home I kept glancing at the overhead rack. Had the thief been sitting behind me? How did I miss him? I don't think I dozed off. Was I the stupid one for putting the case on the rack? My mind was racing faster than the train.

If there was a little electronic gismo, say the size of one of those cheap lighters, you'd drop it in your case and while the case is up on the rack you activate the gismo remotely from, say, a wristband. Once activated, if anybody tries to steal the case it sets off the alarm and screams. Then when you're ready to pick your case up you deactivate it and away you go. An invention.

By the time I got to Oswestry – a hundred a fifty miles away – five minutes later, it was now also working in the lining of a lady's handbag: if somebody snatches her bag as she's walking down the street she can activate it remotely so the bag starts screaming at the robber. He's going to drop the bag. A similar system would work in the home. All your expensive stuff, TVs, Hi-Fis, and so on, have a similar gadget installed. When you leave the house you activate them all from one button. So then, not only is your house alarmed, but every individual item in it can be as well.

A friend of mine, Keith Samuels, an electronics expert, said, 'Yes, no problem. That can be done.' A big part of Keith's job was electronic surveillance equipment. He told me a story about a large supermarket that had a big problem with pilferage and they couldn't work out who or how. Keith moved his team in and said to the supermarket manager, 'Don't tell anybody what we're doing. If anybody asks, we're installing a new computer system.' What he actually did was put in a number of cameras, with tiny lenses that were completely invisible unless you knew. The thieves turned out to be the store's security guards themselves – as usual. What they were doing during their night shift was getting giant-sized packs of soap powder, emptying the contents, and re-filling them with expensive goodies. Then they'd put a small mark on the packet and replace it on the shelf. The next morning their friends visited the store, selected the chosen packs and paid for soap powder at the check-out.

I didn't do anything about my gismo, but it's a good idea.

I did some research on IKEA frames. Well, I went to their store near Warrington. What an industry IKEA is. The car park big enough for thousands of sheep to park their cars, and then guided by the invisible sheepdog to go through that door there, and follow the arrows as if programmed by the great shepherd in Sweden. I knew the area I needed was towards the very end of this wonderland, and I tried to go in reverse and cut corners, but no chance. They know how to handle renegades like me. The only way was the sheep track. At last I arrived at the frames area, and there were thousands and thousands of them, mostly cheap and cheerful.

Curl Up n' Stand may have looked a bit bulky on these simple frames. Slim, round wire would look much more suitable. I'd been toying with this idea since Martha Lee in Hong Kong, but without success. Now with IKEA there was a much stronger motivation.

The solution I came up with was pretty technical, but well within the scope of Rudolf Mark. Using round wire gave the whole system a lighter, simpler appearance, perfect for the majority of the frames IKEA were selling.

I'd already discussed the possibility of the round wire with Rudolf, but now it had an urgency to it. I was buzzing with excitement – not just for me and the project, for Mark as well. Up to now, Curl Up n' Stand had been simple – any metal stampers could do it – and Mark knew I was having the parts made in Asia, in other words cheap. The round wire solution wasn't easy to manufacture, so it gave Mark the edge, and there was a significant saving in raw materials.

The move into D's house was seamless, or pretty well. She never once accused me of being irresponsible or foolhardy in the way I ran Genesis. She knew as well as me that the company had been assassinated. She also believed in the inventions, and knew once a tiny part of their potential was realised all the pain would go away.

I went to see Gaynor in IKEA's offices in Stockport. By now she knew about the Curl Up n' Stand project, and said the whole team of IKEA would be visiting the NEC in February. That was three months away – enough time for Mark to produce samples of the round wire system.

The last time I'd visited Mark, D had been with me, so no trouble with the logistics of the hotel, but this time I was back on my own and the memories and horrors of the staircase came flooding back. I stood, staring at it, memorising every detail, how it turned the corner, the particular burgundy shade of the carpet, how it stopped at the reception level. Definitely did not go down to the labyrinth below.

I know it's stupid to blame the staircase. There had to be another somewhere that went down one more flight. I could have asked reception if, or better still, where the other staircase was but decided against it. Some things are best left alone.

In the morning, the round wire samples were on the boardroom table. They were nickel finish. We chose nickel because that seemed to be the preferred finish of Northern Europe, as opposed to the brass finish preferred in the States. They gleamed like silver in a jeweller's shop.

The meeting with IKEA took place in one of the restaurants at the NEC Spring Fair. D and I, my son Jake who was working with us at the time – and five executives from IKEA. Catherina, Gaynor, their product engineer, one other, and Patrick Wir, Purchasing Strategist. The meeting lasted an hour and a quarter. Twice, the restaurant staff asked us if we could vacate the table, as they had a queue. We stayed. As the meeting went on, it became clear it wasn't a question of whether they were going to use Curl Up n' Stand, it was just a question of which type. I wanted them to select the round wire system that Mark had done such a superb job with.

It was only as the meeting was drawing to a close that Patrick Wir said, 'How much?'

'If you hang me up by the thumbs for a fortnight you'll buy it for three or four Euro cents.'

Patrick's face twitched with agreeable surprise. That was the only time during the meeting his inscrutability dropped.

They took away all the information to prepare for the next stage. I was dazed. We had just spent an hour and a quarter with five executives from IKEA. They had to be the most serious buyers of photo frames in Europe, if not further. Price wasn't an issue. That's why Patrick didn't raise the subject until the end of the meeting. He too saw that the simplicity of Curl Up n' Stand had to make it economical, yet he was still agreeably surprised when I told him the ball park figures. They never mentioned exclusivity of any sort, though I'd probably have given it.

The majority of IKEA's frames were produced at various sites in Asia. It then became a question of sorting out the logistics with their man in Asia to implement the system.

I told Nico the news about IKEA. He was always a good listener to the stories of the Wandering Inventor. He had been CEO of a number of companies in Europe, and knew the potential with IKEA. He was as chuffed as me, and not one to enthuse lightly. Once they were on board, the whole world would be dragged along whether it wanted to or not, and IKEA were now breaking into the States.

The following morning Nico came into the workshop. He told me he had a meeting next door with Bromilow at twelve-thirty, and asked me to keep the noise down a bit – don't give him anything to moan about. He'd got to know Bromilow a little bit by now. An hour later Nico came back in, beaming, laughing. 'Guess what's just happened!'

He'd got to the meeting to find that Bromilow had called in Wrexham Council as well. He'd told the Council that he and his wife Jenny were suffering from severe chest coughs, and had been ill all over Christmas, and they were sure this had been caused by the asbestos in the boiler room.

Below Bromilow's offices there was an enormous old boiler that years ago had heated the whole building, and which had been heavily insulated with asbestos, as they did in those days. Bromilow knew that. What he didn't know was that about two years earlier I had considered recommissioning the boiler but the engineers couldn't touch any maintenance on it until all the asbestos was removed. It's common knowledge these days that asbestos is a very toxic substance, and I'd paid two thousand pounds to have it all removed by a firm of specialists. Bromilow was blaming this asbestos for causing the chest infections of himself and his wife. The operation to remove all the asbestos had taken place over a weekend – that's probably why it was away from his prying eyes. Nico hadn't known why Bromilow had called the meeting, he just thought it was a typical landlord/tenant chat, and he certainly didn't know anything about asbestos in the boiler room.

Nico, the Council Officer and Bromilow marched down the steps and into the boiler room to examine the offending asbestos. The boiler was about the size of a garden shed, pipes sprouting from various parts, dials, wheels. All this would have been caked in two inches of asbestos. But now it was all perfectly clean and clear. Not a speck. I'd love to have seen the look on Bromilow's face.

It made Nico's day. And mine. We never heard anything more about it. But what goes through that devious git's mind… and his wife's for that matter? All the planning and conniving that went on to create a situation that would enable him to claim financial compensation of some sort. And it was all fiction.

This reminded me of the time when I was in Taiwan and had a call from Wrexham County Borough Council. Bromilow was trying to claim something very similar then. That was pure fantasy as well.

For IKEA to have spent an hour and a quarter of their NEC time with us illustrated the impact it would have for them. I thought it would all be straightforward after that. Nothing ever is. Patience was the order of the day. A commitment from IKEA would consolidate the relationship with Mark. I kept in close touch with Patrick Wir. He was always agreeable to chat. The future of the project was now in the hands of their men in China; they were the ones that had to bell the cat.

I spoke to Lundgren, the IKEA guy in China, but I didn't pick up much enthusiasm. I began to wonder if he was happy with the way things were and all I was doing was rattling his cage. He could well have had a cosy relationship among all his vendors. Bringing Curl Up n' Stand into the mix would be bound to replace some products. When I heard that Lundgren would be back in Sweden for a couple of days, I phoned Patrick Wir to try to arrange a meeting. He said, 'Oh, I've just written to you, Ken.' I asked him if he could give me the gist of the letter. He said, 'They're going to decline Curl Up n' Stand on the grounds that their customers won't understand it.' Curl Up n' Stand is blindingly obvious, but if you haven't seen it before it can look confusing, as would anything radically new. I asked Patrick if we could put a VDU in store. 'We don't do that,' he said.

I was devasted. How on earth was I going to break down that kind of barrier?

Curl Up n' Stand is a brilliant invention and wouldn't that bring more customers to IKEA – isn't that something of the point? Five executives from IKEA wouldn't have wasted an hour and a quarter if it wasn't. It would just take one customer to see it, then others surely would, but it's no good my shouting all this to a closed door.

I was travelling to South Yorkshire to see a customer when I got a phone call from D, excited. She'd just had a call from a Tony Mendes from Texas, Development Engineer with Intercraft – Burnes Group. He'd said, 'I've been working on Ken's stuff for a couple of years now, and I've just seen his latest development. How quickly can he get over here?' I'd thought the Burnes Group was dead in the water after they closed the Boston office. Apparently not.

I called Tony back. He was so enthusiastic. Amongst other things, Intercraft were supplying WalMart with one million frames per week, all manufactured in Texas. A million photo frames a week to WalMart, and the rest – Target, Dollar Store. I started to make plans to go out there. 'I'll brief all the people,' he said. 'You come over and knock 'em dead.'

He sent over a thirty-page market research document that had been commissioned jointly by Intercraft and WalMart on who buys frames, what for, when, and how many. Serious stuff.

I arranged another trip to the States. I wanted to see Cynthia Zeller at Fetco in Boston following my meeting with Jones in Hong Kong, and another company, Logan Graphics in Chicago. I told Tony I was visiting other companies during my trip – just letting him know that Curl Up n' Stand was gaining momentum.

I flew to Chicago first, the Windy City… and so it was, and cold. Curt Logan's business was supplying craft and hobby stores with framing accessories for the DIY trade. With the slip-on bracket, Curl Up n' Stand now fitted that market. Curt was going to do all the blister packing and the artwork. I just had to ensure that Curl Up n' Stand got its brand name in and patent number. Sooner or later someone was going to try and copy it – the more title of ownership we had, the better. This was a new market for us. Curt ordered a few thousand to get started. From there I flew to Texas.

I didn't expect Texas to look like it did, and where were the cowboys? I suppose there must have been cowboys somewhere, but there weren't any at my hotel, which was stuck in the middle of nowhere… I mean Nowhere. Out of the big window I could see the vast flat barren land stretching forever, broken up only by the endless line of telegraph poles getting closer and closer together, smaller and smaller. My room was big, but not big enough to require the two enormous televisions. I tried to stretch out to see if a toe could touch one television and the tips of my fingers could touch the other, just for something to do. I couldn't quite… perhaps I wasn't trying hard enough. Do they think if you have two enormous televisions it makes everything alright?

At Intercraft, there wasn't the fanfare and the big red carpet that I might have expected. Tony was the great guy he'd seemed on the phone. 'Wait there,' he said, 'I've just got to sort a couple of things.' I waited *there* about two or three hours, occasionally standing up and reminding somebody, then waited some more.

Tony arrived with some excuse or other, and gave me a tour of the factory. They certainly made a lot of frames. But I know how to make frames and, frankly, I think our way of doing it was better than theirs. I started mulling over at what point of the production the Curl Up n' Stand would come in.

When the meeting eventually did come to order there was Lee Cielonko, Vladimir Gonzales, Cesar Rojas... *Aah, the cowboys have come to town after all.* Everybody made the right noises, until the subject of WalMart came up on which so much depended. The WalMart frames were not shrinkwrapped, and that was a big problem. We always attached the leg with a little sticky info label and then shrinkwrapped the frame. If it wasn't shrinkwrapped the leg could come adrift. Despite everybody saying how good Curl Up n' Stand was, if it was no good for WalMart it was no good for Intercraft. All frames I've ever come across are shrinkwrapped, and if not they're boxed – it keeps them clean. Once that problem came into the meeting, it was difficult to get away from it. And that was that, more or less. Their concerns were real. They weren't shrinkwrapped to save cost. But it meant Curl Up n' Stand could come adrift. Tony Mendes knew the WalMart frames weren't wrapped, and he's not stupid, and yet he didn't think of it before I went. *Have I done it again – travelled 3,000 miles for a waste of time?*

Tony knew all about Curl Up n' Stand and how it worked, and so did the others. Why the hell was I asked to go all that way? I wanted to say something but I had to contain it. I don't know what I was thinking on the flights to Boston. I was still seething with anger. *What the hell have I got to do?* A flight from Austin to Dallas, then a connection to Boston. That gave me something to think about instead of wallowing in my own self-pity.

By the following morning I'd calmed down. The Boston hotel was pretty basic, but whatever part of the world you're in there are breakfast rituals that must be obeyed: you pick up a tray, some juice, some coffee, plonk some bread on your plate, maybe some jam and butter – and that was about it. Then you choose one of the various small tables, making sure you sit with a perfect view of the god in the top right-hand corner. The god was spewing out mindless drivel, with everybody hooked on every word. There was a stack of newspapers neatly piled up. I guessed they must be freebies so I helped myself to one, the Today newspaper. I browsed through it, trying to find something a bit more interesting than the god in the corner. I was struck by an article somewhere near the back, about President Kennedy, and how before he was assassinated he was absolutely riddled with disease, ailments of all kinds. Addison's disease, crippling back pain, being pumped full of pain killers – it went on and on.

I glanced round at my fellow inmates in case I was missing something. As, one by one, they came and went, so did their trays. *What happened to their trays?* There wasn't any bustling Eastern European student to take it away as you might expect. Nobody. The inmates disposed of the tray themselves, but how? There appeared to be a stand over in the corner, a facility for such things. Obviously one compartment for the debris, one for this, and one for that. *But which is which? I must watch the next inmate as he leaves.*

My focus was drawn back to the newspaper and Kennedy. I didn't know anything about this. He was always smiling, charming, in control – charismatic, not the zombie I'm reading about here. All of this had been kept hidden. The man was very seriously ill, and should have been in intensive care by the sounds of it. Instead he was being wheeled around as a figurehead. Are we always fed carefully edited bits of information to ensure we support a particular agenda?

I looked for the inmate who'd nearly finished to observe the procedure. He'd already gone, and so had his tray... *and now I've got to go, I'll have to wing it.* I stood up, folded my newspaper and stretched a bit to show anyone that was still there I was being casual. Without a care in the world, I moseyed up to the unit in the corner, shuffled the tray and contents into it... and legged it for the door.

I'd arranged for a car to take me to Fetco. We arrived at a big office block, grand reception, big car park, and this was just the administration offices – the manufacturing was all in Asia.

I know why I rack up all these air miles. I've got to sell it. Am I a useless salesman? Is that where I'm going wrong? No – IKEA wouldn't have gone that far down the line if I couldn't sell. It had been something else that blocked IKEA... and all the others.

I was looking forward to meeting Cynthia again. We'd always got on well. However, in the aftermath of Texas I was still feeling uneasy but, as they say, the show goes on. *For Christ's sake, Curl Up n' Stand's a great product – just go and sell it!*

Cynthia had had a good report from Jones in Hong Kong. She decided to call her marketing people into the meeting with us to get their opinion. The more the merrier. Initially, they said, 'That's a good idea.' But then one became concerned that, as Curl Up n' Stand was in two parts, the leg could come adrift. The marketing team were very familiar with store practice; they knew exactly how the frames were displayed, how many, and in what manner. The concern was that if somebody picked up the display frame and the leg was dislodged, the store could see it as a problem.

The leg didn't come apart when in use, but a big negative had been thrown into the ring, again. She could just as well have said, 'What if somebody takes the top off the pen and spills ink onto their white dress?' Just as unlikely, but not impossible. I tried to say that for demonstration purposes we could superglue the leg in, but she'd sown the seed of doubt. I felt like the judge who said, 'That's totally irrelevant and the jury must disregard it.' How can the jury disregard it when they've heard it?

I didn't see that coming, and neither did Cynthia – and she'd known Curl Up n' Stand for two or three years now. So had Tony Mendes.

Even Trish, with her sharp eye for the negative, didn't try to use that, neither did IKEA see it as a problem, and yet Fetco and Intercraft had raised it as an issue at exactly the same time.

Curl Up n' Stand has always been a two-part product. There are many products on the high street that involve two parts: the pencil that goes with the pocket diary, the fork attached to the pre-packed snack in the salad bar, the cap of a lipstick, the expensive pen with the removable top – a cup and saucer, for Christ's sake – all familiar items and all perfectly acceptable. Part of the trouble is that Curl Up n' Stand isn't a known item. But how the hell is it going to become a known item unless somebody decides it's a great product and puts their commitment where their heart is?

On the plane back to Heathrow there was something else I found disturbing. I'd read about it several times over the last few days. There'd apparently been widespread sexual abuse, paedophilia, within the Catholic Church over a long period of time. So-called pillars of the community, trusted, highly respected members of the clergy, were found to be abusing children, and apparently had been doing so for years. There must have been hundreds, if not thousands, of people in the Church aware of this who did nothing. The families may not have known, the children would be too terrified, ashamed, to speak out, and who would believe them if they did? How could that happen? Clergy, who are supposedly representing God and all things that are good, abuse children and go on undetected for years. The truth is it was known about, but everybody kept quiet. Aren't they as guilty? Why did they not expose the practice? What was their motivation for keeping quiet?

Then there was Kennedy. Had we been fed lies for all these years on this charismatic man who held the future of war and peace in his hand? The man who had stood strong and told Cuba to disconnect the warheads or he'd blow them to bits. Was he being kept together by concoctions from the medicine men? Kennedy was in the early Sixties – I think it was sixty-three when he was shot, so probably too long ago to mean anything to a lot of people – but he was big at the time. I was appalled; not that he was ill, but that it was covered up. I told D about it when I got back home and we checked on the internet. There were thirteen pages on his ill health. It also said the Bay of Pigs invasion in Cuba in 1961 was orchestrated by the CIA. This is a long time ago, but the same thing would happen today, and not just in America, worldwide. We are just fed information that suits the powers that be. Truth has nothing to do with it.

Politicians, like businessmen, like most prople, a lot of time just say what they think they can get away with to suit their cause. I can't help thinking the same would, and does, happen today.

International Fowl
Goosey Goosey propaganda
Wither shall I wander?
The Middle East? Afghanistan?
Vietnam? Iraq?
Whatever I decide to do
The evidence will back.
But this is wrong – it can't be right

Hold back! I hear you holler.
Unless of course the outcome
Will support the Yankee Dollar.

But I kept coming back to my own selfish world, as usual. So much for being wise. *How could I have been so stupid?* I was still furious. Not with Tony – he didn't see it coming; he'd sent us a thirty-page report on why WalMart buy. Not Cynthia Zeller, either – she didn't see it. I suppose I was going through all of this to somehow mitigate my own shortcomings. What I was really furious about was coming so close and not getting it.

By the time I got off the plane at Heathrow an answer was building. The old wives were pretty smart people: 'Necessity is the mother of invention'. In the dark recesses of a foggy mind I could see the possible solution tumbling round. Intense thought, racing around as if my life depended on it. It *is* possible for it to be one piece.

People talk about women being better at multi-tasking than men. Surely everybody multi-tasks? I wouldn't know what it was like to play with just one ball. It appears that the mind has the capacity to deal with millions of subjects at any one time. That's the way my mind appears to work, anyway. One of the disciplines of meditation is not to think about anything, make your mind blank, which is very difficult and takes the utmost concentration, but it does help to get some sanity into the chaos.

On that same flight I had the idea for another screenplay, The Disciple. God is pissed off with the behaviour of his ambassadors on Earth because of what he's read in the papers, and tells his archangels to find a new disciple. Archangel Voice, drunk on moon juice, selects Jimmie Downie, the head of a dysfunctional Liverpool family, as the Disciple. Jimmie begins to realise he has the power to perform miracles and it starts to scare the life out of him. It's a comedy, which is sometimes the best way to make a serious point.

The whole story played out in front of me like a dream, only I wasn't asleep. People, places, tables, chairs, dialogue, all there – all I had to to was write it down. I'm sure that's not unique, but it amazes me. I wish I saw my own life as clearly. But, even seeing it clearly, how do you write tones of voices, sniggers, a sidelong glance from somebody who's not actually involved in the dialogue, and countless other bits?

The idea of the one-piece frame support was one of those situations where I knew the solution was there, but it wouldn't come to the surface. While I was wallowing in this mire, we had a phone call from QVC, the shopping channel. I had contacted them two years or more before and gone down to see the buyer, Fiona Sanderson, to show them Curl Up n' Stand. She thought it was a good idea, great for television, but nothing came of it. Now, out of the blue, they wanted to order. She asked me if I would be willing to go on television to present it. *Willing? I was born to perform.* I had to go to London for an audition. I had ninety seconds for the presentation. I rehearsed over and over again making sure everything fitted in within the ninety seconds. 'Don't wear anything too bold or garish,' they'd said. I hadn't thought of that; I bought a buff-coloured shirt from Boss.

Their office was right on Chelsea Bridge. I knew parking was limited so I took a taxi from the hotel. The driver was well impressed when he heard where I was going and what for. He had me down as a television star – did my ego no harm at all before the audition.

I was was soon deflated when I met my host presenter – a surly prima donna with deep contempt for low-life. While I was waiting I had been given a cup of coffee in a plastic cup. She greeted me with a sharp, 'Don't put that on the table, put it there,' pointing to the floor. Ninety seconds plus, say, ten seconds either side, and it was over. I didn't know whether I'd got the part or not. I thought it had gone OK, but there was no discussion. I was just left wondering. I didn't even get an, 'OK, we'll be in touch.' I wandered out, hoping I didn't get the same taxi driver who'd dropped me off three and a half minutes earlier. Some time the following week I was told I'd failed.

They'd said it was always better if somebody from the company promoted the product. But not me, apparently. D went down for an audition. She failed too.

It was still going to go on television, but this time with a QVC demonstrator appearing with the prima donna. OK, I wasn't going to be a TV star this time, but what the hell – so long as it sold. I spoke to the demonstrator on the phone two or three times, and sent her a demo pack to illustrate. She understood everything and was impressed with the idea.

The pack we had sold to QVC consisted of three photo frames all fitted with Curl Up n' Stand. QVC ordered five hundred sets. The form was if they sold out on the first airing they would re-order double; if they continued to sell it would become a regular item. I knew this was going to work – we were going straight to the end user. Explained simply on television, it was bound to work.

Five hundred packs were made, all boxed neatly, and we shipped them out to their warehouse, the understanding being if they didn't sell we would take them back.

We couldn't get the QVC channel on our television so we arranged to go and watch it in a pub up the road. It was going to be on at about four in the afternoon. We panicked for a bit because the landlord couldn't get the right channel, but then he found it, and I sat nervously waiting for our moment of fame, like an expectant father.

Our moment came. The QVC presenter announced the various items coming up in this section. When he came to us he said, 'As you can imagine at QVC we see all the new ideas, and occasionally a brilliant product comes up and this is one of them. This item is going to become the new standard for the way picture frames are stood up.' I was tingling all over. *He's talking about me.* I couldn't have wished for a better introduction; we'd been singled out above all the others.

Then our ninety seconds… of hell.

It was a nightmare. The demonstrator totally cocked up. What she should have done was simply take the back out of the frame, fit Curl Up n' Stand, replace the back, and stand the frame up. For some reason best known to herself, she didn't use the demo pack I'd sent her, the one I'd discussed with her on the phone that clearly demonstrated how simple and effective Curl Up n' Stand is to use. Instead, she'd brought one of her own frames from home. She fumbled and stumbled, trying to prise the back out with a butter knife… and the ninety seconds were ticking by. The prima donna, for something to say to fill the embarrassing gap, was reduced to discussing the photograph of the pretty little girl in the frame. It was a total disaster. Time was up, and nobody knew anything about Curl Up n' Stand.

I watched in horror as the camera panned back to the presenter who'd given us the glowing introduction a few minutes earlier, who now said, 'We'll try and get back to that later if we have time,' but that didn't happen.

The demonstrator had known what to do and how to present Curl Up n' Stand. I'd gone through it with her over the phone with the pack I'd sent. Why on earth she decided to disregard that and bring her own frame from home I don't know.

To our surprise, a few of the items sold, but not enough, and QVC decided they would send the rest back. I phoned QVC telling them to put it on air again because the demonstration had been a cock-up and a waste of time.

All the frames and the boxes had been made specially for QVC and now they were coming back. I told QVC it wasn't our fault and I refused to accept the consignment back. But then they did a stupid thing, and paid our bill in full. I'm sure they didn't intend to do that, but they did. I was all the more determined now not to accept the stock back. I tried again to persuade them to put it back on air because I knew it would work. Their own buyer wouldn't have selected it in the first place without being convinced of its potential. They must have known it was their own cock-up that blew the presentation.

In other areas, though, Curl Up n' Stand was selling well. We were getting distributors throughout Europe who bought our products in bulk and sold onward to framing shops, craft and hobby outlets and smaller manufacturers, but it still wasn't putting the yacht in the harbour. At this rate, the only thing to finish up in the harbour would be me. The idea for a one-piece picture frame support had started to form as the plane landed in Heathrow, but how would it work? It was like trying to do a puzzle blindfolded. Perhaps it shouldn't be metal, perhaps the solution had to be in plastic?

Injection moulding. That's the way this kind of plastic part is made. A whole new industry. I went to visit a number of plastic injection moulders. As we solved one problem another would crop up, and the costs were looking horrendous. Perhaps one day, but not now.

I shouldn't be complaining; life was pretty good. We'd been at D's house for eighteen months now. But I was restless – impatient, I suppose.

There was still an overwhelming feeling that things could, and should, be a lot better.

D was wandering around her garden contemplating her estate. I was inside watching a programme on the TV about the Bangkok Hilton, perhaps the most notorious prison in the world – ninety percent of the occupants in for drug-related crimes. The conditions in the prison were appalling, horrendous. I went upstairs to the loo. D had come in and changed the channel. 'I was watching that,' I said. She didn't mind; her head was still wandering around outside. A few minutes later I switched the TV off and joined her in the garden. It was a pleasant evening, we had a glass of wine, laughed about something that had happened during the day. We came back inside but as soon as I sat down I went off into some kind of trance, crying uncontrollably. I was aware of what I was doing, but couldn't stop. It carried on for some time. Eventually it subsided and I said, 'It's gone now, I'm alright now'. What I saw during those few moments, or few minutes, were nightclubs – music, dancing, bars, young people enjoying themselves – the sort of places where casual drug-taking is commonplace. But there were TV screens showing graphic images of the effects of drug addiction. Pretty horrifying images shown on a continuous loop. No sound track, just there for everyone to see what experimenting with drugs could well lead to. These screens had to be installed by law in any places where drugs may be offered in order to drive the message home in no uncertain manner to both the drug users and the people who were selling them.

I've thought of that experience thousands of times since. What I saw in that trance or whatever it was, is a good idea. I don't know why that sort of thing happens, apart from I have no control over it, no conscious control anyway. It may sound crazy, but isn't it more crazy to do nothing about it or pretend it didn't happen?

It wouldn't be the first time people had thought I was mad, and it won't be the last. Drug addiction is a very serious problem, and getting worse. Isn't that madder? We don't admit that any of our children are likely to be involved: 'Our kids wouldn't do that.' But somebody's kids are doing it, and there are millions of them. It would illustrate what horrors the kids could be walking into, and if it doesn't disturb the kids it might disturb the rest of society.

CHAPTER 14

We needed a break from it all. I don't know how long it was since we'd been on holiday. D went out on a Friday afternoon to check with the travel agent. She phoned me, 'I've found something. Sicily. But we need to fly tomorrow morning.' 'Book it,' I said.

By eight o'clock the following morning we were at Manchester Airport. Queuing up with the hordes of travellers my eye was caught by a beautiful young woman. Black hair, black suit, red shirt. She was stunning. Once or twice I had to stop myself from staring. I thought she noticed. She was with another woman, older. She'd be about twenty-five. Looked Italian. She appeared to be getting on our flight. Must be Italian.

We arrived at Sicily, the usual chaos. Thousands of people rushing to get somewhere, but not quite sure where. Outside, the usual row of fifteen coaches. We found the right one to take us to our hotel. After four stops came ours. Six people got off... including her.

I dumped my case on the bed, looked at the bathroom, and glanced out of the window. D wanted to hang her clothes in the wardrobe as usual. I needed to go and find the bar as usual.

I passed her in the lobby. She made some remark about the world cup. I made a stupid reply and said, 'I'm going to the bar. D'you want to join me?' She did. A few minutes later, Zoë's mother joined us, and a few minutes after that so did D. The four of us became pretty well inseparable for the next seven days. Zoë and I were simply drawn like magnets. D was chatting with mum, so it all seemed very convenient. We went to the beach, Zoë, her mum, me and D. I went to get some bottled water, Mum rearranged the towels so she was next to D, and I was talking to Zoë. It seemed ridiculous, but that's the way it was. Of an evening strolling down to the square, Zoë and I were way in front. The other two were distracted by the shops.

We were standing in the square watching some break dancers when D arrived, saw the apparent intimacy of the two of us, and got very upset. Zoë said I can't do this to D, and proceeded to be a bitch for the next couple of days. But I was smitten, like a lovesick teenager. Somehow we got through the next seven days.

Zoë and I stayed in touch a bit after we got back. I was over twice her age. She said that didn't matter. I knew it didn't. But then she started to pour cold water. I wasn't having that, and one day went up to Cumbria to see her. I never did get to see her. But at that moment any feeling I had for her went instantly, as if waking up from a dream. I'd behaved appallingly. Why? I thought the world of D, yet I behaved like an absolute bastard. What drives men to behave like that? I expect it's nearly always men.

> *Someone broke my heart today*
> *I must have put it in the way*
> *I really must stop doing that*
> *I am a dozy twat*

I had taken a lot of my guidance from the Wise Man, but now I felt totally disillusioned. I didn't meditate for months. I felt I was so right about Zoë, and yet so wrong. Eventually I went to ask the Wise Man why. He said, 'You had to go there to get here.'

My old dad worked hard all his life, night school for years and years, always trying to make things better. Liverpool supporter. When they won the European Cup, I think it was, he said, 'That's it, I can go now.' His life was complete. But he didn't go – it was some time later he said, 'I don't know what the point is. I don't know what it's all about.' Liverpool being champions of Europe wasn't enough. We never talked a lot, so it never went any further, but he left me with the riddle: What's the point?

That phrase has haunted me every since. What is the meaning of life, the point, and all the stuff that goes with it?

The Meaning of Life and Associated Stuff

About ten or fifteen years ago, having been married for about ten or fifteen years, the marriage was over and had been for some time. But how to get out of it without proving to the world I was the bastard they all knew I was anyway? And the kids, five of them.

But then it dawned on me one morning: animals don't stay together for life, apart from some like the swan for instance, but the rutting stag has a whole harem, and so does the lion; the black widow spider eats her mate. That's nature. Don't the same laws of nature apply to us? Who was it said 'till death us do part'?

Such joy... I felt as though the weight of the world had been lifted off my shoulders. It's not my fault, it's nature.

That simple realisation happened a few years ago, but, I felt I'd discovered something really profound: of course it's nature. I didn't tell anybody. I wasn't sure anyone else would see it. Society holds up the human race as being superior to animals – we have rules and regulations to keep order because we're intelligent.

I'd gone to a party. It was pretty early on, at that time when everybody was there but it hadn't yet really got going. I said to Louise, 'Come over and ask me can the law of man override the law of nature.' Louise was pretty switched on; she didn't need any explanation, she just did it. I said, 'No, I don't think so. Won't the law of nature win every time? Man can't change that.' "The law must override nature, otherwise you'd have anarchy,' one said. 'But you can't change nature,' said another. Within minutes everybody was talking about it. They all had an opinion.

If there were a law that told the female black widow spider not to eat her mate, it wouldn't make the slightest difference. And the mate knows exactly what he's risking, but does it anyway. That's nature.

I reflected on how many couples I'd known over the years, and how many were still together. I'd lost touch with most of them, so it wasn't very scientific, but I knew a few had fallen by the wayside. A lot of the couples I knew now were either on unsteady ground, or on their second or third attempt. I'm sure they all started out with the very best of intentions. Why do the best intentions go so catastrophically wrong?

Is there a point in the urge to breed that might be more complex? The rutting stag and the lion: all the males want the top job, but they've got to fight for it. The strongest wins. 'Survival of the fittest.' All the elaborate mating procedures are part of the selection process in order to make the species fitter, stronger, wiser. That's widely understood. Isn't that exactly the same in the human race – we are trying to advance the species, we want something better for our children... isn't that what we're trying to do?

We're obsessed with how we look. We go to ridiculous lengths to make ourselves look more attractive. When I shave, I try to make sure my sideburns are exactly the same shape and length. If they are not, I go demented. How's anybody going to find me attractive today? As if anybody's going to notice. Absolutely ridiculous – and we all do it. Change the colour of our hair, make it curly, make it straight, surgery to make some bits bigger, some bits smaller. As far as I know, animals don't do that. Imagine two tigers walking through the jungle: 'Have you heard? Stripes are out... they're so last year.'

Despite what everybody believes, it's not just physical appearance that attracts us. It's much more complex than that. Isn't the intellect, personality, charisma, character, and so on – more relevant? Aren't they the qualities that are going to advance the species? And doesn't real beauty come from within? If George Clooney was weak-willed, no sense of humour, no charisma, would he have the same pull? You could hardly call Jack Nicholson good-looking, but he seems to do alright. Is it the eyes that do it? We always focus on the eyes first, and then check out the real estate. But then, what the eyes see is infinitely variable.

A person in love may say, 'Isn't she the most beautiful girl in the world?' when to somebody else she most definitely isn't. But it doesn't change what the person in love sees. 'Beauty is in the eye of the beholder.' Time and time again that sort of phrase crops up.

Whatever it is that attracts, or repels for that matter, is often instant. Love at first sight – how does that work? Are we able to read that much information in such a short time? Are we all so transparent?

At a glance we may often form a very detailed opinion of someone, whether we like or dislike them, even before they've said anything. I don't think we could do that without seeing their eyes, and so often it's correct.

Is our very soul, whatever that is, mirrored in our eyes? Why was Zoë so bewitching? Yet whatever spell there was disappeared just as quickly. Infatuation? Easy to put a name on it as though it's nicely pigeon-holed and therefore requires no further information. But surely it does. Everything has a reason. It can't just be a dress rehearsal, or can it? Infatuation is powerful, all-consuming maybe, one-sided maybe, short-lived maybe. All very vague.

We refer to animals as if they are separate from us, which perhaps is incorrect. There are plants and there are animals. We are animals, and as such aren't we governed by the laws of nature, just like chimpanzees, lions or earwigs? Like all species, we are trying to secure and improve our future. We know that breeding isn't a lottery. Horse breeding has gone on for centuries; by selective pairing we have a pretty good idea of what the outcome may be. Are we humans trying unaware to do exactly the same thing? It would explain how difficult it is to find the right partner. It would also go some way to explain why we take so much trouble over our appearance. We're trying to advance the species – and that's a biggie.

We'll wrap ourselves in the latest fashion, do everything we can to improve our physical appearance, but it's the characteristics such as charm, wisdom, humour, self-confidence and so on, that are the real attractions. The power of the jungle may be that of the strongest and fittest; in humans we may say the power is in the mind – intellect, intelligence, whatever you want to call it – although we still have powerful animal instincts.

Power itself may well be the biggest attraction and, like wisdom, often comes with age and experience. Whether the power is used for good or evil doesn't seem to make a great deal of difference. The bad guys get the dolls too.

It also appears that, as we mature or become more confident, the characteristics that make us attractive become stronger. It doesn't necessarily make you a better person – you're just the same, only more so. We keep adding to those intellectual qualities as we get older, until we peak, or are peaking, and that may happen at any time from fifteen to seventy or more. Then, once peaked, the rate of intellectual growth will slow down or stop. Does that mean we are not at our most attractive until we peak? But we've still got to be young enough to breed. And then in there somewhere there's love.

The worst investment of my life,
Apart from the cars and of course the wife.
Instead of heaven it brought me hell
When I threw that coin in the wishing well.

I was nine. She was ten.
Put us worlds apart back then.
But I was so in love with her.
I think she knew. I think she cared.

Never a single day goes by
When I don't see the twinkle in her eye.
I'm getting on now, nearly seventy-eight.
I know she'll come before too late.

Hang on a mo, someone's at the door.
A note's just fallen on the floor.
There's a tear in my eye, a lump in my throat.
I can't carry on… I've just read the note.

What of the young couple who are madly in love in their twenties and by the time they're forty they've matured in slightly different ways or directions, and perhaps find they don't have much to talk about any more. How often do we hear 'my wife doesn't understand me' or 'he's changed, he never used to be like that'. Perhaps they weren't in love in the first place.

Why wasn't any of this taught at school? Love: the most important thing in the world, and we don't know anything about it. All I was told was, 'you introduce a man rabbit to a lady rabbit' … and you get a field full of pies. I suppose there were lessons and diagrams on the reproductive system, but it was all pretty meaningless and skirted round by a mile the real issues of man's obsession with sex, and that sissy word, love.

We don't even know what to call it. Love is the most amazing thing on the planet and we don't know anything about it. The education system totally ignores it, and yet we all believe in it, or most of us anyway. Money can't buy it, so the song says. We give it the name love, but we love a Mars bar, love the kids, I love my car, I loved my holiday. How can they be compared? The English language has such a rich choice of labels for any given subject, but we haven't found a way of differentiating between our most powerful emotion, and the desire for a chocolate snack. We call sexual intercourse 'making love'. How pathetic. We can't call sexual intercourse 'fucking' in polite society because it's crude, rude and vulgar. We can call it 'sleeping together'. That's just as pathetic. Sleeping is the last thing on the mind. We can't 'make' love – it just happens, for reasons way beyond our comprehension – unless we happen to make a fortunate career choice and work in a Mars bar factory.

In all these thousands of years of so-called advancement we haven't learned a great deal. We're obsessed with money and material things, and probably always have been. So was I – I loved my first car more than anything in the world – there, I just said it. Money appeared to be the solution to everything, which of course it wasn't. In fact, it wasn't the solution to anything. The more I had, the more I needed.

We are programmed by a society that's obsessed with material wealth. The only way you're going to pull the cutest chick in the farmyard is with the fastest car, career – and money, always money. Millions of people do the lottery and it's not going to make a blind bit of difference. An idiot with money is still an idiot. Probably more so. And all the time the real you is struggling to get out.

When I was about twenty, working on the building sites, for reasons I can't recall I came up with a series of searching questions about life and love. I put these questions to some of the hardened, hard-drinking navvies. I was amazed at how sensitive, loving and caring these men were, and how honestly they responded. Others came up to me and said, 'Ask me the questions.'

Various governments encourage and discourage population growth to suit the fashion of the time. What if we begin to dislike the society we have created, and decide not to add to it? Or if homosexuality becomes more popular? If the whole human race became gay, that would solve our problems, save us worrying about the economy or tsunamis or unemployment. We wouldn't be here. I wonder if that's what happened to the dinosaurs – they became gay? Two dinosaurs walking along holding hands – one says to the other, 'D'you like my hair?' That would work.

Could it be that love binds the couple together while they have children and care for them in the vulnerable early years, then love may fade, but then why does it fade? Perhaps it didn't exist in the first place. How would you know whether what you felt was love or not? I learned what I could on the street, like I learnt everything worthwhile. The education system was useless.

It's not just gays who need to come out of the closet – we all do. But you've got to admire gay people who do – it takes a lot of guts. A few years ago that would have been illegal. Gay people and childless couples fall in love just the same; the only difference is their houses are tidier. Children are messy, and yet most of us can't wait to have them.

The only thing I have against gays is they've stolen a word out of our language. Gay used to mean happy-go-lucky, carefree. It seems it's not just the word that's gone. Being happy and carefree was an ideal. It appears that's no longer fashionable – somebody's stolen that as well.

If it isn't to bind the couple together, what the hell is love for? All the other emotions: happy, sad, laughter, crying, have an understandable origin. We know what makes us sad, we know what makes us happy. Anger, rage, despair even, can pretty well always be traced back to the root cause. Sex is a chemical reaction. It doesn't necessarily have anything to do with love. So what causes love, and why is it there?

Everything has a reason. That's one of the laws of the universe, and I would guess that law is right up there near the top, one of the early ones.

Because I learnt it on the street, I got it wrong. At fifteen I believed you had to fall in love by the time you were thirty. After that you take the kids to the park and get drunk in the working men's clubs. Thirty-five or forty was definitely the cut-off point.

Whatever the reason, love is not there by accident, and it's not like waiting for a bus: you wait for ages and then three come along. Love is too powerful a phenomenon for it to be so casual. You wait for ages and, if you're very fortunate, one might come. Whatever it is. Society and the media are wrong when they imply it's commonplace. The suggestion seems to be that if you have not fallen in love four times by the time you're twenty-five then there's something wrong with you. But how are you able to give yourself completely if you're not yet yourself complete?

If, as I now believe, true love may only happen once in a lifetime, there has to be a much deeper significant reason. True love is an extremely powerful phenomenon and we know nothing about it. Yet it may dominate most of our thinking time for most of our lives. I also believe that true love is always reciprocated; unrequited love does not exist. That's only intuition, but I know it to be true. Something so all-consuming can't be a game of chance.

What is it, and why?

CHAPTER 15

Is that right? There's no such thing as unrequited love? It's the only thing that makes sense. The alternative – that there is such a thing as unrequited love – *that* doesn't make sense.

So here I was. Not where I intended to be. Not the millionaire I promised myself. I've gone to great lengths to say that money doesn't matter, and now I drag myself back into the mire.

But has the fame and fortune now got a purpose, to help bring a more enlightened approach to the reasons for and effects of addiction… and love, the meaning of life? It will take money. How else would anybody listen?

I needed to buy cheaper. Taiwan wasn't cheap any more. The labour rates were becoming on par with America. The fixed bracket was still selling better than the slip-on bracket, much to my surprise, but it needed a cheap, efficient press to apply it.

Our big customer was Venture, up-market modern portrait photographers. Curl Up n' Stand suited their image, and had done since the beginning. We supplied them with photo frame backs in two sizes with two brackets fitted on each, and Venture ordered them by the thousand. It was labour-intensive because of the manual presses we were using, but Venture saw the value, so it worked. They'd take five, sometimes ten thousand at a time, and ten thousand legs went with them. Ten thousand people a month were being introduced to Curl Up n' Stand through Venture alone.

I came up with the idea of a very small press to apply the fixed brackets – something we could supply to small craft shops and framers – and, with help from Dave Broadhurst as usual, built a prototype. I disregarded the traditional ways of applying pressure manually. Instead, I used a cam. Cams are used in engineering, though not in this situation, but it worked. It could apply a lot of pressure with very little effort. It was small, neat and very powerful.

Our largest distributor was Lion Picture Framing Supplies in Birmingham. Martin Harrold was as enthusiastic as me when Curl Up n' Stand was first launched. His hobby was racing 2CVs, and he actually blazoned Curl Up n' Stand on the side of his racing car. Martin introduced me to Dev, an engineer in Kolkata, who could manufacture our press. He also introduced me to Mr Wang in China as a possible manufacturer of the Curl Up n' Stand hardware.

I sent sketches of our press to Dev in Kolkata and Curl Up n' Stand samples to Mr Wang in China. There was no doubt that Dev was the guy to make the press. He understood the principles instantly and responded with detailed drawings. The slight modification Dev made to the profile sent D off on one: she just added a few squiggles and turned the profile into the shape of a mouse. Dev thought the drawing was hilarious, and so Mighty Mouce was born. [15]

Mr Wang sent back his samples of Curl Up n' Stand – a good product. I placed a trial order with him and when he had production under way I went to visit his factory in China.

Wang met me at Pu Dong Airport Shanghai with one of his engineers and his secretary, Miss Fang, who could speak English when it suited her. Our first stop was the restaurant in the airport. I wasn't expecting that, and I wasn't really hungry, but apparently it's the thing to do. We all eat – in China everything revolves around eating. I took to Wang straight away, though all communication was via Miss Fang. I didn't know what food to order and as a result finished up with very little, but that was my fault.

Four hours' drive to Tonglu. As we drove through the outskirts of Shanghai, I started to get a slight idea of how big the place was. Enormous high-rise flats going on for ever. Tonglu was a busy town – shops, cars, people scurrying about. I don't know why I should seem surprised. I didn't expect it to be all paddy fields for goodness' sake.

The hotel was big, and clean, and tidy. It could have been an English hotel fifty years ago, though nobody spoke English, but it didn't matter: Wang was with me. He chatted away to reception, the conversation becoming a bit animated. I gathered I had to pay for the room in advance. But they wouldn't take a credit card. I had some Chinese money but whatever I had, it wasn't enough. In the end I understood that Wang was going to take me to the bank tomorrow, so the problem went away for the moment. How vulnerable you feel when you're taken way out of your comfort zone.

It was pretty late by the time all this was sorted out, and on top of the four hour drive, and the twelve hour flight, I was knackered. The plan was for Wang to pick me up at nine-thirty the following morning. I tried to memorise all I could about the reception so I could find my way back after a night's sleep.

In the morning the little chap behind the reception desk hurriedly pointed to his right, shouting something. My 'little boy lost' look must be internationally recognised. There was no need to hurry, it was just the way he was. When I found the room, it was big – about thirty tables, two or three in the middle that would seat about fifteen or twenty. I took a table by the window, trying to work out what happened next. The answer was nothing.

There were only about three or four tables occupied, and they were quite content with nothing. I had my trusty writing pad, as always. Whether I'm writing or not, it makes me look important or intelligent, and if anybody's watching I'll occasionally stare into space and then write something – but really I'm scanning the restaurant to see how, when or what people do to get something to eat. Then two diners got up, followed by two others, and walked to the end of the room, where there was a long table full of dishes of stuff. Guess that's the buffet.

OK, so you start from that end, miss that one out, have some of that one, and the one next to it, miss a couple more... How was I going to remember all that? I walked up purposefully to get my selection. There was a big bowl of some sort of milky liquid. Shall I have some of that? I got the big ladle and put some of the milky liquid in my bowl with some of the sludge from the bottom. I was half expecting somebody to say, 'You don't eat that. That's what we clean the floor with.' Then I found some boiled eggs, well that's easy enough; chickens must be the same no matter what planet you're on. There was loads of stuff, all different. None of it appeared to be moving. I got a few bits and pieces, and an Eccles cake. That'll do to finish. This is not a bit like proper Chinese food. But it was really tasty. Even the milky sludge was edible. I broke the Eccles cake in half. It was full of dead flies inside, just like home. But it wasn't sweet, it was savoury. I ate it.

Through the window was the garden. I finished my breakfast, and, duly fed and watered, I wandered out. The garden led to a wide path which ran along the edge of the river. In the UK you would have seen blonde ponytails with sweatbands jogging along the path, but here were people of all ages, mostly elderly, doing their T'ai Chi. Magical.

A short drive in Wang's car and we arrived at big steel gates at the entrance to the factory. A little man in the gatehouse acknowledged Wang, pressed a button and the gates opened. I watched Wang, expecting him to say, 'Thanks, Jimmy,' but nothing – Wang ignored him. Was all this his? Impressive.

It wasn't impressive like Mark was impressive, but it was certainly much more impressive than I had expected. Big, loads of room for expansion. I was given the guided tour. Curl Up n' Stand bumping off the presses, albeit primitive. One bend here, another bend over there. I got goose bumps as I watched my little invention taking shape.

It seemed we'd only been there an hour or so and it was time for lunch, apparently. Different people arrived, and ten of us went out for lunch. It wasn't lunch: it was a banquet. Enormous restaurant. Big plates of the most delicious-looking food kept coming, one after the other, everybody diving in. There was no effort made to show me what to do, but pretty soon I was diving in with the best of them. Glass of wine or a beer as well if you wanted it. Then after lunch, siesta time. I thought it was a siesta for my benefit; I wanted to work. But it wasn't for my benefit. Perhaps it was Wang's usual procedure. A bit more work at five o'clock, then out to another even bigger restaurant for an even bigger banquet. The food was superb. The form is you put a big lump of fish in your mouth, chopsticks of course, and you spit the bones out – on the floor, or on the tablecloth next to your plate. That might sound disgusting, but you don't put your fingers in your mouth to take the bones out – *that's* disgusting. Then Mrs Wang would stand, drink in hand, look at me and say 'Campai! Campai!' And, as I'd found out on my China trip with Rik Mansson, you have to drink your glass of wine. All of it... whether you've got a big lump of fish (unfilleted at that stage) in your mouth or not. My mind flashed to a story I'd heard in

Singapore – a bus accident in downtown Shanghai. All kinds of injured people staggered off the bus, sitting down on the pavement. No ambulances, nobody came to help. One by one they managed to get themselves mobile again, and left. No National Health here if I swallow a fish bone.

The next morning, full of confidence now, I knew the score with the breakfast, but it was too early. I wandered out into the garden and along the river bank. A proper river, with little fishing boats chugging along. The long path led to a wide flight of steps leading down into the water. Three or four fishing boats doing their housework. Men and women laughing as they got their day started. It was six-thirty in the morning, so probably it was their day finishing.

No stern-faced pinstripes here, heading for their nine-thirty meeting and another million ound takeover. Who's the richer?

Two or three women with big baskets of laundry appeared behind me and went down the steps into the water, skirts tucked up or not, and bashed their laundry into the water, sometimes on a stone, sometimes not. I sat on the steps, writing. One of the ladies came up the steps and looked over my shoulder to see what I was doing. She'd never seen anything so funny and started laughing. I had to laugh at her laughing, which made her laugh more. She was laughing at my silly writing, and I laughed because I couldn't help it.

Now time for breakfast. I came up with my own formula for 'have that… miss that… have that…' I knew how to get some tea, Chinese of course. You just look at the right person, wait, and she brings it. It's all very easy when you know how.

Wang picked me up and we went to the factory. There was something wrong. He started arguing with a couple of workers outside his office. It became heated, animated – something to do with the dogs. There were three or four dogs wandering round the yard. They weren't guard dogs, and didn't seem to be pets. Somewhere in between. I later found out from Miss Fang that a couple of dogs had gone missing the day before. Somebody's banquet I expect. Miss Fang could speak quite good English but to find out what was going on was like trying to extract teeth.

The same procedure followed for the day: a little bit of work, banquet, siesta, little bit more work, then of course it's time for a banquet.

I had thought the other restaurants were big, but not compared to this one. No menu – none of the restaurants seemed to have a menu. We went into a room that was about sixty feet long. Fish tanks all the way along one wall – every manner of fish swimming around, waiting to be chosen. On the floor big barrels of crabs or something, climbing over each other, and turtles climbing over each other. And other things, that mightn't have been climbing, but you wouldn't touch one. I am the guest of honour, and have to choose the fish. There was some flat fish that looked like plaice or Dover sole. I know plaice so I chose one of them. The waiter scooped one out with a big fishing net, carefully placed it in a brown paper bag, then just dropped it. I watched as it slapped down on to the hard floor. It was motionless for a moment, until it realised Oh-my-God-I'm-in-a-Bag, and started flapping round the floor still in the bag. I looked around to see if anybody else was as shocked as me, but nobody took any notice. I turned my attention to the big cold slab of fish behind me. I thought, I'll choose a dead one next. I pointed to one that must have been about thirty inches long. I gestured about ten inches. He chopped about ten inches off and gave it to us. Apparently I'd chosen the head.

During the meal I was eating some of the plaice. The women in the company looked amazed as I ate some of the flesh, peeling it back off the bone with my chopsticks, and then flipped the fish over to eat the flesh from the other side, leaving the bone still intact. They seemed quite impressed: they'd never thought of doing that before. They looked at each other as if to say, 'Look! The skeleton's still on the plate.' I appeared to have bypassed the chewing and spitting on the floor procedure. The men didn't notice, they were busy devouring the fish head. That's why I was given the fish head! And here was I thinking he was giving me the bit that we normally throw in the bin. Then of course, being the guest of honour, I was given the fish eye. It was still in its socket, about the size of a small golf ball – that was the socket size – the eye was floating around inside. I didn't know it was the socket until I put it in my mouth. It was a hard shell. I had to suck the eye out.

There was always busy chatter at the meal, but I hadn't a clue what anybody was talking about. Towards the end, Wang's secretary said, 'Mr Holmez. Mr Wang say you want go for Chinese Baff.' *Chinese Baff?* I glanced around. Mrs Wang didn't look too impressed. Miss Fang repeated it: 'Mr Wang say you want go for Chinese Baff?' I agreed, of course… when in Rome.

Outside, everybody got in cars and went off that way, and Wang and I got in his car and we went the other way. *What have I got into here?* To my delight, we arrived back at my hotel, but we went to a different entrance. Wang had a very intense exchange with the guy inside, animated as usual; any minute you think they're going to start fighting.

The chatter stopped. Wang followed the man, and I followed Wang, and we were led into some changing rooms with wooden benches and steel lockers. Wang started getting undressed, so I guessed I had to to do the same. Then he led me to another room with about half a dozen big wooden baths. A similar chat with another man; apparently the water wasn't right. Our two baths were drained and we got in. The man then started turning big brass wheels out of some ship's engine room, and water started gushing in at full belt through a two inch hole at the bottom. Wang shouted at the man because he knew how to say 'It's too fuckin' hot!' All I could do was leap up in the air. Eventually, the water reached our shoulders. Wang started splashing water over his arms. He looked at me, mouthing, 'Isn't this great fun!' without a sound coming out of his mouth. I nodded, wishing I was somewhere else. The man comes along and pours a packet of powder into the water, which turns the water into wallpaper paste. I'm now sitting in a tub of warm Polycell pretending this is the best fun I've ever had in my life.

The best fun was about to happen. Two young flopsies came in. Naked. Giggling a bit. One climbed into Wang's bath, and one climbed into mine. The bath was barely big enough for one, so it was quite cosy, the wallpaper paste splashing over the side.

It was time to get out. I climbed out first, and Flopsie showed me where the showers were to wash off the Polycell. As I came back, Wang was just getting out, but he looked unsteady, his head was rolling. *God, he's going to faint.* I grabbed hold of him to steady him, but I couldn't – he was slippery because of the Polycell. I held him tighter. Luckily he was slipping downwards – he could easily have flicked up to the ceiling like a bar of soap. The pair of us bollock-naked. I sat him on the side of the bath. He was out of it. He pointed to the changing room and tried to tell me to get dressed. His mouth was moving, but there was no sound coming out – as if speaking Chinese without the volume made it all understandable. Our clothes were in the lockers. There, on the benches, were two neat stacks of the girls' clothes. On top of one of the stacks was a Burberry scarf. I put the Burberry scarf on and walked back into the bath house. 'No, No!' he shouted, and gestured to me to get dressed. Me and my flopsie got dressed. I know why now – she led me through the hotel reception to a room already organised. Well, I've had some useless fucks before, but that's all the information you're getting.

I went back with my flopsie to try to find Wang. He was dressed by then, and had recovered a bit. He told me to take his flopsie now. I thought, 'Oh God.' She thought it was a good idea. But there's only so much you can do for Queen and Country. I pretended my leg was sore from an old riding accident, and was excused.

The next day Wang, Miss Fang and I were driving to an electro-plating factory. The cars slowed – there had been an accident just in front. As we passed a lorry the driver was slumped over the wheel. There were one or two people there, but that was all. I looked in horror at this, but we didn't stop. It was unimportant. A bit further down the road Wang had missed our turning and drove into a factory yard to turn round. I think he touched the bumper of another car, and an almighty row started. This was going to kick off, for sure – they were many, and we were two. I got my back against a fence and planned to take out the short fat one. The screaming and shouting lasted for a few minutes, then we got back in our car, the argument still raging, and drove off.

Our choice of banquet that evening was at a small restaurant. We were in the room upstairs because we were VIPs. The owner of the restaurant, I took her to be, dashed upstairs shouting something to Wang. He immediately sprang up and dashed down the stairs, quickly followed by his son. This was obviously a man thing, so I shoved my chair back and dashed after them without having a clue why. Another blazing row had kicked off in the street, between Wang and a man in some sort of uniform. Wang's son joined in. I gathered the man in uniform was a parking attendant and Wang had been given a ticket. That's got to start a street war, hasn't it. Across the other side of a very busy road, the back doors of a van opened up. Six more uniforms jumped out and dashed across the road to join in. Apparently traffic wardens go around mob-handed in this neck of the woods. This didn't deter Wang, though, he'd have taken them all on. Eventually it all subsided without a blow being thrown, and we went back to our chilli fish, which I'd found too hot before the affray, but was much milder now after the heat of battle.

I never did find out the full reason for the traffic warden incident. There was a lot of chat about this and other things during my visit, and especially at mealtimes, which I couldn't understand and were never explained. I'd asked Miss Fang a number of times if she could translate, but she wasn't very forthcoming. When I asked her to explain what had happened with the traffic wardens, she told me abruptly to, 'Stop talking.' I was absolutely furious. That was the only moment of impoliteness and disrespect I encountered during the whole trip, and I was powerless to do anything about it – nobody else would understand what she'd just said, and there was no way I could explain.

There was such a lot I wanted to know about the Chinese culture. Despite Wang's little sparks of anger, he's basically a kind, honest man, and I'm very pleased to have him as a partner.

Sex, on the other hand – I have my own ideas of what the ground rules are. I declined another offer of a Chinese Bath. I hope I didn't offend my host's hospitality. I just wanted my own adventure.

I came out of my hotel, crossed over the road, and headed for the nightlife. I made sure I was only carrying about fifty quid, just in case. There were little cathouses all over the place. The front would be a hairdressing salon. You could recognise them with the mauve neon. As I approached one, four or five young girls ran out, waving, smiling, 'Hello! Hello!' 'Not tonight, thank you,' I said. They started giggling hysterically, and scrambled over each other to get to the room at the back of the shop, then one by one heads popped round the doorway, one on top of the other as in a cartoon. I found a bar-type cafe. I pointed to a bottle of beer on the shelf behind the counter, and sat down at a table. I then realised I should have got the cold one out of the fridge. There was a group of about eight lads and girls. I became the subject of their amusement. I had taken a book with me. I think it was called 'Memoirs of a Geisha'. I'd bought the book in the UK. I now read on the back it had been banned in China. I had two or three beers, and I kept being given cups of Chinese tea. Nice gesture. I wandered off into the main hub of Sin City, had a couple more beers somewhere, then decided to wander back to the hotel before I forgot where I was. Like a coward I crossed over the road before I passed the hairdressing salon, and back to the hotel. The small hotel bar was about to close, but she kept it open for me. We had quite a long chat, of sorts. I pointed to a bottle of what looked like spirits for a taste. She gave me the bottle. Time for bed. She told me to take the bottle with me. I don't know whether I paid for it or not. I counted my money. My night of drunken debauchery had cost me thirty-one pence.

A pattern had developed: each morning I'd rise and be on the riverbank at six o'clock in the morning, by now doing my version of T'ai Chi along with all my other Comrades of the Republic.

After my five days, Wang drove me back to the airport. Between banquets we'd got to understand something of each other's needs, and Wang and I had bonded – there was no doubt about that – and that was really why I'd gone. He suggested I come to live in China and he'd find me a Chinese wife then I could make my own Chinese baff arrangements.

I couldn't help wondering how big the prostitute business was. Wang's wife definitely knew what he had in mind. So did his secretary.

In the New York telephone book there are about twenty pages of escorts and call girls with pretty graphic illustrations. If you're ever in New York and you want to see the sights, forget about Times Square or the Empire State Building – if you're suffering from jet lag just take a walk about four o'clock in the morning. What you see will leave you open-mouthed. Girls and guys, and transvestites in full make up and all their glory, skipping and hopping from one hotel to another. I've never seen them advertised in the British yellow pages, though. I mean, they're nasty people aren't they. Sex is a nasty thing. Only practised by nasty people in nasty situations.

CHAPTER 16

A few weeks later I went to see Dev in Kolkata. When I handed in my tickets and case at the airport, she looked at the destination and said, 'What have you done to deserve that?' I was to find out what she meant.

At the airport I was met by Dev, my host for the next few days, a gentleman of the highest order. Kolkata was every bit the image you get from old movies. Once I left the airport I wasn't to see another white man again until I was back in the airport. As that, I stuck out like a sore thumb. I was a curiosity.

Dev and I travelled around a lot by train, meeting different engineers. While we waited on the platform for the next train a crowd would gather round to stare at this curious individual. Quite bizarre.

Of an evening I'd wander down to an hotel nearby that had a bigger bar. The barman smiled as he poured my beer, 'I saw you today on the station platform.'

Oh dear. 'Did I look the odd one out?' I'd been wearing my favourite shorts and Jesus sandals – not the done thing in Kolkata. Everybody else seemed to wear tunics or pantaloons two inches off the floor. I wasn't sure if I was being a bit disrespectful, but apparently not.

'No, you looked great.'

The atmosphere in Kolkata was hot and sticky – made hotter and stickier by the squalour and rubbish piled up in the streets. I suppose that's why I went round in my shorts and sandals.

The barman tried to involve me in a pool game that was going on at the other side of the bar. I declined. I wanted to let the thoughts of the day file themselves neatly in my head somewhere, and I'm not very good at pool anyway.

I remembered the railway station. I was bemused at everybody's being bemused at me. Dev and I were sitting on a long bench on the platform. I became conscious of the person next to me staring, and when I looked round there were four young men, all sitting on a bench, all staring, the next one leaning out a bit further than the one before so as to get a better view. Like a perfectly fanned pack of playing cards. They didn't look away when I noticed their gaze. I nudged Dev so he could see too. We got up and walked along the platform, and they followed like a line of ducklings. I didn't find them intrusive or invasive; they were just intensely curious. They certainly weren't begging for money, either. I didn't come across any of that at all, despite the abject poverty. Squalour was everywhere. Waste food, vegetables, anything – littered the streets. No public toilets, or none that I found – men would just urinate against the wall in full view.

The district of Kolkata I was staying in was called Maiden, near the cricket ground. I tried to explain to Dev the meaning of the word 'maiden'. I embarrassed him; one doesn't talk about that.

All around Kolkata there is evidence of the British influence. On Dumdum Road were decaying engineering workshops that at one time had been busy making munitions. They were proud to show me examples of the enormous shells they had made. I remember the word 'dumdum' made familiar in my young childhood as the name of a bullet or bomb in the war. No longer needed. It seemed Kolkata was surplus to requirements.

We were invited to lunch by one engineering company. A special meal was laid on. Only the men ate, though. The women were the servants. It was an enormous spread. They ate with their fingers, so of course I did the same. Well, not quite the same. I was given a huge pile of food. It tasted great but, despite my best efforts, I was making little impression. I am a slow eater at the best of times, and this was not the best of times. Everybody else appeared to have finished, and I looked as though I hadn't started. I pushed it around my plate to make it look less. Then I noticed I was the source of much amusement to the women standing in the background. I kept asking for more water, hoping it would help – hoping it was bottled. It arrived in a bottle, but I'm not sure how it got there. I realised to my huge embarrassment that my glass was caked in orange mud – that translucent orange you get from

Indian curry. Everybody else's glass was clean, and it dawned on me: you eat with one hand and drink the water with the other. How stupid. I've been in some embarrassing situations before, and this was right up there with the best. The food was good, and it would have been OK if I had been able to help myself and just take small portions as I required, as I had done in China. But that wasn't the way they did it here. They eventually accepted the fact that I wasn't going to be able to finish it, and as the meal concluded the offending plate and glass were removed from my sight, if not my memory.

Why were the women not allowed to eat with us? Were they second-class citizens? Men do seem to have a high opinion of themselves worldwide. They would argue that they're doing all the work and bringing all the money in. I don't know.

We continued our tour of the factory. I needed a loo. All the water was finding its way through. I asked Dev and he passed the request down the line. I was shown an alleyway down the side of the building. I walked down it expecting to find a toilet. No sign of one. As I approached the corner I could smell it. There was a grid in the corner. Was that it? Smelled like it. There was nowhere else. Did I have to pee in the corner of this alleyway? I was dying to go. I couldn't wait. I expected at any second to hear a voice boom out: 'Hey! What are you doing?' If I had have done, I couldn't have stopped. Please God, let this be the right place. Nobody shouted.

Dev's apartment was clean and tidy, albeit modest. Dev had known about Curl Up n' Stand for a couple of years. He couldn't believe that the inventor was actually in his home. It was a very humbling moment. His apartment was on the top of a three storey building. Down below I could see the makeshift shacks where cattle and people lived. Old ladies collected handfuls of cow dung which they clapped on to the sides of the buildings in little mounds. I asked Dev why they were doing that, and then I saw. The cow dung that had been put on the previous day was now dry. The same old ladies came and flicked it off the wall, collected it into sacks and sold it as fuel.

There must have been a particular religious ceremony when Dev took me to the temple. There were crowds inside the temple and all around. You had to go barefoot. All the shoes were piled everywhere outside. The temple was a very splendid and grand building, though I couldn't see a great deal because of the crowds. At the side of the temple a wide flight of steps led down to the Ganges, where the people bathed in some kind of purification rite. I went down the steps too and paddled in the Ganges. It was filthy, but I had to do it. I kept thinking my shoes were not going to be there when I got back. Five hundred pounds' worth of blue Louis Vuitton. That would have fed everybody for a year. They were still there.

In the morning we were at another engineers. As we wandered round, I found I was becoming the centre of attraction again. There was Dev, the boss of the engineering company, and about three or four engineers hanging on my every word. I'm no engineer; they all knew more about the problems that needed solving and how to go about it, but I'm centre stage. I decided to talk about the project from the point of view of people who would use Mighty Mouce.

'This little machine is going to be operated by women.' I assumed that half my audience couldn't speak English, and adopted the international sign for women by gesturing the hour-glass shape with my hands. That brought a broad grin to everybody's face. That was all I needed. 'The lever must be easy to use, otherwise they'll get...' I gestured again, 'One big breast and one small one.' 'Also the machine must be able to be used by left-handed as well as right,' switching the big breast in gesture to the left side. I don't know how much was achieved as far as the project went, but everybody saw it as funny. Humour is the same worldwide.

The main production of one factory we visited was spring clips (circlips) of all shapes and sizes. I saw, as if for the first time, how powerful spring steel could be. It wasn't why we had visited the factory, but now it was all I could think about.

The idea of spring steel occupied the whole of the flight back to the UK. I could see how a spring clip of some sort could clip over a round bar to form a one-piece stand. I think it must take the most intense thought to actually compose it in your mind but, as as had often happened in the past, the long-haul flight did it again.

Dev organised the manufacturing of Mighty Mouce. He made a superb job of it. We ordered the first forty presses, knowing it would turn into hundreds, if not thousands. Every frame maker around the world would want one.

I showed the press to Nico. 'It's a good idea,' he said, 'but you could do with it applying something else, not just the fixed bracket.' It would also fit D-rings, and in that moment it appeared I had invented something else.

Generally, two D-rings are attached to the back of a frame with screws, and a cord strung between them to hang the picture. I got a pencil and sketched. Instead of two holes to receive the screws, there could be two arrowheads punched in the metal to stick out of the back at ninety degrees. The tips of the arrowhead wings curved slightly.

Dev made samples of the D-ring. They needed a bit of tweaking like all prototypes, but they were good enough to illustrate the potential. [16]

I pushed one of them into the back of a picture frame moulding, then tried to pull it out to test the strength. But it wouldn't come out without damaging the frame. It was a very secure fix.

I was puzzled why it gripped so tightly, then I realised the arrowheads had twisted slightly as they were pushed in making it difficult, or impossible, for them to come out the way they went in. It was the little curved wingtips of the arrowheads that had caused it. Of course it was. I'd designed the Dragonstail with the curved arrow tips without realising why until now.

It would be very easy to say I designed it that way in order to create that action, and I'm sure it's what I would have said at the time – but that's not true. It came as a complete surprise to me. I designed it, and of course that's what would happen, but I didn't tell *me*. The mind can be pretty complex.

I showed the idea of Dragonstail to David Huntingford at W P Thompson. David showed little interest in the idea until I said, 'The arrowhead wingtips are twisted.' His attention immediately switched to a hundred percent: 'Say that again.' He leant back in his chair and said, 'It never ceases to amaze me how the inventor's mind works. Let me know when you want me to work on it.' It never ceases to amaze me, either, how the inventor's mind works. I appeared to have invented a fixing.

Martin Harrold of Lion wasn't impressed, though. I was convinced he would see the potential, especially as they were produced by his contact in India. In his catalogue he's got pages of D-rings. But I was wrong again. He said, 'Our customers like putting screws in.' Well I've heard some stupid comments to throw cold water on a good idea before, but that's got to be one of the best. Small screws are a pain to put in. I thought anybody would see that, and I'm offering an alternative where they can just be pushed in under pressure without the need for screws at all.

I took the Dragonstail D-ring to show Venture, who were using thousands and thousands of D-rings on a weekly basis. They questioned the strength of the Dragonstail and the ability to carry the weight of their heaviest frames. That was a reasonable comment, so I tested the strength by taking one of their heavier frames. I fitted it with six pieces of glass to add substantial weight, well above its expected use, and hung the frame for thirty days. It never budged. But I've not been able to convince them.

It's very frustrating. Of course it's going to work. The principle is sound, and the cost savings are enormous. Less labour and no screws.

Perhaps the world will see it one day.

Patent costs were soaring. As the patent for Curl Up n' Stand was maturing, we had to decide in what countries in Europe we wished to have cover. I thought all of them. No chance. The notion that the inventor of a good idea sat back and enjoyed the royalties was the stuff of fiction. It was just constant fire-fighting. All the prototyping costs, all the development costs, the production costs, marketing costs – and now rocketing patent costs.

When you file a patent you then have a certain period of time from the filing date to extend it pretty well worldwide. To get cover in a foreign country you have to pay for translation, and it could be fifteen or twenty pages. Also the individual patent laws of that country have to be considered, and then you pay renewal fees year by year, country by country. Each year those fees rack up. The assumption is you're making the money. The initial filing fees per country can be £2000 or more, then you've got translation fees and foreign solicitors' charges as well as your own patent lawyers; multiply that by at least ten or fifteen countries and we started to get an indication of the enormous pit we were diving into. The fees are absolutely prohibitive, unless you're ICI or Ford. It was D who found this out herself by looking at the German

Patent Office website. Thompsons knew from the beginning my wish to extend the patent worldwide; why hadn't they warned me about this? They knew these fees would become totally prohibitive to any small company or individual, and yet they let me go deeper and deeper, until I found out for myself. I began to have doubts about the ethics of Thompsons.

I wasn't sure how much time or money to spend on patenting Dragonstail, but the new idea for a one-piece picture frame support which we'd decided to name StandEasle definitely needed patenting, especially now I could see how the idea could work with spring steel.

I wrote to Robin Bartle at Thompsons and told him we needed to file another patent application, specifically asking him to keep a close watch on the charges as finances were running tight. I told him that I'd like D to do the official drawings to keep costs down. He was reluctant; he wanted to use their own artist, but I was adamant. Patent drawings are very basic profiles illustrating the function rather than aesthetics. We submitted our patent application for StandEasle along with five drawings.

Robin Bartle wrote back saying the Patent Office had rejected two of the drawings but their artist would be able to re-draw them and the charge would be about £400. A bill for £400 from Thompsons was nothing – their invoices often ran into thousands – but this one stuck out like a sore thumb. If two of the drawings were wrong D could re-do them. Whatever it needed, it couldn't be more than an hour's work. What had happened to his watchful eye on the charges?

I argued that D could alter the drawings, and asked what was required. He wouldn't say. When I insisted he said if D did the drawings they would not be able to underwrite it. They were implying for reasons best known to themselves that if their artist didn't do this very simple drawing, at some stage down the line a patent could be rejected and it would be our own stupid fault. I still insisted and they sent me a copy of the drawings that needed adjusting. In the envelope with their letter was the reply they had received from the Patent Office detailing the problem. On one drawing some feint lines needed to be firmed up, and a second drawing needed to be reduced in size slightly so that the prescribed margins were clear. The size of the drawing could have been reduced on a photocopier by an office junior and the feint lines easily hardened – and they wanted to charge me four hundred pounds. I couldn't help wondering how many other times similar things had happened. They were adamant that their charges were perfectly justified. What – to have straight lines hardened, and an image to be reduced in size slightly – and then to suggest that if we did it ourselves they wouldn't be responsible for the consequences?

I had always considered the advice I received, from David Huntingford in particular, to be of the highest order and I expected his integrity to run through the firm and be reflected in its fees. I now had reasons to doubt that was the case.

We would normally get an invoice from Thompsons along the general lines of 'in attending to...' and 'preparing documents as per your instructions...' We had no way of knowing how the bill was arrived at and accepted it as being perfectly justified, even though the amount sometimes appeared a bit steep. But now, on one small invoice, because they'd inadvertently sent me the note they'd received from the Patent Office, I was able to see exactly what we were being charged for. From then on, every time I looked at an invoice now I was left with a bad taste, so I decided to report what I considered overcharging to the Patent Lawyers' Association. I knew that would rattle Thompsons, but what they were trying to charge me was wrong. The Association said first of all I should exhaust the complaints procedure at Thompsons.

I wrote an official letter of complaint to Thompsons, and had a reply from Doug McCall, senior partner, who went to great lengths to defend Thompsons' ethics and justify their charges. But I was far from satisfied and went ahead with my complaint to the Patent Lawyers' Association. They went through the motions of an investigation, and responded with so much waffle. Then I noticed on their letterhead that one of the principals on the board of the Association was Doug McCall himself.

Doug McCall, senior partner of Thompsons, was also on the board of the Patent Lawyers' Association. He was going to be investigating himself – how was that going to give us an unbiased adjudication?

Making a serious charge against a firm of lawyers is heavy stuff, and Thompsons' adamant rebuttal made me re-examine my accusations. Was I missing something? After all, they are a respected, long-standing firm of patent attorneys. Doug McCall made an appointment to meet with me at my office in North Wales to try to reach an amicable solution. That must have hurt – people like him don't drive to see anybody; they demand anybodies come to see them. In preparation for that meeting and to make sure I was on solid ground, I went over all the correspondence we'd received regarding the drawings and saw again the note from the Patent Office clearly stating very minor requirements. That was a stupid mistake by Thompsons – they had surely never intended to send me the letter from the Patent Office. As far as I could see, that letter damned them completely.

Doug McCall arrived, full of venom. Didn't like him – he was a bully. I could see the meeting could turn volatile, so I took him away from the office and we went to the Bryn Howel, by way of neutral ground. I showed him the Patent Office note. He was stunned. He did his best to cover up, but the rug had gone from under him. My accusations were now undeniable and all his holier-than-thou arguments were crushed. I demanded the £400 bill be quoshed, a few thousand pounds in compensation – I can't remember how much exactly – and a written apology.

He found that a very bitter pill to swallow but had no alternative; the bill was duly cancelled and we received a written apology. Giving the bully a bloody nose was compensation enough.

The air must have been blue when he got back to his office in Liverpool. That note from the Patent Office had been for their eyes only. Sending it to me had given me all the evidence I needed. Strange… lawyers in particular don't make fundamental mistakes like that, and I couldn't help wondering what made me notice Doug McCall's name on the Association's letterheading. I would normally just scan a letter like that to pick up the pertinent bit, and that would be it. Life does seem to have a habit of helping you when you really need it.

Now the only person I trusted at Thompsons was David Huntingford. I insisted if I was going to continue using them as patent lawyers everything would have to be handled by David. They agreed.

CHAPTER 17

Of a weekend D and I would occasionally take ourselves away from the maddening world and the stupidity of it all. Erddig Hall is a beautiful house and only five or ten miles away from where we lived. I was fascinated by how people got through their day in the relatively recent past. On another occasion we went to Warwick Castle but, having seen Erddig, I didn't feel that could be bettered and was content to wander round the gardens while D did the full tour. The magnificent castles of days gone by are now just tourist attractions.

Old King Cole made love on the dole
For times were 'ard at the palace.
But he had his evil way three times a day
With Betty, Doris and Alice.

They worked, so I'm told, counting the gold
For a monarch from a different story.
Cole thought to himself, 'If I acquire that wealth
I'll return to my former glory.'

He concocted a ploy with a colleague called Roy
And invited the girls to a party.
'If I may be so bold, why not bring all the gold?
And I'll bring the ale, to be hearty.'

They should have said 'Cole – get knotted'
But the girls were besotted
'Cause the King had a way with the wenches.

So did as he told
And brought all the gold.
He said, 'Put it down there on the benches.'

Now cheats never prosper,
'Cause a tailor from Gloucester
With a pension for twenty-four carat,
Did the same in reverse
and relieved the King's purse.

Now Coley's as sick as a parrot.

Old King Cole saw money as the solution to everything, but lost it again as fast as he got it.

I decided to take myself off to Lanzarote for a week to try and come up with some direction and, as my old Dad said, the 'point of it all'. A week on my own, regain some focus.

I needed to re-write 'Do you remember '92... So do I', after it had been stolen with my briefcase on the train... and it was driving me mad.

The place I stayed in was good enough, cheap. But I needed a haircut – fancy coming away on holiday without having had a haircut. Every time I settled down to write or meditate all I could think of was I needed a haircut. I found a hairdressing salon, of sorts. It wasn't a barbers but they all do men's hair in places like this. I smiled at the woman I took to be the hairdresser. She didn't smile back, it was more of a glare, and pointed to a chair then stood behind me and without a word started hacking away. 'Not much,' I stuttered. Waste of time. Bits of hair flew off this way and that. I tried to engage her in conversation. It only made her more angry. I prayed for somebody to come in. Somebody did: another hairdresser. They didn't speak. The new one went into the back room for a few moments then came out, totally ignoring the vampire behind me who was about to claim her next victim. Eventually I plucked up courage and said, 'Oh, that's much better,' and stood up. I pulled some money out of my pocket. She took all of it and I made for the door, glad to escape with my life. I looked back towards the shop to see if it was still there, and wondered whether I should have seen from the outside what was waiting for me within, or whether I should tell somebody. I didn't. I went back to the blank page and wrote, 'Be careful what you wish for'.

In re-writing ''92' it was impossible to create flow of the first draft. Writing is very solitary and can be very frustrating at times, with occasional bits of inspiration… only to read it back the next day and realise it's rubbish and you start again… and again.

It wasn't just the writing to sort out, it was the invention. That's where the money had to be. Why wasn't Curl Up n' Stand selling better? Perhaps it's the D-ring idea that will be successful? And now the biggest one of all, the one-piece picture frame support, StandEasle.

Going away to get shut of distractions only goes so far; wherever you go, you take your head with you. Meditation helps to clear the head, but it's not always easy. I don't know how it works. Trying to clear your mind of all thought takes a lot of concentration. I suppose it's a kind of brain-washing, but it does help to keep things in perspective and clear out the trivia.

The bars in Lanzarote are OK, as far as they go, but they're all touristy – full of English or Germans. I got a taxi, and asked him if he knew a decent bar away from this rubbish. 'Yes,' he said, 'I'll take you where I go.' I was hoping to find a Spanish bar where the old guys are sat outside leaning on their sticks, putting the world to right. They all know more about the world than me.

We went down the side streets into the suburbs and stopped in a quiet street, nice houses. I was intrigued. He pointed to one. I went in, he drove off. It was a bar, well decked-out, though quiet. *Must be just because I'm early.* I bought a drink and chatted to the lady behind the bar, then the girls came in – about eight of them – and sat in a semi-circle facing me and the bar. I'm to choose one, apparently. I'd walked into a cathouse. I tried to laugh it off and let them know politely that I wasn't interested. They got the message, and one by one they left. It wasn't that I wasn't interested. What is it they say? Men think of sex once every ten seconds. I'd have thought it was more often than that. I must see it differently from everybody else. I didn't see a bunch of girls being paraded out like that as sexy in the slightest. I hadn't told the taxi driver I was looking for a girl of any sort. He just assumed. I'd have happily chatted to the girl behind the bar for a while, but it wasn't that kind of place. It was a cathouse – I don't like the word 'cathouse', but 'brothel' is worse, it always sounds degrading to me, both to the girls and the men who go there. But whatever you call it, that's what it was. I don't know what the neighbours made of it, in the middle of quiet suburban streets. I can't stand the word 'snog', either. It's strange, the way some words just don't treat the subject with respect.

It's the total lack of subtlety I don't understand. Sex should intrigue, excite, surprise – not be so blatant. Am I the only one who can see that? Without that, you may as well stay at home and do it yourself.

I've always known I see the world differently. It seems I see women differently as well. The girl behind the bar told me of another place, more what I was after. I believed her, and went. It was a livelier bar, and seemed OK until I realised it was the same. I was chatting to a girl at the bar when another girl came up and said in a strong German accent, 'She vould like you to buy her a trink, or…' I took one look at the aggression on the face of Frau, and decided on 'or', and left. At least this one was in a part of the town that I vaguely knew. I made my way back to the Gary Linneker bars.

The last time I'd come to the Canaries was on holiday with Mike (my neighbour at Fron Haul) and Martin – that was to Fuerte Ventura, not far away. Mike, who can rival me in the outrageous stakes, bought an Andy Pandy suit – or that's what we called it – in one of those surf shops. It had knee-length shorts with a bib and brace front, multi-coloured, tight-fitting, and stupid. He bought it for going to the gym, so he said.

We were half way through the two weeks. It would be about nine o'clock in the evening, quite a lot of people around. Martin left the bar and came back a few minutes later wearing Mike's Andy Pandy suit and nothing else. Everybody thought it was hilarious. There was a middle-aged couple who ran a pub in Yorkshire – he had a go at the Andy Pandy suit, and eventually I had to have my turn.

There were two German girls, one very pretty, the other butch – a bruiser. Once or twice I'd caught the eye of the pretty one, smiled, and got a smile back. Butch didn't like that and gave me such an evil scowl. They were in the bar.

I finished my stint, changed, came back into the bar. I pointed at Butch and said, 'You're next.' I went back to join the lads, carrying the suit, and nothing was said for a few minutes. Then I got up, went over to the two girls, threw the suit at Butch and in my best Gestapo voice shouted:

'You vill go and try on ze Komfy Klozing!'

To my astonishment, she cowered. 'No! No! Please No!'

'You vill go in zere,' pointing to the toilet, 'and put on ze Komfy Klozing!'

'No! No! No, I can't!'

I stamped on the floor. 'Achtung! Achtung! You *vill* put on ze Klozing!'

'I can't. I'm not wearing anything underneath.' She opened her top a bit to show she wasn't wearing a bra. I don't know anything about bra sizes, but if she had been wearing a bra it would have had to be two buckets.

Now the whole bar was jumping up and cheering at the cabaret. 'You vill take off ze right blouzen, zen ze left blouzen, and down viz ze pantaloons...' I mimed what she had to do.

She grabbed the suit and disappeared to the loo. I sat down and started talking to Pretty. She said, 'I wouldn't do it – unless you give me five hundred Euros.' There was something about the way she said it that made me realise the two of them were on the game.

Butch came back wearing the 'comfy clothing', bib and brace stretched to the limit. The evening descended into a riot. The bar was busy. I don't know how many Germans were there. I was in danger of starting World War III. I know there was a group from Holland who joined in the affray.

The next night one of the waitresses told me that three of them nearly got sacked. The manager wasn't happy at all. 'Oh God, I've upset him.' But it wasn't me. They'd tried to persuade the manager to go and put on the comfy clothing and he didn't like it.

I never saw Pretty and Butch again.

The week served its purpose, though. The screenplay was much better and, above all, so was the new invention, StandEasle. I could see how it was going to work now. D enjoyed the break too – away from the manic lifestyle I seem to carry with me.

Whether D and I were destined to live together for ever was another thing. Recently the house next door to hers had come on the market. She said why didn't I buy that.

A propos of nothing, a poem I wrote a couple of years ago…

Life
I think I've reached that time of life
You know, when I should swap the wife.
Don't get me wrong, she's good to me
But for heaven's sake she's forty-three.
She'll understand, I'm sure she will.
I'll tell her tonight after The Bill.
Funny thing, she's not come home,
Hasn't called, hasn't phoned.
I went next door to see if he knows where.
Funny thing… He's not there.

After the IVA we'd switched banks to NatWest, and had been with them for some time by now. At first my manager had been Wendy – a rare commodity, a lady – but she was good, in a lot of ways like John. But she did the unthinkable and got pregnant and eventually left. My account was transferred to an idiot, an imbecile. I'm not going to waste time talking about him, or his area manager, but they know who they are. The sort of men who get a little power and become fascist dictators.

I missed the intelligent counsel I'd had with John Pitchford of Barclays. I wrote to the chairman of Barclays and told him what high regard I had for John. I must have given them a good yarn, because I had a very positive response. As a result I moved back to Barclays. John had gone much higher up the ladder so he couldn't directly manage my account, but he introduced me to Wyn Read, local business manager. I got on well with Wyn. He wasn't John, but very few people were.

Now I knew how to make StandEasle in steel. It would be elegant, cool and sexy. The design had to be right, more so than Curl Up n' Stand, and I'd spent a lot of time on that. I started looking in shops at household items, at cars, for inspiration. Eventually it was a teaspoon in

Habitat. I hoped Rudolf Mark in Austria would manufacture it, but he was losing interest. Even though he could see how StandEasle would work, the numbers just hadn't happened as I'd promised. Maybe I overplayed the possibilities with IKEA, I don't know. They stopped replying to phone calls and emails. I felt really hurt – I thought we had a good relationship there, but they just disappeared. He knew of my involvement with China and the obviously lower labour rates there. But China's there – it can't be ignored. Mark's excellence in engineering would have balanced that. It's terrible when you don't know the reason – you have to concoct something so you can try and put it to bed, and you invariably get it wrong. But I never got the chance to find out. Nico said, 'How're you getting on with Mark?' I told him. It seems like I've had a enthusiastic supporters over the years, and it's as though they take me as far as they can then leave me at the edge of the forest and disappear, and I'm left to go on alone again. Nico said, 'That won't happen to us, will it?'

Now at last I'm not alone
Because I've got my mobile phone.
It looks so smart, all black and chrome.
I love my little mobile phone.

It's really bril and great you see
Cos all my friends can contact me
And when I'm busy doing things
I make sure I can hear it ring.

Though I haven't heard it ring today.
I guess my friends must be away.
I'm surprised that no-one's tried at all.
Check to see – no, no missed calls.

Surely someone wants to talk to me?
Must be a faulty battery.

I got Wang to make the prototype of StandEasle; it was superb. All those years I'd spent in designing, developing, redesigning, and producing Curl Up n' Stand, knowing it was far better than any other photo frame support – and now I'd beaten it, that was scary. What if it had been somebody else? All the work, all the years, I'd put in to developing Curl Up n' Stand. I'd invested my life, and D had gone with me every step of the way, I'd realised all my assets – house gone, car gone, Japanese garden gone, and not regretted for one moment because of the sure-fire knowledge that sooner or later the world would see Curl Up n' Stand for what it is – and I did it. But now here's a new one, completely different, and ten times better. How on earth had that happened?

StandEasle had turned into something elegant and beautiful and, above all, effectively one piece. It needed a better name. 'StandEasle' sounded too downmarket.

I sometimes booked a hotel at the weekend, to think, meditate, write and give us both some space.

In the Chester Chronicle there were about eight ads for escorts, massage parlours. 'Busty blonde available for discerning gent.' I picked one that sounded better than the rest. The receptionist, Maureen, I think it was, didn't sound very *femme fatale*-ish. She sounded a bit mumsie – not what I expected. She described the girls in detail – the colour of their hair, their shape, the size of their tits.

Why do people talk like that? I'm not interested in the colour of her hair or the size of her tits. You fuck with the mind. I want intelligent, liberated, style. 'You're talking about Ava,' she said. A shiver ran down my spine. I knew exactly who I was talking about, but how did she know?

It's ten to nine. Why am I so nervous? I've been with escorts before. Why is this so different? But it was, and that was it. That was the first time I met her.

Singapore's motto is Kiasu – 'refuse to fail'. I adopted Kiasu Easel for the name of the new stand. It was perfect – much better than StandEasle. I felt a new focus, a new determination. [17 and 18]

D and I both needed space of our own. It was stupid paying for hotels. I discovered a superb apartment on the outskirts of Chester in the grounds of Old Hall Country Club. A couple of rooms in a beautiful old house that was the administration for a pretty posh leisure club – gym, swimming pool, beauty spa. Perfect. D came along to have a look, just to make sure I wasn't kidding myself. She could see the magic.

There were just three apartments in the house: mine, a much smaller one, and the third was Sue's, who owned the place. It was superb. Behind the house next to the orchard was a big outdoor swimming pool. I took the cover off in the morning, a perfect way to start the day.

Ava had an apartment in Chester. Sometimes she came to mine, sometimes I went to hers.

> *I wandered lonely, cock in hand*
> *Searching for the promised land.*
> *Kissing pussy, licking cunt,*
> *On and onward in my hunt.*
> *But will I ever find my goal*
> *And be swallowed by the Holy hole.*
> *I scream to the skies in silent rage*
> *When will my quest come of age.*
> *But every cloud has a silver liner.*
> *I've fallen for a Swede's vagina.*
> *This pretty cunt did smile at me*
> *And asked me in to have some tea.*
> *She looked across just like a friend.*
> *I became consumed, and that's the end.*

She snatched the poem out of my hand, and put it in her bag.

We amended the patent application for StandEasle to include all the bits that had now become Kiasu. Then, as usual, the Patent Office searched for prior art. During the searches that had been carried out for Curl Up n' Stand, I'd seen every possible picture frame support filed in the last two hundred years, so I knew that was academic.

But I was wrong. The search by the Patent Office came up with prior art. I stared at it in disbelief – a patent that had been filed in 1943.

It was exactly the same as Kiasu. I could have drawn it myself. [19]

I was in D's kitchen at the time, staring at the drawing. My head was about to explode. The similarity was uncanny. Why had I never seen this before? I thought I knew every picture frame support that had ever been considered since Adam was a lad. And there it was, staring at me: a small bracket clipped on to the back of a frame, and a leg with a horizontal bar that clicked in to the bracket and rotated into position to support the frame. Exactly the same as Kiasu.

I had to find a way to claim original thought, or I couldn't patent it. But I couldn't – it was the same as mine. I don't know why it didn't get on the market, because it works – I know it works. Now, all I'd be doing would be showing the rest of the world how to make it, without any commercial rights whatsoever.

For some reason the 1943 model didn't get on the market, but that didn't alter the fact that it was in the public domain. The patent protection from 1943 had now lapsed so I could still make Kiasu, but so could anybody else. It just meant Kiasu couldn't be patented.

It must have been week later when I noticed a very slight difference. The spring steel grip on the 1943 invention wrapped round the bar clockwise, and my invention wrapped round the bar anti-clockwise. That tiny difference was major. There was greater friction grip on the bar when the leg was rotated against the spring than with it. The effect was that on the 1943 invention the friction grip was weaker in the working position, and on my invention it was stronger in the working position. I was sure that difference would be enough to give my claim originality. Why the original inventor hadn't perceived it, I don't know, but that's the way it was.

David Huntingford hadn't spotted it, but why should he? When I explained the difference between the two logics I could tell by the tone of his voice that he could see the importance of the difference.

The implications of Kiasu – effectively one piece – took away the doubts raised by Fetco and Intercraft, and the concerns raised by IKEA on how to educate shop customers on how Curl Up n' Stand works. The Kiasu Easel was obvious.

A guy called Doug owned the escort agency, but Ava ran it. Escorts, or prostitutes, are considered to be the lowest of the low, linked to drug addiction and crime. I dare say there are some. '*They'll steal your money*' – I've never come across that, though many other so-called honourable people have tried. If the roles were switched and men were the prostitutes, they would consider themselves studs, and so would the rest of society. 'The oldest profession in the world', and the most disrespected. Was it a woman who said, 'Sex is too good to give away'? And not only is it too good to give away, but that men should pay and women get the money. I would have thought that was pretty clever.

The girls are no different from any group of girls you'd meet anywhere. In a lot of ways, much more interesting because they've got the balls to do what they do. Some smart, intelligent, well-dressed. Some brassy, overpainted. Some are single mums trying to make ends meet, or disillusioned housewives.

> *She'll awake with a smile in her eyes.*
> *She'll try but her eyes can't disguise*
> *Last night she was home very late.*
> *Been a bad girl, been a naughty girl,*
> *It was great.*
> *It's a long time since she'd heard her heart sing*
> *But what pain will the ecstasy bring?*
> *Is she guilty? Will you know?*
> *Will you find out? Does it show?*
> *It's a long time since he really cared.*
> *They lived together but nothing was shared.*
> *Will remorse and regret fuel her sorrow?*
> *Or will she forget this and meet him tomorrow?*
> *He said she was the best of the best*
> *Great body, great legs, great breasts.*
> *She showers the body he laid*
> *then smiles as she remembers… he paid.*

Life in Old Hall was luxury – a beautiful apartment, a gym I could use whenever I wanted. Occasionally Sue would organise a ball, big marquee in the grounds, dancing, champagne, beautiful people… and me.

The Kiasu Easel stock came in. The quality was terrible. The spring clip was too weak or too brittle and would break, the finish was poor. I couldn't send them back – they were from China and paid for in advance. Every single one had to be checked by hand, and half were thrown away. Painful. I told Wang, of course, and he assured me they'd get it right – next time. I'd ordered too many. I should have just ordered a few thousand, but I didn't, I ordered a lot. Greedy.

We were doing well with Curl Up n' Stand through our European distributors, so we added Kiasu to that market, being the easiest way to get it started. A good distributor in the States had to be equal to all our European distributors in one go, then we'd be up and running. The biggest distributor in the States was UMS.

I arranged a meeting with Tom Moscato of UMS in Syossett, near New York. If I could convince them to stock our products and market them to the small framers throughout the States alongside their other framing sundries, the trip would be paid for after the first two or three orders. That was the plan.

I stayed in the Chelsea Hotel in New York – still my favourite – and went to a taxi office to arrange a car for the next day. I told them, 'I'd like a car tomorrow for Syossett, wait an hour and bring me back.' I went through to the back office while they worked out where Syossett was. There were twenty or thirty guys and girls manning phones. A voice boomed out from the back: 'There's no such place.' I boomed back: 'Oh yes there is, and I want the best driver and the best car you've got. This is the best job you're getting out of here today.' The whole room fell silent, whispering, 'Who the hell spoke to Joe like that?'

I got the best car and the best driver: Lennie, a big man, dark skinned, dark well-tailored suit. Took his jacket off while he was driving; crisp white shirt. He looked more like a diamond merchant than a taxi driver. We got on brilliantly, as if we'd been two childhood friends brought back together after forty years.

We arrived at UMS and as I got out of the car, Lennie said, 'Knock 'em dead, Ken!' In the short time I'd known him, I knew he meant that, just as he would have done if we'd been kids going into battle.

UMS placed a trial order. The Atlanta trade show was just two weeks away, and I agreed we'd go and promote our products on their stand.

Outside the offices Lennie had parked next to one of those enormous

SUVs, about twice the size of a Range Rover. Stickers in the back read: 'Boycott France', 'UN out', 'The Riflemens' Association'. The number plate said it was Peter Ackerman's – the owner of the company who had joined us at the meeting. He seems to have a few issues.

CHAPTER 18

Ava wanted out of the industry. I told her we'd open a club in Liverpool. A 1920's – 30's style club with live music and dancing of the era. She said it would have to be sexy. Of course. What should we call it?

'4Play,' she said.

'I was thinking Aphrodisiac.'

'Are you going to be a millionaire?'

I was confused. 'Of course,' I said. I could see the club: small tables, two-seaters, four at the most, table cloths, intimate, stylish, elegant, straight out of a old Hollywood film set.

I told her dirty stories, which drove her wild. I thought everybody did that, but apparently not. She told me I should write them down and sell them, any woman would love them.

I started to write a story, but I wrote it so fast it was easy. To be more correct, it wrote itself. I called it 'Je t'aime'. It was only when I'd finished it that I realised the story was about us. I wept and wept uncontrollably. Not out of sadness but out of some sort of overwhelming joy. I went to bed and in the morning I saw the couch six inches deep in spent tissues and wept again. Last night, she and I had fallen in love. I knew she must have felt the same thing.

I gave Ava the story. A couple of days later she called me and said, 'I can't see you any more.'

'Why?'

'The story's about me. You're falling in love with me.'

'So are you.'

The story had been a sort of catalyst; it had just accelerated what I knew with absolute certainty.

'You said we'll buy a house and live in Paris.'

'Well why not?'
'I can't speak French.'
'You can learn.'
It was becoming impossible to separate fantasy from fiction.
'We need to see each other,' I said, 'so I can explain.'
'I can't. You'll cry. You're emotional.'
'I won't.'
'I will,' she said.

Kind of crazy, kind of smart
Then something went and broke my heart.
I thought that I was in control.
Own goal.

Was it something stupid that I said
That landed twisted in her head?
Never meant, just misread.
Whatever, empty bed.

A careless phrase floats on the wind.
I tried but I can not rescind.
All my hopes and dreams are binned.
The sinner sinned.

Is that me walking in the rain?
Did I watch my soul float down the drain?
If he is me, then what's my name?
Am I insane?

Staring at the silent phone
Terrified of the twighlight zone.
There to reap what he has sown.
He slept alone.

I knew what I felt was right. I became more determined, angry, she didn't believe me, she didn't let me explain. Didn't she trust me? Honour is everything.

Some people liken me to Don Quixote. I liken myself to Don Quixote. I've never read the book, but there's something about the character. I had a framed Picasso print at Fron Haul of Don Quixote for many years. I needed to slay the giants and then I could claim the fair maid. The giants were the greed, corruption and arrogance of a society that was blocking my way. But there was something bigger – a force, unseen, without logic, I didn't understand. Had I just met my Dulcinea too soon?

Isn't it strange, or so it seems,
The way we live inside our dreams?
The way we drift and fantasize
On a life we'd like to realize?
In all the things I want to do
There is always, always you.
So many things are left unsaid
Wandering in and out my head.

CHAPTER 19

There were major cock-ups on the flight to Atlanta. Our plane couldn't fly out of Heathrow, and we were bussed to Gatwick. The trade show with UMS was starting the next day and we should have been in Atlanta by seven o'clock in the evening – but instead we were in New York at midnight with no flight out to Atlanta until the morning. No hotel to be had for love nor money. We slept, or rather didn't, in JFK, and didn't arrive in Atlanta until ten o'clock the following morning and the show had already started. No suitcases, wearing the same clothes for the past twenty-four hours, no sleep.

My son Jake, D and I got to the show, unwashed, unchanged and knackered – but the show must go on.

The American framers loved Kiasu. That kept us going for the rest of the day, fed on adrenaline. Our suitcases had arrived at the hotel by the time we got back.

We were at the show bright and early the following morning. Jake and I wandered around, inadvertently walking past the Craft stand. Four or five of the Craft boys busying about, getting their day ready. A voice shouted out, 'Ken! Hiya Ken!' I turned round, to see Tony Mendes of Intercraft with Ron Morin.

Tony rushed over and shook my hand warmly: 'Great to see you! We need to talk. Where can I find you?'

I glanced at Ron. He was furious. He'd have been spitting flames if he could. 'We're on the UMS stand, just over there.'

'OK,' he said, 'I'll be finished here shortly.'

If at that moment a bolt of lightening had come down and taken me out, I'd have died happy.

We waited for Tony Mendes to turn up, but he didn't. Ron Morin did, though. I came back to our stand at one point to find Ron staring at the Kiasu Easel. He saw me and scuttled away, just three yards, turned and stared at the easel again, almost open-mouthed. Now, you don't do that. If you see something in the enemy's camp that gives you cause for concern you don't stand open-mouthed gawping at it, you scurry back to your own camp and send a subordinate over to pinch one. You don't show your hand like he did. What he saw frightened the living daylights out of him.

The next day D and I were walking down one of the aisles on our way to get a coffee. D spotted some small writing on the top of one of the stands that read 'Burnes Group'. How she noticed that, God knows. There was nothing else to say it was the Burnes Group.

I stopped and asked the representative, 'Are you the Burnes Group?'

'Yes,' he said, 'Are you Ken Holmes?'

'Yes.'

'Tony Mendes said we've got to speak to you, but he's had to go.'

'Oh, right. OK, could you hang on a minute, I've got to show you something.'

D and I hurried back to our stand, grabbed a couple of Kiasu samples and returned to the Burnes Group.

As soon as I started to show them the magic of Kiasu, Ron Morin burst on to the stand like the SAS, saw me and skidded to halt. He grabbed one of their brochures and flicked through it, trying to look casual, but he was flicking through it at such a rate it had the opposite effect. He was straining his ears to try and hear what I was saying – if he was a cartoon character his neck would have stretched three feet. D went and stood between Ron and me and started edging back quietly, pushing him out of earshot. The Burnes reps were well impressed with my little demo, totally unaware of the guerilla tactics that were going on behind them. They gave me new contacts to follow up after the show: 'This is the head of sales of the Burnes Group – he may be more helpful to you than Tony.' We left. Ron Morin, still animated, leapt past us on to the stand and started jabbering away to the two reps. I guess he'd be telling them I was the most evil person on the planet, and responsible for everything that was wrong in the world.

It had taken no more than five minutes for us to get the samples and return to Burnes' stand. In that time Ron Morin had somehow found out I had ventured on to hallowed ground and must be dealt with swiftly… you've got to laugh.

We saw Atlanta in a much better light this time, staying in a different part of town – perhaps that was it. Any black guys we met, mostly taxi drivers, were friendly, full of fun, no confrontations in the streets. We came away with a glowing introduction to the Burnes Group – and a decent order from UMS though we didn't get to know their people much. I'd tried to talk to Peter Ackerman a few times. I suggested we put a joint ad in Decor Magazine, the big picture framing publication in the States. I knew the editor and persuaded Peter to come with me to meet her, but he seemed edgy, uncomfortable. Probably me – I do make people behave oddly sometimes. But it was only an ad, to promote Kiasu with UMS – surely that would have been of benefit to both of us. He told D and I he had a gun, something to do with a staff problem. Why does that mean you need a gun – and why did he tell us about it?

There was nearly another mini-incident at that show. D and I eventually got to sit down for our cup of coffee, at a cafe area in open space a little way from the exhibitors' stands. In the distance I saw the unmistakable outline of Joe Eichert bumbling towards us. As his familiar smirk got within speaking distance, 'I recognised that voice,' he said.

I just said, 'Fuck off, Joe.'

He'd probably seen the Kiasu Easel and wanted to be friends again. Did he think I'd forgotten he was just a liar and a thief? Amazing. He got the message, just turned round and walked back the way he came.

How did D see that small 'Burnes Group' sign at the show?

It was actually on the side of the stand, not meant to be a promotion in any way, just a small ID that the organisers put on all the stands. In amongst hundreds of stands, all crammed with glitzy framing stuff and flashy signs, she noticed that one. We didn't expect the Burnes Group to have a stand there, otherwise I'd have asked Tony where it was. What the Burnes Group was exhibiting was bizarre in itself: a framed picture that had a built-in spirit level set into the moulding, so that when you hung the picture on a wall… you could ensure it was level, I suppose. I'm finding it too ridiculous to talk about. The cost of producing it must have been ridiculous – the whole thing was ridiculous.

We shipped the order out to UMS, then had to spend months chasing payment for it. Customers we'd met in Atlanta phoned us in the UK asking where could they get hold of the Kiasu Easel; they'd tried UMS, who apparently said they'd never heard of it.

I eventually spoke to Peter Ackerman and told him I could do with the bill being paid. He just said, 'I'm not paying it.' No reason, no explanation; he just thought he was being clever. I don't think he intended not to pay. He was just announcing his superiority. After all, he did have a gun.

He paid us eventually but I didn't see there was any point in doing further business with the man. All the effort we'd gone to, getting ourselves and the stock over to the States – the show had been a great success, and sales would have only got better – all wasted.

I followed up the sales director of Burnes Group a number of times. I sent him samples, and he certainly received them, but he kept making excuses. He was nervous, hesitant – he didn't seem to know what he wanted to do. Had somebody got at him? Of course they had – it was Ron Morin, though neither of them would ever admit it.

Ava was in my head all day and every day. I just had to be patient. I'd kept in touch with what she was up to through Andrea, one of the agency girls, a good friend. She was now living with Doug, the guy who ran the agency, or pretended to. Didn't bother me in the slightest – he was never any competition.

I could tell by the far away look in her eyes
She would never have settled for him.
She was born to fly like a bird in the skies
I could tell by the far away look in her eyes
She would never be caged within.
In the morning she'd rise
And I could tell by the far away look in her eyes
Her journey's about to begin.
But who has arrived at the land of the free
And I think of the far away look in my eyes.
Please let it be me.

I sent an application to get on the BBC Dragons' Den TV programme. Within two or three days I had a phone call from the BBC. Talk about a pressure interview. I was interrogated for three quarters of an hour by a girl who knew exactly how to do it. I thought I put my case forward well. She wouldn't have interrogated me for so long if I'd been wasting her time. Serious funds from a serious entrepreneur would be brilliant; not just the money – another brain to bounce ideas off.

But I never heard back from them. I managed to track down the researcher I'd spoken to at the BBC and found my application had been denied. So much for coming over well in the interview. The reason for rejection was that we'd already 'done it' and didn't need the Dragons. If we'd already done it, how come I was so broke? I can't watch Dragons' Den any more. I feel cynical about the whole programme – the majority of applicants have no idea about marketing, cash flow, distribution. If they went through the same pressure interview as me, why were they on the programme? Unless they were just brought in to be humiliated. I don't think the programme is genuinely interested in helping people at all – just in making sensational TV and themselves look clever.

I replayed over and over again the last thing she had said, trying to make sense of it. I know I'd sent her a copy of 'Je t'aime'. 'The story's about me,' she'd said. She was right, even though the similarities were pretty sketchy.

The applications for the Fine Art Trade Guild Awards had been closed for a month or so. I wasn't going to bother this time, but then I saw their stand at a trade show and showed them the Kiasu Easel. 'Put an application in quick,' they said, 'You might just be in time.' We were short-listed for the Innovation of the Year Award.

One of the other finalists was Martin Harrold of Lion. I sent him an email saying, 'I see we're going head to head on the Innovation Award – best of luck.' He replied, 'We're pretty sanguine about it.' What does sanguine mean? D tried to explain, and I looked it up in the dictionary. He thinks he's won, the arrogant bastard.

The award ceremony was a black tie affair at a big hotel in Coventry. I hate those things, but you've got to do stuff like that, I suppose.

Charles Downing sent D and me an invitation to join his table, which was kind of him, and it saved us a lot of money. Charles was one of the big boys at the NEC these days. I don't know why he sent us the tickets, but it was good of him to think of us. We arrived to find hundreds of penguins walking around all over the place. *This is not for me.* At the drinks reception before the dinner, we went over to say hello to Martin and his wife. They looked at bit subdued. None of the usual, 'What's the mad inventor come up with this time?'

I started to become very uneasy. Something was seriously bothering me. I didn't want to be there. I couldn't talk to anybody. I said to D, 'I need to go.' She got very angry. 'No,' she said, 'I've just driven for three hours to get here!' I began to believe I was on some sort of crazy mission, nothing at all to do with a stupid bit of bent wire; I was being given some colossal responsibility. I began to think I wasn't just like Don Quixote – I *was* Don Quixote. I was the character Cervantes had seen four hundred years ago. As crazy as this may seem, that's what I felt with absolute certainty. I also felt that Cervantes got the story wrong – or perhaps he was just misunderstood.

I felt as though my head was exploding. What if Don Quixote wasn't mad, wasn't stupid? Somehow, I was to put the story right.

The feeling subsided slightly and I decided to stay.

I said to Charles, 'Please excuse me if I seem a bit out of it this evening – there's something bothering me, and it's far bigger than this.' Charles knew me and understood.

An hour or so later I was perfectly relaxed, flirting with the girl from Trinidad on reception. There were ten or twelve round our table. I was sitting next to Ros, one of Charles' sales people – very funny, very entertaining. D was chatting away to someone else. An enjoyable evening. Then the dreaded award presentations. I knew we had won the Innovation of the Year – we were the best by miles. I said to D, 'I don't want to go and collect the award. You go and get it.' She refused. I wasn't sure what I would say, but D wouldn't go. It was going to be the usual scenario – read out the list of finalists, dramatic pause, then the winner's name's announced, everybody claps, and the unsuspecting winner walks up to the stage pretending to be embarrassed and humble. What was I going to say? The best I could think of would be 'Thanks,' and get off the stage as quickly as possible. I just hoped I wouldn't say what I thought about a few people, and the industry in general. This wasn't the time or the place.

When they announced the winner of the Innovation Award, it was Lion Picture Framing Supplies… I stood up and clapped louder than anybody else in the room. I was so relieved not to have to make a speech – not that I would normally shy away from the limelight. As the evening wound on, it started to dawn on me: Martin should never have won it. The Award was rigged.

It was coming up to eleven o'clock. Trinidad was knocking off, so I went to say *au revoir*. One of the young hotel stewards was trying to roll up the red carpet. He was having difficulty because penguins kept walking on it. I knelt down next to him, grabbed hold of a corner of the carpet, and said, 'We'll wait till the biggest prats get on it, and we'll yank it.' Muscles in my arms built up like Popeye. He fell over laughing; he couldn't do anything. A few minutes later, I saw the steward in the corner of reception, leaning on the carpet he'd just rolled up. He saw me, smiled broadly, and did a thumbs up. I can see myself, looking at the carpet, then across to the clusters of penguins milling about, and back to the carpet again. I remember thinking, *'What's he going to do?'* Meaning me.

I walked over to the steward and said to him, 'I'm going to give you a laugh.' I picked up the carpet and put it on my shoulder. It must have been thirty inches in diameter, like a big roll of stair carpet. I marched off into the clusters of penguins, and burst into each group in turn shouting, 'I didn't come here to carry this fucking carpet around all night, you know!' and, 'Isn't it time somebody else carried this fucking carpet?'

There was a look of horror on the face of the outgoing Chairman of the Guild as he got the red carpet treatment. A voice behind me said, 'Ken!' It was Paula. Paula's one of the few good guys. I just dumped the carpet in the middle of the melee and went to talk to Paula.

On the Monday morning I sent three emails. One to Charles Downing that said, 'Thank you very much for your kind hospitality, though most of the people there were prats,' or something to that effect. One to the Editor of the Fine Art Trade Guild magazine that said, 'The Innovation Award was rigged. Bet you haven't got the balls to publish that either. And you'll have to live with that for a long time'. (He had previously refused to publish a poem.) And one to Martin Harrold that just said, 'You knew before.'

His winning entry was a square metal plate for fixing to the back of a canvas painting to act as a hanger. It wasn't worthy of an entry in the first place.

I got a reply from Charles Downing that said, 'It was great to see you and D again. I can't comment about anybody else.' No reply from the Fine Art Trade Guild.

I was out of the office when Martin Harrold replied. Two full pages of protestations, demanding my retraction by the end of the day or I would be reported to the Fine Art Trade Guild, and on, and on, and on. He obviously didn't know I'd already told the Fine Art Trade Guild what I thought of them.

I came back to the office. D was upset – well, concerned – who wouldn't be? A two-page letter from our biggest distributor. Why was it two pages? All I'd said was 'You knew before'. I sent an email to Martin Harrold saying, 'Don't send me any more emails. If you do send any more they won't be read. I have instructed D to delete them unopened. If you wish to communicate any further do so in private and confidential mail.' And I waited for the litigation.

Through all the years and all the battles Simon Wallwork stayed with me. 'It's going to happen, Simon,' I said, 'You know that, don't you?' He nodded. 'Because I'm determined, aren't I?' He nodded again. I'd arranged to meet him at the roadside services on the A55. He knew sooner or later we'd pin down one of the big boys and then he'd have a proper job to do. 'Speaking of proper jobs, I might have one for you anyway.' I told him about the Fine Art Trade Guild and the reaction from Martin Harrold. He laughed. I think he already knew I was Don Quixote. 'Keep me posted,' he said, and we both went on our way.

A few days later I received a letter from the Fine Art Trade Guild. 'This is it,' I thought, expecting litigation. It wasn't. It was a note saying, 'Thank you for applying for the Innovation Award, and congratulations on becoming a finalist. We know what hard word goes into this,' and a certificate. I tore it into tiny pieces, wrote 'Joke' over the Fine Art Trade Guild logo, and posted it back in the envelope it had arrived in.

No more emails from Lion. No solicitors' letters. I've accused them of corruption, and they've not countered it.

At the very least I've lost my best distributor at a time when I need every penny I can get. But that didn't happen either. How many people at the dinner knew the award was rigged, and thought it was clever – or knew it was wrong but didn't have the balls to do anything about it?

A pathetic Fine Art Trade Guild Innovation Award, and they've got to cheat. They just can't play fair.

Now the dust had settled, if dust ever does, I'm still Don Quixote and I have to set the record straight. Three things: Don Quixote wasn't mad, quite the opposite. He may have confused the odd windmill but he knew evil had to be dealt with. His sidekick wouldn't have been a simpleton; he would have chosen someone with an ability to go much nearer to understanding his aspirations. Probably a women because of his respect for the fair sex. And he would win the heart of the beautiful Dulcinea. All his battles would not have been in vain.

I wasn't getting anywhere with the sales director at Burnes, and decided to go over his head, to the CEO. He hadn't held that position very long, but he gave me a good hearing and was very interested in the Kiasu Easel, though he had never seen it. It had obviously never left the sales director's desk. I sent samples to him, and followed up in a few days. He said, 'It looks good. Cute idea. I'll speak to a few people – could you call me back in about a month.'

I called him back in about a month, and he'd left the company. His secretary survived, Donna Robinson. She told me who his successor was, but he'd need a little time to settle in and find out where the coffee was – and then I'd have to start again from scratch.

I'd still kept the possibilities open with IKEA, though. I sent Kiasu samples over to Patrik Wir.

He said, 'It looks very interesting. What's that word at the top of the drawing?'

'Kiasu. It's our company motto.'

'What does that mean?'

'It means cannot fail,' I told him.

He chuckled. 'I'll pass it on to Product Development, and I'll know more than them, won't I?'

I hadn't really thought about it being our company motto until then – that just came out.

A month later, I followed up Ulrika Walgren in Product Development. No welcome voice there: she was very curt, abrupt. With a 'piss-off-I-don't-want-to-talk-to-you' tone in her voice, she said they were developing a stand in a particular IKEA way.

When I got my breath back, my first reaction was they were going to steal my idea. *How am I goind to find that out – and what can I do to stop them?* I couldn't phone Patrick back, I couldn't do anything.

As one door opens another one slams shut.

It all seemed to confirm what I'd known for some time – I was being tested, as if I was part of some almighty plan in this fiasco we call life. Too many weird things going on. All my hopes built up then crashed to the ground. And I fall for it every time.

Yet through it all I felt blessed, privileged, immensely fortunate to be me. But I'm not special – what if we're all being tested? It's the only thing that seems to make sense.

I love that woman so much every bit of me aches. Where's the sense in that? I hadn't spoken to her for some time. I got all the news from Andrea, which was really a bit sly, a bit deceitful, I was feeling guilty – certainly not very honourable.

I phoned her. She shouted at me.

'Don't sulk because we had a row. We've got to keep talking.'

'I wasn't sulking. I was annoyed with you because you didn't trust me.'

'Oh.'

The following night I had a phone call from Andrea. Ava had just called her. 'She's thrilled that you're back.'

'What did she say?'

'She told me to keep my weekend clear.'

I woke up with the word 'verbane' stuck in my mind. Nothing else, just that. I asked D what it meant. She said there was no such word.

'There must be.'

'No,' she said, 'Verbatim?'

'No, that's not it.' The word wouldn't go away.

'There's Urbane,' she said.

'Oh, that could be it. What does that mean?'

'From urban, I suppose.'

We looked up urbane – 'adjective (especially of a man) suave, courteous and refined'. *That'll do. That's me. Don't care if nobody else agrees. Goes with the Don Quixote bit.*

I designed some business cards. *Don Quixote – urbane statesman.* D designed them with me, actually, though she's refusing to admit it now. We spent ages on the 'Q', for instance. That's one of those letters you do spend ages on in Design School.

I don't care in the slightest if anybody thinks this Don Quixote thing is mad. I think all the greed, corruption and dishonesty that's rife in society is far more insane.

I'd missed Ava so much. At least we were speaking again.

Isn't it strange or so it seems
The way we live inside our dreams.
Six months, now probably more,
Since we fucked upon the bedroom floor.

The longer that we're kept apart
The stronger you are within my heart.
Fulfilling dreams dreamt as a boy
But then again I'm still a boy.

How much joy can one behold
As this little boy grows old.
Surely all this can't be fair.
Am I receiving someone else's share?

Now three score years and one have passed
I see the purpose, the point, at last.
I've been given all this wealth
Not to keep boxed high up on the shelf.

For the moon and the stars and the sky above
Are yours Miss Jurgensson, with love.

We were invited to the Bologna show by our Italian distributor, Giorgio Rinaldin. To be strictly truthful, we asked him if we could join him. It meant we got to exhibit at the show without all the fuss and expense of our own stand. Giorgio – a good man, honest, a gentleman.

Close to Rinaldin's stand was Bienfang, an American company, promoting their foam board products. Foam board isn't widely used in the UK, but it sells by the ton in the States and a lot of it is used for picture frame backing board. The Kiasu and Curl Up n' Stand easels were developed with foam board in mind. The prongs on the brackets can pierce the core of the foam board and stand it up. I went over to the Bienfang stand to show them the Kiasu, and just happened to pick the moment when Conni, the Vice-President, was there. When I demonstrated it, her face lit up with excitement, 'Can we try it on this? Can we try it on that?' The Kiasu worked perfectly on everything.

'We've got to have it exclusive,' she said.

'But I'm already talking to some very big companies. Photo frame manufacturers are very interested.'

She looked confused. 'But photo frames already have a stand,' she said, but then realised photo frames weren't her competition so it wasn't relevant. 'Oh, you can do what you like with them.'

Conni's sales director was standing next to us, and said, 'Have you any idea how much foam board we sell?'

I didn't really, but I liked the way he was talking.

Conni repeated, 'We must have exclusive.' What she meant was exclusive to the foam board industry.

'I want a yacht,' I said, following the superlatives that were flying around.

The sales director said, 'You give us exclusive – you get a jet!'

I sent samples over to Conni to be on her desk when she got back to the States. She responded immediately, introducing me to Joe Wetli at a company called Elmer's.

Elmer's owned Bienfang, along with a lot of other companies. Their main product was glue. Glue doesn't sound much – photo frames don't sound much – but multiply by the numbers sold by WalMart and Dollar Store, etc., and it's colossal.

Intercraft were selling a million frames a week to WalMart alone. One cent royalty on that equals… a hell of a lot. And now Conni is talking about them again, with a different product. Whether I was driven by the lust for wealth or power, or both, doesn't matter… they're the sort of numbers.

Within two months I was on my way to Columbus, Ohio – Elmer's head office.

'Elmer' was the name of the cow from whose hooves the first glue was made. Elmer's Glue became a household name in the States for sticky stuff. Alongside the sticky stuff Elmers sold tons of foam board, and craft and stationery stuff.

Columbus seemed typical of a certain kind of America. Hardly anyone walking, all the shops looked the same, the bars looked the same, the restaurants looked the same, everybody ate the same food. Clean, tidy, and soulless. Thank God for places like the Chelsea to keep hope alive.

Joe wasn't particularly excited about the Kiasu Easel. Some people see it instantly, and Joe was one of the guys who just didn't. Still, the momentum fired up by Conni carried it along, and we agreed the basis of a starter pack to promote the Kiasu Easel alongside the foam board.

I phoned Ava to tell her I was in Columbus, Ohio, and was about to slay the biggest giant ever, expecting it to impress. It didn't. It never did.

'Bring me back a fridge magnet,' she said.

'I am Don Quixote. Give me a challenge more worthy.'

'OK, then. Bring me back the Fire of Liberty.'

Fuck, that's a biggie – 'I'll need till Tuesday on that.'

'OK.'

How am I going to bring back the Fire of Liberty? Pondering that got me back to the UK.

I was introduced to Max to finalise the Elmers deal. He had some query over the prices. 'Can't we buy it cheaper?' he said. I sent him an email:

'Whenever anybody asks about price I think of the ballpoint pen. You get a little brass cone about 10 mm long, drill a hole down the centre of it, and put a little ball bearing in that hole, and attach a polythene tube at the opposite end to the ball bearing. You fill that tube with ink – sticky ink so it won't flow out the wrong end. Then you can scratch the little brass cone along the paper and the ball bearing dispenses a line of ink. Then you put that tube inside a plastic sleeve so the little cone peeps out of the end. And you put a plastic cap on the end where the tip is, so it won't mess up your pocket. You put a metal clip on the cap so it will clip on to your pocket. And you put a spring inside the plastic tube so the little brass cone can click in and out as required. And, here's the really clever bit – you make it for a penny.'

One of Elmer's core products was a ball-point pen. He understood the analogy, and we agreed prices.

'I am the Fire of Liberty,' I told her when I got back to the UK.

'I can't put you on my fridge.'

My mind flitted back to the Fine Art Trade Guild awards. I knew I was what Cervantes saw four hundred years ago. I told Ava. She said, 'You're definitely Don Quixote.' She knew the book very well; she'd studied it at university.

'Cervantes went mad,' she said.

'I'm not surprised he went mad. He got it wrong. Don Quixote wasn't stupid. Eccentric probably, but intelligent. And his sidekick would probably be a woman, not a man, and not stupid either. And Dulcinea, the most beautiful woman in the world, had to be intelligent.'

'She didn't exist,' Ava said.

That scared me a bit.

I had to write the story and put the record straight, so Cervantes can rest in peace.

I gave her one of my Don Quixote business cards.

'It's your telephone number,' she said, as she put it in her purse.

She knew my number from memory? The next day I told her I was her knight, a fearless and ferocious fighter.

'Nice,' she said. Not in a sarcastic or patronising way, perhaps a little disbelieving.

I had a meeting with Simon Wallwork to start the heads of agreement with Elmer's. I must have been working with Simon for about six years by then. He'd see me any time I asked him and I'd never had a bill. A while ago I'd asked him how the bill was doing. He said, 'It was six thousand last time I looked.' 'Are you getting any pressure from upstairs?' 'No,' he said, 'Don't worry about it.' I told Simon everything, including Ava and Don Quixote. He agreed the best looking woman in the world had to be intelligent. I asked him if he would be best man. 'Yes,' he said.

I needed to firm up the American patent. Elmer's wouldn't have been interested without that. It wasn't a question now of whether I was going to become a millionaire; it was just a matter of time. Elmers would do that in one.

Patent coverage for Kiasu in the States was crucial for the deal with Elmer's, and that was going to cost a few thousand. I applied to Barclays for a loan to cover this. I'd been working with Wyn Read for some time by now. He knew there wasn't any collateral to back up the loan, and said a personal guarantee would cover that.

I'd forgotten that John Pitchford had said Barclays would never lend again – but then so had John, otherwise he wouldn't have invited me back. After all, the only reason you change banks is to improve your financial structure. In any case, that had been a few years ago and a lot had happened since.

'What's this for?' D asked. She was reconciling the current account.
'I don't know.'
'Did you agree something when you were with Wyn?'
There was an amount of £15.80 coming out of the current account. She showed me the figures, 'And look, the same thing came out last month.'
'I never agreed anything like that.'
D checked with Barclays and was told it was a direct debit in favour of a company called Clearly Business.
She phoned Clearly Business and was told that it was for our software package. D asked them, 'What software package? We haven't had any software package, so please cancel the direct debit.' She was told curtly, 'You can't just cancel it. You've signed a contract.'
'You've signed a contract,' D told me angrily, transferring on to me some of the aggression she'd just received.

I tried to rack my brains. I'd had two meetings with Wyn Read. Had I signed something? No, I couldn't have done, could I?

'No, I didn't!' I was getting angry now.

I asked D to get a copy of the agreement from Clearly Business. Two documents arrived.

'Look, she said, 'You have signed it'.

'That's not my signature.'

'You must have done it in a rush or something.'

'It's not a bit like my signature.'

It wasn't anything like my signature, but D refused to believe it – the alternative was unthinkable. What I was telling her was the signature on that paper was a forgery. We both fell silent. I wrote my signature on the pad – the signature she'd seen a thousand times before. The signatures on the two documents from Clearly Business were forgeries.

D could see it of course. It was not a bit like mine… and these are Barclays Bank documents. One of them was a binding contract and the other was a bank mandate authorising Clearly Business to take £15.80 out of the account every month.

I phoned Wyn and left a message on his voicemail asking if he could explain. He got back to me, 'Don't worry, Ken, it'll save you money.'

'How can it save me money if it's costing fifteen pounds a month, and what's it for anyway?'

'It's for a software package to help you do your cashflow.'

A software package. I wouldn't know a software package from a cushion. 'Well we don't need it, Wyn, whatever it is. In any case, we never got anything.'

'I'll drop it round in a couple of days,' he said.

I left it at that for the time being.

Two or three weeks went by and we still hadn't received the software. I had no idea what a 'software package' was – D looked after all the computer stuff. It eventually arrived.

'That's no good,' D said.

'Why?'

Because it'll foul up our own system. It says we'll have to uninstall our own bookkeeping system to put this on, and what we have is ten times better.'

What Wyn had tried to sell us was a baby version of the professional software we already had – OK if you're just opening a corner shop. What we were using was a professional system of book-keeping. If we had tried to install Wyn's version we would have been going back to kindergarten. D remembered Wyn had tried to sell us the same package six months earlier.

He'd tried to sell us the same thing six months ago, and we'd refused it then – and now he was trying to dump the same thing on us again?

Right now, I had to swallow my anger. The loan was the priority. The Kiasu Easel was going to have a major impact worldwide. That was my focus, and the financial structure to go with it.

Whenever I have applied for a loan, or gone into any important meeting for that matter, I have always played the scenario over and over again in my head – starting with the answer 'Yes', and working backwards countering every stumbling block along the way that might lead to a negative result. The Kiasu Easel was the biggest 'yes' I could possibly have imagined. The implications and potential with Elmer's were obvious – and so was the need for the American patent.

The loan was to ensure we could cover the cost Thompsons were likely to charge for complying with the particular requirements of American patent law.

Doing cash flow projections and profit and loss forecasts had become second nature. With Geoff's help, doing twelve month, three year, five year projections was easy. But in reality they're worth little more than the paper they're written on. Either you see the project with the value it has, or you don't.

Wyn and I had a blazing row on the best procedure. Nothing to do with Clearly Business, but it was so bad it made our continuing relationship untenable. Nevertheless, the loan application went in and Paul Jones became our manager at Barclays.

I was talking to Max on the phone every two or three days. He was easy to talk with. We both understood each other's requirements. Elmers had a number of manufacturers of various kinds in China, but it made sense for us to carry on with the manufacturing of Kiasu at Wang's factory, certainly for the time being. Wang would then despatch it to one of Elmer's factories in China for final packaging – blister packs, that sort of thing. Then it would be shipped back to the States for distribution throughout all the major outlets. All very exciting. First order to be placed in January, two months away.

> *It wasn't philosophy,*
> *More frontal lobotomy,*
> *But somehow she got to me during the storm.*

> *The wind it was freezing.*
> *I couldn't stop sneezing,*
> *But something from Sweden was keeping me warm.*

> *I found it amusing,*
> *Though rather confusing,*
> *A blonde-haired illusion I kind of recall.*

> *Appeared in front of me,*
> *Trying to comfort me,*
> *Then Humpety-Dumpety fell off the wall.*

> *But something attracted me,*
> *Disturbed and distracted me,*
> *Pleasantly knackered me,*
> *quite slim and quite tall.*

> *Rearranged my ability,*
> *Completely, deliberately.*
> *Felt totally pigletty when she came to call.*

'Who else do you know from Sweden?'

'It's you, you stupid woman. But I didn't write it, I couldn't have done. That's good. I just happened to be holding the pen at the time. I'm not that clever, but I'm clever enough to know that.' Same as Kiasu – I didn't do that either, unless there's a lot more to me than I'm aware of. I don't even know what frontal lobotomy is.

I put the telly on – an Ingmar Bergman film. I don't like him really, too heavy – I was just going to watch it because he was Swedish. Two men in the back of a car discussing frontal lobotomy. I know what it means now.

She sent me a text inviting me to a party. I knew she had these parties from time to time; it was an agency thing. I never went, they were of no interest to me, she knew that, but this was one way to break the ice.

> *I've just had a text from a one-time friend.*
> *She fucked me till I fell in love then drove me round the bend.*
> *An invitation to a kind of party.*
> *Slim, nice smile, perhaps a little tarty.*
> *I dreamed of her the other night.*
> *We were on a plane, a midnight flight.*
> *When we landed in the aerodrome*
> *We were going to see her folks back home.*
> *I got on well with Ma and Pa,*
> *apart from that incident in the car.*
> *And picnic basket in the lake*
> *Anyone could make that mistake.*
> *Mr Holmes is rather nice,*
> *But me and Dad – don't you think – a little mad?*
> *As a child you were Oh so cute,*
> *We kind of hoped you'd be a prostitute.*
> *And so the party is tonight.*
> *Will we fall in love or fight?*
> *She's sending a car.*
> *I'll be there by ten.*
> *One thing's certain:*
> *I'll never find another Ava,*
> *And she'll never find another Ken.*

'It's not a lake, it's a fjord,' she said.

'Poetic licence.'

'I'll never meet another Ken, that's for sure.'

'Will we fall in love or fight? I'll call you back,' and she put the phone down.

There were about a dozen girls at the party, though Andrea wasn't

264

there. I'd tried to persuade her to go. 'I can't,' she said, 'I'll give the game away. We'll be talking all night, giggling.' There was another teacher there, a nurse who worked in A&E, one or two rough-looking, and Laura – the sort of woman that some men would give their right arm for. The rich tapestry that went to make up the oldest profession.

I'd met Laura a couple of weeks before. Ava phoned me, 'I've got a new girl. You've got to see her. She's got that look that Irish girls have – so pretty, so dirty.' She was right. 'How does she ever get out of bed?' But tonight Ava was keeping Laura well out of my reach.

I wore a dinner suit for no particular reason. 'You and I should be going to Covent Garden,' she said. Doug was at the party. It was the first time I'd met him. Seemed a nice guy. He was walking around making sure everybody had a drink. He asked her, 'Where's your ring?' She was looking down at the floor, 'It must be in the bedroom somewhere.' 'I'll take it to Boodle & Dunthorne,' he said, 'and get it altered.' I didn't see him as competition. I just thought if they got married it would slow things down a bit.

I was talking to Jane for quite a while, a Scouser, so full of fun. A porn star in London during the week, an escort at the weekend. The money she got from being a porn star was good, but was it good enough to compensate for the way she was treated? I told Jane, 'Ava and I love each other'. 'I know,' she said. She knew. And she also knew that Doug was trying to put a ring on her finger. Laura knew as well. 'How do you know?' I said. 'The way she talks about you, the way you talk about her.'

I spent most of the evening on my own. 'Somebody go and talk to Ken,' Ava shouted to nobody in particular.

'I don't do talk.'

'He doesn't do talk,' she corrected herself.

One of the girls did come over to talk to me. 'I like the way you keep yourself to yourself,' she said. 'I like to do that.'

Later on I was dancing with Gabbie. Gabbie grabbed hold of Ava's hand to join us. Ava declined. 'But it's Ken,' she said.

The room was pretty big, plenty of space for everybody to mill around. Two bedrooms somewhere – I couldn't care less. I was sitting on the couch talking to one of the girls whose main job was an A&E nurse. Ava was walking round with two phones, directing operations.

As I watched her walk across the room something totally weird happened, her whole appearance changed: she became much older, slightly stooped. She was still wearing the same clothes. It only happened for about four or five seconds and then went back. I remember thinking, 'I'd better be quick, I want that woman to get pregnant.'

I didn't say anything to Ava at the time. I couldn't – it was too stupid. Nobody else saw it. I knew nobody else would have seen it. For those few seconds she became thirty years older.

I stood up and recited a poem.

Pretty Polly Flopsie who lived in Dingley Dell
Was coming to the time of life when her breasts began to swell.
She unbuttoned her little blouse before the looking glass
And there she stood firm and pround, such a pretty lass.

Pulled up her skirt, took her knickers down, and sat upon a chair
And examined her vagina for signs of pubic hair.
She poked and prodded all around examined every bit
But not a single hair was found, but it was good fun doing it.

In the morning Polly got up early
Sat upon the loo to see if there were signs of short and curly
While she had her morning wee
And there she saw four or more, much to her delight.

The Hairy Fairy'd been and done it some time in the night.
The next day there were more and more.
They then came in a rush, and before apple blossom time
Polly had herself a bush.

Polly called out to her mother, Mummy come and see
Just look what I've been and gone and grown, around where I do my wee.
Of course mum had noticed all these changes,
Now Polly you beware. There lies the root of all your dangers

So listen and take care
The men out there are bastards – they'll fancy some of that

Tey'll play Nick Nack Paddy Wack on your tits
And stick all sorts up your twat.

One of the girls was a bit disgusted. It didn't offend Ava or anybody else. She just said, to nobody in particular, 'Didn't I tell you Ken was a poet?'

I didn't tell her what I saw. I didn't know how to say it. The party was due to run again the next night, but when I arrived it had been cancelled. Doug was asleep somewhere. We talked until about five o'clock. It started to become light. Doug slept through. 'He's not going to sleep for ever you know.'

CHAPTER 20

On Monday morning I had a phone call from Paul Jones. He told me they'd refused the loan.

'Why?' I said, trying to hold back my anger.

'They don't give a reason.'

'Who didn't give a reason? Who are 'they'?'

He wouldn't, or couldn't answer me.

I told him repeatedly, 'I want to speak to 'them'. They've made a mistake.'

No loan meant no American patent. No American patent meant no Elmers. I was furious. We had a very powerful invention. Conni could see that, but she wouldn't convince the others without the patent.

There's none so blind as those that cannot see (whoever 'they' are). I wrote to the Chairman of Barclays, Matthew Barrett. Two days later I had a phone call from Alison Leary from the Chairman's office. We must have spoken for about half an hour. She seemed impressed with my argument. 'Leave it with me,' she said, 'Let me see what I can do.' I felt I now had somebody in the Chairman's office fighting my corner.

I had a good feeling about Alison Leary. She could see the project, and she recognised my determination and ability to see it through. I still wasn't able to get to the mysterious man who made the decision, but I had confidence in Alison. She wouldn't have her position in the Chairman's office for nothing. People were bound to listen to her arguments. But they didn't. Her apparent best efforts didn't work. The loan was rejected again.

It wasn't just that the loan was rejected, it was the matter-of-fact way that she said it, as if she was discussing the weather. 'At least we tried,' she said.

They'd got no idea, no vision whatsoever. Can't they see the Kiasu Easel is going to change how a photo frame stands up – on every table from Bangkok to Boston.

I couldn't tell Elmer's we couldn't afford the patent; they had to believe everything in the garden was rosy. It was, apart from stupid Barclays. I had a conversation with Max. He was keen to go with it. We had some difference of opinion on how many per week WalMart would sell. It wasn't that he didn't think it would sell, it was just the volumes. I said, 'We can let the Great American Public decide, and adjust from there, can't we?'

'Absolutely right,' he said.

Somehow I managed to scrape together the funds for the American patent, but it drained my working capital. Even when I received the initial order from Elmers, I wouldn't have the pathetic amount I needed to ask Wang to make it. I couldn't let Elmer's know we were strapped for cash, but I had no alternative but to ask them for an advance. I hated doing it – I knew it was too much to ask. And I was right. I tried to be matter of fact about it, as if it didn't really matter.

He wanted to pay us thirty days after the stock landed in America, which would have been two or three months after I'd paid for it. That meant that I would have to place three or four orders with Wang before I started to get some back.

'How about,' I said, 'You pay us thirty days after it arrives at your packing people in China?'

'Yes,' he said, 'We can live with that.'

'It sounds like we've got a deal then, Max?'

'Sounds like it to me.'

'So what do we do now?'

'We don't want to be messing about with lawyers, they just cost more money. Set it down on an email, and that'll do.'

I put the phone down. Sweat was pouring off my hand. D was standing alongside me. 'We've done it!' I said. His agreeing to pay thirty days after the stock arriving at their people in China made all the difference in the world. I put the details down exactly as we'd just discussed, and sent the email.

The following day, Max emailed back, 'I never agreed to any of that.'

It all blew up in my face. I'd written it down exactly as we had agreed it. It had been a very amicable phone conversation. There wasn't one point of argument. D had been standing alongside me. She'd heard every word – or my half of it anyway. She was as stunned as me.

I phoned Conni to see if she could find out what the hell had happened. She phoned me back, 'Apparently there have been some big budget cuts. It's a bad time. Give him a month and try again.'

A bad time? Was there ever going to be a good one?

What's the word worth
I pondered lonely as a clown
And dined on pies and thistledown
When all at once I saw a frown,
A ghost from years of Watney's Brown.

I must be drunk, I said to me,
And wandered home to have some tea.
But that became no use, you see.
I couldn't find the fucking key.

But then I saw before my eyes,
Fluttering and dancing, a row of pies.
But they were all just in disguise.
Enough, I screamed, of all these lies.

And started out to climb the hills
And saw the dark satanic mills
So I swallowed one of my little pills
And became a host of daffodils.

I'd told Ava I was going to slay the giants and make my fortune – and failed again. She'd said, 'It takes ten years for an invention to work.' Does she know more about the scale of things than I do?

I blamed Barclays for the Elmer's thing blowing up. I'd been forced to push Elmer's too hard for the money. There may well have been budget cuts – those sort of things happen all the time. But I could see some big suits in the Elmer's office saying, 'We're not paying for it until we've got hold of it – not for a product that hasn't got a history.'

What I did feel now, though, was that Barclays weren't giving me any respect at all. I hadn't been able to discuss the loan with the person who made the decision; there might have been a different way to structure. But they'd knocked it back without any explanation, no reasons given – just a blank 'No'.

We may be just a small company, but we've discovered something unique with great commercial potential worldwide, and what I was looking for, what I expected, was financial guidance on the best way forward. But instead all I got was contempt. They didn't even grant me the courtesy of discussion. They'd also ignored my complaint about a forged signature. I may not have been able to do anything about them refusing a loan, but I wasn't going to let the forgery thing drop.

I wrote to Alison Leary demanding a response to my accusation of forgery. Alison had a habit of phoning, so I told her to respond in writing. I wanted all communications recorded from now on. Despite that, she phoned me. I told her abruptly that I had said in my letter to respond in writing, 'Do that,' and put the phone down. The gloves were off.

D had her garden to go into at weekends and downtime – her bit of escape from the insanity. I started doing a bit of wood carving – I've always liked mucking about with wood. I was never really that good at it, but I thought I was, and because I could see what I wanted to achieve it would take my utmost concentration to get there... the perfect antidote.

They mostly turned into sculptures, figurines, without any real recognisable form. Yet they were OK – people seemed to like them, so they said. I actually sold a couple.

One of the sculptures took the form of a woman – naked, could be a dancer. It was only after I'd been working on it for two or three weekends I realised it was Ava. I was pleased with the way it was going, but then I noticed something that stunned me – stopped me in my tracks.

She'd left Doug and we'd become lovers again. She'd been talking about breast implants, and brought a girlie magazine round to show me some pictures for my opinion. Made no difference to me. It wasn't the body I loved.

'There can be complications,' she said.

'Well don't do it then.'

'I've paid a thousand pound deposit. I'm not wasting that. Everybody's got something about themselves they'd like to change.'

'What would you change about me?'

'Nothing.'

I was the only one who knew, apparently.

I noticed the breasts on the sculpture were tipped with two tiny knots in the wood, exactly where the nipples would be. I stopped, put it down, and looked at it again. I'd probably done that bit about a week ago. How could that happen?

I couldn't finish the carving. I was scared – no, not scared – but I was frightened of breaking the spell, or whatever it was. There were two tiny little knots in perfect position. You can't plan something like that.

I knew it was something to do with her implants. I couldn't wait to tell her it was proof – of what, I didn't know – but proof of something.

And there was that thing at the party. I told her what I saw: that for just about three or four seconds she'd changed to a woman thirty years older.

'I've not changed.'

'No, I know.'

'And I'm certainly not going to be using two phones when I'm sixty.'

'I'm not saying that's what will happen. I'm just saying it's what I saw.'

'No, I don't believe it.'

'You don't have to. Just believe I believe that's what I saw.'

Weird stuff has happened to me all my life, but now it was happening more often. I didn't talk about it much. It was stupid – I had trouble believing it myself.

She wouldn't have it. 'There's a knot there… and there's a knot there. And my bum's not like that.' Trying to change the subject.

'You're so romantic,' she said.

She'd said that before. Doug wasn't romantic, but Ava was. I don't know whether I won that battle or not. Romantic's a good thing, isn't it?

'You're a dreamer,' she said. She'd called me that before.

'You have to be a dreamer to be romantic, and if you're not romantic you're dead inside.'

You may say that I'm a dreamer,
I know that's how it seems,
But really I'm a schemer,
a-scheming at my schemes.
But then again you're right my love,
For the schemes provide the means,
To leave the world a better place,
And fulfill all my dreams.

Alison Leary sent me an email saying she'd had a long chat with Wyn Read. Wyn had apparently told her he'd discussed the Clearly Business software package with me at length. Then she said that although the signature appeared to differ from the one they had on file, 'it would be difficult for either of us to substantiate it'.

From childhood I remember practising my signature over and over again. Trying to make it special, knowing that this was going to be my badge of honour for the rest of my life. Didn't we all do that? Every time I signed a letter, I looked to see if it was me. I always thought I could do it better… but it was always the same. [20]

Difficult for either of us to substantiate it? I couldn't believe what I was reading. A child of five could see it was a forgery.

It was a blatant forgery, anybody could see that. She bloodywell knew it wasn't my signature, which had to make it a forgery. No apology, no 'I'll look into this right away', no concern whatsoever that my signature may have been used illegally.

Alison Leary has a senior position in the Chairman's office at Barclays and she's saying it would be difficult for either of us to substantiate it. Substantiate it? Everybody's signature is different – isn't that the whole point? Isn't that why we give the bank a specimen signature when we open an account?

If there had been an explanation, an apology, and an assurance it wouldn't happen again, I would have accepted it, but there wasn't.

Part III

THE ALCHEMIST

CHAPTER 21

Life deals you a set of cards. You make the best of what you have. Then, when all the cards are stacked against you, you've played all your aces and there's nowhere else to turn, you find additional cards you hadn't noticed before. No, they just weren't there before. This repeats itself as long as you have the balls to play the game. If it didn't, there'd be a steady line of people following the lemmings. Those Old Wives knew 'every cloud has a silver lining', 'don't worry, something will turn up', 'it won't seem so bad in the morning'. All mean the same thing. Perhaps the best, although slightly different: 'what doesn't kill you makes you stronger'.

I've lost count of the number of times my castle came crumbling down. A couple of years ago all our framing activities had practically dried up because of our supply problems, apart from a few small accounts. We shouldn't have survived, but then out of the blue I had a phone call from somebody I hadn't spoken to for quite some time and we landed a new contract – pretty specialist work, but it was right up our street. We invested in two fork lift trucks to handle the volume and two months later we were as profitable as we had been at the height of Spielmanns'. Hard work, but nothing wrong with that. We ceased framing activities altogether and concentrated on the new contract. Our customer was very happy with the arrangement, and it looked like we were back on track again. But after eighteen months the contract stopped overnight without any warning. That should have been the death knell.

Have you ever stopped to think
While feeling in the pink
Of the pleasant things that life has got in store?

And while you're deep in thought
Your concentration's caught
By the phone or by a knock upon the door.
Then everything is changed
And your life is rearranged
And nothing is the way it was at all.
But then, as if insane,
You do the same again
Till fate decides to make another call.

All we had now was the income from the picture framing hardware – the inventions. Despite all the accolades thrown at us over the years, the sales were pathetic. We disposed of our framing equipment for practically nothing. Staff who had been with me for years were forced to find other employment and left, or were made redundant. We moved to a much smaller unit, reducing our overheads. And yet, through all of this we knew one day it would all work out; it was just a matter of time.

I'd become something of an expert juggler – I had to be – paying people when absolutely necessary, making sure the wheels of industry kept turning. Always something of a balancing act – any company knows that. What compounded our cash flow problems beyond the norm was that we had to pay in advance for our stock coming in from China and then wait for two or three months or more to sell, and receive payment.

Our biggest customer by far was still Venture, and they were buying the Curl Up n' Stand system with the two brackets we fixed on the back. We'd been doing this for a few years now. Labour-intensive, as always, but it worked.

We hired casual labour to do this as required from an employment agency, Travail Recruitment. D handled all that side of things, booking temps when we had a decent order. It was a Dickensian way of doing things, manually fixing two brackets on each back using small hand presses, and there could be twenty thousand backs to do at a time. It was a pretty simple operation, but even the simplest of things would go wrong – brackets not fitted properly, in the wrong position, upside down, wrong quantities in the boxes. Over the years all this kind of simple mistake had been ironed out with staff training, but with temps we didn't have that.

I knew we owed Travail – they had to wait alongside everybody else. But they wouldn't wait and quickly became hostile. The bill amounted to £1,200 and they started Court proceedings.

We received a summons through the Small Claims Court stating we either pay the debt in full, dispute the claim, or propose terms of repayment to the claimant. We thought this was all a bit high-handed. We knew we owed them the money, we never disputed that.

We filled in the required Court forms, making an offer of £80 per month, and sent them to Travail. I know it doesn't sound very much, but in twelve months it would be nearly paid up. It was worth a try.

We then received a letter from Thomas Higgins, the solicitors acting for Travail, ignoring our response and stating the case was now going to the High Court for Judgment. We'd made an offer to Travail following the Court's procedure, on the correct forms and within the deadline. We wrote back to Thomas Higgins immediately, asking did that mean our offer had not been accepted.

Instead of an explanation of what happened to our offer, we received a notification from the High Court to say the Judgment had gone against us. This was now looking serious – why would it go to the High Court for judgment when we'd never disputed the debt – why did it go to the High Court at all?

The next morning D and I were working at the bench at the entrance to the warehouse, fitting the brackets on the backs ourselves, to save labour costs.

I saw a car moving slowly on an adjacent road. I got an overwhelming feeling of foreboding. I said to D, 'There's somebody coming here. Leave it to me. I'm going to get shut of them as quick as possible.' The car turned into our road and pulled up.

'Is the gaffer in?' he said as he walked towards us. Braided hair, sunglasses, gold jewellery. I could feel anger welling up.

'What d'you want?'

'Are you the gaffer?' he said, smirking.

'Just get to the point and fuck off.'

D was shocked, 'Why are you talking like that?'

'Leave it to me.'

'Are you the gaffer?' he said again.

'What if I am? Just get to the point.'

D said, 'Who are you? Are you selling something?'

The smirk never left his face. I just wanted him to go. This hostile conflict continued, until eventually he told us he was a High Court Enforcement Officer – a bailiff.

He produced a clipboard and flashed some piece of paper which apparently gave him the authority to enter the building. He demanded we pay him £1,800 there and then, or he would seize our goods to that value. The £1,200 debt was apparently now £1,800.

He moved past me into the warehouse. Was I supposed to stop him? How would I? He was half my age and this was his job; I wasn't going to win. And apparently he had some sort of authority – from the High Court was it?

He walked round with clipboard and pen, listing things. I was seething with anger. I told D to get the cheque book. She wrote a cheque for the £1,800. He insisted it be made out in favour of John Marston & Co. I shouted at him, 'I knew what you were about before you got out of the car.' He looked up. 'I just want you to know that,' I said, and glared at him. I gave him the cheque and said, 'If you're not legitimate, that cheque gets stopped.' He muttered something about, 'don't shoot the messenger'. When he left D immediately got on the phone to Thomas Higgins. I watched him as he walked to his car. He only drove a few yards away and I could still see him, then he spent about ten minutes talking on the phone. I expected him back any moment. He hadn't wanted a cheque, he wanted cash. Eventually he drove away.

D's telephone conversation was brief. Thomas Higgins & Co. had instructed John Marston & Co., High Court Law Enforcement Officers, to act on their behalf. Her call didn't need to go beyond the telephonist.

He'd listed six items for seizure: the two manual presses D and I had been working on when he arrived, the computer and the desk and chairs out of the office, a pallet truck, and a few other items of no value to anybody except us. Any two or three of these items would have brought an immediate halt to our company's activities. That was his intention.

His demeanour was hostile and threatening – that was also his intention. He didn't list the expensive fork-lift truck in the corner because it was obviously not in regular use, nor the twenty-four pallets of new stock, which could all have been realised for cash if that had been his intent – but it wasn't. He just listed the few items that would cause an instant halt to our company's activities.

We owed Travail £1,200. We had never disputed that. We'd offered them £80 a month. What had happened to that offer? D checked with the High Court in Northampton, and the Small Claims Court in Wrexham. Both said any offer made to the claimant must be put before the Court for adjudication. They may not have liked the offer, but they couldn't just ignore it.

We'd made an offer under the correct procedure. They could choose to accept that offer, or submit it to the Court for adjudication. They chose to do neither.

Because the correct procedure had not been adhered to, we applied to the Court to have the Judgment set aside. D had worked in a legal office for a number of years in a previous life and understood the procedure.

Travail had appointed Thomas Higgins, a firm of solicitors specialising in debt collection. Travail knew an offer had been made and, by the reaction and denials coming from Thomas Higgins, they too knew an offer had been made, and chose to deny it. Instead they went for Judgment as if we'd totally ignored the summons. The Judgment was fast-tracked and then John Marston & Co. were instructed to act as bailiffs. It was one of John Marston's enforcement officers who had entered our building. It seemed to be a tried and trusted procedure.

I immediately wrote to John Marston & Co., telling them the correct procedure had not been adhered to. I also told them that we had applied for the Judgment to be set aside, and that the cheque given to the officer for £1,800 must not be presented. I contacted my bank and put a stop on the cheque.

On Monday morning three days later I had a meeting first thing, and didn't arrive at the warehouse until eleven-thirty. D's car was parked in a different place. The big doors to the warehouse were closed – and locked. They're never locked – they're never even closed. I had to knock hard on the doors, and shouted 'D!' The office was some way away. She eventually heard me and and opened up.

D had locked herself in. Not only that, she'd wedged an iron bar against the doors from the inside, just in case he came back. That's how much the evil bastard had scared her.

I wrote again to Marstons and told them what I had just witnessed, and how dare they cause D such distress. I demanded an immediate apology and compensation of £15,000 made payable to D in consideration for the distress caused. They haven't responded yet.

The next day I heard D on the telephone saying something like, 'We've applied for the Judgment to be set aside.' I realised she was talking to the bailiffs and took the phone off her. The voice on the other end was very hostile and aggressive. The correct legal procedure meant nothing to them. The fact that we'd applied for the Judgment to be set aside was of no consequence. I put the phone down and said to D, 'They're on their way back to seize our stuff.' We locked up immediately and went straight to the police station in Wrexham – knowing that the law was on our side, and believing they would acknowledge that.

The police were sympathetic, saying, 'We don't like them either, but there's nothing we can do.' I tried to argue they were breaking the law, but I was wasting my time. The bailiffs could just walk into our place – or anybody's for that matter – take whatever they wanted and, more specifically, threaten people to such an extent you'd rob your own grandmother to pay them off. They carry the title of High Court Enforcement Officers, but they are little more than thugs. If they are working within the law, there is something very wrong with the law. They appear to be able to do what they like, and charge what they like for doing it.

I got to the warehouse the next morning not knowing whether I'd be met by a van load of thugs, or the place broken into. Nothing. D arrived shortly afterwards, and our day began without event.

I learned years ago: at times like this you put everything in writing.

I wrote to Thomas Higgins telling them we'd made an offer in the correct manner, why was this ignored? Tracy McIver, solicitor at Thomas Higgins, responded saying they had 'not received an offer at this office', and if an offer had been made to Travail they had 'declined to accept it'.

I read McIver's letter a few times. She *knew* an offer had been made to Travail. That was clear from her denial. Whether Travail had told her an offer had been received and she'd told them to keep quiet, doesn't matter. The manner of her response told me she knew an offer had been made. As a solicitor, she also knew that an offer must be put to the Court for adjudication. That is the law.

Every time Thomas Higgins responded, they damned themselves further.

I phoned Simon Wallwork and told him, 'If I'm not mistaken, I've unearthed a high level of illegal activity being practised by a large firm of solicitors specialising in debt collection, and the bailiffs they use for enforcement.' I knew I couldn't ask him for his official professional advice because of the cost implications, but Simon was a mate. I sent him copies of all the correspondence, just in case.

There was something very wrong with all of this. I'd heard about an organisation called the Law Society, but knew nothing about it. I looked at their website and wondered whether I should put in an official complaint about Thomas Higgins.

I spoke to Simon a few days later on another matter and told him, 'I'm going for Thomas Higgins and the bailiffs.' 'Good,' he said. He'd obviously taken a look at the correspondence. I asked him how powerful the Law Society was.

'Very,' he said.

CHAPTER 22

Life goes on. It was now just before Christmas, 2006. I hadn't spoken to IKEA for about eighteen months. I decided to phone them. I didn't think Ulrika would remember me, but she did. 'Oh hi, Ken! Yes, I've got a Kiasu Easel on my desk now.' I couldn't believe it. 'But I'm not buying frames any more,' she said, 'Nicole Johannessen's taken over now. She sits right behind me. If you hang on I'll pass the easel over to her and put you through.' My little boy's heart started beating like a drum again.

'We sell a lot of photo frames,' Nicole said.

'Well if you've just taken over, shall I let you find out where the coffee's kept and call you back in the New Year?'

'Yes,' she said, 'Please do that.'

Little cameos of the conversation kept running through my mind over and over again. *Oh hi, Ken... I've got a Kiasu Easel on my desk...* and *...We sell a lot of photo frames...* Eighteen months since I spoke to IKEA, and the Kiasu Easel's on Ulrika's desk. They're serious at last. And they sell millions. The best Christmas present we could have had.

I couldn't wait to tell Ava. She'd be impressed. She knew how big IKEA is – she's Swedish.

'You spoke to their Manchester office?'

'No, Sweden – the new buyer, Nicole Jorgenssen.'

'Jorgenssen?'

'Yes'.

'That's my name.'

I'd called her Nicole Jorgenssen instead of Johannessen. I just couldn't think of Nicole's second name. I wanted to tell her the buyer had a Kiasu Easel on her desk. I'd wanted her to be impressed – I expected her to be impressed – but I blew it.

She'd said it took years and years for an invention to be accepted. I was going to prove her wrong, but I wasn't doing my cause much good at the moment. The conversation switched to something else. Soon it'll be the New Year, and IKEA will become a reality.

I'd written to the Matthew Barrett, the Chairman of Barclays in October expressing disbelief that a forgery within his bank was being treated so casually. I eventually got a reply stating that as they'd stopped the direct debit and refunded the money the matter was at an end. No apology, no explanation. Why did they cancel the direct debit? Why did they refund the money? They were guilty, and they knew it. They'd committed forgery and they were trying to brush it under the carpet. I always thought forgery was a criminal offence, and not to be dismissed so lightly as though it were a minor clerical error. If they had put their hands up and apologised I would probably have accepted it, but they didn't, they blatantly denied it – '*try and prove it*'. They thought they were untouchable. And me – I'm just low-life.

Barclays were trying to bully me! Take away Savile Row and the Financial Times, and replace it with Primark and the Sun – and you've got a bailiff.

Not that John Marston would be Primark – he'll be Savile Row. His stationery says John Marston OBE. Order of the British Empire – what did he get that for? Apparently he was awarded the OBE for his services to enforcement. What a load of rubbish.

Thomas Higgins had gone quiet since we complained to the Law Society. Perhaps we'd struck a nerve. The bailiffs' equivalent is the High Court Enforcement Officers' Association. Assuming it has the same influence over its members, we sent a very vigorous complaint about the practice and behaviour of John Marston & Co. It took a while to get a response, and when that came it was pretty vague and dismissive, rambling on about how we must ensure we have followed the complaints procedure at John Marston's offices before approaching the Association.

John Marston & Co. had had enough complaints from me to fill a book, but nevertheless we made an official complaint, without response.

I then wrote a number of letters to Pauline Hayward, Secretary at the High Court Enforcement Officers' Association. Then we discovered that John Marston himself was chairman of the High Court Enforcement Officers' Association. It became patently obvious that Pauline Hayward was a puppet of John Marston & Co. How convenient for the criminal to be judge and jury of his own case. Is that how he got his OBE? I wonder if he made a donation to the Labour Party too?

Pauline Hayward knew Marston was corrupt. I wrote and told her, 'If you don't stand up to corruption, you are part of it.' Sooner or later she'll have to answer to her conscience.

The same goes for Alison Leary. Why did she say she'd had a long conversation with Wyn Read? What was there to talk about unless my signature had been forged? Why did she say it would be difficult to prove forgery unless she knew it was?

Doug McCall of Thompsons was on the board of their professional association. Who do these people think they are – divine beings?

What's the point of having a professional association to monitor the practice and behaviour of the footsoldiers when the board of the association comprises the very same footsoldiers?

Now, whenever I wrote to John Marston & Co., I always addressed the correspondence direct to 'John Marston, Order of the British Empire', giving him his title in full.

The world is run by men obsessed with money and greedy for power, who will bend or break any law if they think they will get away with it. Right and wrong has nothing to do with it, although we all instinctively know the difference between right and wrong – that is one of the laws set by the universe. But because bullies are in charge we allow ourselves to be manipulated to behave like performing seals, terrified to step out of line, even though it's wrong or there's a better way. In the meantime, the bullies charge ahead unhindered, while the young bullies work their way up through the ranks. We talk about the bullies in the playground – aren't the real bullies in the boardroom, and because nobody stands up to them the practice becomes the norm? Perhaps the biggest crime of all is that they're worshipped as supermen, and admired.

So you've put on a suit
And washed your face
You've become a rat
So join the race
You've taken a sip from the tainted wine
And fucked with the corporate concubine.
Your soul is mine. It's here to stay.
Welcome to the American Way.

For some time I'd been hooked on a TV programme, Sixth Sense, watching the way Colin Fry spoke to the audience about their friends and relatives who had passed to 'the other side', as he referred to it. He'd shock and astound them, reliving and revealing memories of the departed which he could not possibly have known.

His honest, matter of fact, way of discussing the afterlife convinced me that there is another life, more meaningful, after we have departed this one. I think I always knew there was something going on after this, but I didn't expect to have such graphic evidence.

If this life is just a stepping stone, what's the relevance, what's the point? There has to be one. Everything has a reason.

As fortune – money of any sort – became harder to come by, I found I desired it less and less. I started to make my life as simple and uncluttered as possible. I removed all the pictures off the walls of my apartment and the knick-knacks around the place. Anything that wasn't essential went. Suits out of the wardrobe folded up neatly in carrier bags for Oxfam. I just kept the basics. I didn't throw the hangers away. We do some stupid things – I was throwing away clothes I'd spent thousands of pounds on and keeping the empty hangers just in case. I kept my dinner suit – not for formal occasions, just because it's a bit wacky and I wear it now and then for no particular reason.

As my wine glasses got broken, as they do, I started drinking my wine out of an empty pesto jar. It was glass, and about the right size, so why not? I'm still using the same jar now, years later – it's unbreakable. Ava thought this was amusing at first, but then when I offered her a glass of wine she said, 'I'll share yours.' She understood the logic. I'm sure she'll understand everything if she gives it a chance.

I asked her if she'd heard of Colin Fry, and found out she'd been hooked as well. She laughed about her grandparents watching her, saying, 'I'm no angel!'

She told me to ask my grandfather and father for help.

'I do,' I told her.

'Do you say it out loud?'

'It doesn't matter. They know anyway.'

'It does – you've got to say it out loud.'

We almost had an argument on whether the spirits have to be told audibly or whether the thought is enough.

The following evening on Colin Fry's programme, he said, 'You don't have to speak out loud – the other side know what you're thinking' – as if he was saying it to settle an argument.

This wasn't how I'd planned my life to turn out; wasn't where I thought I'd be. But for some reason it felt a pretty cool place to be. If I'd made my fortune when I knew I was going to, I would more than likely have wrapped myself in the trappings that money buys and felt smugly superior. But superior to what, to whom? We are all individuals – the only person we're competing with is ourself. It's not whether you win or lose, it's how you play the game. I used to think that was a patronising remark to give the loser something to hold on to. Now I know it's the only thing that matters.

Everybody is an individual, unique – a tribe of one. Each of us is infinitely variable, and we are not qualified to put those variants in order of merit. The old wives said, 'You're as good as anybody else, and don't let anybody tell you different'. Secretly we all know that, but money is such a potent drug we tend to list people's importance in order of their bank balance. Money appears to be a panacea, but that's just an illusion.

I tried to impress a ten year old boy with Kiasu. He wasn't having any. I told him I was a magician, an alchemist, turning worthless metal into gold. Made no difference to him, but it impressed me. Invention is alchemy. The fact that it hadn't made my fortune had nothing to do with it. It still turned comparatively worthless metal into something special.

I had to use the passcode on the gate; there to deter intruders like me. She was surprised to hear my voice on the intercom. Perhaps that's why she let me in. It was the same room the party had been held in. Ava was sitting in an armchair. I sat on the couch and called to Shakira to come and join me. She came over and snuggled up. Another girl came in, dripping wet, wrapped in a big white towel, and went into the kitchen to make coffee. I recited the poem:

Six months ago, no maybe more
Since we fucked upon the bedroom floor.

When I got to the part that said,

Fulfilling dreams dreamt as a boy,
But then again I'm still a boy.
How much joy can one behold
As this little boy grows old?

Shakira looked up. 'Did you write that?'

I nodded.

'That's beautiful.'

'He loves me,' Ava said, a bit dramatic.

'You love him too.' Shakira stood up and signalled to the girl with the towel, and they both left the room.

'It was there I saw you change at the party. You walked from there to there, then changed back again.'

'Do you know what frontal lobotomy is?' She drew a finger across her forehead. 'Does that mean I've got to put up with you for the next twenty years?'

'Thirty,' I said.

I wanted her to see the Journey poem. I said, 'I'll bring it round tomorrow night.'

The next night I went round. I think it was Shakira who answered the intercom. Then immediately Ava took over and wouldn't let me in. She was curt, abrupt, vile. I felt the knife go deep inside. I stuck the poem in the letterbox and wandered off in a daze.

'Forget about her and move on,' someone said. I wouldn't, even if I could. Have they never been there? Memories flash in and out, good or bad, whether we want them to or not, like a recurring dream.

'She'll come running when you make your fortune.'

'I'll allow you to say that once.'

A couple of weeks later, that same person said, 'I wonder if I'll ever fall in love?'

Memories have a life of their own. We're just the unwitting receivers. They don't take into account the pain or the joy that goes with them. They just say 'deal with it'.

At times like this
We question the risk.
Such a mix of powerful forces.

This kind of strain
Confuses the brain.
The kind this problem causes.

I must resist
And try to desist,
But my mind is bent to distraction.

For my aching heart
Is breaking apart
Because of the fatal attraction.

CHAPTER 23

Sue, my landlady, was going away on holiday and I was in charge of locking up the house. She made a point of making sure I knew exactly which key did what, and stressed I should make sure I left the house fully locked. Her brother's house had recently been broken into. I asked her, 'Are you sure it's wise leaving an inventor in charge of security?' She knew my head was on a different planet most of the time. 'Will you try especially hard, for me?' I left in the morning making sure the new deadlock was set on the door. That was a bit of overkill. The ordinary locks would have been perfectly OK – the office was going to be opened up again before long. That evening, Sue's mother Arlene asked me had I brought in the mail before I left. I said no.

'You must have done,' she said, 'It was on the sideboard.'

I said I couldn't have done; I'd left at seven-thirty and the mail always arrived at about eight-fifteen.

Somehow the mail had got on to the sideboard when all the doors were locked.

I told Arlene, 'It's me. Things like that happen to me.'

'No, no,' she said, and waved her hand in dismissal, 'I don't believe in that.'

Years back, when I was still married, we were going to a party and I decided to wear my dinner suit. My bow tie was always kept in the sock drawer. I couldn't find it. It wasn't there. Pat, who found everything, searched the sock drawer. It wasn't there. Even the kids looked. The next day, it was there. I think that sort of thing happens to everybody. Things drop into a vortex and then reappear days, weeks, sometimes years, later exactly where they should have been.

I call these weird things Aardvarks – unexplainable phenomena. One of my favourites was the holly leaves.

The holly leaves had started appearing outside the warehouse doors. Nothing strange about that: it's outside. I dismissed it for a while, but they kept arriving. Always holly leaves, only holly. One or two – or sometimes five on a good day. I tried to impress D with this new phenomenon – no success whatsoever. I decided to find the tree so I could burst this stupid bubble and get it out of my head. I wandered around the industrial estate – rowan trees, sycamore. No holly anywhere. There seemed to be a pattern to this – the leaves only appeared during times of crisis. I reached the conclusion they were harbingers of doom. D wouldn't accept that there was anything odd going on. Of course she was right. Didn't make sense. Nevertheless we both walked round the estate and then up and down the road a bit to find the source. It was quite surprising we didn't find a holly tree at all. It was stupid – they were just holly leaves, but where had they come from?

Mike, in the unit next door to us, began to notice the holly leaves. He'd looked for the tree too. 'Weird, isn't it?' he said.

When I'd thrown all my clothes away, there were a few items that I just couldn't. In particular, a pair of shorts that I must have had more than ten years. They were becoming pretty threadbare. I tried to replace them, searching the specialist sports shops and surf shops, but nothing came close.

I borrowed a sewing machine and taught myself how to sew – or, rather, D did. I bought a pattern for shorts, and we went to a fabric warehouse. Row upon row of bales of fabric, stacked to head height, and I'm a kid in a sweet factory. I wandered round in silent awe – and so did D if she'd admit it. From time to time one of us would pop our head up: 'What d'you think of this?' Then we saw it. And that was the one. Perfectly outrageous. Because it was upholstery cloth D told me to put it through the washing machine to pre-shrink the material before I made it up. After washing, the material had frayed at the edges, which now meant I had a fringe on the hem of the shorts. It was just getting better and better. Belt loops each with a tiny fringe of its own. I got a tie-cord from the same shop for a belt. Knee-length, including an inch and a half of fringe, patch pocket on the back, and two side pockets.

They were great. As good as my old shorts? I think so, when they've travelled a few thousand miles.

Then, for some reason, and I still don't know why, I decided to adapt the basic idea of the shorts and make a skirt.

The skirt idea seemed perfectly natural, obvious and logical to me. We went back to the fabric warehouse. D wasn't very happy at the thought of my making a skirt, but then we saw it – Nefertiti. Rich fabric with an Egyptian design. If I thought I'd discovered perfectly outrageous before, I'd just blown it out of the water. So much so that it overruled D's horror at the thought of my wearing a skirt, for the moment anyway. Same belt loops as before, with a patch pocket on the back, but now I put another patch pocket on the front, a diagonal one. What was I doing making a skirt? But it looked good. No, *great*.

I came down the stairs from my apartment wearing the skirt. Sue and Arlene were in the doorway of the office. They just nodded in quiet approval, as if it was all perfectly natural.

Sue and Arlene are great people. Sue's a great chef. Once or twice a week she'd invite me for a meal and we'd chat for hours.

Ava said, 'Doesn't she ever ask you about the girls visiting?'

'No. She knows they're escorts.'

'What d'you tell her?'

'I told her it's an exercise in the master class.'

'You don't need it. Every time is different.'

I didn't know that. I kind of wished she hadn't said it.

Rocket Man

Doctor I hope that you can help.
My life is in a mess.
Can't satisfy the wife, you see,
And it's caused a lot of stress.

D'you think that you can change its shape,
Make it look more like a rocket?
Of course I can. The very pills are
Right here in my pocket.

Take one pill in the morning
And another one at night,
And before too long I think you'll find
They will relieve your plight.

The doctor was quite right, you know.
The pills worked very soon.
The long-haired one is thrilled to bits,
In fact she's over the moon.

I had to wear it when I went for my early evening drink in Chester: face the demons and all that, and I was scared stiff. What the hell was I doing?

To get to my pub in City Road I had to walk past two others before I could cross over. There were bouncers on the door of one pub, to keep away the low life. Forty-inch neck, dinner suit, shaven head. I could feel their stares, but passed without incident.

The people in my pub just seemed to accept it – most, anyway. One the barmen just wondered what I was going to do when I went to the loo. Frankly, so was I.

Having done it once, the next night was easier, and I actually got a friendly, 'Good evening' as I passed the forty-inch necks. 'Good evening,' I said. Inside I was going, *Yess!*

My pub was quite busy; groups of lads, some not knowing whether to cheer, jeer or throw stones. One of them came over to me, 'I used to wear the kilt when I was in the army.' Broad Scottish accent. He knew my skirt wasn't a kilt, but he also knew what it meant. We chatted for a few minutes then he returned to his mates. I've now got the army on my side!

I made another one. More formal, black, with a vague pale grey fleck. This second one had a lining. That's how I spent Christmas.

'You don't know how much love I've got to give,' she said, and put the phone down.

I called her back. *'You've got what you've got for a reason,'* I told her, *'Use it.'*

Making the black skirt totally occupied my thinking time. Christmas means nothing to me – a boring waste of time, and it will remain that way until Ava and I are together. D is off for a week or two now, doing her own thing with family, like most people. I never buy presents or send cards, haven't done for years. I used to sweat blood wondering what to buy, and then got it wrong. So do millions of others, just going through the ritual because that's what they're expected to do. The stores are full of crap, stuff you don't need, and millions of people fighting to buy it. Celebrations are great, but they don't have to cost a fortune. Society is just brainwashed into parting with as much money as possible, especially on presents for the kids. And then the kids spend more time playing with the box than with the contents.

Years ago when my kids were small I cut a hole in a box and the cat went in. The kids would lie on the floor daring to walk their fingers towards the hole, until a lethal paw shot out and the kids screamed. But they couldn't resist doing it again, and played for hours.

'Totally occupied my thinking time' – that's a laugh. I knew with absolute certainty that I had more to offer her than money. I searched and searched until I ached, and then searched some more, to find the words to explain what I meant. I knew a world that was totally obsessed with money was wrong, but every time I tried to explain it just sounded like an excuse from somebody who's got none.

I did get one Christmas gift I treasured: a greetings card from Travail, signed by all the members of staff. The dispute with Travail had been going on for months now, and since the beginning of October it had been hostile to say the least. Everybody in their company must have known about it – and they'd sent me a Christmas card. Wonderful. I think that was a little aardvark; why didn't one of the people who signed the cards say, 'Are you sure this is a good idea?'

Roderick Marsden of Travail phoned. D took the call. He's a nasty shit. He accused D of making all kinds of promises, which she did not. I won't have anybody talking to D like that. I told her if he called again just pass the phone to me.

He did call, and I took the phone. He was ranting and raving. He threatened to instigate a winding-up procedure and have my company closed within twenty-one days. Threats like that just wash over me. He got more and more frustrated, repeating himself. I told him, 'You've said that already.' I knew that would annoy him. I knew what he was really pissed off about: a few days before we'd received a letter from Thomas Higgins saying they were no longer acting for Travail. No wonder Marsden was angry – I'm surprised he didn't blow a gasket – he hadn't got a solicitor now. I told him, 'The Chinese say repeating yourself like that is a sign of madness, you know. The Court will decide on the eighteenth,' and put the phone down. *I forgot to thank him for his Christmas card.*

The Law Society responded to our complaint saying that a solicitor is obliged to act on its clients' instructions. (Even if they are aware their client is lying?) It's a very thin line from being aware that your client is lying to suggesting they do so. There is no doubt Thomas Higgins knew an offer had been sent in the proper manner. Do they not have a duty to uphold truth? Apparently not. For the Law Society to arrive at their conclusion they would have had to approach Thomas Higgins. No solicitor would like being approached by the Law Society regarding an official complaint. Maybe that was why they were no longer acting for Travail. He was now without a solicitor, and he was trying to bully us into submission before the Court hearing. Thomas Higgins are corrupt, and they didn't want to have their involvement with Travail discussed any more. Travail, Thomas Higgins and the bailiffs knew exactly what they were doing, and it was obviously common practice.

Every day, I'd been thinking about the conversation with IKEA just before Christmas: *'Oh, Hi Ken... I've got the Kiasu Easel on my desk...'* and *'We sell a lot of photo frames.'*

I phoned Nicole Johannesson. 'Hi Nicole. Ken, Lade-Back Company.'

Silence.

'Ken Holmes? The Lade-Back Company?'

'Yes?'

'I said I'd call you about now – about our Kiasu Easel.'

Gone was the friendly conversation of a month ago. Her tone was abrupt, curt. 'If we're going to do anything about a picture frame stand, we'll do it our way.'

And that was about the extent of the conversation. I was cut dead.

It was almost an exact replica of the door being slammed in my face eighteen months before – and still I didn't see it coming.

D said, 'What happened?'

'I don't know.' I tried to repeat what Nicole had just said. It didn't make sense.

'What else did she say?'

'I don't know. That was it.'

What the hell had just happened? What had happened to, 'Oh, hi Ken,' and, 'I've got a Kiasu Easel on my desk,' and, 'We sell a lot of photo frames,' and the rest of it from four weeks earlier? Gone, and replaced with a knife in the guts. Again.

I replayed that short conversation over and over again, just as I had four weeks before, but this was different. She'd left me with no chance to call her back, no negotiation, no 'keep in touch'. Any bridges there might have been weren't just burnt; they'd been blown up.

It didn't make sense. Time and time again the welcoming door swung wide open, only to have it slammed in my face.

IKEA don't waste time. They wouldn't have a Kiasu Easel on their desk unless… and yet they did.

What doesn't kill you makes you stronger. Well I'd go along with that, but why? What's the point? I was becoming more and more like Don Quixote. But was I destined to spend my life tilting at windmills? I knew I had to slay the giants – but who are they?

In years gone by to neutralise the stress I may have gone out for a weekend, drinking with my mates until the early hours. Now poetry was a kind of substitute. Might give you a headache at the time, but you don't get the hangover.

All the poems I'd written for Ava over the last couple of years I knew had a life of their own, and now together they began to tell a story. Not necessarily in the order they were written, but one by one they were finding the place they were meant to be. Then music and dance came in, making a kind of modern ballet.

Writing poetry is like doing a jigsaw puzzle without the picture. Bits fit together, move up, down, sideways, until they slot in with other bits. Only when it's finished does the picture become clear.

I'd written the Polly Flopsie poem months ago, for no apparent reason.

I read it to Ava. 'You should get that published,' she said. 'There are magazines that would pay for stuff like that.'

I don't know what magazines she meant, and I never did anything about it; now Polly Flopsie is the heroine in the ballet.

The ballet centres around an escort agency in Manhattan. Polly, from a little village in Sweden, wanted to be a dancer but instead goes to university, following her parents' wishes. There, she discovers sex. Ten years later she's running the best escort agency in Manhattan. But it doesn't fulfil her dream as a little girl growing up in Dingly Dell. She sits at the corner of the stage and sings 'Someone to Watch Over Me'. Three thousand miles away, Don Quixote, an aging poet, inventor, frustrated, angry because his inventions are not receiving the respect they deserve, puts a record on his old record player and plays the same song. During the song he has his biggest idea yet. 'Sanchez,' he says, 'We are going on a big adventure.'

'Where?'

He looks up at the world map. 'There,' he says, 'The Americas. We're going to capture an island. There it is – the Isle of Manhattan.'

And so the story begins.

CHAPTER 24

I thought the giants were the industry, but perhaps they were bigger than that. Perhaps the real giants were the bailiffs and Barclays. They had to be slain.

Eighteenth of January – the Court case with Roderick Marsden of Travail. Our case was scheduled to be heard at 1240.

We arrived at the Court at noon and reported to reception. Scary places, Courtrooms – so they should be I suppose. We waited in one of the side rooms. There were four or five of these, so you could wait in private, away from the enemy. There was a schedule on the wall of the cases to be heard in Courts 1 and 2. Four more, then us.

The room was silent, apart from our muted conversation, interrupted periodically by the tannoy calling the next case. At twelve thirty-five the case before ours was announced. Looked like we'd be in before lunch. At twelve fifty D needed to go the loo. I went to the reception to see if we were likely to be called before lunch. The receptionist said, 'Well the Judge is still in there, and he hasn't had his lunch yet.' She glanced round at a plate of salad under cling film.

One-fifteen, still no sign. I went back to reception. 'Oh! Your case has been heard,' she said, 'The Judge has gone to lunch.'

'How could it have been? We've been waiting!'

'Well it came over the tannoy,' she said, 'and it's been dealt with.'

'But we've been here all the time. We've been here since twelve o'clock.'

She knew that, and sensed my anger. 'Wait here a moment. I'll try and have a word with the Judge.'

She was back within a few minutes. 'The Judge said he's dealt with it, but he'll explain if you come back at two o'clock.'

D was upset, with shock and disbelief. I was able to stay calm and focused, but inside I was seething.

At two o'clock we were standing outside the Courtroom. I said to D, 'Please leave it to me.' Judge Jones called us in. Judge Hoffmann was also sitting at the back of the Court as an observer.

'I called the case myself,' Judge Jones said.

I had no doubt about that. 'We never heard you, Sir.'

'The Claimant heard it, and in your absence I had no alternative but to find in his favour.'

'We've been here since twelve o'clock, Sir. We heard all the other cases being called but not ours.'

He thought deeply, and said, 'I suppose you're wondering what I'm going to do?'

'Yes, Sir.'

'Well I'm going to have your case heard again.'

A wave of relief washed through me. 'When might that be, Sir?'

'Well, as soon as the schedule comes up.'

'Because the Claimant will believe he's won and the bailiffs will come in again.'

He would have seen the reams of correspondence, and would also have seen the look of distress on D's face, and understood exactly what it meant.

'I'll do it now,' he said, and got up and left the Court.

We weren't sure whether we were to follow him or not. We stood up and started to make our way towards reception. Judge Hoffmann said, 'We'll have all the tannoys checked tomorrow.' I knew they would find nothing wrong with the tannoy. Even if our tannoy had failed we would have heard it from the adjoining waiting rooms – they weren't sound-proofed. Our ears had been blocked from hearing it, for some reason.

I said to Judge Hoffmann, 'You're going to find there's nothing wrong with the tannoy. It's me. Those sort of things happen to me.'

He waved his hand in dismissal, 'No, no, I'm not going there!'

A few minutes later Judge Jones appeared back at reception and we were handed a Court Order overturning the Judgment from that morning and stating a new hearing date.

He'd gone to a great deal of trouble to reschedule the hearing there and then. He knew that I was speaking the truth – for whatever reason, we hadn't heard the tannoy. He also knew what the implications would have been.

We left the Court, dazed. D was still very angry. Why had we not heard the tannoy? Something had made that happen. We crossed over the road to a cafe, to get some tea and calm down a bit. Through the window I saw Judge Hoffmann pass by. We smiled at each other broadly. He was bemused too. He knew the tannoy had worked, but he also accepted that we hadn't heard it.

That piece of paper in our hands was our protection. The bailiffs couldn't do anything now – at least not until the case was heard again on 15 February.

But the following morning a letter from the bailiffs arrived saying they were sending in a removal van to take away our goods, and the contractors were under instructions to break in if necessary. In order to avoid their attendance we must pay the debt in full immediately. If we failed to pay and the removal contractors attended, '... *you will be responsible for their charges whatever the outcome of the visit. Charges vary, depending on such factors as the journey time to your premises and the equipment the contractors bring with them. As a guide expect to pay £300.00 plus vat for the first hour and £200.00 per hour after that.*'

The letter insisted we contact them immediately to advise our method of payment.

I phoned the bailiffs and told them the Court had set aside the Judgment, and a new hearing date had been allocated.

'Prove it,' he said.

'I've got the paper in front of me.'

'Fax it over to me and call me back in ten minutes.'

'No! If you want to speak to me – you call me back!'

He did: 'That makes no difference,' he said. 'We're coming in anyway.'

I slammed the phone down. I couldn't believe they had such contempt for the law.

D phoned Wrexham County Court and spoke to the Court Manager, who said, 'Well, they can't.' D explained, 'They're ignoring that, they're going to come in anyway.' The Court Manager offered to intervene on our behalf and said she would phone Travail. That was our only hope. For the rest of the day we were nervous, anxious – had she called Travail? It had been good of her to offer, but she was the manager of a busy Court with a thousand and one demands on her day.

She eventually phoned us back to tell us she'd spoken to Travail. He must have been spouting like a volcano. He thought he'd won. He must have phoned the bailiffs the instant he left the Courtroom, instructing them to go in heavy, but he'd been thwarted – again.

What doesn't kill you makes you stronger, and I'm not dead – far from it. Despite all the bloody battles something deep inside tells me I'm blessed with good fortune.

I had believed the holly leaves were acting as harbingers of doom. They always arrived at moments of stress, but now I realised they arrived to tell me there was a greater force on my side. The number of holly leaves that arrived was an indication of the size of my army. The Court tannoy thing was the weirdest aardvark yet. It worked out alright in the end, but why didn't we hear the tannoy in the first place?

How could I explain all of this to Ava? All this was scaring the life out of her. 'Can't you just pay him?' she said. She knew as well as I did that this wasn't a great amount of money, but this had gone way beyond 'just paying him'; I needed to see justice was done. I told her, 'Believe me – I'll sort it,' but I was having trouble convincing her.

> *I'm not surprised you think it's scary.*
> *I'm not surprised one bit at all.*
> *This is not about the short and curly.*
> *That's just become the bonus ball.*

> *There's a greater force outside control*
> *Driving us to the Holy hole.*
> *A supreme intelligence up above*
> *Has decided you and I will fall in love.*

I was fighting our corner harder than ever, and enjoying every minute of it. D would never admit enjoying it, but she was with me every step of the way and did what had to be done. It was as though there is some sort of force that guides you and gives you strength when right is on your side.

302

Despite all the chaos and battles, business was OK. Not great, but OK, and that was good enough. We were doing the backs for Venture – D and I. The monotonous, boring fixing of two brackets on twelve thousand backs, twice a month sometimes; the job we used to give to casual labour – the casual labour recruited from Travail which was how the problem started in the first place.

The strange thing was that we had time to do it. It's well known that work expands to fit the time available. It also appears that time expands to fit the work you have to do.

As well as doing the backs for Venture, I still needed to keep promoting the inventions worldwide. It was coming up to the NEC Spring Fair, the major trade show that I'd gone to every year for the last… God knows how long. We'd been going to give it a miss this year, with all the shit flying around, but I changed my mind.

I decided to get dressed up. It was probably a mixture of bloody-mindedness and a determination to show the world I didn't give a damn.

I'd been wearing the skirt for about a month or so by then. At my favourite watering hole I got to listen to music that I'd never come across before. There was one particular CD they played. I found myself turning it into part of the ballet doing bits of choreography while nobody was looking. Nobody bothered anyway – I was just accepted.

If I was going to the NEC wearing my skirt, I had to finish off the outfit. I went to a fancy dress shop in Liverpool, Lily Bizarre, and hired a period coat and Bobby Shaftoe shoes. The coat was three-quarter length, gold-coloured velvet, with turned-up cuffs. I made a jabot in a similar colour. I already had a black 'granddad' shirt I'd acquired in Kolkata. It wasn't perfect, but nobody would see that. We went to the NEC.

I think D was more self-conscious than me. It was as though when I got dressed up I became a warrior and rose to meet the occasion. We didn't need to stay at the show long, just sufficient time to cover the business we had to do. I couldn't have wished for a better reaction. Complete strangers smiled in approval, and a few old adversaries gawped, open-mouthed. What have I started?

Promoting the inventions was my passion, but it wasn't the only thing;

I was determined to bring John Marston & Co. to book. I knew their activities had to be illegal, but what was the charge? What was the crime he'd committed? It wasn't as obvious as I thought. If he'd seized the items he'd listed he would have stopped us functioning as a company. I understood that part of the bailiffs' brief is you must not take away the tools of trade.

And Barclays? I'd decided a while ago that they were going to answer to the Court. That's got to be straightforward enough... that's forgery.

I phoned the Court to speak to the manager and thank her for her intervention with the bailiffs. She said, 'Oh, by the way we checked the tannoy and found there was nothing wrong with it.'

'I knew there wouldn't be,' I said, 'but I'll have to explain why when we can get out to the pub.' She laughed.

The tannoy had been working correctly. It would have been loud and clear in each of the waiting rooms. That would be essential. And yet D and I, nervously, patiently waiting for our case to come up, one eye on the clock, the other on the list of cases, didn't hear it. Nobody questioned us about that. They accepted that we didn't hear it, and they also accepted that it was not due to carelessness or disrespect.

15th February – the new hearing with Travail. This time we heard the tannoy and appeared before Judge Hoffmann, face to face for the first time with Marsden. The Judge said, 'Both of you go away into a room, reach an agreement, and come back in fifteen minutes.'

Perfectly reasonable I thought, until we got into the side room. Disputes happen in business all the time, but this was never in dispute – we'd had an unexpected cash flow problem and needed time to pay. Pushing it through the Court was heavy-handed, but surely we can now discuss a reasonable solution like intelligent people? I hadn't met the guy until now but, as I suspected, he was just a shit. The Court's position in this situation is to adjudicate over a settlement. Judge Hoffmann gave us the opportunity to reach agreement. Marsden was in no mood whatsoever to negotiate; he just demanded the full amount be paid there and then, and would not discuss.

We had been paying the £80 per month as I originally offered. I offered to double it to £160. He wouldn't consider it. He was as charming in person as he had been on the phone. It was Pink Floyd that said about bullies in 'The Wall': *When they get home at night their fat and psychopathic wives would thrash them within inches of their lives.*

We went back to Judge Hoffmann, who had no hesitation in accepting my new offer as being perfectly reasonable, and that was his Judgment. Marsden was not happy, but that was the end of that.

I'd been at my apartment in Old Hall now for about two years. It was cleaned every week, bed linen and towels changed. That was the problem: privacy. Ava would visit. Sue knew – she didn't mind at all. The cleaner didn't approve, though it was bugger all to do with her. Sometimes, I'd find Ava's statue turned to the wall. I didn't like that. Then I found it lying on the floor face down. That was it. I would not have it treated with disrespect.

I told Sue I didn't want the cleaner entering my apartment any more.

'What about the cleaning?' she said.

'I'll do it myself.'

'Mary can sometimes be clumsy,' she said, 'It was probably an accident.'

It wasn't an accident. But, even so, if it had been knocked over carelessly she'd have known. I took the statue out of the apartment. All this created a bit of an atmosphere, and I decided to look for somewhere new.

I told Ava I was leaving Old Hall.

'Why?' she asked.

I told her I won't have my stuff, especially that, treated with disrespect. She squealed.

If it was possible, I found a place with even more magic – Foxhill Lodge in Frodsham; the lodge to a big house owned by the Church of England Diocese of Chester and just used once a week or so for ecclesiastical meetings and such. Set in acres and acres of landscaped grounds, parkland, woodland. The lodge itself could have been plucked from some distant fantasy; ideal for an aspiring Don Quixote. I showed Ava a photograph. [21]

'Oh, that looks great,' she said, 'Have you got an apartment in there?'

It did look bigger in the photograph than it was. 'All of it,' I said.

'Frodsham – I can easily get there by train.'

It was perfect – wacky, kind of surreal, private and lots and lots of space. I started making it my own. It had just been completely renovated; brand new kitchen, carpets, two bedrooms, lounge, bathroom, dining room. I bought two small sofas from Homebase for £200, and a second-hand telly. The rest of the furniture I made.

The front door was too magnificent to fit a letterbox. I made a postbox and fitted it in the porch outside the front door. Little lid on the top – not locked – if anybody wanted to steal my private correspondence they'd be welcome. Painted black with bold red 'POST' painted on it, courtesy of D.

Behind the house there was a wooded area. I found a clearing and tidied it up for my space. I dug a hole in the ground and lined it with stones for the campfire. Over the next few weeks I made some seats around the fire in case I had company. I was happy. It was idyllic. I had a grill propped up on bricks for cooking. Loads of wood. I've always liked playing fires. I dug a narrow trench around the fire, and flooded it every now and then to keep the ground wet. About five yards away there was a badger's set and, if I was quiet, as the light started to fade, out he'd come.

Life in my castle wasn't quite idyllic. It was cold. I know castles are supposed to be cold, damp and draughty, but not twenty-first century ones, surely? There was central heating, but it never seemed to quite hit the spot. The agents said the place was probably still drying out and warming up following the renovation. Which made sense.

All the people at Foxhill were very friendly. The warden, Ian, and his wife, Sue, lived in the bungalow fifty yards up the drive. A modern bungalow – not a proper castle like mine. Another neighbour, Roy, would come along most evenings with his dog and his gun. I never heard the rifle – it had a silencer on it. The trick was not to scare the others, so they could carry on munching and breeding, as rabbits do. I had the idea of arming the rabbits – they could hide behind the trees with their guns when the gamekeeper came to call. But life doesn't work out like that. Some of us have guns and some don't.

Roy asked me if I wanted one or two rabbits. *If I say yes, am I encouraging the slaughter? Will he shoot more?*

'If you don't want it,' he said, 'I'll leave it for the fox.'

That answered my question. My needs are equal to the fox's.

I was presented with a couple of rabbits two or three times a week, so the fox got his as well. I learned how to gut them, but never got used to it – my stomach heaved every time as I pulled out the guts, but I also learned how to make the most delicious rabbit pie.

Ava would come by once a week or so. We went for a little walk into the meadow.

'This is beautiful,' she said. 'Why haven't you shown me this before?'

There was so much to show her, so much to say. But where to begin?

Tucked away in a far distant corner of the grounds was a Japanese garden in need of a bit of t.l.c. The grounds were maintained, but this part had been neglected. There was also a maze in the grounds, but I didn't need a maze – life was throwing up enough mysteries.

I thought I'd solved the point of everything with The Meaning of Life, but it goes much further and probably always will. Every time I think I've discovered why, another why takes its place – but each one takes me nearer the truth.

Outside my magical world the other world was still revolving. 3 April – received another letter from the bailiffs:

"This execution has not been settled and I now write to give you fair warning that my Officers will attend at your premises with REMOVAL CONTRACTORS on 11/04/07.

They will be under instructions to break in if necessary so please ensure that someone is there to meet them on that day.

In order to avoid their attendance the arrears must be paid immediately to this office in the sum of £2005.89.

Should you fail to pay and the removal contractors attend you will be responsible for their charges whatever the outcome of the visit. Charges vary, depending on such factors as the journey time to your premises and the equipment the contractors bring with them. As a guide expect to pay £300.00 plus vat for the first hour and £200.00 per hour after that.

I strongly advise you to contact me at once with your immediate proposals for payment. I accept cash, banker's draft and some credit / debit cards."

Are they denying we'd sent the money? We had sent Travail the

£160, right on the button. Was he denying he'd received that too? We should have sent it by Recorded Delivery – you've got to be so sharp with these bastards.

We checked our bank – they'd received the money, and paid it in. It might have been one day late – is that all it takes for them to jump down our throat in such a violent manner? For them to act so quickly and so aggressively, they must have been watching for my payment and been absolutely delighted when it was a day late.

I sent the bailiffs my reply:

4 April 2007

Attention: John Marston, Order of the British Empire

Dear Sir,

Please let me know if you still intend stealing my property on 11 April, so I can decide what to wear.

Yours faithfully,

K Holmes

I'm not that tough. I'd worked out if they came in mob-handed I'd let them take whatever they wanted. By now D had backed up everything on her computer, and plan B was in place for all the other bits. We'd be up and running again within twenty-four hours for £500.

I knew while we stood strong we would win. There's a funeral director near our warehouse. I was going to ask them if we could borrow three coffins and prop them up open against the wall, in order to greet the bailiffs in an appropriate manner. Clint Eastwood did something like that.

I had to go over to Liverpool to see our boxes man. I phoned Ava, 'Come on, let's meet up for a coffee, you'll laugh your socks off.'

'Right, I'm getting ready. See you soon.'

I was really looking forward to it and so was she. The chance to talk at last, without the not-so-hidden agenda.

As a boy, I always had plenty of friends, but I never really had the best one like you're supposed to. I always thought I was on a different flight path to everybody else, and it kind of worked both ways. When I was a misplaced choir boy I never had to go through the initiation bit. I don't quite know why – I wasn't going to run off and tell somebody. In any case, if you're the sort of boy who would do that you got it worse. And then in Scout camp – hundreds and hundreds of Scouts, and the new boys had to swing on the rope over the stream while boys from either bank threw mud. The only way to escape was to drop into the water. I didn't get that either. It was as though I was invisible. I certainly wasn't going to volunteer. I've gone under the radar, or over it, all my life.

I knew from an early age I was going to go mad, or that's what people would think, and the only thing that was going to stop that was becoming incredibly rich. In that case, you're not mad: you're eccentric.

You can't be mad if you've got lots of money. What if I'm not mad? What if it's that the people who lust after money are mad? Money is the root of all evil… It's money that's driving John Marston, Order of the British Empire.

We sat chatting all afternoon. I thought the coffin idea was funny. It just scared her more. She's tough enough. She doesn't scare easily. I was just going a bit too far. 'They'll just take the coffins as well,' she said. We're sitting in a busy cafe in the middle of Liverpool – and I'm wearing a skirt. It amused the young couple sitting at the next table, and it amused Ava – she had to take some photographs on her mobile.

We knew the bailiffs' activities were very wrong, but how to prove it in law? Nevertheless, we started Court proceedings against them. The guidelines on do's and don'ts for bailiffs were vague and inconclusive. We went to the local Court and asked to see the Court Bailiff. We explained a little of what had gone on. He said, 'Well, we wouldn't do that.' It appeared that the Court-appointed bailiffs adhere to pretty fixed guidelines, but the private bailiffs are a law unto themselves.

11 April – Bailiffs Day. I didn't get the coffins. There's something about funeral people – they always look a bit morbid. I didn't think they would see the funny side. I didn't ask them. I did think about borrowing crash hats from Biker Mike next door: one for him, one for D, one for me, and doing a line dance when they arrived, to the tune of 'Nathan Jones' as sung by Bananarama. It was nothing to do with anything in particular, we just thought it would be funny.

They didn't turn up.

Springtime. Lighter nights meant I could cook my evening meal on my campfire. I got the longest garden hose I could, and it just about made it from the house, up through the scrubland and along the tree line to the fire, so that from time to time I could flood the little moat around the fire and keep the ground damp. Two days later, the water dried up. I checked the connection in the house – everything seemed to be OK. I traced the hose along the tree line, and there I found the leak: a little hole had been chewed in the hose. That had to be my friend 'Ratachewie'.

I first met Rat shortly after I'd moved to Foxhill. There were three or four steps on the path that led up to the woods. The steps were edged by a dry stone wall. As I walked up, my path was blocked. There he stood, on guard on the top of the dry stone wall, a formidable figure. He was only about six or eight inches tall, but big enough to stop me. I froze, transfixed. Standing up to his full height, matchstick arms waving as high as they could, his little head and fat belly wobbled and gyrated in some sort of tribal dance. Our Mexican Stand-Off didn't last long – I think we both retreated at the same speed. I raced back to the kitchen to put the kettle on and make some tea while I thought about it.

I told D about this incident the next day and she Googled 'rat belly dance' on the internet, and there it was, described exactly as I'd seen him. He was defending his territory. The dry stone wall was his house, and had been for some time. It was me who shouldn't have been there; I was the intruder.

I repaired the hose. I had no doubt that Rat had bitten the piece out of it. From then on he became 'Ratachewie'. He kindly left me and the hose alone after that. I'd been punished enough for disturbing his territory.

Barclays changed their Chairman. I think at this time it was Marcus Agius. Anyway I sent him a letter demanding £5,000 payable immediately as some small compensation for the stress and all the time I was spending in trying to clear my name. £5,000 was the limit you could claim in the Small Claims Court. He wasn't going to pay it, but now we had a figure to hang our hat on.

We started proceedings in the Small Claims Court. Our claim charged Barclays plc with forgery of my signature on two documents which authorised a subsidiary company of theirs to extract money from my company's account. I demanded £5,000 in compensation for some of the time spent in an effort to resolve this.

The Court sent the official claim to Barclays, which they could not ignore.

Barclays responded to the Court in the following manner:

"We, Barclays Bank plc, intend to apply for an order that the claim be struck out pursuant to CPRr 3.4 for non compliance with CPRr 16.2 and CPRr 16.4, with summary judgment for the Defendant pursuant to CPRr 24.2 together with costs in favour of the Defendant because the Claim Form discloses no reasonable grounds for bringing the Claim, is an abuse of the Court's process, fails to comply with CPRr 16.2 and 16.4 and the Claimant has no real prospect of succeeding on his claim."

We hadn't a clue what all the CPRr references were. Barclays then went on with a further five paragraphs, the fifth one being:

"'In the circumstances, Mr Holmes is the incorrect party to have issued this Claim and as such it is an abuse of the Court's process and does not disloses no reasonable grounds (sic) *for bringing the case. For the above reasons the Claimant does not have a real prospect of succeeding on his Claim and I respectfully request that it be struck out under the Court's inherent case management powers."*

All five paragraphs were in a similar vein. I don't know whether it was some sort of legal jargon, but it appeared to me some of the grammar was atrocious. Or was it just some sort of legal gobbledegook designed to confuse and deter peasants like me?

The Court had set a date for the hearing of Barclays' application, at 10:45 on the 21 June. The hearing was to decide if Barclays had a case to answer.

We had a month to prepare for the hearing. In my mind, the claim was straightforward – either they forged my signature or they did not. But then Barclays probably had a Legal Department bigger than the Wrexham Court. And what were all these CPRr things?

Even though I was delving into an area in which I had no experience whatsoever, it didn't phase me in the slightest because we knew we had right on our side – and D was there to do the paperwork. And the good guys win, don't they? Though whoever wins they're going to be in charge of the media, so they're going to be the good guys anyway.

There was a lot of correspondence to and from the legal department of Barclays, as well as from Marstons. As usual, I addressed my correspondence to 'John Marston Order of the British Empire'; it was him I was after. I wanted to make sure he personally was getting the letters, and that wasn't clear from the correspondence, so I phoned his office.

'This is The Lade-Back Company,' I said. 'We've just received a letter and I want to clarify – was the letter from John Marston?'

An excited voice at the other end said, 'Are you Ken?'

'Yes,' I said. I had visions of him covering up the mouthpiece and saying to the rest of the office, 'I've got *Ken* on the phone!' as if I was some kind of local hero standing up to the ogre. The letter was from John Marston.

The day before the Barclays hearing, we received a letter from Adrian Ruffhead of their Legal Department threatening me with very high legal costs and the costs for the barrister they would be appointing, stating that we would have to pay all Barclays' costs *when* we lost, and suggesting we withdraw. Did he think I was going to buckle under a threat like that? It only made me more determined. If he was so sure he was going to win, why was he threatening me the day before the hearing with liability for the costs? He wasn't so sure he was going to win, was he?

Now it was 21 June, and we were to come face to face with Barclays in Wrexham County Court. The list of cases was pinned up on the wall, as before: K Holmes vs Barclays Bank plc. I liked the sound of that.

Barclays' barrister introduced herself outside the Courtroom. Confident, self-assured, she informed us of the procedure in a somewhat patronising manner. She obviously saw all this as a foregone conclusion, and I was just an irritant to be dealt with swiftly and with minimal inconvenience.

The hearing was informal, the barrister sitting on one side of the table, D and I on the other, the Judge at the head.

She had a very clear agenda, confidently and authoritatively saying to the Judge that it should never have come to Court. Instantly I sensed there was something of an Old Boys' network here, and I wasn't part of it; this was her turf.

She knew exactly what buttons to press, or thought she did. She prattled on saying that if there was any case to answer it should have been brought by the parties to the contract, in other words The Lade-Back Company Limited should be the Claimant, not me; and Clearly Business should be the Defendant, not Barclays. She told the Judge I was totally irresponsible and wasting the Court's time. She went on like this at some length as if I'd just crawled out from under a stone.

I told the Judge that I had never entered into a contract with Clearly Business; I had never even heard of a company called Clearly Business. Clearly Business was only acting on instructions from Barclays, and it was Barclays that had forged my signature, and that my signature was my property, and not the property of The Lade-Back Company. It was my property that had been fraudulently used. *And if you don't stop talking about me like this I'm going to take my ball away.*

She knew perfectly well my claim was one of forgery, but repeatedly tried to distract the Judge on points of contract law. For a while it worked. Deputy District Judge Jones-Evans seemed somewhat confused over what my claim actually was, which was probably her intention.

D tried to interject, and was abruptly silenced by the Judge. There was no doubt his sympathies leaned towards the barrister. After all, she came from the same school he did. And who were we to dare take on the establishment?

'And how did you arrive at this £5,000?' he said.

D and I had spent hours arriving at £5,000. It was listed in full detail before him. The barrister had a copy of it too. She said, mockingly, 'You can't claim £40 per hour for drafting correspondence.'

I smiled sarcastically and looked at her. 'I can't claim £40 per hour? What are you charging – £400 per hour – and you're questioning my £40 per hour!' She shut up.

Eventually the Judge began his summing up. I didn't like the way it was going. He'd done everything he possibly could during the hearing to get me to drop my claim. As he concluded his summing up, he said, 'It is with much regret…' My heart sank – he had found against us. 'It is with much regret,' he said, 'that the case goes to trial.' That's what I wanted. His phrase flashed over and over in a split second. I glanced at the barrister. She looked angry and shocked. The regret he felt was definitely not for me. He could see there was a likelihood that forgery had been committed and that Barclays were possibly the perpetrators. He was regretting the fact that Barclays had to answer to the Court and he couldn't think of a way to stop it.

He then went on to say that it would be extremely unlikely for me to win, still trying to goad me into dropping the case. He could see it was having no effect but continued, saying even if I did win I would not receive anything like the £5,000 I was claiming. At the very most I would be awarded a nominal amount of around £50 to £100.

'This is not about money any more, it's about justice and principle,' I said.

'This is not a court of morals.'

'Perhaps it should be,' I said.

He didn't respond further. That seemed to strike home. He just went on to say that not only would I have to prove forgery, I'd have to prove who did it, and that Barclays knew about it. He concluded, saying, 'I'm allocating four hours for the trial.'

In the corridor outside the Court room, I stopped the barrister and told her everybody in the Court knew it was a forgery. Her superior, self-assured confident manner long gone, she tried to brush past me. I wouldn't let it go.

'Everybody in the Court knew it was a forgery.' There had only been four of us in the room, of course, but I was in drama mode.

'I can't possibly discuss this.'

'It's a blatant forgery, and you know it.'

Flustered and agitated, she said, 'My client is Barclays,' and hurried past me to the sanctuary of the solicitors' room, and probably locked herself in.

D and I left the Court. The first blood was ours, and against the odds. She'd been certain she was going to win. Her cocky attitude was evidence of that. And the Judge? Supposed to be an impartial upholder of the law. We were in the Small Claims Court, and Barclays had sent a barrister charging £400 per hour. The Judge was arrogant and abrupt, telling D to be quiet when she'd attempted to clarify something. OK, there are rules to be obeyed, and perhaps all the discussions should have been handled by me, but we're not trained barristers. The Small Claims Court – a court for the common man? Don't you believe it.

'It is with much regret,' he'd said, *'that the case goes to trial.'* That

phrase spoke volumes, and was now running round my head: it's not just Barclays we're taking on, it's the prejudice of the Courts now. And he's allocated four hours for the trial. Four hours? Little cameos of what had been said in the Court played over and over in my head, and still do. *'It is with much regret that the case goes to trial.'* It is with much regret? Barclays have committed forgery, and he's saying *it's with much regret?* If the roles had been reversed, and I'd been the one who'd committed forgery, he'd have been giving me one of those sinister looks and putting the black cloth on his head.

A few days later we received another letter from Adrian Ruffhead offering £160 in full and final settlement of my claim, subject to my agreeing that the existence and terms of the offer remain confidential between the parties.

That was the value he placed on a charge of forgery, and a measure of his gross arrogance to think that my demand for justice was going to be bought for £160.

It would be about nine o'clock in the morning. D and I were bashing away at the Venture backs in the doorway of the warehouse as usual. It was a good way of getting rid of the pent-up emotion from yesterday's trial. Though there wasn't any really; we'd won.

A car pulled up nearby, and a man in a suit suit got out. D looked at me nervously. 'Don't worry,' I said, 'It's OK'. He walked towards us. Had we seen Mr Rowlands, he asked. He was due to meet with him about now. Colin Rowlands was the landlord. 'No,' I said, 'But come in and make yourself a cup of tea if you like, while you're waiting.' It was starting to rain a bit. He came in, but declined the tea. He was very interested in what we were doing. I told him about my inventions. I don't need a lot of encouragement to talk about myself. I eventually asked him what his business was. He hesitated, then said quietly, 'Inland Revenue'. 'Oh, you're just the guy I want to see!' I said. He was a bit taken aback – he'd never had that reaction before. I told him we were way behind with our PAYE and the VAT. Between them we owed over £8,000. He said, 'Right, well this is what you do... contact so and so at the Tax Office, explain your position, and they'll listen. You'll be surprised.'

Colin Rowlands arrived and my visitor walked to meet him. He turned and said, 'Good luck with the invention.'

'Luck doesn't exist, you know.'

He stopped and came back.

'Luck doesn't exist. It was invented by fools and losers. Life helps those who go for it.'

'I agree with that,' he said, and went on his way.

That afternoon I spoke to Gwen Roberts at the Revenue office, and arranged a meeting.

Gwen was one of the senior managers at the Revenue office. It was a very bizarre meeting. We must have been talking for about twenty minutes or half an hour before the subject of money cropped up. By that time she knew all about the inventions. We'd even discussed at some length our mutual belief in the existence of another life beyond this. She knew just as well as I that another life existed, and she was looking forward to seeing her sister again.

Eventually it came to the money. I told her our finances were stretched to the limit and the bank wouldn't lend us any money – no security. She nodded towards the Kiasu Easel on the desk as if to say: if that's not an asset, what is? I totally agree, but the banks have never considered the inventions as an asset, despite the obvious potential. She started scribbling down some numbers and running them through the calculator. She worked out a very reasonable schedule to enable us to pay back the arrears. She also offered to negotiate with the VAT on our behalf.

I'd been dreading facing the tax problem, and now I wondered why – everything appears to have a solution. That was down to a chance meeting with a Revenue man – or perhaps it wasn't by chance – and Gwen Roberts with her intelligent approach to the problem. She's convinced of an afterlife as much as I am, and not through religious doctrine. *Perhaps she'll introduce me to her sister. No, that sounds like some sort of date, doesn't it. Do they have dates? I'm sure they do. I mean, anything goes doesn't it? You might be able to go on a date with Moll Flanders or Boudicca.* I even talked with Gwen about some of the poetry I was writing. She and her partner loved poetry.

CHAPTER 25

Two trials coming up. There's always enough to fill your day.

Judgment Day

And so as the trial begins
And you're brought to account for your sins
Every law you have broken
Every slander you've spoken
Every crime you've committed
There'll be not one omitted
Every lie you have told
Now the truth will unfold
Every small misdemeanour
Every penny you've pilfered
Despite the amount
You'll be brought to account
Every thoughtless deed
Your obsession with greed
The Court will consider
Now how do you plead

Now the gallows are ready
Your head wracked with pain
Your legs are unsteady
And it's starting to rain
I admit to the court
I committed the crime

But I did some washing this morning
And it's still on the line
And it's still there now
'Cause I didn't have time
I promise the court
I won't do it again
Please have mercy m'lord
'Cause it's started to rain

Silence in court
While I try to decide
You say you did some washing
And it's all still outside
Well invoking the powers
Vested in me
I declare to the court
You're allowed to go free
So calm down young man
There's no need to shout
You're guilty as charged
There was never a doubt
But you can't hang a man
While his washing's still out.

Ava was in my castle sitting on the coffee table, leaning back against the radiator to keep warm. I read the poem. She snatched it off me like an excited child, as usual. She loved the poetry. She loved me. But then the barrier would come down. A brick wall, impenetrable. I don't know why. I don't think she did really. I said, 'There's something blocking this.' I've said that before.

Of an evening I'd wander around by my camp fire, practising my day in Court, hooking my thumbs under my imaginary lapels as the barrister for the prosecution addressing the dock, and the twelve good men and true:

I put it to you that on the night in question you did not go to Milton Keynes. Instead, you took the overnight train from St Pancras through the

Channel Tunnel and, instead of going to Paris, you bribed the train driver to take you straight to Morocco (pause as gasps ripple through the Court room) and there, disguised as a bedouin tribesman, you went to the Grand Hotel, Casablanca, where, as part of your carefully contrived plan, you administered the poison in the Contessa's night-time glass of warm milk. Then you hired a racing camel and rode with all speed back to the Channel Tunnel, cleverly disguising the camel as a parcel van. You drove to the Majestic Hotel, Milton Keynes (pause, as more gasps ripple round the Court room), and there you had previously hidden in the grounds of the Majestic Hotel a pair of beige corduroy trousers and a cardigan. You quickly changed, mingled with the guests coming down for breakfast at nine-thirty...

At this point the accused breaks down and admits everything. Cheers from the gallery.

I wondered whether to get dressed up for Court. Couldn't tell D – she'd go mad. If I do, I'll need to get a coat and Bobby Shaftoe shoes again. The coat I'd hired had been fine for the NEC, but not for the Court. I'd need something more sombre, in keeping with the occasion – certainly not gold velvet. The shoes were OK – in fact they were great – but I didn't want to hire them. I wanted my own pair.

Gary at Lily Bizarre got me a new pair of shoes from his supplier for fifty pounds. Brilliant. But he didn't have a suitable coat. He reckoned he could get one made, but that was getting complicated and it sounded expensive. I could make one – I'd made the skirt. But when I say 'I', I mean D. I'll have to tell her.

I hadn't a clue how to go about making a coat. But D did. She knew exactly how. Despite her protestations that the whole idea was stupid, we got a pattern for a period coat, circa sixteenth century, and went to Aberkhan with a shopping list. We bought about three and a half yards of slate grey velvet with just a touch of burgundy in it. Superb. Grey lining. Six yards of black edging braid. The whole lot cost me about £20, plus the pattern.

I made a mock-up coat out of some old curtains just to see. It seemed to work. And now for the proper job. But not just yet – the hearing with the bailiffs was looming, so the coat went on the back burner.

We received a witness statement from the bailiffs. And now, for the first time, they have included D's car, her own private car, for seizure.

D was furious and very, very upset. She phoned them and told them it was her own private car. 'Prove it,' they said. They'd use whatever lever or tool they could to get at me and support their evil mission, and cause as much stress as possible. These people don't know much about human nature – mine, anyway. It just made me more incensed, and more determined to bury him.

My castle in Frodsham was just the place for this medieval knight to plan his campaigns – stuck on the side of a hill, surrounded by countryside, about a mile away from the village centre. For a long time I've liked going out for an early pint or two, though I don't drink pints any more – I drink halves – for no other reason than just to be different. Three or four halves does me. I'd been to Frodsham before with D and a couple of friends. Nice place. A number of pubs, a couple of restaurants, take-aways, that sort of thing. The usual stuff. But now there was a difference – I was wearing a skirt.

It was only seven o'clock in the evening. At least the good old lads wouldn't have had their six or eight pints yet. I had my three halves. There were a couple of sniggers, sidelong looks, but pretty uneventful. I left the pub, walked down the high street, and turned left on to the main street to get to my car. There was a gang of lads in front, outside a pub. A warm summer evening, nice place to be.

Do I walk round, or try and cross over? No, can't do that. Can't stop, either. Just keep walking. The heckles started. *Why the fuck am I wearing a skirt? Have I got some sort of death wish?* Amidst the jeers I heard a voice: 'I tell you what, that lad's got some bottle.' *That's a good thing. Do I stop, give him some money? No! Keep going. Why the hell do I put myself through this?*

Why am I wearing a skirt? I've asked myself that question thousands of times. I now know: it wasn't my idea, it was the Gods'. One day, while I was busy trying to do something else, they said to me: 'You will go from this place and make a skirt, and then you will go forth wearing the skirt.' And that's what happened. You can't goeth against the Gods. If you don't believe the Gods exist – where have all the socks gone?

How many times have you sorted out the washing and found a sock missing? First of all you check the ones you've paired up to see if it's been matched with another one, which is a bit stupid really because even if you do you're still left with an odd sock. And you check the empty washing machine just in case it's stuck at the top of the drum. It's not important. Just annoying, and you've got more important things to worry about. But still, when you're putting the socks away you make sure it wasn't in your sock drawer all the time – but it's not. And that's about it. You know it's going to turn up somewhere. You always keep the spare one. Because wouldn't you be the stupid one if you threw it away and it turned up the next day. It never does.

Well, I've got news for you: the Gods have got them. There, I've said it. And they've been doing it for years. I don't care if I've blown their cover; I owe them one for making me wear a skirt.

'You know the socks that go missing in the washing machine?'
'Yes.'
'I know where they've gone.'
'I *know* where they've gone.'
'The Gods have taken them.'
'No they haven't. It's the little green pixie who lives behind the washing machine – eats them.'
I'll get her one day. I just hope it's on this planet.

My trips to the highlights of Frodsham became a regular event. I became quite good friends with the landlord and lady of one of the pubs. They never asked me why I wore a skirt, they just accepted it. Most of the men thought it weird or stupid – but the women didn't. Women I'd never met before would strike up conversation. They were coming on to me. They thought it was sexy! This confused the men even more – and me, for that matter.

As my confidence grew I travelled further afield. I went to a big posh pub. It looked as though it doubled as a night club towards the weekend. Right now, midweek, it was pretty well empty apart from a gang of about a dozen lads in a big circle, all sitting around chatting, probably about football or cars – the usual stuff. I sensed a reaction as I walked past them to the bar. I got my drink and went and sat at a table nearby. If they were going to have a go at me, bring it on. I could hear the muttering and sniggers. I went back up to the bar for another half, and there was a wolf whistle. I turned round and walked over to them.

I stared at them all, one by one, as if I was in some kind of spaghetti western, until one by one they backed down. The last one said: 'Oh, it's just a joke.'

'Oh, you're a comedian.' I said, and went back to my half. Nothing more was said.

I would never have had the guts to behave like that before. Is that how Superman felt when he put his underpants on the outside? No, it's nothing to do with that at all – I had no choice.

My castle was still cold, and it was summertime. The Diocese's promise of double glazing hadn't happened yet. There was central heating, but putting that on in summer wasn't right. I'd built a fitted wardrobe in the bedroom and, because I am me, it had to be wacky. It was built across the corner with separate compartments for all my socks and shoes, the front screened with full length heavy curtains. I kept reminding the Diocese about the damp atmosphere. Nothing was done. They had tidied up and painted the outside, and it looked really smart... but cold.

When she came round we'd share a glass of wine out of my pesto jar. She loved me from the very first night. I kind of thought that would have been it. I mean, love at first sight – isn't that what the fairy tale says? How did I know there was a whole pile of other stuff? The trouble with fairy tales is you've got to slay the giants. And this slaying giants business is hard work, and don't let anybody tell you different. Telling her I'm going to slay the giants isn't enough, apparently. You don't talk about it – you do it.

CHAPTER 26

The hearing with the bailiffs was now just one week away. We received a letter enclosing a statement of their costs in readiness for the hearing: £3,478.09. A Small Claims Court hearing, and they were throwing a very expensive barrister at it.

Again D trawled through the minefield on enforcement law on the internet. A comparatively new law of harassment came up. We'd been accusing the bailiffs of threatening and menacing behaviour, and bullying – that had to be harassment, hadn't it? We were trying to turn ourselves into lawyers and barristers overnight and pit our wits against the Judiciary's finest, and now it's just one week away. John Marston, Order of the British Empire – he hadn't selected his barrister out of the Yellow Pages, had he? Harassment should have been our claim, but how the hell were we supposed to know that? And it was too late now.

I wore the only suit I now possessed – the dinner suit. I went to the hearing with some trepidation, nervous anticipation. Was he going to be there? Was I going to confront him at last?

He wasn't. I suppose I was somewhat relieved. It was just the Judge, D, me and Mr Brennan, Marstons' barrister. Pretty soon after the hearing got under way, the atmosphere relaxed, not a bit like I'd expected. An air of mutual respect. Mr Brennan noticed that and said something to that effect. It seems he was expecting a different atmosphere also. He was good. Very good. Well practised in his familiar arena. Not pompous or arrogant as I might have expected, but courteous, intelligent, respectful. He began reciting similar cases, similar scenarios, in great detail. Each one illustrated claims similar to mine that had failed.

My claim, that the bailiffs were taking away the ability of The Lade-

Back Company to function, i.e. removing the company's computer, etc., was linked to the law which says the bailiff is not entitled to take away the tools of trade. I knew that it was meant to refer to the plumber's spanner or the joiner's saw, but I was trying to argue that The Lade-Back Company was itself a tool, my tool. I'd created the company to promote and develop my inventions and without that tool I would not be able to practise my trade. That might be a clever argument in some courtroom drama on the television, but we knew it was a grey area.

The Judge also pointed out that the bailiffs don't have to list item for item the goods they wish to seize – they are entitled to take everything. Their powers are colossal. They listed items to draw to our attention that they could close us down within minutes.

Mr Brennan had come prepared with a number of precedents to support his defence regarding seizure of tools of trade. Perhaps it was part of his plan to list them out in great detail. The Judge commented at one point, as he noticed me leaning back on my chair, 'He's using this against you, you know.' I said, 'Oh yes, I know what he's doing. I haven't nodded off yet.' Mr Brennan continued his articulate recital. I realise now that was probably his ploy, to wear me down.

I guided my argument towards the bullying tactics the bailiffs had employed. I showed the Judge the latest letter we'd received from the bailiff. The second 'Van letter'. He read it and handed it back, then Mr Brennan asked if he could read it. Neither commented on it at that stage, but they both understood what effect that kind of letter was intended to have. They both would have reflected on the effect of receiving such a letter themselves.

The Judge, realising where my argument was leading, commented, 'As you've learned more about the law you have focused your arguments towards the charge of harassment.' He wasn't being critical, it was just his observation.

Harassment! I'd known all along the bailiffs had to be breaking some law but I couldn't identify it. I thought I'd found it a month before with blackmail. I must have read half a dozen dictionary definitions of the word blackmail to make it fit. It wasn't right. Extortion wasn't right either. Menacing, threatening, bullying. I'd gone back to blackmail. I had written to John Marston accusing him of blackmail and told him we were taking legal advice, but all the time the clock had been ticking, and I had nobody to give me legal advice anyway. It was down to us. We'd discovered the crime of harassment all too late – that bloody word the Judge had just used.

We were in a Court of Law; I couldn't just change my claim to one of harassment, much as I wanted to. My claim was that he was taking away the tools of my trade.

Both the Judge and Mr Brennan were well aware of what tactics the bailiffs had employed. In their defence, the Judge said, 'The bailiffs are just the piggy in the middle.' 'A good description,' I said. He laughed.

It was probably drifting towards the end when the Judge referred to the bailiff's tactics as 'robust'. As I heard that word I realised which way the judgment was going to go. Robust? Heavy-handed? Maybe, but not illegal.

Whether I was beaten by a better man on the day, or whether I was charging him with the wrong crime, it doesn't really matter. I'd given it my best shot, and felt calm and relaxed throughout the whole procedure. The Judge asked me if I had anything more to add. I searched deep inside. The well was dry. 'What time does the pub open?' They both laughed.

The Judge gave his lengthy summing up. The outcome was inevitable. After his judgment he said, 'Well you know now there's a matter of expenses.'

'I go bankrupt,' I said.

'Don't do that,' said the Judge.

Mr Brennan turned to me, 'That's not as easy as you think.'

'This was easy?'

He didn't respond. He knew more than anyone how much effort we'd gone to.

The Judge addressed the matter of costs.

'The number of hours spent on that seems excessive…'

Mr Brennan acknowledged, without comment.

'The solicitor's hourly rate for preparing that document is high… that would be the sort of thing handled by…' and so on.

Mr Brennan didn't argue at all. He made it clear he wasn't there to defend the costs.

I'd kind of switched off now. I'd lost the case. I was about as interested in the costs as the barrister. Whatever they came down to, I couldn't afford it. The Judge must have seen this and said, 'I'm arguing on your behalf.' I told him, 'There's not a lot of point. I can't afford it anyway.' But he continued.

The Judge reduced the expenses to £2,000.

'Can you afford £75 a month?'

I didn't expect that, and woke up. I nodded, 'Yes, sir.'

'Have you any other County Court Judgments against you?'

'No, sir, apart from the High Court Judgment relating to this.'

He addressed Mr Brennan, suggesting if the judgment were to be recorded in such and such a manner it would not appear as a County Court Judgment against me. Mr Brennan nodded in full agreement. The Judge turned to me and said, 'As long as you keep up the payments, it won't affect your credit rating.' He didn't have to do that. He'd also reduced the charges by nearly half; the £2,000 was fixed with no interest accruing, and even I could afford £75 per month.

Mr Brennan then addressed the Judge,

'It is my experience that when something goes wrong it continues to do so. Can we stay the Writ of Fi Fa?'

The fi-fi what? I thought.

The Judge agreed.

D looked past me to Mr Brennan and said a heartfelt, 'Thank you'. Fi-fi apparently meant a lot to D, and that was enough for me.

That was it – the end. Mr Brennan was standing next to me, as he had been all the time. He turned and said, 'You really put the wind up him.'

I looked at him in disbelief.

'You could have brought him down.'

'That was my intention, and still is.'

'He could have had his licence revoked.'

The enormity of what he had just said went right through me.

I thought for a moment, then turned to him, 'Thanks for that.'

'That's OK.'

It would be easy to forget what had brought about this whole procedure. It started as a simple late payment of a bill, that can happen to all businesses at any time. A debt that started off at £1,200 had now apparently, according to the bailiffs, inflated to over £1,900, and according to Travail it was over £2,000. I'd asked them to justify the inflated price and they hadn't.

I said to the Judge, 'There seem to be some differing opinions on what we're being asked to pay Travail.' He said, 'Well that's clear. I can tell you that.' He left the Court room and reappeared with a copy of the Court Order that said the Judgment Debt was £1,609.58. This was considerably less than the bailiffs and Travail were demanding – but now we had been advised of the correct amount by the Judge himself, and as far as I was concerned that was the law. Any additional money claimed by Travail or the bailiffs was pure fantasy.

I had been very impressed with the courtesy and professionalism of the Court. Even though the outcome wasn't in our favour I felt the victory was ours.

It was probably something to do with the respect shown by Judge Perry and Mr Brennan, staying the Writ of Fi Fa, but above all Mr Brennan telling me effectively that John Marston OBE was scared. Three things Brennan said: You really put the wind up him; You could have brought him down; He could have had his licence revoked. Marston knew he was abusing his authority. He'll openly brag about this victory, but when he goes to bed at night he'll wonder how close he came and whether it might happen again.

On reflection, we were never going to achieve victory in the usually accepted sense. It would have set a precedent that could have had serious ramifications. Bailiffs have a necessary position in society. To stop that position being abused would be very complex, and not for this day. But perhaps we gave a bully a bloody nose and something to think about.

The remarks made by Mr Brennan at the end of the hearing about the concerns of John Marston OBE, and also his request for the Writ of Fi Fa to be stayed (which I now understand meant cancelling the authority for the bailiffs to act against us) will stay with me for ever.

This case should not have come to Court, this whole procedure had been unnecessary, and the Judge and the barrister knew that. They knew we had behaved correctly throughout. The charges brought by Travail and the subsequent involvement by Thomas Higgins, Solicitors, and the bailiffs they selected for the debt collection, were instigated by greed and abuse of the law.

I was extremely proud of what D and I achieved that day, but it's only now, as I attempt to write the story, that I realise the true level of that achievement. Although Judge Perry was chairing a Small Claims Court on this occasion, he was a District Judge, called upon when necessary to preside over criminal proceedings. Likewise, Mr Brennan was at the top of his profession. How often in their careers had they been able to speak in such a favourable manner to the losing party?

The offer we had made to Travail was received within the time scale. Travail knew that, Thomas Higgins knew that, and the bailiffs knew that. Should we have sent it by Recorded Delivery? Maybe. But is that what the world is now – full of liars and cheats? Lust for money, whether it's within the law or not. Where there are ruthless and dishonest people the law doesn't always come down on the side of truth. Not in this life, anyway. But there will be justice one day. Of that I am certain.

On reflection, we were never going to win. If we had, the ramifications of setting such a precedent would have been enormous. Although if we hadn't have gone for it with the absolute certainty that we were going to win we would never have achieved what we did. But then, how does one evaluate victory? Was it a victory for truth and honesty?

Should I have conducted myself better in the trial? Could I have done? What would I do differently if I faced it again? Because I was going to – in four weeks I was going head to head with Barclays in the same Court. There's always something you wish you'd said, or perhaps could have said better, with more punch – though I can't think what it was. Apart from one occasion when Mr Brennan addressed Judge Perry saying something like, 'I'm sure the Judge has forgotten more than I've ever learned.' I just wish I'd said, 'Is my learned colleague suggesting the Judge is forgetful?'

CHAPTER 27

'What is it you love about me?'

'It's not you I love, it's your soul.'

'Where is my soul? Is it in my face, in my body?'

'Somewhere near your cunt I expect.'

I never talked about the incident at the party again. It wasn't some dark premonition – no point in that. It might have been a warning of what might happen if…

We stood outside Foxhill for a while.

'You're so cute.'

It was as though she was looking deep inside, seeing me for the first time. The first time anybody has seen me.

I've secretly harboured the notion that I have been cute all my life, but nobody's ever said it until now. And it had to be her.

Over the last couple of months the environment in my castle had become more and more uncomfortable, and there was still no sign of the promised double-glazing. The main problem was in the bedroom, damp patches were now appearing on the walls, black mould in the corners and my clothes in the wardrobe were always damp. I moved out of the bedroom. The second bedroom wasn't any better, so I moved my bed into the dining room, which seemed less of a problem. I took what clothes I needed out of the wardrobe and put them in a box by the bed. I was just never able to make the place warm and cosy.

I'd already told the Diocese either they make the property good now or I move out until they do. I was addressing my complaint to the agents, who supposedly passed it on to the Diocese. I was told in an abrupt manner that as I had signed a six-month lease if I did move out I would still be liable for the rent. Pay the rent on a property that was not fit to live in? I sent them photographs of my clothes, shoes and furniture that were now growing green mould, and told them that as one third of the property was uninhabitable I wanted the rent reducing by that amount. The Diocese apparently refused. The Diocese was hiding behind the skirts of the agents, and in turn the agents were blaming the Diocese – very convenient. I was being ignored. I wrote to the agents telling them if they didn't do something about the situation immediately I would send a report to ARLA, their trade association. That pressed the right buttons.

The agents sent a surveyor round to check the damp. He told me he'd found an excessively high level of 'ambient moisture' in the property. Despite this surveyor's report, the Diocese still maintained the property wasn't damp. If 'excessively high levels of ambient moisture' doesn't constitute damp, what does? The whole situation was becoming bizarre. I asked the Diocese to send a representative round to discuss it. Every situation has a solution, but without dialogue there could never be one. The Diocese declined.

I had loved my time in Foxhill, and that was the point: it was in the past. Now I'd lost interest totally. No more camp fires, no more rabbit pie. I sent the agents a bill for £1200 being one-third of the rent I'd paid to date. They didn't pay it, of course – I wasn't surprised. I told them if they didn't pay it I would go to the Small Claims Court. I knew how to do that now.

It was a perfectly justified complaint and now, instead of its being resolved amicably, they've got an angry tenant – and this isn't some rogue landlord, this is the Church of England.

I asked the agents for copies of all the correspondence they'd had with the Diocese regarding this matter. At first they declined, until I pointed out that the Court would require this, and the Judge would draw his own conclusions if they refused. All the correspondence was delivered by hand the following day. From this point, I directed my complaint to the Diocese. The Diocese responded, saying that the person dealing with this matter was away for a few days. But then contradicted themselves – pretending they didn't know something when it was clear from their later correspondence that they knew all the time.

Lying never works – you'd think they'd know that. *Oh, what tangled webs we weave, when first we practise to deceive.*

We got an email from Peter Gowrley at the Diocese saying the person attending to this matter was 'away for a few days'. The next day we got a letter from Birch Cullimore, their solicitors – highlighting all the points that reportedly couldn't be addressed until the person dealing with it was available a few days later. Obviously divine intervention had taken place. The only reason why I'm regurgitating all this is because it was the Church of England – they were just as guilty as the bailiffs and Barclays of lying, cheating and bullying.

In the end, I received a bundle of correspondence from the Diocese's solicitor, Birch Cullimore, including a number of case history reports of a similar nature, going to great lengths to illustrate that if the case did go to Court I would not succeed. Their accompanying letter also advised me that I should take legal advice, and concluded with enclosing a cheque for £900.

I opened the heavy envelope and saw the cheque for £900 – that'll do. I wrote back saying, 'You have gone to a great deal of trouble to illustrate that I have no chance of success in Court. You also suggest I take legal advice. You would not have done that unless it was in your best interests. If, on the other hand, your advice was well meant, I apologize, but then I would suggest the Diocese appoint different advisers. Then you enclose a cheque for £900. Very interesting.'

I waited for the cheque to clear before I sent that letter, and that was the end of it.

How I'd misjudged Foxhill. When I first saw it I knew destiny was weaving its magic spell – I was meant to be there. I'd envisaged having deep philosophical discussions with the leaders of the Church on the Meaning of Life. From time to time the main house was used as a conference centre, bringing together different religions – predominantly Roman Catholic and Church of England – who would discuss their common ground. Ian, the warden, told me this, but he also said the discussions never came to anything, and never would. They were all preoccupied with their own best interests, and little better than the other so-called leaders of our society.

I returned my castle to Ratachewie, and hoped he would have more success.

Pretty well everybody in Barclays must have known about the dispute and pending court case. Nevertheless they were still my bankers and I was getting good service from Paul Jones, my new man. We got on well. I knew he was aware of the history. I said to him once, 'Whatever happens, I've tried.'

'Tried?' he said, looking at me, chuckling, 'You can say that again.'

I moved to an apartment in Lavister about three miles South of Chester. It didn't have the charm of Foxhill, but it was warm and dry, and pleasant enough – what I needed.

I shouldn't have been forced to leave Foxhill, and that's what it had amounted to. The conditions of the property were wrong, but the real crime was not that there was a damp and unpleasant atmosphere – the real crime was that they lied. Not a big lie in the scale of things, but the way they lied convinced me they were capable of lying about far greater things.

Shouldn't they be the ones to know that honesty and truth is the only way? Don't they say there's another life beyond this? Isn't honesty one of the prerequisites to getting yourself a decent job there?

Am I as wise as I thought I would be?
I'm not surprised, though perhaps I should be.
I don't tell lies, or is that the smug me?
And when I cry, is she there to hug me?

Here I lie –
in the pit I dug me.

I don't imagine there'll be jobs for bankers there, or bailiffs. They won't be needed. But there will be jobs. The pubs aren't open all the time.

KINGDOM OF GODS – VACANCIES

Visionary:	*Discussing practical philosophy with the marsupials; exploring the benefits of the modern pouch in the overall scheme of things.*
Politician:	*No longer required.*
Philosopher:	*You tell us.*
Inventor:	*Assessing life expectancy of a good idea, and the*

	ramifications; and should these be considered before you have the idea in the first place.
Honest Man:	To assess why truth is such a rare commodity; and what would happen if it wasn't. (No applications received to date.)
Ostrich:	Bring your own sand.
Everybody:	Consider the consequences of your actions.
Somebody:	Eliminate the last vacancy because nothing's getting done.
Geronimo:	Ready Steady Go-ist for the lemmings. Urgent please – there's a big queue.

The trial with Barclays was just four weeks away, and I had no idea what to expect. The trial with the bailiffs didn't seem to have given me anything to draw on. This was much bigger – four hours – and I hadn't the slightest idea what the procedure would be. Who speaks first? Who cross-examines who? Who calls witnesses? What witnesses? All I know about this kind of thing is what I've seen in courtroom dramas on the telly – the barristers with their long black robes and white curly wigs.

Is that why I decided to get dressed up? I don't know. I did say to D and Mike next door it was to level the playing field.

Me and my skirt were now joined at the hip. But I needed the rest of it. I looked at numerous period costumes, robbed a bit from this, and a bit from that, until the picture formed clearly. I don't know what period of history it belonged to, maybe one we haven't had yet. Now, in less than four weeks, the trial to prepare, wheels of industry to turn – and make me a warrior.

A warrior has to have the right battledress. D objected. Of course she did. Who in their right mind wouldn't? And yet she helped me make the coat. No – she made it. I helped a little bit whenever I could and did what I was told to the best of my ability. And the shirt, with its frilled collar and cuffs. And the jabot. I don't think I knew what a jabot was – I do now.

I had the skirt – that was made: the black skirt I'd made at Christmas for formal occasions. I decided to test the water. We went to the Court on the pretext of something else. I wanted to say thank you to the Court Manager who had intervened and helped us stop the bailiffs after the first hearing. I framed a copy of the Judgment Day poem, and put a Kiasu Easel on the back to stand it up (you don't want to waste an opportunity). Court officials would never be allowed to accept a present. But this was not a present, it was just a bit of fun. We entered the Court building – *confidence essential, act as though you dress like this all the time, talk casually as you walk through the foyer, a polite nod or 'Good Morning' if appropriate. Don't stop.* I might have been aware of one or two looks of open-mouthed astonishment, but nothing was said. Then into the lift up to the third floor, and down the long corridor to the courtrooms. If the receptionist noticed anything, she didn't say. Possibly distracted by my handing her the framed poem. 'Could you pass this to Cathy Howells.' She swivelled her chair, looking round the office. 'OK. She's not here at the moment.' She couldn't resist reading the poem, and chuckled. 'OK,' she smiled. We left. Back down the corridor, back through the foyer, and out to the car. A little clenched fist: *Yess!*

I needed to know the procedure, the etiquette, the protocol. A crime had been committed, there was no doubt about that. Now my task was to prove it in a Court of Law. Against Barclays Bank plc., a household name worldwide. It wasn't a matter of revenge – it was a matter of bringing them to account. But how to do it? What if the case gets thrown out on a stupid technicality because I've said the wrong thing in the wrong place?

We were sent a Statement of Truth from Adrian Ruffhead. He stated how irresponsible I was, wasting the Court's time, emphasising that I had no prospect of winning.

And then he stated – and this is a Statement of Truth – that I had attended the meeting with Wyn Read with the express purpose of discussing the Clearly Business software package, that I had signed the documents, that D was also there, and that we had taken the software away with us at the end of the meeting.

I asked D, 'What does a Statement of Truth mean?'

'It means he's on oath. It's the same as being on oath in Court.'

'How could he possibly say that was true? He knew full well it wasn't.'

He'd admitted that Barclays prepared the two documents, in other words filled in the relevant details, and stated that I'd signed both of them at the meeting.

334

Statement of Truth? I was speechless.

What was that phrase? Something like, 'Power corrupts, absolute power corrupts absolutely'. D checked on the internet and got the original quote. It arose in a letter from Lord Acton to Bishop Mandell Creighton in 1887: *'Power tends to corrupt, and absolutely power corrupts absolutely. Great men are almost always bad men.'*

This Statement of Truth came from the Legal Department of Barclays, one of the biggest banks worldwide. We're not talking about two men in the pub arguing about whether the goal was offside or not. They are well-versed, well-practised, in Courtroom procedure. Why is he lying so blatantly? He obviously thinks he's going to get away with it, and he calls it a Statement of Truth. Is that the way the law works – victory goes to the most convincing liar? I needed advice.

I contacted a firm of solicitors in Wrexham, Allinson Hughes. Among other things they handled criminal law. As soon as they heard Barclays were involved they wouldn't even discuss it. I wasn't asking for legal representation, just advice on the procedure. But as soon as the B word was mentioned, they ran scared.

I also called Barry Ashton, a solicitor in Llangollen I'd known for a good number of years and considered something of a friend. He almost got hysterical, as though I'd told him I was just about to go and murder the Queen.

Ava had said some time back, 'You can't fight them. You haven't got the money.' Perhaps it was just as well I hadn't got the money and was doing it on my own. If the solicitors scared that easily their representation would be useless.

I remembered a solicitor in Liverpool – Rex Makin. A reputation for taking on cases perhaps others would not. He'll do it, I thought. I contacted his firm: they wanted their fee paid in advance. £750. A hell of a lot, I thought, for what would be about a ten minute chat, but it may be money well spent in the long run.

I drove to Rex Makin's offices in Liverpool and was greeted by an office junior, Mr Baker, who said, 'OK, leave it with us. We'll let you know.' I said, 'I haven't paid £750 to leave it with you. I've driven from North Wales for this meeting.' I had to raise my voice before I was eventually granted an audience with one of the partners, Mr Carruthers.

Mr Carruthers breezed in, straight off an LA film set – he didn't have the red braces but that's about all that was missing. He listened to what I had to say, then asked, 'You want us to tell you what your chances of winning are?' 'No,' I said, 'I just want to know the procedure, what to expect, who does what, in what order, that sort of thing.' He appeared to understand, or I thought he did.

Then I got a six-page letter – their terms and conditions. Well, it was mostly about money, actually; £250 per hour for Mr Carruthers, and £150 for Mr Baker, and, 'Thank you for providing us with payment… We will write to you with our advice in 7 days.' I couldn't help wondering how much of the £750 I'd already spent. I really don't like the society we've created.

I received a letter from Mr Carruthers, which didn't tell me what I wanted to know. I was still none the wiser about Court procedure. I phoned them and tried to say that wasn't what I wanted to know, but I couldn't get past Mr Baker, and he was no help. If I was dissatisfied with the advice, I was to put it in writing. There wasn't time.

The case hinged on whether I could prove that forgery had been committed. I knew forgery had been committed. Barclays knew forgery had been committed. But what constituted proof?

There are handwriting experts who specialise in this area. Yet again D trawled the internet, this time to find out who these handwriting experts were. We were now entering an extremely specialized area. They all appeared to be in and around London. It became apparent that their advice could never be considered as an absolute; one expert's opinion could differ from that of another – and it doesn't bear thinking about what their fees would be for an official opinion anyway.

That brought us back to Wyn Read. Apart from myself, he had been the only other person at the meeting. I knew Wyn wouldn't lie – it wasn't in the nature of the man. But I wasn't sure Wyn was going to be attending the trial. If he told the truth it would make a mockery of the statements of truth issued by Adrian Ruffhead and everything else Barclays had said.

It was essential that Wyn Read attend the trial. Could I subpoena Wyn to attend the Court hearing? I wasn't even sure what the word subpoena meant, and was I in a position to do so?

There was a simple matter of expenses to be offered to any witness being called. Do I pay Wyn the expenses in advance? A nominal fee,

£70. I didn't know. Not wishing to fall foul of Court procedure, I contacted Rex Makin's to clarify. Mr Baker was no longer in the employ of Rex Makin, and I got the feeling my credit had been exhausted – if I wanted any further advice another fee would be involved. £750 and a trip to Liverpool for advice, and it was worth nothing. I sent the subpoena and the expenses fee in the form of a postal order to Wyn Read care of Barclays.

The day of the trial was looming fast. I'd had a number of conversations with Wyn around the time we'd discovered the direct debits being taken out of our account. I remembered when I asked him about it, he'd said, 'Trust me, Ken. It'll save you money,' and 'I'll drop the software package round to you in a few days.' I knew I'd said something like, 'I don't need this Wyn. People are already doubting my sanity. D thought I'd signed something and not told her.'

I knew this exchange with Wyn had been by emails, but we couldn't find them. D reminded me there had been a problem with the computer a while back and a lot of stuff had been lost.

I would arrive at Quarry Road at about eight-thirty, click the kettle on, put the computer on and switch on the CD player. D would arrive about nine-fifteen. Each morning I played the Karl Jenkins 'Armed Man – A Mass for Peace' CD. The trick was to get to the end of the Benedictus track – and that lasted seven and a half minutes – before D arrived because it upset her, made her angry. It upset me as well. It was meant to.

I already had eighteen tracks on the CD I was making for the ballet. The first time I heard Benedictus I knew Don Quixote had died. I didn't know he was going to die until that moment. It's now played at the end of the ballet. One by one the dancers appear on the stage, preparing for the celebrations that are going to happen that evening. As the music starts, a sombre atmosphere develops. One by one they begin whispering to each other, then go and stand in a line at the front of the stage, eventually joined by Polly. As the music slowly develops, the power and the emotion of the moment build. As it reaches its climax, all the cast sit down, apart from Polly Flopsie who screams to the skies, 'Why!'

And every morning at that moment I break, and weep.

I have to stage this before D arrives, for obvious reasons. She caught me once or twice and said, crossly, 'Don't play it if it upsets you that much.' I wasn't upset because he'd died; I was upset because Don Quixote was no longer there to look after Polly. It was an extremely emotional part of the ballet. I had to re-live it over and over again so I could see what effect it was going to have on the whole work. Don Quixote was the hero – I couldn't believe that was the end of him. It was only by playing it over and over again that I could really examine the cause and effect. I now knew what happens after the curtain comes down.

The coat was on the table, a little bit further advanced than it had been yesterday. It now had one sleeve. Earlier in the day that sleeve had been attached by fifty pins, each one making a tiny, tiny gather in order that A fitted to B precisely. The coat was going to be magnificent. I made sure there was a relatively clean cup for D's coffee, and set up the bench in the doorway for another blast at the Venture backs in the sunshine.

I checked the emails to see what bounteous offerings had appeared overnight. There may have arrived an order from some obscure part of the world, among the usual rubbish. I somehow felt a bit detached, and didn't really care one way or the other greatly. I was still immersed in the music.

The music subsided, and D arrived bang on cue.

Venture pulled rank on everything. They had to – they paid the bills. It was very convenient, actually. It meant that everything else had to be put on the back-burner. The mindless act of pressing two brackets on to a piece of MDF didn't allow for any intense conversation, so we occupied ourselves with trivia, and the need to do one box of 10 x 8s in a quarter of an hour, or one box of 7 x 5s in half an hour, to give us some kind of indication of when we'd complete the 6,000 backs required by Monday. It didn't always work out that way because the monotony was punctuated from time to time by the phone, or Mike from next door calling round for a coffee – that was always a welcome diversion, and forty minutes gone – then back on with the race against the clock to reach the despatch deadline. Mike's business was pulling motorbikes apart and putting them back together again. Our chats very quickly descended into philosophy and the meaning of things. He laughed one day, when he reflected he used to come to work and talk about the soaps on the television the night before.

One of our favourite bits of occupational trivia was Alphabeticals: a subject category is selected and each player in turn has to come up with an example in alphabetical order. For example, Round Things: Antelope's nose, Bullring, Circumnavigate, Dogcollar, and so on. To give the game more scope for argument, we had more obscure subjects. For example, Little-known Pastimes of the Arapajo Indian (arrow-making couldn't be allowed, for instance, because it was more of an occupation than a pastime). From time to time we have to remind ourselves that this is supposed to be trivia, and not meant to cause deep discussion/argument.

Then of course there was the trial preparation, and the coat.

Ava pretended not to listen whenever I talked about the ballet until I told her, 'Don Quixote has died.'

'Why? How did he die?'

'I don't know. Polly was distraught.'

I just thought she ought to know – prepare, I suppose – in case it's some kind of stupid premonition.

But it can't be a premonition. Like that thing at the party where she appeared to be thirty years older just for a few seconds. There's no point in predicting something that's going to happen anyway, no matter what. It doesn't make sense. Everything has a reason.

I don't mean DQ won't die – of course he will, at some point. The warning is: she must prepare, she must understand, she must know their love is eternal. Perhaps that's why he comes back.

Who's that lying on the floor?
Fuck! It's me – what's that for?
I'm getting up. There's a smile on my face.
What the fuck is this place?

And so as the party started,
A selection from the dearly departed,
Returned to pursue
the ultimate screw.

We received a Witness Statement from Helen Tyson at Barclays, Wyn's manager, in which she too stated that D had also attended my meeting with Wyn Read with a view to purchasing their software package. How can these people lie so readily, and in such a blatant manner? These are people we're supposed to trust with our financial and personal details.

Even though Wyn and I had disagreed on best procedure, I still held him in high regard as a man of integrity. It was a stupid mistake for Wyn to make, because it was pretty obvious it was he who forged my signature. Whether or not that's actually what the Court would decide remained to be seen.

An obvious act of forgery had been denied by a number of people within Barclays' organisation – blatantly lying on the assumption that 'We're Barclays, and we're too big and powerful for you to do anything about it – and in any case, you can't prove it because you're a little man. Now go away and leave us to do important things'. That's the real crime: they think because of who they are that they are above the law.

D's attention to detail sometimes borders on obsessive. Detail's important, but so is the clock, and it's ticking towards Court Day. Our Particulars of Claim were extensive, thorough and detailed. This led to an equally extensive response from Adrian Ruffhead. Was it all his years of training and experience in law that taught him to lie so fluently, or was it just pure arrogance? Whatever it was, that is exactly what he did, and signed it as a statement of truth. Helen Tyson's statement was also in the realms of fantasy.

D replied to both statements, responding to each numbered paragraph in turn. A lengthy procedure, and it had to be done… but the coat's only got one sleeve.

D arrived at Quarry Road clutching a bundle of papers – five A4 sheets – the missing emails from Wyn. I scanned through them. And there they were, those few phrases that had been haunting me. '*Trust me, Ken, it'll save you money,*' and another one: '*I'll drop it round in the next few days*' (meaning the Clearly Business software).

'They were on my computer at home,' she said.

Of course they were. From time to time we worked on D's computer at home. Why hadn't we checked there? Didn't matter. We'd got them now – and in time. Just.

The emails confirmed that I didn't know anything about the Clearly Business package, it wasn't discussed at the meeting, D didn't attend the meeting, and I didn't walk away from the meeting with the package. Surely it proved beyond question that a lot of Adrian Ruffhead's Statement of Truth was lies.

We sent the evidence to Adrian Ruffhead at Barclays (I wouldn't have minded being a fly on the wall when he read it) and copied it to the Court.

I'd told Ava I would probably die before her, just simply by the age difference, but I'd wait. She said, 'While you're waiting, teach the men how to find the clit.' I told her the next day, 'That's going in the ballet!' She laughed, 'Your story's not quite the same as Romeo and Juliet, is it?'

'I'll be coming back, you know.'

'Yes, I know.'

I expected Barclays to put their hands up and make some kind of pathetic offer. Instead, they continued with their threats. Still convinced that they would win, they told me if I didn't drop the case which I was sure to lose, I'd be facing legal costs in excess of £3,000.

One more sleeve in the coat, and the Venture order despatched on time, as always. I'd made the jabot in a rich deep purple silk (well, not silk, but near enough), secured with a little black stud of the Devil, a Cesar Manrique design I'd picked up in Lanzarote a few years before.

There was a belt to be attached to the back of the coat. Design rather than functional, but essential. It acted as a T-bar at the top of the vent. It needed two buttons. The smallest detail can sometimes be the hardest to solve. We searched for the right size and colour. I finished up taking two buttons off my beloved denim jacket bought in Paris.

We'd made and fitted the lining. Nobody would see that apart from us, but we would. Now all that remained was the braiding to edge all the coat, lapels and cuffs. The sewing machine had already stated the limits to which it was prepared to go as far as strength and resistance of the cloth were concerned. The braiding was a step too far.

D's approach was it had to be done by hand. But now I'm like a caged lion, pacing. The trial was imminent. The coat was the last thing to be put in place. This was one of the few times I had to override. I needed every element to be put in nice little piles so I could prepare for the battle. I got in early the next morning and set myself the task of attaching the braiding with my trusty machine. I had three of the strongest needles available. In true Hollywood fashion I broke the last needle on the final stitch.

The holly leaves would appear sometimes in twos and threes, and occasionally there would be five, say. Not every day, just when the occasion required. But that day, the day before the Court, they came in like a storm, over and over again. I collected them and kept them in a box. Too many to count.

I can't be sure, but I'm sure I'm right
They came again last night.
The Gods of love, the Gods of war
The power of the universe, the power of all.
Building the power within,
Building my strength for the fight.
And now the battles begin.
I will win.

CHAPTER 28

The Court entrance was just a short walk from the car park. For the first time I was in my magnificent coat, frilled shirt, jabot, skirt and Bobby Shaftoe shoes. I was a warrior. [22,23]

All the past battles now faded into insignificance, merely skirmishes, minor obstacles to be dealt with in order to get here.

We checked in at reception. No comments on my clothing. There, on the schedule, K Holmes v. Barclays Bank plc. Judge Perry would be presiding again – the same Judge who had adjudicated with the bailiffs four weeks earlier. Four weeks? Seemed like four months. D wandered around, casually gazing at the various noticeboards as if she was on the look-out for a second-hand washing machine or a sofa in good condition.

'Come and stand here.' *Can't she see I'm terrified? Can't she understand I need her here in case anyone speaks to me.* I'm sure if anybody had said, 'Can I help you?' to me at that moment I would have snapped back, 'That's a lie!' I didn't have the opportunity. The next thing I remember I was standing in the Courtroom.

No big gallery with crowds of onlookers jeering and shouting. No twelve good men and true waiting to cast judgment. Just D and I at one end of the front row of desks, and a barrister representing Barclays to my right – a Ms Candlin. No flowing black robe, no white wig with tight curls at the sides. Was I the only one who had dressed for the occasion? Helen Tyson chose to sit a few rows back. No sign of Wyn. Surely he would have come in to the Courtroom at the same time as the others? Somehow, I wasn't surprised. And no Adrian Ruffhead – where was he? He should have been there. I wanted him there.

Judge Perry entered. He didn't take a second glance at my

appearance. It seemed I'd got away with it. His bench, facing us, was slightly raised.

I don't know how long the trial lasted. It couldn't have been four hours, could it? I've no idea. I just remember being calm, relaxed, focused, totally in control – far from the quivering wreck I'd been a little while earlier. My recollection of the trial is rather like a train thundering along a track, going in and out of tunnels, remembering bits as the train emerges again into the light.

Judge Perry introduced the parties and the purpose of the trial. He made it clear that I would need to prove forgery had taken place.

The Judge then invited Ms Candlin to start the proceedings.

She said, 'I've outlined the skeleton of our defence,' and handed Judge Perry a copy.

'Has Mr Holmes had a copy of this?'

'No, I couldn't find him.'

'It's hardly a very big Court.'

We were handed a copy of the skeleton defence and the proceedings were adjourned while we read it.

D read the skeleton defence. I could see from the speed at which she was reading through it there was nothing new. She confirmed that and we returned to the Courtroom.

Judge Perry looked for my reaction to the skeleton defence. I said, 'There's nothing new in there, and we covered all the points in our last reply.'

We'd sent in our reply to the defence, including the additional evidence, a week before, but it was clear from his reaction that Judge Perry had not received it. Ms Candlin had. This reply was crucial. It contained the emails from Wyn Read which had only resurfaced a few days ago.

D handed the Judge her copy, and he adjourned the proceedings once more for a further fifteen minutes while he read it.

We were recalled and the Judge glanced towards our desk, 'A very informative document,' he said. He was now fully aware of the contents of Wyn Read's emails.

Ms Candlin began her attack, for that's what it was – carefully wrapped in the niceties of Courtroom etiquette. Time and time again she questioned my credibility in every possible way. She did her best to paint a picture of an absent-minded delusional megalomaniac, only interested in his own self-importance, glamour, globe-trotting and the high life, without any interest in, consideration for – or memory of – the detail; the implication being 'that was for others, wasn't it'.

I said to Judge Perry, 'I don't know why Ms Candlin is pursuing this line, but I can talk about this all day if she wishes.' Judge Perry said, 'I understand what she's trying to do. Let her continue.'

One of the first things you learn at knight school is chivalry, and to defend truth and honour at all costs. Perhaps these are not taught – perhaps you're either born honourable or you're not. Or perhaps you are but choose to ignore it. Everybody knows the difference between right and wrong; that is one of the laws of the Universe. The more she attacked, the sharper my sword became – simply because I was relying solely on the truth, and that's easy.

She was trying to lure me into a trap, trying to flatter me into agreeing with her. Did she do her training at the Perry Mason School of Courtroom Drama?

'You're more interested in the big picture, aren't you, the grand scheme of things. The detail is not important to you, is it? Ms Page looks after all that, doesn't she?'

Does she think I'm an imbecile?

I told her that during the course of business I'd travelled round the world a number of times on my own: trade shows in the States, business trips in India, Taiwan and China, trade missions to Australia and Singapore. In Singapore I'd booked a flight to Hong Kong, travelled around Hong Kong by train to three meetings, all arranged by me.

'I guess that's a 'no' then,' said the Judge. I must have gone on a bit.

'I'm an inventor,' I said to Ms Candlin, 'If that doesn't involve detail I don't know what does.'

She fell silent. If there was a pit being dug, she was the one falling into it.

She suggested I'd attended the meeting, signed the documents and completely forgotten I'd done so, and that D had watched me sign the documents and forgotten about it, too. Her motive was now transparent, and very offensive.

The email evidence from Wyn Read was being totally disregarded.

Judge Perry asked me, 'Was Ms Page with you at the meeting?'

'No, Sir.'

He didn't look to D for confirmation – that was sufficient.

Ms Candlin continued with her attempts to assassinate my character, implying that I was an extremely difficult person to deal with; that I'd been through a succession of bank managers, therefore an impossible client.

'John Pitchford, for instance, he wouldn't take you back as a client, would he?'

'John Pitchford was a very good friend of mine,' I said, 'and still is, but he's been promoted within Barclays and he now only has a few accounts with turnovers of £5 million or more. John and I used to have breakfast meetings at Carden Park two or three times a year. That's the way we did business.'

I'd been with Barclays for close on thirty years, and of course I would have had a number of managers over the years. These days you're rarely with a bank manager for more than three or four years – banks tend to shuffle the pack as a matter of course.

If she'd have taken the trouble to speak to John Pitchford, she would have known that I held John in the highest regard, and I feel John would have reciprocated. There was a lot of mutual respect.

'I put it to you,' she said, 'that your grievance was not about forgery. You were angry because your loan had been turned down.'

'Angry?' I said, 'I was livid.'

'You also thought it was outside the scope and understanding of your local managers, and took your request over their heads direct to the Chairman's office.'

'Yes it was, and it still is.' I turned to the Judge, 'May I explain what the loan was for?'

'Yes,' he said, 'I'd be very interested. It was quite a lot of money.'

'I'm an inventor, Sir.' I had a Kiasu Easel with me. I passed it over to the Judge, then demonstrated how it worked on a frame in front of me.

'Pass the frame over here.' He stood it up on his bench. 'What a good idea.'

'It's actually got my name on it, if your eyesight's better than mine.'

'These are very good glasses,' he said as he fitted his specs, 'Oh, I see'.

346

'The loan, Sir, was for the American patent.'

He saw instantly the importance of the American market for the Kiasu Easel, and the cost implications in achieving the US patent; he could also see what the implications would be if we didn't get it.

The cross-examination by Ms Candlin continued.

A few minutes later I was able to address the Judge, 'By the way, I got the American patent.'

'Good,' he said.

She lost her train of thought a number of times, and there were long moments of silence as she looked through her notes.

Eventually Judge Perry said, 'Mr Holmes isn't going to say what you want him to say.'

'I've just got a few more questions,' she said.

'Be quick, then, this is getting rather tedious.'

He's calling her tedious. I like that.

I held up in front of her a copy of the document with the forged signature.

'Look! You can see it's a forgery, can't you.'

She didn't reply. I waited. She just stared at me silently, expressionless, blinking occasionally.

No response. I realised I wasn't going to get one. 'You're not going to answer me, are you!'

'Actually, it's she who's supposed to be cross-examining you,' the Judge observed.

'Oh! Sorry Sir.' I slapped the back of my hand.

He saw the whole scene as bizarre, as I did. For those few moments I'd wiped her slate clean. She'd lost her train of thought completely. She just looked expressionless, frozen in a vacuum. I've done that to people before. I don't know what actually happens, but all of a sudden the person I'm talking to goes blank, and totally forgets what they were doing or saying, and why.

I turned to my left to see if D was approving of the proceedings so far. She was looking away from me, to her left, out of the window. She appeared to be trying to stifle a grin. I couldn't tell. I continued.

I took that moment to address the Court: '*Power tends to corrupt. Absolute power corrupts absolutely. Nearly all great men are bad men.* That was in a letter from Lord Acton to Bishop Mandell Creighton written in 1887 and it still applies today, and I will fight corruption whenever I come across it.'

Earlier in the hearing, I had raised the subject of handwriting experts. I told the Judge that we'd researched the possibility of this, but it may well have meant getting a report on the handwriting of every employee in the branch and, even if that were possible, the costs of such experts were prohibitive. It had also become apparent that graphology was not an exact science, more an opinion, and the opinion of two experts could differ.

So when Ms Candlin raised the question of expert evidence, Judge Perry told her, 'Mr Holmes has already covered that.' I pointed out to the Judge that Barclays had admitted they'd filled in the forms, and there appeared to be a good deal of similarity between the handwriting of the signature and that on the forms themselves. For instance, that the K and the H in the signature looked very similar to those in the name at the top of the form. I could see the Judge's eyes focusing from the bottom of the document to the top.

Ms Candlin had lost the attacking, confident air she'd begun with, and was beginning to look distressed, hesitant, her demeanour unsure, flickering *like a candlin the wind.*

Judge Perry knew I was implying that Wyn Read had forged the signature, and asked the barrister why such an important party had not attended the hearing. He was told Wyn Read was absent on sick leave.

'Too sick to offer a witness statement?'

Ms Candlin didn't reply.

He turned to me, 'What would the motivation have been?'

'I imagine there's a certain amount of pressure to sell on accessories like the software package supplied by Clearly Business. It's like when you buy an appliance from Dixons, they always try to sell you the insurance. There would be pressure within the banks to encourage this kind of sale, either on individuals or branch-to-branch to reach their quota. Ms Tyson will be able to enlarge on that.' I turned to Helen Tyson, who had been silent throughout the hearing; she remained so.

Judge Perry was indicating he'd really heard all he needed to, but then said, 'Oh, we haven't addressed this witness statement by Helen Tyson.'

'Oh, that's just so much waffle,' I said.

He chuckled to himself, 'I suppose it is all a bit hearsay.' He considered it would be of no constructive benefit to the hearing.

His lengthy summing up concluded by saying that a forgery had indeed been committed, that Barclays knew about it, but since there was no prejudice intended when the forgery was committed it could not be deemed a criminal act in law.

I accepted the Judge's summing up in every detail. There was never any malice intended by Wyn. My singular objective from the beginning had been to expose the lies and deceit perpetrated by Barclays. What had started with a stupid mistake by Wyn had turned into a catalogue of blatant lies and false accusations by Barclays from their highest office, time and time again accusing me of signing a document that they knew perfectly well I did not, and D of witnessing such action. They continued with their lies, under oath, even when faced with categoric evidence to the contrary.

Why was Wyn not at the hearing? Why was he off sick? Why did he not even produce a witness statement? Was it because Wyn is an honourable man, so he couldn't have lied under oath?

Perhaps this all started with Alison Leary's email from the Chairman's office saying my signature appeared to differ from the one they held on file, but it would be difficult for either of us to prove it. She knew as clearly as anybody else involved that it was forgery.

It had taken eighteen months of single-minded determination for two people to take on the might of Barclays. There was no doubt that the day's hearing had been a major victory. Judge Perry made that quite clear. But what was the conclusion? There was no acknowledgment from Barclays, no apology, no reprimand in law. They are free to take the same action over and over again, with hardly a hair out of place.

Ms Candlin, barrister for Barclays Bank plc, and Helen Tyson left the Courtroom immediately.

As D and I collected our papers, Judge Perry rose and said, 'Good luck with the invention.'

This was not the moment to tell him that luck doesn't exist. I just said, 'I expect our swords will cross again.'

'I look forward to it,' he smiled.

As we arrived at the car park, we saw Ms Candlin and Helen Tyson standing by their car. We went over. I wanted to ask why Wyn was off sick and how was he.

Ms Candlin asked, 'Did you know the Judge?'

'Yes, we were in Court four weeks ago against a firm of bailiffs.' But I was more interested in the welfare of Wyn Read. I turned to Helen Tyson, 'How's Wyn?'

Very distressed and uncomfortable, backing away, she muttered, 'He's on sick leave.' She'd lied on her statement of truth, and she knew I knew.

*****

The victory was ours. The moral victory anyway. Had they paid for their evil? They will think not. A few thousand pounds in legal costs, and a barrister – a tiny bit of petty cash.

John Marston OBE, Bailiff. Thomas Higgins, Solicitors. Roderick Marsdon of Travail. Alison Leary of Barclays. Joe Eichert. Numerous other fools and miscreants, too many to mention but they know who they are.

All appear to have escaped without retribution. Or have they?

How does this humble knight deserve the hand of the fair Dulcinea, when the evil giants still walk free?

If the laws of the land can't administer justice... perhaps I'll write the book. Kiasu.

FINALE

There isn't an end, just a series of beginnings, each one taking me further – taking me nearer the truth. After every skirmish, 'I'll learn from that,' I'd say, 'No point in making mistakes if you don't learn from them – no point in making anything if you don't learn from it.'

Sixty-two years gone in the blink of an eye. I can still see the little boy who saw the pain and danger of the holly leaves asking his mother how much money he would get if he jumped off the roof on to a bed of prickles.

That same little boy a few years later, when his car broke down at the entrance to the Mersey Tunnel, being pushed into the tunnel by a policeman.

A little while later the boy as an aspiring businessman running out of petrol in his old Anglia van but there on the side of the road the battered Mazola cooking oil can came to his rescue.

The little boy didn't dream of becoming prime minister or playing for England – he dreamt of being the biggest pull on the planet. What he really meant was to fall in love. That was the best, the only, way he could describe it. How could he know what love was?

Snapshots of a distant past. Little cameos, as clear now as when they were captured. Hundreds, thousands of them stored in the scrapbook we call memory. Millions, if you include taste, smell, and a song on the radio that can send you careering back decades.

They come skipping into focus, sometimes for no apparent reason – or perhaps I'm just not aware of the reason. I didn't have any control over what I put in the scrapbook. How many times did I say 'I'll remember that,' but didn't.

Is it time now to consider the cost?
Bloody battles won and lost.

Each morning in the bathroom mirror
Is he a saint today – or sinner?

The same little boy looks back at me as always. A few lines here and there. I've still got quite nice hair, but then I've always had quite nice hair. I used to say that to the kids when they were small – just to annoy them, like fathers are supposed to.

It must have been fifteen years ago or more when my daughter spotted two grey hairs, and said, 'Ah, look at that. You're getting old.' I never thought anything about it, though I haven't seen the grey hairs for a while. They appear to have gone. And there are some days when I think my hair's better now than it's ever been.

The body's old, and creaks a bit, but my heart's getting younger. Has anything really changed? Maybe. Maybe not.

Life is a jigsaw puzzle, and I was trying to complete it, searching for one piece at a time. I was thrilled when I found it, but then realised there was another piece needed. Then when I found that, I knew it was the one I was looking for all the time. But yet again I realised there was another one missing – but I wouldn't have known that if I hadn't found the other pieces first… I had to go there to get here.

Each piece of the puzzle led to greater fulfillment as the picture slowly started to emerge, until there's only one piece left. Even though I can now see the picture, it will not be complete until the last piece slots into place. I will search and search until that piece is found.

The wise man told me ten years ago to write. If Ava and I had been together from the beginning as we should have been, this book would not exist. It would not have been necessary. I said to her, 'Something's blocking us.' Was it the wise man, making sure I wrote the book? He can play hard ball sometimes.

Somebody once asked me what sort of stuff did I write – I said, 'I'm a Writer of Wrongs.' I thought at the time it was just a smart-arse answer, but now I'm not so sure.

She

... Rearranged my ability,
Completely, deliberately.
Felt totally pigletty when she came to call.

I will find the last piece of the puzzle. If I happen to die in the process, that won't stop me.

The universe knows what the completed picture in the jigsaw is. It was up to me how I went about it, and whether I completed it or not. Then when I saw the picture, it had been there all the time – I was just too blind to see. It was completely different from what I expected but far more fulfilling than I could have hoped for.

Towards the back end of last year, was it – difficult to be sure – I told her I would get to the Holy Hole in the New Year.

'That's only two months away,' she said.

I'd never heard the phrase before until I wrote it in a poem. Neither had she. Yet we both knew without explanation what it meant. A sacred place, a place of enlightenment, a place of supreme peace and fulfillment.

'I don't read anybody else's poetry now. Only yours.'

Neither do I, but then I never did. Everything is there – though the poetry isn't mine. The words came out of the deep recesses of my subconscious somewhere and I rearranged them to make them fit. It was only then that I realised what they meant. I've learned such a lot from the poetry that I wasn't aware of.

When I wrote,

> *'It will take all you've got*
> *and don't you forget it*
> *the whole fucking lot*
> *and still you don't get it',*

I remember thinking *Shit, I didn't see that coming.*

And in the Judgement Day poem,

> *Now the gallows are ready*
> *Your head wracked with pain*
> *Your legs are unsteady...*

I remember thinking, *How am I going to get out of this?*

353

Then I wrote,

And it started to rain

and I knew everything was going to be alright.

It's just an observation – I'm sure it must happen to everyone – but it's spooky.

As always, it had been staring me in the face.

Alchemy. What if wealth has nothing to do with money? What if the pot of gold was inside me all the time?

Did I know all those years ago when I asked my mother how much money I would get if I jumped off the roof on to a bed of prickles that the journey was going to be scary and full of pain?

Eventually, the holly leaves arrived – not with pain as I expected, but as an army.

I can't be sure, but I'm sure I'm right
They came again last night.
The Gods of love, the Gods of war
The power of the universe, the power of all.
Building the power within,
Building my strength for the fight.
And now the battles begin.
I will win.

The holly leaves weren't the cause of the pain; they told me I wasn't alone, and I would win – if...

The mind goes far beyond the limitations and boundaries I shackled myself with. Perhaps boundaries do not exist at all, except in my imagination. I had belief in my own intuition and instincts, and the guts to follow my dreams. It's instinct that has driven my whole life. Time will tell if my instinct had any merit. But I was intoxicated with the desire for money, and it is a very potent drug – but the lust was insatiable. But then the dreams were there for a reason and they didn't go away.

Money is a false god, fool's gold. We wrap ourself in possessions, the big house, cars, trophies, all carrying a need for maintenance and repairs, insurance, security. We don't own the possessions. We are owned by them. How many of these possessions are actually needed? How much pleasure and reward do we get from them when we balance it against the cost? Are they just acquired to impress others?

Real wealth has nothing at all to do with material possessions or money. Money doesn't bring freedom or liberation as I once thought. When I was so-called successful in business I wasn't free – I was trapped, a prisoner of what I'd created.

In my late twenties a friend said I was making a lot of money. 'Only compared to other people,' I replied flippantly. But it's true – there's no point in comparing ourselves to others. Ultimately it is only ourselves we can impress or disappoint.

I used to believe money brought power, but aren't powerful people trapped in the worlds they've created, unable to think freely without considering the ramifications to the material world they can't see beyond? They are obsessed with making more money, and at the same time terrified of losing what they have.

Money doesn't bring power, as I once thought – quite the opposite. Things are very often the opposite of what they appear. Power comes from within. Fulfillment, honesty, self-liberation. Isn't that true alchemy?

When I was about twenty I was working in the City of London, Throgmorton Passage, beautiful old buildings. We were modifying one to bring it into the computer age. One morning I was trying to manoeuvre a long ladder and broke a small window high up. The commissionaire of the building, ex-army, saw the broken window and boomed out, 'Who broke that?' It could have been any one of thirty-odd contractors. 'I did,' I said. His anger diminished immediately. 'OK,' he replied, 'So long as I know,' and that was the end of that. Just because he knew I was telling the truth. Is honesty that powerful? That small incident has stayed with me all these years.

A very good friend told me, 'Look for the signs'. I thought I was the only one who knew about the signs, but her saying it gave them more meaning. Whether the signs are from the material world or the supernatural doesn't matter. She also said, 'Never give up'. The signs are what have driven me and given me the strength to know that so long as I don't give up I will win. That is inevitable.

I doesn't really matter if you believe in unexplained phenomena or not, just believe I believe it. Everybody's signs are different, and you must learn to have belief in your own. Unfortunately, not everybody will recognise the signs even though they are there. There's none so blind as those who cannot see, or perhaps simply refuse to see.

We consider ourselves somehow to be part of a chosen race, just because of the piece of land we happen to drop on at birth. We claim a divine right to all the privileges that go with that piece of land, and woe betide any outsider who tries to take them away. We also adopt the pride and prejudices that go with it and, perhaps the most bizarre of all, the religious beliefs of that land, and we prepare to fight wars and die for that land, just because of a freak of birth.

There is an obsession to discover what are considered to be other intelligent life forms on distant planets that we may be able to communicate with. If that happens, how will those life forms view all the wars that are going on here, all fuelled by greed? We are not an intelligent species. If we were we would find a way of solving disputes by reasoned argument, not by physical violence. I hope nobody tells them I'm here – I'd be so embarrassed.

When we do reach distant planets, the government that happens to own the spaceship will only be interested in the commercial rights anyway. The first thing America did when they landed on the moon was to plant a flag. At least we know the moon isn't made out of cheese, or it would be in the shops by now.

I realised many years ago when I was living in Llantysilio that everything has two functions; one designed by man and one by the universe. I thought everybody knew that, but perhaps not. A framed picture is designed by man to hang on the wall, and designed by the universe to hide the hole you put in the wall to hang it.

Nobody ever did ask me when the Battle of Hastings was. Was that memory wasted? Perhaps the universe kept it there to draw attention to the gross inadequacies of the education system that just perpetuates the status quo. They don't say the best qualification for a well-paid career is avarice and the path to the top is littered with bullies, corruption, lies and deceit. Education totally ignores the power of love, or why it's there, or what we can learn from it. But I can't just blame the education system – it's just a symptom of a society that totally misunderstands the point of everything. Love is the most important thing on our planet, and we treat it so casually, like if you've missed your bus there'll be another one along, but there won't.

I invented stuff to make my fortune. Perhaps the universe invented them so I would learn how to fight for what I believe in.

Every task we do successfully gives us a sense of achievement, a buzz, inside. But society doesn't recognise it unless the achievement earns monetary reward.

The warm buzz I had was from achievement. Any satisfaction I had from making money was shallow and insatiable – and just left me wanting more.

The Japanese Garden, or inventing a doofy, or writing a poem, were never done for money, although I thought the doofies were at the time. Do all the achievements add up to fulfillment? Did those nice people in the universe put the buzz there? Do all those fulfillments build the Brownie points to enlightenment? I image the buzz has to be honourable to qualify, which excludes the liars and the cheats – the buzz they get from that doesn't count, and I think they know that if they care to admit it. I hope it also includes the professional foul, and the people who add the canned laughter to tell you something is funny.

The little boy was seduced by a pretty face, but what is that – skin and flesh stretched over a skull, a membrane animated by thought, emotion and the soul. It's not the skull – I haven't heard of anybody being captivated by the beauty of a skull. They all look the same. And yet every single face is different. Even identical twins are different. Throughout the whole world, no two people are the same, making a glance, a smile, unique to that one person. We're all searching for that one piece of the jigsaw puzzle, but you don't fall in love with a jigsaw piece that only nearly fits.

When I did find the right piece of the jigsaw no-one else in the world would fit quite the same.

Love has little to do with physical appearance – it goes right to the soul, and only one person can hit that spot completely. I now know unrequited love doesn't exist. True love is reciprocated. All the movies and songs that say different are wrong. Anybody who has truly been in love knows that.

'Everybody's got something about themselves they'd like to change.'
'What would you change about me?'
'Nothing.'

What are the chances of finding that one piece in the whole world – unless it's not by chance?

If I could slide inside her mind,
And fornicate 'til I go blind,
Do you think that I might find…
No chance!

Surely I can change the plot,
If I'm pissed off with what I've got,
And spent more time begetting and begot,
No chance!

The cards are dealt with you in mind,
You're on your own to bump and grind,
The future's now, the past behind,
Get to it!

Just realise you've nowt to fear,
Except that thing between your ears,
Just get your fucking arse in gear,
And Do It!

You have the strength, you have the might,
To climb the very highest height,
And change the darkness into light,
Just Do It!

If you just search inside your soul,
You'll learn to conquer any goal,
Walk tall and straight from pole to pole,
Then you will reach the Holy Hole
Do It…

Just Do It!